T0320150

The Microfoundations Delusion

To the memory of Alan Huntington Charnley (1929–2011),
an inspiring teacher of economics

The Microfoundations Delusion

Metaphor and Dogma in the History of Macroeconomics

J.E. King

Professor of Economics, School of Economics, La Trobe University, Australia

Edward Elgar

Cheltenham, UK • Northampton, MA, USA

Published by
Edward Elgar Publishing Limited
The Lypiatts
15 Lansdown Road
Cheltenham
Glos GL50 2JA
UK

Edward Elgar Publishing, Inc.
William Pratt House
9 Dewey Court
Northampton
Massachusetts 01060
USA

A catalogue record for this book
is available from the British Library

Library of Congress Control Number: 2012935277

ISBN 978 1 84980 317 5 (cased)

Typeset by Columns Design XML Ltd, Reading
Printed and bound by MPG Books Group, UK

Contents

1. Introduction

1.1 THE NATURE OF THE PROBLEM

Take any advanced text in macroeconomics, written from a mainstream perspective. Wickens (2008) is a good example: it is an authoritative graduate text published by an Ivy League university press (Princeton). Here are the opening words of Chapter 1:

> Modern macroeconomics seeks to explain the aggregate economy using theories based on strong microeconomic foundations. This is in contrast to the traditional Keynesian approach to macroeconomics, which is based on ad hoc theorizing about the relations between macroeconomic aggregates. In modern macroeconomics the economy is portrayed as a dynamic general equilibrium (DGE) system that reflects the collective decisions of rational individuals over a range of variables that relate to both the present and the future. These individual decisions are then coordinated through markets to produce the macroeconomy. (Wickens 2008, p. 1)

Wickens proceeds by setting out a formal model of the behaviour of a RARE individual (a representative agent with rational expectations), a model that is supposedly derived from the work of Frank Ramsey (1928), to provide the purported microfoundations of the macroeconomic analysis that follows. (Lance Taylor (2004) denotes them as 'MIRA microfoundations': methodological individualism with representative agents.) I say 'supposedly derived', because Ramsey himself was quite clear that he was modelling the decisions of a socialist government and made no claim that his analysis might be applied to individual economic agents under capitalism. The reference that Wickens makes to 'the collective decisions of rational individuals' unwittingly points to the difficulty: it is, of course, *individual* and not collective decisions that are, supposedly, being aggregated. If they really were *collective* decisions, the aggregation would be unnecessary.

An initial and utterly insuperable problem with RARE microfoundations, as many critics have noted, is the assumption of a single representative agent, which implies that all individuals in the economy that is being modelled are identical. There is thus no reason for them to trade with each other, no reason why their decisions should be coordinated, and therefore no role for markets (Kirman 1992; see also Acemoglu 2009, pp. 149–55). Wickens soon acknowledges the problem:

> The basic Ramsey model can be roughly interpreted as that of a closed economy without a market structure in which the decisions are coordinated by a central planner. A first step towards greater realism is to allow decisions to be decentralized. This requires us to add markets – which act to coordinate decisions, and thereby enable us to abandon the device of the central planner. (Wickens, 2008, p. 2)

This is not a 'rough' interpretation of the Ramsey model, but a precise statement of its domain (though his central planner *makes* decisions rather than 'coordinating' them). Whether the 'greater realism' that Wickens claims to provide has in fact been attained is very doubtful. 'Firms act as the agents of households' in his DGE model of 'the decentralized economy', not as their employers (ibid., p. 54). Neither employment nor unemployment plays any significant role. Since 'including labor caused only minor changes to the previous results … we shall also exclude labor where appropriate and feasible' (ibid., p. 83). This proves to be almost always; there is no entry in the index for 'unemployment'. Such is 'modern macroeconomics', 'based on strong microeconomic foundations' that effectively eliminate the defining characteristic of the capitalist mode of production, the capital–wage labour (or employment) relationship.

These are important questions, for several reasons. Most obviously, the scientific status and (especially) the autonomy of macroeconomics are at stake. If the microfoundations dogma is correct, and the macroeconomy is 'produced' *à la* Wickens simply by aggregating the decisions of RARE individuals, then macroeconomics becomes nothing more than an application of microeconomic theory. There is no longer a case for teaching it as part of the core of graduate education in economics; it should instead be offered as an option, like industrial organization or environmental economics. This conclusion has been embraced with enthusiasm by the neoclassical labour economist Daniel Hamermesh (2008), and – in an amazing *volte-face* from his earlier advocacy of an autonomous 'Post-Walrasian macroeconomics' – by David Colander (2007), though in his case rather more tentatively. As we shall see in Chapter 6, this is the culmination of a lengthy process. A quarter of a century ago, Robert Lucas (1987) was both foreshadowing and welcoming the disappearance of macroeconomics as a separate intellectual discipline.

Even if things do not go quite this far, it is clear that the survival of any form of Keynesian (not just Post Keynesian) macroeconomics is now in question. Wickens's claim that DGE theory 'incorporates both Keynesian and New Keynesian macroeconomics' is contentious, since on the very next page he praises the work of the avowedly anti-Keynesian Robert Barro and reports that he himself 'had strongly disliked the Keynesian approach to macroeconomics, even from my undergraduate days at the London School of Economics' (Wickens 2008, pp. xiii, xiv). The 'New Keynesian' theory that is supposedly incorporated in DGE models is in fact a travesty of Keynes, eliminating the principle of effective demand and with it any notion of involuntary unemployment as a consequence of effective demand failures (Dullien 2011). Keynes's own reaction, had he been confronted with a graduate text in macroeconomics in which the index contained no entry for 'unemployment', can easily be imagined.

Finally, and most important, there is the issue of academic economists' reactions to the global financial crisis that began in 2008. The microfoundations dogma has played an important role in the 'business as usual' strategy of the mainstream of the profession, in terms of both theory and policy. This is depressingly evident in the widespread popular support for 'fiscal consolidation' in many European countries, where public services are being slashed in the name of 'debt reduction', reducing effective demand and further increasing unemployment – and government debt. This is impossible to explain in terms of self-interest: only the very rich make no use of public libraries, schools, hospitals and swimming pools, and even they have found their property incomes threatened by the contractionary multiplier effects of government spending cuts. There seems instead to be a deep-rooted belief that the financial problems faced by governments are qualitatively identical to those confronting individual agents and must therefore have the same solution, albeit on a very much larger scale. When an individual or a household gets increasingly into debt, reducing expenditure is often a sensible course of action (not always, of course: taking out a mortgage to buy a family home is in normal circumstances a prudent decision). But the principles of 'sound finance' cannot be applied to governments without committing a serious fallacy of composition, as Abba Lerner (1943) demonstrated many years ago. The microfoundations dogma makes for bad politics, in addition to bad economics.

This book is part history of economic thought and part economic methodology. In it I trace the protracted and tortuous history of the microfoundations dogma since the earliest days of macroeconomics as a separate branch of economic theory in the early 1930s, having first scoured the literature of the philosophy of science in an attempt to make sense of it all. I am conscious of trespassing here: I am an historian of ideas by trade, and have no training and very little experience in the philosophy of science. But I believe that the issues raised by the microfoundations dogma are so important that they have to be confronted by anyone with an interest in the future of macroeconomics. This book is an initial salvo in this confrontation.

I should make my own position very clear. As you will already have concluded, I am not a neutral observer. I am a heterodox economist, and on questions of macroeconomics my sympathies are with Post Keynesian theory, especially in the form of the Keynes–Marx synthesis sketched out by Michał Kalecki (1899–1970) and further developed by later writers in the Kaleckian tradition. Since the early 1990s I have become increasingly irritated by the microfoundations dogma, in particular by the regular apologies that authors, conference participants and seminar presenters seem obliged to offer for writing perfectly sensible papers on macroeconomics without having provided any microfoundations. I firmly believe that the critics of the microfoundations dogma are correct, for all that they are in a small minority in today's economics profession. I object not just to RARE (or MIRA) microfoundations but also to the claim that superior, non-RARE microfoundations have been, must be or should be provided for heterodox macroeconomic theory. I strongly advocate the relative autonomy of macroeconomics as a separate 'special science', and agree with Robert Skidelsky (2009) that it should be taught by specialist macroeconomists and not by practitioners of mainstream microeconomics. I only wish that all Post Keynesians, and indeed all heterodox economists of other persuasions, agreed with me.

1.2 THE STRUCTURE OF THE BOOK

The next three chapters, which constitute Part I, focus on methodological and philosophical questions. Chapter 2 discusses the use of metaphors and analogies in scientific discourse, with particular reference to economics. I argue that 'microfoundations' is a bad metaphor and an unacceptable analogy. In Chapter 3 I consider some of the issues raised by another questionable metaphor, 'micro-reduction', drawing on the substantial literature on this question in the philosophy of science before criticizing its application to economics. I next consider (and reject) the suggestion that it is necessary to provide 'macrofoundations' for microeconomics. Then, in

Chapter 4, I consider two case studies: the continuing debate on micro-reduction in the life sciences, and the protracted controversy that took place in the 1950s and 1960s on the principle of methodological individualism in social science. The chapter concludes with a discussion of the growing interest in the study of emergent properties, which have very important and largely negative implications for attempts at micro-reduction. There are important lessons here, I will suggest, for economics.

Part II is devoted to 'microfoundations' in the history of economics and the other social sciences. Chapters 5 and 6 trace the very convoluted history of the word and the doctrine since 1936. Note that the two are separable: you can assert the dogma without using the word, as J.R. Hicks (1939) did in *Value and Capital*, and indeed all its adherents did before 1956 (when the Post Keynesian Sidney Weintraub became the first to use it in print), and often for some years thereafter. Conversely, it was possible to use the word while denying the dogma, as Weintraub himself did and many other Post Keynesians have done since. I have chosen to end Chapter 5 in 1975, when the International Economic Association held an important conference on the issue, a conference whose proceedings revealed continuing doubt and confusion on the whole issue (Harcourt 1977). Only with the rediscovery of the Ramsey model at the end of the decade was the microfoundations dogma really able to take off. Chapter 6 takes the economics story from 1975 down to the present day, while Chapter 7 shows how the word and (to a very much lesser extent) also the dogma of microfoundations have been taken up in the other social sciences: sociology, political science, history and – straddling all three – Analytical Marxism. As will be seen, the fate of microfoundations offers an instructive case study in the failure of 'economics imperialism'.

It will be evident from Chapters 5–6 that not all practitioners of economics have accepted the microfoundations dogma. Part III is devoted to these dissenters. The story is, once again, a complex one. Among heterodox economists, many Post Keynesians have been strong critics of the dogma, but a surprisingly large proportion have been unclear, inconsistent or just plain confused on the issue. Chapter 8 is dedicated to the Post Keynesians, while Chapter 9 deals with other dissidents. Within mainstream economics, some but not all Old Keynesians have been consistently critical of microfoundations, while others have wavered. Austrians, who might have been expected to be firm supporters of the dogma, have been no less divided, along with institutionalists and evolutionary economists. I conclude the chapter by speculating on the reasons for these uncertainties. In Chapter 10 I consider another subset of economists, the economic methodologists.

How have economists with a knowledge of and interest in the philosophy of science dealt with the microfoundations dogma? Not quite as well as one might have hoped, I will suggest.

Finally, in Chapter 11, I try to draw together the various strands of the argument. Why did the microfoundations dogma become so popular, and why did it only take off in the late 1970s and early 1980s, and not (many) decades earlier? Why does the dogma matter? What can we learn from it about the use and abuse of metaphors in economics? What is the future of macroeconomic theory, with or without microfoundations? What are the broader lessons that a new generation of macroeconomists need to learn?

1.3 ACKNOWLEDGEMENTS AND DISCLAIMERS

I have pestered friends and colleagues on these matters for many years. Some of them will disagree fundamentally with the broad position that I defend in this book, or with my interpretation of many of the narrower issues of doctrinal history and methodology that I discuss. I owe them my thanks all the same: Javier López Bernardo, Victoria Chick, Sheila Dow, Tony Endres, Geoff Harcourt, Don Harding, Neil Hart, Jim Hartley, Mike Howard, Therese Jefferson, Tae-Hee Jo, Jakob Kapeller, Harold Kincaid, Peter Kriesler, Fred Lee, Bruce Littleboy, Troy Lynch, Ian McDonald, Robin Pope, Colin Rogers, the late Kurt Rothschild, Michael Schneider, John Smithin, Gerry Steele, Tony Thirlwall, Jan Toporowski and Roberto Veneziani. Earlier versions of some chapters were presented at a staff seminar at La Trobe University in May 2007; at the Berlin conference of the Research Network Macroeconomics and Macroeconomic Policies in October 2008 (this paper was published as King 2009); at a symposium on microfoundations at SOAS, University of London, in October 2009; at the 23rd Conference of the History of Economic Thought Society of Australia, University of Sydney, in July 2010; and at the 3rd International Summer School of the Research Network Macroeconomics and Macroeconomic Policies in Berlin in August 2011. I am very grateful to participants for their comments, suggestions and criticisms. The book was completed while I was a visitor at the University of Graz in the second half of 2011. Once again I must thank Karl Farmer, Christian Gehrke, Heinz Kurz and their colleagues for their hospitality in that most beautiful of Austrian cities.

PART I

Microfoundations and the Philosophy of Science

2. Microfoundations as a (bad) metaphor

2.1 INTRODUCTION

In the 1980s the BBC screened a series of lengthy interviews with leading philosophers (a programming decision that is almost inconceivable today). I have fond memories of one of these broadcasts, in which the interviewer, the philosopher and Labour (later, Social Democrat) MP, Bryan Magee, put a very pertinent question to the great A.J. Ayer. 'What', Magee asked him, 'do you regard as the main difficulty with logical positivism?' 'Well', said Ayer, after a slight pause, in an answer that appeared to be spontaneous but must have been very carefully rehearsed, 'I suppose I'd have to say that the main difficulty with logical positivism is that it is nearly all wrong'.

The main difficulty with the microfoundations dogma, I believe, is that it, too, is nearly all wrong. There are two reasons for this: the fallacy of composition and downward causation. The fallacy of composition entails that an entire economy may behave in ways that cannot be inferred from the behaviour of its individual agents. In Keynesian macroeconomics the classic example is the *paradox of thrift*: a decision by any individual to save a larger proportion of her income will lead to more saving by that individual, but (in the absence of increased investment) this will not be true of an increase in everyone's savings propensity, which will simply reduce their incomes and leave the volume of aggregate saving unchanged. This proposition is at least three hundred years old; as Keynes (1936, pp. 359–62) observed, it was popularized by Bernard Mandeville in his 1714 *Parable of the Bees*. In Chapter 3 I shall provide several further examples of the fallacy of composition. The principle of downward causation states that, in economics, causal processes operate in both directions: not only from the behaviour of individual agents to the behaviour of the entire economy, but also from the economy to the tastes, beliefs, expectations and actions of the individual agents.

Since the microfoundations dogma is inconsistent with both of these principles, the dogma itself must be false. Or, perhaps, in Ayer's words, 'nearly all wrong'. To deny the need for macroeconomics to be derived from 'rigorous' (that is to say, RARE) microfoundations, I do not need to claim – and neither do I claim – that microeconomics is irrelevant to macroeconomics, that the behaviour of individual agents is of no concern to macroeconomic theorists, or that causation runs exclusively (or even predominantly) downwards, from macro to micro. Instead, I shall suggest, microeconomics and macroeconomics are related to each other horizontally, not vertically. The phenomena that they study are rather obviously closely related, and their practitioners most certainly can (and should) cooperate with each other and learn from each other. But neither should be seen as the 'foundation' of the other.

This is the main difficulty with the microfoundations dogma, but it is not the only one. There are at least three more. One, which I touched on in Chapter 1, is the threat that it poses to the autonomy, and indeed the continued existence, of macroeconomics. This is quite widely recognized. As the Austrian economist Herbert Walther relates:

> A few years ago (ironically, just before the financial crisis of 2007) I was at a conference and got into a conversation with a very talented young economist who had an interest in methodology. I happened to mention that our university was advertising a vacancy for a professor of macroeconomics. She smiled and asked me, in some surprise: 'Is there still such a thing as macroeconomics?' (Walther 2011, p. 35; my translation)

The second difficulty is the great confusion that the microfoundations dogma has generated, in the ranks of its supporters almost as much as in those of its critics and among mainstream economists almost as much as for their heterodox opponents; this will be exposed in some detail in Parts II and III of this book. Third, and to my mind the most irritating, is the enormous but entirely spurious advantage that it seems to give to the mainstream, whose microfoundations are apparently far superior to those offered by the various streams of heterodox economics, when indeed the latter have any microeconomics of any consequence to contribute. In sum, the microfoundations dogma has had, and continues to have, a large and pernicious effect: directly on academic economics, and indirectly on economic policy and public discourse on economic issues.

One obvious objection to all this is that it greatly exaggerates the importance of language. 'Microfoundations' is just a word, after all, and whether we should use it – or refrain from using it – has no real significance. It is a metaphor. So what? Metaphors are simply a form of rhetorical decoration, which might interest poets, art critics or students of literature but are irrelevant to economic theorists and policy makers. Insistence on the use of the 'microfoundations' metaphor is nothing more than an instance of what Steven Lukes has described – in the broader context of methodological individualism in the social sciences – as 'futile linguistic purism' (Lukes 1968, p. 125). Thus it does not need to be taken seriously by economists.

This, I think, would be a serious mistake, for several reasons. First, rhetoric matters. As Deirdre (formerly Donald) McCloskey has long argued, economic discourse is intended to persuade, and a good rhetorician will always be more persuasive than a poor one. She cites the unfortunate example of John Muth, whose deeply muddy prose both denied him the credit she believes him to have deserved for discovering the concept of rational expectations and delayed the widespread adoption of the concept itself for some years (McCloskey 1985, p. 88).

Second, and more important, metaphors are *not* (at least, not always) mere embellishment. They sometimes (perhaps often) influence the nature of the ideas that are being presented, and thereby have a substantive rather than a purely decorative or persuasive effect. Cristina Bicchieri, in a paper entitled 'Should a scientist abstain from metaphor?', gives three examples of metaphors in economics: (i) extension of theory of consumer choice to new fields (ii) game theory (iii) 'the recent microfoundations program in macroeconomics ... In all these cases, we represent objects or phenomena "as if" they possessed certain properties or satisfy certain relations' (Bicchieri 1988, p. 107). Bicchieri criticizes McCloskey for denying the substantive significance of metaphors in economic discourse:

> According to McCloskey, because economists make extensive use of metaphors and analogies, they are rhetoricians. Maybe they are. But are metaphors *only* literary devices? Is that [*sic*] true that there is no difference between poetic and economic metaphors, as he repeatedly claims? Are metaphors merely ornamental, or do they convey some knowledge? I believe that they do, and that is the reason why some of them persuade. (Bicchieri 1988, p. 101; original stress)

For Bicchieri, some weighty philosophical issues are involved in this claim:

> Old-fashioned empiricism separates literal and figurative language, associating the latter with rhetorical purposes or stylistic embellishment ... Consistent with this contrast is the idea that metaphor, the chief rhetorical trope, is an elliptical simile that can be translated into a literal paraphrase without loss of content [as suggested by Aristotle] ... Modern positivism did not change the picture. Its distinction between the cognitive and emotional aspects of language, coupled with the belief that scientific knowledge can be reduced to a system of literal sentences, implies that metaphor has no cognitive import. (Ibid., p. 102)

In opposition to this empiricist or positivist position, Bicchieri invokes 'the *interaction view* of metaphor' of I.V.A. Richards and Max Black, according to which '[i]n any metaphor there are two constitutive elements: the primary subject and the secondary subject. In an effective metaphor the two subjects are taken from different domains or modes of discourse and are brought together interactively' (ibid., p. 103; original stress). It follows from this that 'metaphor has a meaning of its own that cannot be reduced to literal paraphrase, since the meaning results from the interaction of two different contexts' (ibid., p. 104).

This recognition of the 'cognitive import' of metaphors suggests a third reason for taking seriously the use of metaphors in economics. It is necessary to distinguish *good* metaphors from *bad* ones, and to do so by applying criteria that go beyond a metaphor's ability to persuade, since a metaphor can be both persuasive and pernicious. 'Microfoundations', I believe, is precisely such a metaphor.

In sum, metaphors are both interesting and contentious, in economics and in science more generally. Spatial and constructional metaphors, in particular, need to be critically assessed. In this chapter I discuss the use of metaphors in the literature of science in general (Section 2.2) and in economics (Section 2.3), before turning to the specific issues raised by spatial metaphors in economic discourse (Section 2.4). In Section 2.5 I argue that 'microfoundations' is a bad metaphor, which involves a highly misleading analogy. The chapter concludes (Section 2.6) by considering the need for economics to have acceptable social and philosophical foundations.

2.2 METAPHORS IN SCIENTIFIC DISCOURSE

According to Alexander Rosenberg, '[t]he role of metaphors in science is not well understood. Indeed, the role of metaphors is still controversial on its home ground in language. It should be no surprise that when we metaphorically or otherwise extend literary metaphor to scientific practice, matters become quickly obscure' (Rosenberg 1994, pp. 406–7). The use of metaphors in science seems often to be ignored by literary theorists. A recent 550-page volume edited by R.W. Gibbs (2008) includes a detailed discussion of the use of metaphors in Artificial Intelligence but contains no index references to science, social science or natural science; the references to the 'aptness' of metaphors are purely subjective, with no objective criteria proposed. Yet it remains true that '[s]o-called purely intellectual concepts, e.g., the concepts in a scientific theory, are often – perhaps always – based on metaphors that have a physical and/or cultural basis' (Lakoff and Johnson 1980, pp. 18–19). And this poses a serious problem, since '[t]he most fundamental values in a culture will be coherent with the metaphorical structure of the most fundamental concepts in the culture ... But ... there are often conflicts among these values and hence conflicts among the metaphors associated with them' (ibid., pp. 22–3).

This is not to say that scientific metaphors are necessarily bad. Indeed, James Bernard Murphy suggests that they are often highly productive: 'The history of science shows that theoretical innovation is usually a matter of seeing analogical resemblances between different phenomena' (Murphy 1994, p. 542). This reinforces the importance of the substantive as well as the decorative function of metaphors. As the organization theorist Gareth Morgan suggests:

> ... metaphor is often regarded just as a device for embellishing discourse, but its significance is much greater than this. The use of metaphor implies *a way of thinking* and *a way of seeing* that pervades how we understand our world generally ... One of the interesting aspects of metaphor is that it always produces this kind of one-sided insight. In highlighting certain interpretations it tends to force others into a background role ... Another interesting feature rests in the fact that metaphor *always* creates distortions ... metaphor uses evocative images to create what may be described as 'constructive falsehoods' which, if taken literally, or to an extreme, become absurd. (Morgan 1997, p. 4)

In Chapter 10, on 'The Challenge of Metaphor', Morgan has a section with the heading, 'Metaphors create ways of seeing and shaping organizational life'. As in natural science, he argues, so also in the study of organizations: metaphors are profoundly important. 'When scientists study light as a wave it reveals itself as a wave. When it is studied as a particle, it reveals itself as a particle. Both tendencies or qualities co-exist. The metaphor that the scientist uses to study these latent tendencies *shapes* what he or she sees'. And the same is true of organizations: 'Think "structure" and you'll see structure. Think "culture" and you'll see all kinds of cultural dimensions. Think "politics" and you'll find politics. Think in terms of system patterns and loops, and you'll find a whole range of them' (ibid., p. 349).

A similar point is made by Bicchieri, who asks

> Is the same process at work in literature, science, and everyday language? ... Max Black thought there was a difference between explicit scientific usage of language and metaphorical usage. According to him, we need metaphors in those cases where the precision of scientific statements is not possible. Hence

> metaphor is appropriate to the prescientific stages of a discipline or, in the case of developed sciences, to heuristics. (Bicchieri 1988, p. 104)

Bicchieri denies this: 'I want to argue that metaphors play an essential role even in mature fields, in the development of new theories as well as in the extension of old ones. They are *constitutive* of scientific discourse' (ibid., p. 104; original stress). Similarly, towards the end of his book on *The Romantic Economist*, Richard Bronk discusses 'the creative use of metaphor' in scientific discourse: 'The incorporation of a new metaphor may help a paradigm evolve, but it may also sometimes lead to a paradigm shift ... metaphor may play a similar role [to poetry] in shaking us out of habitual ways of seeing within economics or any other discipline' (Bronk 2009, p. 273).

Arjo Klamer and Thomas Leonard distinguish three classes of scientific metaphors. The first, and least important, are *pedagogical metaphors*, which 'simply serve to illuminate and clarify an exposition and could be omitted without affecting the argumentation as such' (Klamer and Leonard 1994, p. 31). Second, and rather more influential, are *heuristic metaphors*, which 'serve to catalyze our thinking, helping [us] to approach a phenomenon in a novel way' (ibid., p. 32). Heuristic metaphors encourage the use of analogy, which is 'sustained and systematically elaborated metaphor' (ibid., p. 35). Third, and operating at 'an even more fundamental level', are *constitutive metaphors*, 'those necessary conceptual schemes through which we interpret a world that is either unknowable (the strong position, per Nietzsche) or at least unknown' (ibid., p. 39). Constitutive metaphors are extremely important. They 'frame a discursive practice in the way that the U.S. Constitution frames U.S. legal discourse...They determine what makes sense and what does not' (ibid., p. 40), thereby serving to define the Kuhnian 'disciplinary matrix', or the Lakatosian 'hard core' of any science.

This perhaps explains why, for so many mainstream economists, the requirement for microfoundations is self-evident and seems to need no justification. When I presented an earlier version of the arguments in this book to a seminar audience at La Trobe University this became exasperatingly clear. 'Are you saying that we don't need microfoundations?', asked one young neoclassical theorist. 'Yes', I replied. 'Why do you think that you do need them? 'Because they're micro*foundations* ...'. This circularity of argument seems to be a characteristic product of a constitutive metaphor. Willie Henderson notes a rather similar problem. 'The trouble with metaphor', he observes, 'is that once you start noticing that it is there, it tends to become unmanageable – there being no independent metaphor-free vantage point from which to discuss it' (Henderson 1986, p. 124). None the less, he attempts to distinguish 'between those metaphors that eventually give rise to predictive theory and those that are normative in nature and recommend either "good" action or a "good/bad" way of viewing the world', and also to establish 'criteria for "useful" metaphors or at least some suggestions on how metaphor might be handled in teaching' (ibid., p. 111). It has to be said that Henderson himself does not get very far in suggesting such criteria (but see also Henderson 1993, 1995).

'What remains to be explained', Bicchieri maintains, 'is why some metaphors meet with success, how some of them succeed in becoming so well entrenched as to grow into literal statements. Becoming literal is not just a matter of time' (ibid., p. 106). She discusses the work of the philosophers of science Thomas Kuhn, Mary Hesse and Richard Boyd (ibid., pp. 106–10). All three claim that 'the use of models in science requires the use of metaphors, inasmuch as it requires analogical transfer of a vocabulary and creates similarities ... Indeed, it has been argued that a scientific explanation can be interpreted as a metaphorical redescription of the domain of the explicandum' (here she cites Hesse 1966, pp. 157–77). According to Bicchieri, models 'introduce new predicates' and 'allow new predictions to be made', by 'providing something like a linguistic extension, a new vocabulary' (Bicchieri 1988, p. 108). Of 'fictional models', she writes: 'The fictional character of such models is well captured by the idea of a metaphorical description, attributing a provisional similarity to structures otherwise very different. The metaphoral process reveals new relationships, suggests new ways of looking at the phenomena. Some of them may later come to be rejected. There are the unsuccessful models, the failed metaphors. They can fail precisely because they have cognitive content and are not merely rhetorical devices' (ibid., p. 110).

The final (brief) section of Bicchieri's paper is headed 'Why do metaphors persuade?' Here she argues that, while many poetic and literary metaphors become overused, banal and useless:

> Scientific metaphors, on the contrary, are [intended] to be overused. They undergo public articulation (indeed, this is the mark of a good metaphor), and the proposed similarities between the two subjects are extensively explored, sometimes by entire generations of researchers … . Paradoxically, a successful scientific metaphor is a 'dead' metaphor: It has become well entrenched, part of our body of knowledge. (Ibid., p. 113)

But this is not true of literary metaphors: 'On the contrary, I do not believe that literary metaphors benefit from overuse' (ibid., p. 113). As an example of a dead metaphor, Maurice Lagueux takes 'liquid assets': this is a very dead metaphor indeed, which no longer works metaphorically (Lagueux 1999, p. 10). He cites Nelson Goodman as describing a live metaphor as 'a calculated category-mistake' (ibid., p. 11). Dead metaphors, on the other hand – and these constitute the majority of metaphors that are used in economics – are simply technical terms and are understood by economists as such (ibid., p. 12). Microfoundations, I suggest, is very much a live – and therefore contestable – metaphor.

2.3 METAPHORS IN ECONOMICS

As Henderson notes, economists 'use metaphor on a systematic and/or *ad hoc* basis to help towards building predictive models, to suggest good action or form the basis for judgement, to establish a technical and semi-technical vocabulary, to assist in the framing and reframing of questions as well as to instruct, ridicule or even mislead' (Henderson 1986, p. 125). Several categories of metaphors that have been used in economics can be distinguished, in addition to the constructional metaphors, exemplified by 'microfoundations', which will be discussed in the following section. I discuss them in alphabetical order, since there seems to be no obviously better way of doing it. First, there are the energy metaphors that are brilliantly dissected in Philip Mirowski's *More Heat Than Light* (Mirowski 1989a), a profound critique of neoclassical economics that hinges on 'a critical inquiry into the complex analogies that underlie the energy metaphor in the theory of value' (Murphy 1994, p. 543). Henderson notes the importance of what he terms 'iconic metaphors': 'elementary supply and demand diagrams are in fact *iconic metaphors* i.e. they are like maps of a town that does not exist or, to put it another way, they are maps of all possible towns of a certain type' (Henderson 1986, p. 115; original stress).

Occasionally mathematical metaphors are employed, as for example when Robert Shiller, interviewed by David Colander, compared the micro-macro relationship to that between calculus and geometry (below, p. 178). Much more common are mechanical metaphors. In fact, Henderson distinguishes 'two basic metaphorical traditions: the mechanistic and the organic traditions', and observes that '[t]he machine metaphor is found frequently in economics discussion and not simply in micro-theory' (Henderson 1986, p. 115). 'Whereas the metaphor of the machine in micro-economics helps to build predictive models, at least for certain types of problems', he continues, '*ad hoc* machine metaphors such as "fine-tuning" or inflation as "overheating" need to be questioned. If not, there is a danger that we will be used by metaphor rather than metaphor being used by us' (ibid., p. 116). Organic metaphors are widely used in economics, and they have some interesting implications for the issue of microfoundations. Thus Richard Bronk notes that 'Herder used the organic metaphor to signal that the whole is more than the simple sum of the parts', since it depends on the 'dynamic interrelationship' between the parts (Bronk 2009, p. 88), while Carlo Ginzburg notes that 'vegetal' metaphors are used by postmodernist micro-historians: they claim to deal only with the leaves, not with the trunk or a branch (Ginzberg 1993, p. 31).

There is one final category that deserves a mention: trade metaphors. Asked in an interview in December 1996 whether it was still possible to differentiate between micro and macroeconomics, the real business cycle theorist (and 2011 Nobel laureate) Thomas J. Sargent replied as follows:

> It's increasingly difficult, because macroeconomics imports ideas very rapidly from micro. For example, the equilibrium concept we use. A good macro-economist can talk very well to a good microeconomist, much more easily than, say, 20 or 30 years ago. We are now used to seeing the same equilibrium concepts, Nash equilibrium or some version of perfection, both of us use dynamic programming, a very similar kind of learning is used in game theory and macroeconomics, and so on. (Ibáñez 1999, p. 250)

2.4 SPATIAL AND CONSTRUCTIONAL METAPHORS IN ECONOMICS

Spatial and constructional metaphors are most important for the argument of this book. 'Most of our fundamental concepts are organized in terms of one or more spatialization metaphors', suggest the literary theorists George Lakoff and Mark Johnson (1980, p. 17). In Chapter 10 of their book, entitled 'Some further examples' of metaphors, the first example that they offer is constructional:

> THEORIES (and ARGUMENTS) ARE BUILDINGS
>
> Is that the *foundation* for your theory? The theory needs more *support*. We need some more facts or the argument will *fall apart*. We need to *construct* a *strong* argument for that. I haven't figured out yet what the *form* of the argument will be. Here are some more facts to *shore up* the theory. We need to *buttress* the theory with *solid* arguments. The theory will *stand* or *fall* on the *strength* of that argument. The argument *collapsed*. They *exploded* his latest theory. So far we have put together only the *framework* of the theory. (Ibid., p. 46; original stress)

They note some peculiarities of constructional metaphors:

> BUILDING: The surface is the outer shell and foundation, which define an interior for the building. But in the BUILDING metaphor, unlike the CONTAINER metaphor, the content is not *in* the interior; instead, the foundation and outer shell *constitute* the content. We can see this in examples like: 'The foundation of your argument does not have enough content to support your claims' and 'The framework of your argument does not have enough substance to withstand criticism'. (Ibid., p. 100; original stress)

Such metaphors are very commonly used by economists. Thus Henderson notes that '[w]hat economists themselves (as opposed to students of economic method) do *all the time* is to talk about theories in terms of "theory as a building" as identified by Lakoff and Johnson' (Henderson 1986, p. 109; stress added). He quotes from his personal notes taken at a public lecture by Frank Hahn on inflation ('recently', at Birmingham University): 'Those who hold the rational expectations view do not have a building and should stop pretending that they have. What they have is a scaffold and what they are doing is tidying up the scaffolding by a movement of a few planks here and there, but nothing more than that' (ibid., p. 110). In similar vein, when asked about the relationship between micro and macroeconomics, Paul Samuelson replied: 'We always assumed that the Keynesian underemployment equilibrium floated on a substructure of administered prices and imperfect competition'. Why, he continued, were unemployed workers not able to find work in small companies at low wages? 'Free entry was not a feasible thing and there was overcapacity in all lines. This goes back to the system being floated on imperfect competition and increasing returns technologies' (Colander and Landreth 1996, pp. 160, 161).

Later in this book an amazing range of spatial and constructional metaphors will be encountered. In Chapter 5 alone, we shall find references to 'laws of connection' between micro and macro (Keynes, echoed by Kevin Hoover); to 'one side of the moon' (Keynes again); to 'bridging the gap' between micro and macro (Lawrence Klein); to a 'house' constructed of 'bricks' (Ruttledge Vining); to the 'cornerstone' of economic theory, and to 'building up and down' (Milton Friedman); to the need to 'tie' micro and macro together (Franco Modigliani); to macro propositions being 'built up from' micro ones (Don Patinkin); to micro theories as 'building blocks' of macro, but also to the existence of a 'two-way street' between them (Gardner Ackley); and to the need to 'buttress' macro with micro theory, so that the micro can be 'hooked up to' the macro (E.S. Phelps). There is also my favourite: the desirability of constructing 'a bridge or at least some stepping stones' between them (Takishi Negishi). It seems, sadly, that no-one else has used the stepping stone metaphor, but there are several references in subsequent chapters to the construction of 'bridges' between micro and macro (Lawrence Boland, Frank Hahn, John Hicks, Theodore Rosenof). Other constructional metaphors include the provision of micro 'underpinnings' for macro (John Cornwall) and the need to supply a 'common bond' or to 'bind together' the two areas of study (Alfred Eichner). The number of authors who have referred, approvingly or otherwise, to the 'macrofoundations' of microeconomics, is too great for me to cite them here: I have twenty names on my list, and there will surely be others whom I have missed.

Here is one final example, which neatly combines an organic with a spatial metaphor. In his discussion of the relationship between microeconomics and macroeconomics, which is cited in Chapter 5, Richard Stone uses two metaphors: the 'roots' and 'springs' of human action. Macro models deal with aggregates, he writes, and thus 'tend to be relatively superficial and to ignore any optimizing principle which might be supposed to lie at the roots of human endeavour' (Stone 1962, p. 494). 'In order to replace the *ad hoc* relationships which figure so largely in macroeconomics', he concludes, 'the optimizing model tries to penetrate more deeply into the springs of human action' (ibid., p. 505).

2.5 THE PROBLEM WITH 'MICROFOUNDATIONS'

So, where precisely does the problem lie (so to speak)? 'Metaphor is inherently paradoxical', Gareth Morgan suggests. 'It can create powerful insights that also become distortions, as the way of seeing created through a metaphor becomes a way of not seeing' (Morgan 1997, p. 5). It follows that '[a]ny given metaphor can be incredibly persuasive, but it can also be blinding and block our ability to gain an overall view' (ibid., p. 347). Lakoff and Johnson write about ways in which 'a metaphorical concept can hide an aspect of our experience' (for example, conduit metaphors about communication) (1980, p. 10). As Henderson notes, his own discussion 'puts metaphor in a problem-framing context but metaphor can also be used in a problem-solving context ... The difference between problem-solving and problem-framing is like the difference between answering a given question and changing the question' (Henderson 1986, p. 123). He expresses the hope that awareness of these issues 'will help increase critical understanding of when it is legitimate and illegitimate to make use of metaphor' (ibid., p. 125).

Bronk identifies two dangers, with particular reference to dead metaphors:

> The first is that there may be important distinctions and differences in our vision and analysis because of the structuring effect of the conceptual and logical framework implied by the metaphor. The second danger is that when a metaphor hardens into one of the implicit and unquestioned metaphors of everyday or specialist language, it starts to have an impact not only on the way we see social or market reality, but also on the way we structure that reality and the policies we advocate. (Bronk 2009, p. 23)

He cites Thomas Carlyle on the dangers of seeing society as a machine (ibid., pp. 23–4). 'The danger that hidden metaphors may distort both our vision and social reality itself makes it imperative that – as economists, policy-makers, entrepreneurs and voters – we remain conscious of the metaphorical structuring of economic vision and analysis' (ibid., p. 24).

The theme of Bronk's book is the clash between rationalist and Romantic outlooks, based respectively on mechanical and organic metaphors.

> Carlyle was pointing to the most important truth about such dominant structuring metaphors – that those who have internalized them cease to have access to the same evidence and the same yardsticks in debate as those using different metaphorical schemas would have. To use Carlyle's own image, unless we break free from the metaphorical chains we have made for ourselves, our outlooks remain for ever imprisoned by them and hence divided from the outlooks of those captured by other metaphors. (Ibid., p. 47)

But Bronk himself uses 'microfoundations' in several places uncritically, without realizing that it itself is a metaphor (for example, ibid., pp. 127, 165, 214, 301), even though he doesn't *believe* it: 'The social unit (because it is more than the simple sum of its parts) is an important explanatory force in its own right' (p. 245).

'Microfoundations', then, is simply a bad metaphor. Or perhaps, as a previous reference to Klamer and Leonard might suggest, it is a bad analogy. Murphy notes that there is an Aristotelean 'circle of metaphors': 'laws of physics', 'natural law', custom as 'second nature':

> The use of these expressions to define nature, custom, and law is so ubiquitous that they have lost their metaphorical force; the notion of 'the laws of physics', for example, has become so clichéd that it is now taken literally. These are

> dormant metaphors and we cannot interrogate them until they are awakened; and since a metaphor is a condensed analogy, we awaken it by making explicit the implicit analogy. The first step, then, in making sense of a metaphor is to unpack the implicit analogy. (Murphy 1994, pp. 541–2)

Murphy notes a difficulty: 'Metaphors are obscure in a way that analogies are not … there are always several possible analogies implied by any one metaphor. A metaphor is not simply an abbreviated analogy; it is an abbreviation that may stand for many different analogies' (ibid., p. 545).

Like Murphy, Lagueux notes that not everything which is not to be clearly understood literally is necessarily metaphorical. He stresses that 'there is no hard and fast boundary between "literal" and "metaphorical"', and criticizes McCloskey and her supporters, who tend 'to conflate the use of metaphors and that of abstract concepts'. 'It is correct', Lagueux continues, 'to oppose "metaphorical" to "literal"', but this 'should not be confused with the opposition between what is abstract and what is concrete' (Lagueux 1999, pp. 6, 8). So-called metaphors must therefore be clearly disentangled from explicit analogies, which are metaphorically much more acceptable (ibid., p. 5). Thus he distinguishes metaphors from similes: 'An analogy is to a simile what an allegory is to a metaphor … whereas metaphors and allegory are poetical and essentially suggestive literary tropes, simile and analogy are analytical exercises which are perfectly suited to scientific analysis' (ibid., p. 15; stress deleted). Lagueux's own example of an analogy in economics is 'optimization', originally borrowed from physics but now a perfectly legitimate analytical concept in its own right. 'Liquidity', on the other hand, *is* metaphorical. Lagueux concludes by acknowledging that 'reliance on analogies can, in some circumstances, be misleading and deceptive' (Lagueux 1999, p. 20).

Using Lagueux's terms, I believe that 'microfoundations' is not a 'poetical' or 'essentially suggestive' literary trope but should be interpreted as an analogy, since in requiring the reduction of macroeconomic theory to microeconomics it very clearly specifies a set of 'analytical exercises'. This raises the question of the criteria for identifying 'misleading and deceptive' analogies. How, then, might good and bad analogies be distinguished? Scott Gordon specifies four conditions for a successful analogy (himself using a baseball metaphor in the process):

> Let us symbolize the proposition to be proved as P and the analogy of it as A. To get on first base, it is necessary to show that P and A are indeed similar in certain respects, while recognizing also that they are different in other respects which, for the purpose of the exercise, are construed to be irrelevant. To move to second,

> A must of course be explicable. If it is not, then the process of explaining by reference to A merely replaces one mystery by another. In order to be safe on third, the explanation of A must be *true*; otherwise P is being explained by a second-hand argument that is itself false. Finally, to cross home plate, the causal mechanism known to be at work in A must be explicitly shown to parallel the mechanism at work in P. That is to say, one must be able to demonstrate how P works, since that is the object of the exercise. (Gordon 1991, pp. 50–51)

My argument is that the microfoundations analogy confirms Gordon's more general conclusion: 'The history of the social sciences is replete with analogical argument but these requirements frequently remain unfulfilled' (ibid., p. 541).

'Microfoundations' is a spatial analogy, taken from architecture, from the building trades or from constructional engineering. It has some very clear implications. Foundations have to come first, they must be solid, and they need to be reasonably extensive. (Victoria Chick reminds me that in earthquake zones foundations need also to be quite flexible. This is food for thought – especially perhaps for inflexible mainstream economists – but I do not think that it substantially affects my argument in this book).You cannot construct a high-rise building first and then put in the foundations, as an afterthought. They must be solid: we all know what happened to the foolish man in the Bible who built his house upon sand, and Takishi Negishi's stepping stones would not be a great improvement. Finally, they must be extensive: you would not want an entire shopping centre to have the same meagre foundations as a single suburban house.

Mainstream economists claim that their 'microfoundations' satisfy all three conditions. The model of the rational, forward-looking, utility-maximizing representative agent already exists; it is logically sound; and it has been applied to a very wide range of (micro)economic behaviour, extending imperialistically well beyond the former borders of the discipline to provide microfoundations also for sociology, political science and social psychology (Lazear 2000 is a classic statement of this claim). Heterodox economists are at a considerable disadvantage on all three criteria: their microeconomics is a work-in progress that lacks the rigorous analytical core of neoclassical theory and is in principle incapable of supplanting the other social sciences. Thus the 'microfoundations' analogy places opponents of the mainstream at a very real methodological disadvantage.

Or it would do so, were the analogy a good one. In the context of Gordon's analysis, P is the statement that 'macroeconomic theory must have rigorous microfoundations', while A is the proposition that 'all buildings need secure foundations'. Gordon's second and third requirements are evidently met, since A is both explicable and true, but his first and third requirements are not: P and A differ in ways that are *not* irrelevant to P, and the causal mechanisms that operate in A have no clear parallel in P. There is a simple reason for this: P is false. It is possible to construct at least the outlines of a credible macroeconomic theory with little or no reference to microeconomics.

In a frequently cited passage the neoclassical Keynesian James Meade summarized the Keynesian revolution as replacing a model in which 'a dog called *saving* wagged its tail labelled *investment*' with one in which 'a dog called *investment* wagged its tail labelled *saving*' (Meade 1975, p. 82). As this striking metaphor suggests, any 'Keynesian' macroeconomics worthy of the name must begin with an income–expenditure model of the type first written down by Paul Samuelson in 1948 (see Schneider 2010). This model was implicit in the *General Theory* and was almost stated explicitly, six years before Samuelson, in Michał Kalecki's paper on the theory of aggregate profits, which was itself an elaboration of arguments already found in his first, entirely macroeconomic, model of the trade cycle (Kalecki 1935, 1942). The income–expenditure model lies behind the 'paradox of thrift' (above, p. 9), which hinges on the aggregate relationship between savings and investment. It demonstrates that total output and employment will normally be demand-constrained, not supply-constrained, so that the full employment of labour, and the full utilization of productive capacity, will be the exception rather than the rule. Keynes denied that there were good reasons to believe otherwise, rejecting the Wicksellian mechanism by means of which investment and saving are brought into equality at full employment by variations in the rate of interest. The rate of interest, he argued, is a quite different phenomenon, which equates the demand and supply for money. Savings and investment are brought into equality through variations in the level of income. It is significant that the only diagram in the *General Theory*, which Keynes derived from Roy Harrod, is used to illustrate this fundamental point (Keynes 1936, p. 180).

The income–expenditure model is closely related to the expenditure multiplier, a concept that was discovered independently and almost simultaneously by several writers in the early 1930s (King 1998) including, in addition to a Pole (Kalecki), an Australian (L.F. Giblin), a Dane (Jens Warming) and an Englishman (Richard Kahn). All four variants of the multiplier were based on the simple principle that, when income rises, domestic expenditure rises by a lesser amount, due either to increased saving or to increases in imports, so that the second, third and subsequent rounds of increased expenditure constitute a converging series. This seems obvious now, but it was much less obvious at the time. In a world in which full employment was guaranteed, the multiplier would always equal zero, since an increase in one category of expenditure would automatically be offset by a decrease of the same amount in another category: higher public spending would 'crowd out' an equal quantity of private expenditure, for example.

The crucial point is that these are *macroeconomic* theories, which are consistent with a very wide range of assumptions about individual behaviour and therefore also with a considerable variety of microeconomic models. The law of large numbers suggests that the behaviour of aggregates is often easier to understand and to predict than the behaviour of individuals, as George Shackle (1954) noted long ago (below, pp. 158–9). Geoff Hodgson makes a similar point about the operation of institutions, which function in such a way that 'macroeconomic order and relative stability are reinforced alongside diversity at the microeconomic level ... The concept of an institution, properly handled, points not to a spurious supra-individual objectivity, nor to the uniformity of individual agents, but to the concept of socio-economic order, arising not despite but because of the variety at the micro-level' (Hodgson 2000, pp. 117–18). And Joseph Heath, in criticizing the principle of methodological individualism, notes that 'statistical analysis' may give better explanations than individualistic ones, for example in relation to crime rates and the causes of their increase or decline (Heath 2009, pp. 13–14).

Similarly, the Keynesian income–expenditure model stands or falls by its ability to capture, in a highly simplified form, important features of the real-world capitalist economy, viewed as a whole. It does not *need* microeconomic foundations, neoclassical or otherwise. The two principles of the fallacy of composition and downward causation, which I stated at the beginning of this chapter, are again relevant here. The fallacy of composition entails that the elementary laws of Keynesian macroeconomics could not be inferred even from complete knowledge of the correct microeconomic models, should such models exist. Downward causation entails that the operation of macroeconomic laws may significantly influence individual decisions. I shall provide further examples of both principles in the next chapter.

2.6 CONCLUSION

Again, I am anxious not to be misunderstood. Rejection of the microfoundations dogma does not entail acceptance of 'the doctrines of universalism, conceptual realism, holism, collectivism, and some forms of *Gestaltpsychologie*', according to which 'society is an entity living its own life, independent of and separate from the lives of the various individuals, acting on its own behalf and aiming at its own ends which are different from the ends sought by the individuals' (von Mises 1949, p. 145). It does not require me to deny the relevance of microeconomics to macroeconomic theory, or for that matter the relevance of macroeconomics to microeconomic theory (on which, see Section 3.5 below). Neither does it mean that economics needs no foundations of any sort. On the contrary: there is an urgent need to provide social and philosophical foundations for economic theory, micro and macro, and here it is the mainstream economists who have failed. They need to be aware (as Marx would have said) that they are attempting to model *capitalism*, not simple commodity production. Hence there are two classes of agents, capitalists and workers, and it is the former who own the means of production and control the production and sale of commodities. Firms are *not* simply the agents of households. Production is motivated by *profit*, not – at least, not directly – by the utility functions of asocial, classless 'consumers'. Since profit is by definition the difference between revenue and costs, that is, the difference between two sums of money, it is pointless to model a capitalist economy in terms of barter. These social foundations of any meaningful economic theory are exceedingly obvious, but they are routinely violated in the mainstream models that employ RARE microfoundations, as we have already seen in the case of Wickens (above, p. 2).

As for the philosophical foundations of economics, a minimum requirement is some form of scientific realism. This is a doctrine that comes in a number of varieties, ranging from the minimalist version advocated by Uskali Mäki (2011) to the more restrictive variant proposed by John Searle (1995) right through to the very demanding and precisely specified 'Critical Realism' of Roy Bhaskar and Tony Lawson (see, for example, Lawson 2003). All versions of scientific realism require that economic models display a substantial degree of 'realisticness'. That is to say, they should be immediately recognizable as simplified versions of a very complicated reality. Using the 'iconic metaphor' considered previously, economic models should resemble the city models that are sometimes on display in local history museums and not the fantastic constructions that feature in futuristic

Hollywood movies (and were brilliantly foreshadowed in the 1925 Fritz Lang film, *Metropolis*). Economic theory should bear a close resemblance to 'the economic society in which we actually live' (Keynes 1936, p. 3). As we have seen, Wickens also fails this test (above, pp. 2–3).

In his interpretation of Kalecki, Peter Kriesler (1996, p. 66) argues that 'micro and macro stand side by side, with important feedbacks between them'. This spatial metaphor, I think, is spot on. Returning to the constructional metaphor, microeconomics and macroeconomics should be thought of as two separate buildings, equal in height, adjacent to each other and connected by footbridges. Both rest on a single, solid and extensive set of social and philosophical foundations. The people who work in the two buildings are on friendly terms and in frequent (preferably, increasingly frequent) contact with each other. What they do in their own building is different from what their colleagues in the other building do, but it is not incompatible, and they both aim to reduce the inconsistencies over time. These efforts, however, should not consume all their energies. There are no methodological grounds for evacuating the macro building and moving all its occupants into the micro building (and also none for the opposite course of action).

In sum: 'microfoundations' is a very bad metaphor, which has caused considerable confusion and has been used to justify some very bad decisions by macroeconomic theorists. The full extent of the confusion will be revealed in Parts II and III. But we have not yet finished with metaphors. Quite early in the development of the microfoundations dogma, the philosopher of science Alan Nelson (1984) recognized it as an example of *micro-reduction*, a contentious doctrine that has been debated for generations (if not centuries) by both natural and social scientists; it is also itself a (contentious) metaphor. In the particular context of economics, Nelson doubted that micro-reduction would succeed. The same doctrine was proposed for the social sciences by Joseph Schumpeter and Max Weber, who advocated (more or less consistently) the pursuit of *methodological individualism*. In the life sciences its most prominent advocate is Richard Dawkins, who uses the slightly different term, *hierarchical reductionism*. To illustrate the principle, Dawkins uses metaphors that are so spectacularly bad that they almost become good, since they expose the weaknesses of the reductionist analogy more clearly than any literal statement could ever do. The next two chapters are devoted to these issues.

3. Microfoundations as micro-reduction

3.1 INTRODUCTION

What then, exactly, is meant by the 'reduction' of one theory to another? The philosopher of science Kenneth Schaffner offers the following brief, general definition: 'Intertheoretic explanation, in which one theory is explained by another theory, usually formulated for a different domain, is generally termed *theory reduction*' (Schaffner 1967, p. 137; original stress). 'Hierarchical reduction' or 'micro-reduction', as exemplified by the microfoundations dogma, is a special case of this general principle.

The word 'reduction', however, turns out to be a rather slippery term, at least in English (it would be instructive to know if similar complications arise in other languages), and in Section 3.2 of this chapter I consider some of the problems that it poses. The remarkably bad metaphors used by Richard Dawkins to justify the reduction of the life sciences to genetics are exposed in Section 3.3, while Section 3.4 outlines some of the objections raised by philosophers of science to the general principle of inter-theoretic reduction. In Section 3.5 I apply these criticisms to the microfoundations dogma in economics. This raises the question of possible macrofoundations for microeconomics, which I discuss – and reject – in Section 3.6. The chapter concludes, in Section 3.7, with some brief reflections on the failure of the micro-reduction project, in economics and in other areas of thought.

3.2 'REDUCTION' AS A METAPHOR

The common meaning of 'reduction', of course, is to make smaller, to diminish in number or size. This is the way in which it is used in arithmetic, and also in cookery (where 'reducing' a stock or sauce means boiling off some of the liquid, leaving a smaller volume). The *Shorter Oxford Dictionary*, however, gives no less than ten definitions of 'reduction' and 23 of 'reduce', including the one that is most relevant to the philosophy of science: 'decompose or resolve (a compound) into a simple compound or its constituent elements'. This is taken from chemistry, where it is apparently now obsolete and has been replaced by a rather different meaning: 'cause to combine with hydrogen or to undergo reduction; add an electron to, lower the oxidation number of, (an atom)'. No clear diminution in number or quantity is implied here, and hence no necessary movement from higher-level entities (the 'macro') to lower-level entities (the 'micro').

The American sociologist Howard Becker documents the plain, non-metaphorical, commonsense use of 'reduction' in empirical sociology. As Becker relates, the eminent Austrian émigré Paul Lazarsfeld advocated a process of simplification in which the number of categories of observed variables could be diminished without any loss of information. There were similarities with the age-old principle of Occam's Razor: 'avoid the proliferation of unnecessary entities'. When investigating social disadvantage, for example, it was found to be generally unnecessary to group individuals by race, place of birth and education. Since non-white people – in the United States or in Australia – are likely to be disadvantaged on all counts, one dichotomy (white/non-white) will do the work of the three that the researcher might be tempted to use (white/non-white, native born/born overseas, graduate/non-graduate). The details of such a reduction process might be disputed, in any particular case, but it would be difficult to object to the procedure in principle (Becker 1998, pp. 177–8). And it was intended as a pragmatic device to make research easier, not as a methodological dogma. Lazarsfeld also advocated a reverse process of splitting categories and thereby increasing their number, to which he gave the rather awkward name 'substruction'. Either reduction or substruction might be appropriate in the context of a particular piece of research: it all depended on the circumstances (ibid., p. 181).

If only matters were quite that simple. 'Reduction' is indeed used metaphorically in the context of the philosophy of science, as is apparent from the frequent references in the literature to the 'bridge laws' that supposedly connect theories from different domains. And micro-reduction is a special case of the general principle of inter-theoretic reduction. Philosophers of science have argued about it for centuries, since it raises some fundamental questions, including the mind–body problem; the relationship between genes, organisms, species and environments; and the possibility that the laws of physics might provide 'rock bottom' explanations for all scientific phenomena (Wilson 1998). There is also a long and very important tradition in economics (and the social sciences more generally) of 'methodological individualism', which I shall discuss in Chapter 4.

In order for the microfoundations dogma in economics to be correct, three propositions concerning inter-theoretic reduction must be true. First, reduction is both possible and mandatory. Second, reduction must take place in the vertical (and not the horizontal) plane, since a bridge is not a foundation. Third, vertical reduction must be downwards, from macro to micro, not upwards, from micro to macro. All three propositions are dubious. As we shall see in Section 3.3, there is a big question mark over the possibility of successful theory reduction, and no compelling reason to make it mandatory. The second proposition fares no better: even if inter-theoretic reduction were possible, and mandatory, it need not be vertical, since it could legitimately take place in the horizontal plane (Kuipers 2001, p. 156). I shall return to this question in Section 3.5.

Finally, the third proposition is also not a trivial matter:

> Purely formal criteria, however, prove to be insufficient to determine the direction of the reduction ... Unfortunately, merely formal criteria for reduction would permit, say, an economic theory to reduce a formally isomorphic chemical theory. The envisioned reduction therefore would fail to capture the physicalist's commitment that higher-level phenomena depend on the physical phenomena that compose them. (Trout 1991, pp. 387–8)

It is not difficult to think of 'reductions' that operate in the opposite direction. For example, in vulgar Marxism (and sometimes also in more sophisticated versions), an individual's beliefs are explained in terms of her class position, in the context of the hegemonic ideology of capitalist society: 'in the final analysis', that is to say, such individual characteristics as national identity or religious affiliation are attributed to the demands of capital accumulation (Halliday 1992).

There is a long tradition of this form of reductionism, going back in the case of religious beliefs to Ludwig Feuerbach, Karl Marx and the later literature inspired by Richard Tawney (1926) and Max Weber (1930). While you may find their materialist explanations of developments in religious thought to be unconvincing, they are not obviously absurd or contradictory. This, then, is a legitimate form of reductionism, and it operates *upwards*, from micro to macro. Another example comes from sociobiology. There is some difficulty in providing a Darwinian explanation of altruistic behaviour: how are the genes of an unselfish individual transmitted from one generation to the next when such an individual is more likely to be killed and eaten than a non-altruistic member of the species? One answer runs in terms of group selection. Groups made up of unselfish individuals are more likely to survive than groups dominated by selfish ones (Kropotkin 1902; van den Bergh and Gowdy 2003, pp. 71–3). Again, this may as a matter of fact be incorrect, but it is not absurd or contradictory, and it involves a reduction upwards, this time from the individual to the group. You can probably think of other examples. I shall have more to say in Section 3.5 about upward reduction in economics.

3.3 MORE BAD METAPHORS

In his best-selling book *The Blind Watchmaker* Richard Dawkins uses mechanical examples – the steam engine, the computer, the car – to defend the principle of hierarchical reductionism (micro-reduction by another name) in the life sciences:

> The behaviour of a motor car is explained in terms of cylinders, carburettors and sparking plugs. It is true that each of these components is nested atop a pyramid of explanations at lower levels. But if you asked me how a motor car worked you would think me somewhat pompous if I answered in terms of Newton's laws and the laws of thermodynamics, and downright obscurantist if I answered in terms of fundamental particles. It is doubtless true that at bottom the behaviour of a motor car is to be explained in terms of interactions between fundamental particles. But it is much more useful to explain it in terms of interactions between pistons, cylinders and sparking plugs. (Dawkins 1996, p. 12)

The hierarchical reductionist, Dawkins continues,

> … explains a complex entity at any particular level in the hierarchy of organization, in terms of entities only one level down the hierarchy, entities which, themselves, are likely to be complex enough to need further reducing to their own constituent parts, and so on … the hierarchical reductionist believes that caburettors are explained in terms of smaller units, … , which are explained in terms of smaller units … , which are ultimately explained in terms of the smallest of fundamental particles. Reductionism, in this sense, is just another name for an honest desire to understand how things work. (Ibid., p. 13)

Well, perhaps. A motor mechanic just might be happy to have a complete knowledge of all the parts, and might not need to know anything else in order to acquire a full knowledge of the operation of the car. I myself am totally unmechanical, and would not be a good person to ask about this. But I do know that cars are not just pieces of machinery. They have social, political, economic and cultural significance. They are studied by traffic engineers, by urban sociologists, by town planners, and even by political economists who are interested in the demise of the so-called 'Fordist' stage of capitalist development (Amin 1997). None of them could conceivably be satisfied with information about car components, not even if it was accompanied by knowledge of metallurgy, chemistry and particle physics. This is not to say that information about the parts might not be useful to them, in some circumstances, or that they should dismiss such information as trivial or misleading. But it would certainly not be sufficient, and would probably not be very enlightening for their particular purposes. The biologist Steven Rose, whose criticisms of micro-reduction will be considered in Chapter 4, also takes issue with Dawkins's argument, which implied (for example) that the speed of a bus could be fully explained by reference to its mechanical properties. 'While this is one perfectly appropriate way of describing *how* it is that the bus drives fast', Rose argued, 'the *why* question relates to the complex framework of public and private transport, schedules, road congestion, driver skills, and so on within which the mechanisms of the bus engine are embedded' (Rose 2005, p. 87; original stress).

The two fundamental principles of the fallacy of composition and downward causation are again helpful in explaining precisely how Dawkins has been misled by his own metaphors. It is not possible to infer all the properties of the car from a complete knowledge of its parts, precisely because of its social, political, economic and cultural significance. And the same applies to the speed of a bus, as Rose suggests. Moreover, changes in the social, political, economic and cultural context in which cars are driven frequently affect not just the car as a whole machine but also some or all of its parts: causation also runs downwards, from the larger to the smaller units, and not just upwards from the smaller to the larger as Dawkins maintains.

The fallacy of composition has recently been invoked by the philosopher Mary Midgley, this time using a biological rather than a mechanical example: 'Complex wholes such as an ant colony or a living body act *as wholes*. The structural properties that make this possible could not be inferred from a knowledge of their separate parts'. Thus it follows that 'in general, the reductive thinking that theorizes about large-scale behaviour from analogy with the behaviour of small parts is not reliable or scientific' (Midgley 2010, p. 8; original stress), and it would not have found favour with Charles Darwin. Dawkins's error, she suggests, results from 'treating microphenomena as if they were a separate cause of the large-scale activities they are involved in, rather than just one aspect of them'. Objections to this 'rather strange way of thinking' have ancient roots:

> Thus, as Socrates pointed out in the *Phaedo*, someone who is asked why he is sitting here may answer by giving a detailed account of how his knees, hips and

> ankles work. But this kind of reply tends to leave the questioner feeling that his question has not been answered. (Ibid., p. 50)

The fallacy of composition is closely related to the concepts of *emergence* and *irreducibility*. The latter is 'often viewed as the sense in which emergent properties are autonomous from the more basic phenomena that give rise to them' (Bedau and Humphreys 2008, p. 9). That is to say:

> ... a state or other feature of a system is emergent if it is impossible to predict the existence of that feature on the basis of a complete theory of basic phenomena in the system ... A closely related idea is that emergent properties cannot be explained given a complete understanding of more basic phenomena. (Ibid., p. 10)

A complete theory of car components would not allow us to explain the social, political, economic and cultural significance of the motor car. These are emergent properties, which cannot be inferred from a theory of the parts and cannot be reduced to it. That is why we need traffic engineers, urban sociologists, town planners and political economists. I shall have much more to say about emergent properties in Chapter 4.

The two principles are linked, since one reason why 'it is not a trivial matter to infer the properties of the whole' is the phenomenon of downward causation. To understand the causes of changes in car components over time, we need more than knowledge of metallurgy, chemistry and particle physics, more even than complete knowledge of these things; we also need to know about society, politics, psychology and economics. There are two well-known examples of downward causation from the mid-twentieth century motor industry. One is provided by the fins and other ornamental embellishments, with no engineering advantages, which were added to cars on the insistence of marketing specialists who drew on studies of consumer psychology in order to suggest ways of increasing brand loyalty and therefore also profitability (Packard 1957). The other was the belated introduction of a range of safety features in the wake of an intense political controversy over the dangers involved in driving cars without them (Nader 1965). In both cases causation ran downwards, from human society to the component parts of its machines – from larger units to smaller units, from macro to micro. In Dawkins's 'hierarchical reductionism', however, causation can only go upwards, from micro to macro. The crucial phrase in the passage previously quoted is 'one level *down* the hierarchy'.

'It goes without saying', Dawkins writes, in an attempt to defend himself against the accusation that he is a non-existent, baby-eating type of reductionist, 'that the kinds of explanations that are suitable at high levels in the hierarchy are quite different from the kinds of explanations which are suitable at lower levels. This was the point of explaining cars in terms of carburettors rather than quarks' (Dawkins 1996, p. 13). A similar argument might also be invoked by mainstream microeconomists to absolve them from having to reformulate their theories in terms of neuro-chemistry or the physiology of the brain. But this is already a retreat from the reductionist position. And the direction of causation in hierarchical reduction is *always* upwards, never downwards. It runs from the smaller unit to the larger unit, from micro to the macro: from the gene to the organism in Dawkins's version of Darwinian biology, from the individual agent to the macroeconomy in the case of the microfoundations dogma, from the car component to the car in his motoring metaphor. Before we consider the microfoundations dogma as an example of an unsuccessful micro-reduction, however, there is a lot more to be said about reductionism as a general principle.

3.4 THE PERILS OF REDUCTIONISM

There is a very substantial literature in the philosophy of science on these questions. More than thirty years ago William Wimsatt's survey article contained 132 references, all of them on the question of reduction in the natural sciences. He himself was broadly favourable to the principle of reduction, but with significant reservations (Wimsatt 1979, p. 361). I suspect that a full bibliography of the relevant literature since then would contain many hundreds of items, especially if it included work on reduction in the social sciences. Steven Horst (2007) has a substantial bibliography on the treatment of reduction in the philosophy of science literature. Some of the more important contributions in the second half of the twentieth century were made by John Kemeny and Paul Oppenheim (1956), Oppenheim and Hilary Putnam (1958), Kenneth Schaffner (1967), Lawrence Sklar (1967), Robert Causey (1972), Thomas Nickles (1973), Kemeny (1976), D.H. Mellor (1982), Gregory Currie (1984) and Rajeev Bhargava (1992). See also Brodbeck (1968, Section 3) and Richard Boyd, Philip Gasper and J.D. Trout (1991, Section III).

This is not the place for a comprehensive survey of the literature on micro-reduction. Instead I will note a few important, relatively recent contributions and will conclude by summarizing the arguments of Horst, who presents a convincing case against reduction, with specific reference to the reduction of psychology to the physiology of the brain. Debates about the possibility of reducing one science to another probably began in classical antiquity. In the modern era, as Horst suggests,

> It is worthy of note that reductionism enjoyed its greatest popularity in two periods: the seventeenth and the twentieth centuries. In both cases, it was developed explicitly on the model of mathematical reasoning. For early modern advocates like Galileo, Hobbes and Descartes, the paradigm to be emulated was geometric construction and proof. For the Positivists and Logical Empiricists, it was the logical syllogism and axiomatic systems .... Reductionists from Hobbes and Descartes to Carnap and Ernest Nagel supposed that complicated physical systems could likewise be understood as derivations or constructions out of characterizations (definitions) and laws (axioms) pertaining to the simplest material bodies. (Horst 2007, p. 36)

I shall return to Nagel's (negative) opinion of the prospects for reduction in the social sciences, and in particular economics, in Chapter 4 (below, pp. 48–9).

In the mid-nineteenth century there was a vigorous 'emergence movement' that denied that micro-reduction was possible in the natural sciences, though apparently no attempt was made to apply the same arguments to the social sciences. Interestingly, this movement involved John Stuart Mill (McLaughlin 1992), who sometimes took a very different line with respect to social science: 'Human beings in society have no properties but those which are derived from, and may be resolved into, the laws of the nature of the individual man. In social phenomena the composition of causes is the universal law' (Mill 1874 [1974], p. 879, cited by Rizvi 1994, p. 359). The nineteenth-century case for emergence failed, as McLaughlin relates, on empirical grounds: the necessary emergent properties were simply not there to be discovered.

Almost a century later, in the 1920s and early 1930s, the Vienna Circle debated the 'unity of science'. One of its members, the Austrian positivist philosopher Otto Neurath, discussed the unification of science with his fellow exile Friedrich von Hayek in the early 1940s. As John O'Neill has noted, this is a complicated issue:

> The project could take a number of forms: (i) a reductionist project in which all the sciences would be logically derivable via bridge-laws from physics; (ii) a programme for a unified method which would be followed by all sciences; (iii) a project for a unified language of science; and (iv) a project that would integrate the different sciences, such that, on any specific problem, all relevant sciences

> could be called upon – a project for the 'orchestration of the sciences'. All four projects were defended by some positivists at different moments in the history of the movement. (O'Neill 2004, p. 436)

Thus the first, reductionist, variant was only one form that the unification of science might take. It was vigorously opposed by Neurath, along with the second variant: 'would it not be preferable to treat all statements and all sciences as coordinated and to abandon for good the traditional hierarchy: physical sciences, biological sciences, social sciences and similar types of "scientific pyramidism"?' (Neurath 1944, p. 8, cited by O'Neill 2004, p. 436). Neurath himself favoured the third and fourth variants, since, he believed, the coordination of the sciences required a unified language. Seventy years on, the prospect of a unified language for all the sciences appears most unlikely, but the 'coordination' and 'orchestration of the sciences' – in this context, of microeconomics and macroeconomics – is a worthy project, and in repudiating 'scientific pyramidism' (Dawkins's 'hierarchical reductionism') Neurath was very firmly on the right side of a much later argument in the methodology of economics (see also Cartwright et al. 1996).

In the 1950s both Michael Polanyi and Herbert Simon came to similar conclusions. Polanyi insisted that different 'levels of reality' cannot be reduced to each other, if only because of the different types of 'personal knowledge' required in each individual science. It would be a mistake, he suggested, to suppose that the reality of a machine could be grasped only by physics. On the contrary, a 'physical and chemical investigation cannot convey the understanding of a machine as expressed by its operational principles. In fact, it can say nothing at all about the way the machine works or ought to work' (Polanyi 1958, p. 329, cited by Coates 1996, p. 113). In complex systems, Simon argued,

> … the whole is more than the sum of the parts, not in an ultimate, metaphysical sense, but in the very important pragmatic sense that, given the properties of the parts and the laws of their interaction, it is not a trivial matter to infer the properties of the whole. In the face of complexity, an in-principle reductionist may be at the same time a pragmatic holist. (Simon 1962, p. 468)

I shall return to this final, very important, question in the final section of this chapter.

Criticism of micro-reduction by philosophers of science continued unabated in subsequent decades. Unlike Simon, Alan Garfinkel was an 'in principle' anti-reductionist: 'Microreduction is sometimes thought of as an ideal', he wrote in 1981, 'something that is possible "in theory" though not "in practice". One can then be a reductionist while conceding a "practical" independence' to higher-level explanations and the special sciences that generate them. 'But my claim is stronger than that: the explanations we want simply do not exist at the underlying level' (Garfinkel 1981 [1991], p. 449). He took an example from population ecology. There are well-known periodic fluctuations in the populations of foxes and rabbits: the foxes eat so many rabbits that there are too few left to sustain the fox population, which collapses, thereby taking the pressure off the rabbits, and so on. This is the familiar macroexplanation of the population dynamics; it is a causal account of the structural relations between the populations of the two species. A convincing microexplanation of the death of rabbit *r*, captured by fox *f*, would contain a great deal of information, much of it irrelevant to the macro question; Garfinkel terms this 'redundant causality'. Like Rose, he maintains that it answers a different question: 'The microexplanation tells us the mechanism by which the macroexplanation operated. The structure gives us the *why*, while the microexplanation gives the *how*' (ibid., p. 448). Individualist explanations in the social sciences invariably contain 'hidden structural presuppositions' that 'rule out the reductionist program in social theory' (ibid., p. 455; here Garfinkel refers to Thomas Hobbes's *Leviathan*).

In a book published three years later, Susan James revealed herself to be no less sceptical regarding the prospects of reducing sociology to individual psychology. 'The individualist case for the reducibility of theories about social wholes', she concludes, is

> ... far from proven, and there are strong grounds for believing that it cannot be completed. But in addition to these theoretical difficulties there is also a pragmatic one, which emerges as soon as we consider what would be involved in the sort of reduction that individualism requires. Whatever their other qualities, individualist explanations will clearly be enormously cumbersome ... A realistic sense of what reductions involve may lead us to question the point, as well as the feasibility, of the reductionist enterprise. If we can understand the social world in holist terms, why should we bother to reduce it to individualist ones? (James 1984, pp. 52–3)

In *Individualism and the Unity of Science*, Harold Kincaid (1997) was also highly critical of reductionist strategies in social science, at least when applied to explanation rather than ontology; there is an excellent brief summary of the arguments of his book in Kincaid (1998). As he notes, wryly, 'The fallacious inference from "W is composed of P" to "W is fully explainable in terms of P" seems irresistible' (Kincaid 1997, p. 6). 'There are three good reasons', Kincaid argues,

> ... to think that reduction will fail on any likely development of social sciences: (1) multiple realizations of social events are likely; (2) individual actions have indefinitely many social descriptions depending on context; and (3) any workable individualist social theory will in all likelihood presuppose social facts. Each of these claims, if true, rules out reduction as defined here. (Ibid., p. 33)

The second and (especially) the third problems are fatal also to the project of methodological individualism in the social sciences, and will be discussed in more detail in Chapter 4 below.

Kincaid's first problem, that of multiple realizations, is connected to the intricate philosophical concept of supervenience (on which, see Hands 2001, pp. 170–71). Kincaid explains:

> Reducing one theory to another requires that we have some lawlike way to connect the vocabulary of the two theories. If, however, the kinds of events described by the higher-level theory are brought about by indefinitely many different kinds of lower-level entities, then such a lawful connection may be lacking. As a result, we will have no way of deducing higher-level explanations from lower-level ones. Reduction will thus fail. (Kincaid 1997, pp. 50–51)

He uses economics as a case study in the difficulties that these three problems pose for any micro-reduction project, arguing that 'optimizing processes' cannot be enlisted as a necessary condition for good explanations of economic (or, more generally, of social) phenomena (ibid., pp. 114–17). 'Of course', he concludes, 'reductionist intuitions are not completely misguided. Complex wholes obviously do not exist nor act independently of their parts. Information about underlying detail can help confirm and can deepen our explanations. But these are anemic reductionist doctrines that leave space for autonomous and essential higher-level explanations' (ibid., pp. 144–5).

A slightly different approach is taken by Theo Kuipers, who rejects both radical reductionism, 'the belief that every macro-concept and macro-law can be reduced', and radical holism, 'the belief that all (interesting) concepts and laws of the domain cannot be reduced', in favour of the intermediate position of 'restricted reductionism'. This is 'the belief that some concepts and laws may be reducible, but others may not be'. In this spirit Kuipers endorses a 'mixed strategy', which 'favors reduction when possible. Roughly speaking, in the mixed strategy one describes the macro-phenomena and their possible relations in macro-terms, and tries to explain them in micro-terms as far as possible, and hence in macro-terms as far as necessary' (Kuipers 2001, p. 156). Kuipers applies his mixed strategy to the relationship between psychology and neuro-physiology (ibid., pp. 175–81).

For Horst, however, any form of reduction represents an outdated remnant of the philosophy of science of the 1950s. 'Often discussed cases of failed or incomplete intertheoretic reduction in the literature' include the reduction of thermodynamics to statistical mechanics; the reduction of thermodynamics/statistical mechanics to quantum mechanics; the reduction of chemistry to quantum mechanics; the reduction of classical mechanics to quantum mechanics; the reduction of evolutionary biology to genetics; and the reduction of genetics to molecular genetics (Horst 2007, p. 59). Horst concludes that 'explanation is not generally derivation, and indeed the majority of scientific explanations cannot even be successfully *reconstructed* as reductions' (ibid., p. 53; original stress). None of these examples is taken from the social sciences; Horst's own interests are in the philosophy of mind, and he has nothing to say about economics. He advocates 'the methodological autonomy of the special sciences', with 'a plurality of explanatory types', 'a variety of separate good-making qualities or explanatory virtues, each of which contributes to the epistemic quality of scientific understanding', and also 'a variety of interdomain relations' (ibid., pp. 56–8; original stress deleted). He concludes that there are 'a variety of fruitful ways that two scientific domains can come into contact with one another, but that fall far short of the kind of derivation relation that is distinctive of broad reduction' (ibid., p. 60).

Whether this entails the fundamental 'disunity of science', as Horst himself suggests (ibid., p. 60), or instead vindicates Kincaid's (1997, p. 1) picture of 'a non-reductive yet unified science' remains open, along with the even more intriguing question as to whether macroeconomics and microeconomics (now) constitute two *separate* – but related – 'special sciences'. I shall return to this issue in Chapter 11. But it is now time to apply the lessons that have been learned from the reduction literature to the particular example of microfoundations for macroeconomics.

3.5 MICRO-REDUCTION IN ECONOMICS

As we saw in the previous chapter, one of the first philosophers of science to pay serious attention to the issue of microfoundations in economics was Alan Nelson, who regarded it as 'a fertile field ... as a source of insights about what may be involved in reducing one theory to another' (Nelson

1984, p. 573). Unlike the mind/body problem, the relationship between microeconomics and macroeconomics seemed to be a relatively simple matter, which did not involve the deep questions raised by Cartesian dualism. Thus, Nelson suggested, 'it does seem that a reduction of macroeconomics to microeconomics would not be plagued with the kind of ontological difficulties which might attend schemes for reducing, say, cognitive psychology to neurophysiology. Consequently, the manner in which this prima facie highly plausible reduction falls short is particularly revealing of the problems facing reductive strategies in general' (ibid., p. 574). As this passage suggests, Nelson concluded that the project was most unlikely to succeed.

Nelson distinguishes three reduction projects. Option 1 starts from the given microtheory, adds to it satisfactory aggregation procedures, and then derives the macrotheory from it. This option faces an apparently insuperable empirical obstacle, revealed in the 'conviction that individual economic behavior is too erratic to support an *economic* theory and that significant microeconomic theorizing must be about some kind of averages' (ibid., p. 582; original stress). Option 2 is to '[t]ake independently determined micro- and macrotheories and *then* find aggregation procedures that entail the macrotheory when conjoined with the microtheory' (ibid., p. 580; original stress). But this will not provide microfoundations; or, rather, 'there is a strong sense in which this undertaking presupposes the existence of *macro*foundations for *micro*economics; namely, it requires the existence of some macroexplanations of some microphenomena', so that 'there is a strong sense in which macroeconomics is methodologically at least as well founded as microeconomics' (ibid., pp. 587, 586; original stress). Option 3 involves taking macrotheory as 'antecedently given', stipulating satisfactory aggregation procedures, and then attempting 'to find restrictions on the form of the microtheory such that the macrotheory can be derived after the fact from the microtheory and the aggregation procedures'. This option, Nelson argues, 'bears little resemblance to popular philosophical models of reduction' (ibid., p. 591), and cannot yield secure microfoundations.

The philosopher Julian Reiss makes the same points in a slightly different way. Admittedly, 'there is a kind of ontological dependence' between micro and macro, he writes, so that 'one could not have macro without micro. But this is a trivial claim' (Reiss 2004, p. 232). More important is the point that 'clearly, macro entities causally influence micro entities (when, for example, agents react to inflation or changes in the federal funds rate'. And Reiss has a second, even more telling, comment:

> The second point is that it is not clear whether one would really 'fix' the macro entities by 'fixing' the micro entities. Imagine we could duplicate all micro entities of some economy. Would that duplicate the macro economy, too? Not necessarily. This is due to the relative liberty with which macro aggregates are constructed. There is no one way in which, say, the price level can be measured. Importantly, different ways of measuring have different, and in some cases very different, results. These results, in turn, may have effects that spread throughout the economy. (Ibid., pp. 232)

Here Reiss cites the controversy in the late 1990s over whether the official Cost of Living index in the United States had been accurately constructed, and in particular whether it had adequately reflected improvements in the quality of consumer electronics. Re-measurement would affect indexed social benefit payments, for example, with potentially significant macro-economic consequences. 'Therefore', he concludes, 'even if one assumes strict determinism at the micro level, copying a micro economy would not ensure that the history of the duplicate would be identical to the history of the original. In order to ensure that, one would also have to fix the methods of measurement, but this is exactly the "additional bit" macro entities have' that reductionists must repudiate (ibid., p. 233).

Reiss's two points are very closely related to my two anti-reductionist principles, the fallacy of composition and downward causation, and thus they have a very direct bearing on the question of whether it is necessary or even possible to provide microfoundations for macroeconomics. The fallacy of composition means that a statement that is true of any individual considered separately may be false when applied to them all taken together. There are some obvious examples in everyday life: with the introduction of all-seater football stadiums in the UK after the 1989 Hillsborough disaster, any individual supporter who stands up to get a better view does indeed get one, but if they all stand up no-one's view is improved. One economic example was discussed in Chapter 2: this is the *paradox of thrift* (above, pp. 9, 23). But there are several other examples.

First, any realistic monetary theory must allow for a *paradox of liquidity*. This term seems to have originated with Sheila Dow (2010), but the principle is long-established in the literature on financial panics, and Keynes himself noted the impossibility of increased liquidity for the community as a whole if the supply of money is unchanged (Keynes 1936, p. 155). If any individual financial company wishes to increase its liquidity, it can always do so (at a price), but if all financial companies attempt to do so the consequence will be a reduction in aggregate liquidity and (in the absence of government intervention) the real possibility that the whole system will collapse. The global financial crisis that began in September 2008 provides a dramatic example of this principle. There is also an inverse principle, the *paradox of debt* (Hewitson 2012, p. 27). When firms in aggregate expand their investment spending the resulting increase in profits will reduce their leverage ratios, and thus also frustrate their plans to finance the increased investment by higher ratios of debt to equity (see also Lavoie 1996; Lavoie and Seccareccia 2001).

This is closely related to *Kalecki's profit equation*: in a closed economy with no government, and on the assumption that workers do not save, aggregate profits are equal to and determined by the sum of capitalist expenditure on consumption and investment. Thus 'capitalists get what they spend', but only as a class; any capitalist who thinks that it applies to him as an individual will end up in jail, like the disgraced media magnate Conrad Black (Kalecki 1942). The Kaleckian *paradox of costs* is rather similar: a wage rise is very bad news for any individual capitalist, but it may be good news for them all, taken together, if the consequent rise in consumption expenditure raises the level of economic activity and thereby increases aggregate profits. It all depends on the values of the relevant parameters (Blecker 2002).

I offer one more example (there will certainly be others). Nicholas Kaldor (1956) rejected the marginal productivity theory of distribution and instead developed a macroeconomic model of the relative shares of capital and labour. In Kaldor's model the wage and profit shares depend only on the ratio of investment to income and on the savings propensities of capitalists and workers. The model was later generalized by Luigi Pasinetti (1962) to allow for the accumulation of capital also by workers, as a result of their saving. 'Modern macroeconomists' like Wickens and Acemoglu would dismiss all this as yet another outmoded example of 'ad hoc theorizing about the relations between macroeconomic aggregates'. Kaldor's contemporaries, the neoclassical Keynesians Franco Modigliani and Paul Samuelson, took a rather different line of attack, claiming only that his conclusions relied on special assumptions about parameter values (Samuelson and Modigliani 1966). To this Kaldor responded by noting that:

> A capitalist system can only function so long as the receipts of entrepreneurs exceed their outlays; in a closed system, and ignoring Government loan expenditure, this will only be the case if entrepreneurial expenditure exceeds workers' savings. Unless one treats the consumption expenditure of entrepreneurs as an exogenous variable, given independently of profits, it is only the 'Kaldor-Pasinetti inequality' (i.e the excess of business investment over non-business savings) which can ensure the existence of profits. (Kaldor 1978, p. xvi)

Once again, the fallacy of composition is implicit in Kaldor's argument. Even complete knowledge of the determinants of the consumption and saving decisions of all individual workers and capitalists would not permit us to infer the Kaldor-Pasinetti inequality, without which profits would be zero and there would be no capitalist economy to be studied. This is an autonomous macroeconomic condition, an emergent property of the economy as a whole.

These are all cases where individual behaviour is governed by macroeconomic requirements. The logic of our macroeconomic analysis tells us that, in aggregate, saving cannot increase unless investment rises; the liquidity of the entire financial system may be threatened by individual firms' quest for increased liquidity; total profits always depend on total spending, and this may frustrate firms' plans to increase leverage; under some circumstances increased wages may lead to higher profits, not lower profits, in aggregate; and individual saving decisions must be consistent with the survival of capitalism. None of these results is immediately obvious, or could be derived from knowledge of microeconomics alone, and every one of them also entails the existence of downward causation, from macro to micro.

3.6 MACROFOUNDATIONS FOR MICROECONOMICS?

The potential significance of downward causation has led some economists to argue that we need macrofoundations for microeconomics. Possibly the first to use this term (perhaps with tongue in cheek) was Takishi Negishi, at the famous S'Agaro conference of the International Economic Association on the microfoundations of macroeconomics (see Harcourt 1977, p. 142, and Chapter 5 below). There are good reasons for taking this argument seriously, first because of the irreducibly macroeconomic nature of many important problems (as noted above), and second because what may be termed the prevailing macroeconomic regime has profound implications for individual behaviour.

This second point was neatly made by David Colander, whose 'Post Walrasian perspective maintains that before there is any hope of undertaking meaningful micro analysis, *one must first determine the macro context within which that micro decision is made*' (Colander 1996, p. 61; original stress). The macro context has both a normative and a positive dimension (if I may be permitted to use this contentious terminology). Ian McDonald (2008, p. 5) cites a well-known neoclassical text by Tibor

Scitovsky, *Welfare and Competition*, the subtitle of which is *The Economics of a Fully Employed Economy*. Right at the start Scitovsky notes that when

> a scarce resource becomes underemployed, it no longer matters whether it is used efficiently or not ... it does not matter if too large a proportion of underemployed resources is devoted to the satisfaction of one particular want, because this again results in less unemployment and not in the lesser satisfaction of other wants. Efficiency in the use of underemployed scarce resources is as irrelevant as it is in the administration of free resources, and for exactly the same reason. (Scitovsky 1952, p. 9)

The early Keynesians also believed that a 'full employment economy' would be quite different from an 'unemployment economy', especially in the labour market, where full employment posed a potentially very serious threat to 'discipline in the factories' (Kalecki 1943).

I think this important question can be developed much further. Perfect competition in the labour market is only *possible* under full employment, since only then is it possible for the supply of labour to the individual firm to be perfectly elastic; only then does the worker have no reason to value her job; only then is there no cost to losing that job; only then are there no wage rents. In an unemployment economy, all employers have some degree of monopsony power, and this has a number of important consequences, even in a rigorously neoclassical model of the labour market. There is no longer a labour demand curve for the individual firm, and hence no market demand curve. There is also no guarantee that an increase in the real wage will reduce the number of workers employed; the introduction of a statutory minimum wage may have no adverse effect on employment, and in some circumstances may actually increase it (Manning 2003). There are, of course, other reasons to doubt the widespread existence of perfect competition in the labour market, even under full employment (Kaufman 2007), so that the absence of full employment is sufficient, but not necessary, to establish the existence of monopsony.

Interestingly enough, the opposite is probably true in the product market, where generalized excess capacity may well be a necessary condition for perfect competition between suppliers. As Alfred Marshall knew, each supplier has its own 'particular market', or group of regular customers, who have good reasons for not abandoning that supplier to take advantage of small and possibly transitory price reductions by its competitors. If customers are uncertain that their orders will be filled immediately by hard-pressed producers in a totally impersonal market, they will face the prospect of substantial 'shopping costs' and will therefore have a strong incentive to form long-term relations with their regular suppliers, whose demand curves will in consequence be downward-sloping, not perfectly elastic (Okun 1981, pp. 138–55). Oddly, Arthur Okun does not mention the cyclical nature of shopping costs. The value to the supplier of repeat orders, which he does emphasize, presumably works in the opposite direction, being greatest when the market is slack. On balance, however, it seems probable that the condition required for perfect competition in the labour market (full employment) is inconsistent with that needed for perfect competition in the product market (excess capacity), and this conclusion is derived from *macroeconomic* considerations.

Whether all this justifies us in requiring macrofoundations for microeconomics is another question. I am inclined to think not. There is something paradoxical, or even perverse, about the idea of 'foundations' that exist at a higher level than the edifice that they are supposed to be foundations of, whether the edifice is physical or intellectual in nature. Perhaps it is an innocuous rhetorical device, though I think not: we saw in the previous chapter that metaphors are often much more than harmless literary devices.

There is also a substantive question of how to think, and how *not* to think, about economic theory. As Peter Kriesler suggests, writing about the work of Michał Kalecki, there are two hypothetical extremes:

> [W]e can regard the first as seeing macroeconomics as a pure aggregation from the micro, with no new information resulting from the aggregation that is not already in the microtheory. On the other hand, the second view can be characterized as regarding the micro as a pure disaggregation from the macro, with no new information about the functioning of the economy being generated by the procedure ... the way in which micro and macro theories are interrelated in Kalecki's analysis is quite different to either of these two approaches. In particular, neither theory dominates nor forms a constraint on the other. Rather than any form of hierarchical relationship, *the two theories lie side by side* (so to speak), and both give information which the other cannot give, while the interrelation of the two yields further information not obtainable from either in isolation. (Kriesler 1989, p. 123; stress added)

Kriesler's horizontal metaphor is a very useful corrective to the vertical metaphor employed by Dawkins, with his 'hierarchical reductionism'.

To claim (as I do) that the microfoundations dogma is an example of a failed micro-reduction does *not* commit me to advocating macrofoundations, still less to any form of radical Hegelian holism of the kind denounced by von Mises (see above, p. 25). Kincaid (1997, p. 14) distinguishes three different 'individualist claims': '1. Full explanation requires reference solely to individuals. 2. Full explanation requires some reference to individuals. 3. Purely individualist theories suffice to fully explain'. I reject the first and third claims, but – obviously – not the second. Rejection of microfoundations does not require me to deny the relevance of microeconomics to macroeconomics (or for that matter *vice versa*). All that I am claiming is that the two bodies of knowledge exist side by side, neither being the foundation of the other. My target is what Steven Pinker rather perversely describes as 'bad', 'greedy' or 'destructive reductionism'. I have no objection to what Pinker terms 'good reductionism', which 'consists not of *replacing* one field of knowledge with another but of *connecting* or *unifying* them. The building blocks used by one field are put under a microscope by the other' (Pinker 2005, pp. 69–70, original stress; cf. Dennett 1996). Whether this should be described as 'reduction' is another matter.

3.7 CONCLUSION

The majority of critics of micro-reduction treat the feasibility of micro-reduction as a matter of *fact*, so that the 'causal features of the world determine which explanatory practices are appropriate' (Trout 1991, p. 391). As Kincaid puts it, whether 'these potential obstacles [to micro-reduction] are real can only be decided empirically; the individualism–holism disputes depend on concrete empirical detail' (Kincaid 1997, pp. 23, 26). The alternative position is defended by Jutta Weldes: 'Since all terms are theoretically defined, intertheoretic reduction is *in principle* infeasible between theories grounded in different ontological and epistemological assumptions' (Weldes 1989, p. 382 n 55; original stress). To me, Weldes seems to be perched precariously at the top of a very slippery slope leading to a wholly unacceptable postmodernist theoretical relativism. I am even prepared to admit the 'in principle' possibility of the reduction of all scientific knowledge to physics because, as David Papineau suggests, this 'need have no practical implications. For the in principle derivability may be practically unfeasible, in which case the reducibility of the human science will make no methodological difference to its practitioners'. On the contrary, it 'would seem to leave plenty of room for human sciences that in practice owe nothing to physical theory' (Papineau 2009, p. 112) – and for a relatively autonomous macroeconomics that will never, in practice, be reduced to microeconomics.

In the next chapter I reinforce these conclusions by means of a more detailed study of two examples of failed micro-reductions: the ('greedy') attempt to reduce the life sciences to genetics, and the (equally greedy) methodological individualism project in the social sciences. In each case it was the two empirical principles of the fallacy of composition and downward causation that did the damage. Or, to express the same principles in slightly different terms, it is the emergent properties of higher-level systems that make hierarchical reduction impossible in practice. Thus the 're-emergence of emergence' is the third and final topic to be considered in Chapter 4.

4. Two case studies: biology and social science

4.1 INTRODUCTION

We saw in the previous chapter just how controversial micro-reduction has been in the philosophy of science, and how the case against it invariably invokes the two principles of the fallacy of composition and downward causation. When applied to economics, these principles provide strong reasons for rejecting the microfoundations dogma. In this chapter I reinforce the case against micro-reduction by means of a much more detailed account of two failed micro-reductions: Dawkins's attempt to reduce the life sciences to genetics (Section 4.2) and the methodological individualism project in the social sciences (Section 4.3). In each case the macro system under investigation displays emergent properties that could not have been inferred from knowledge of the corresponding micro theory, and which exercise a (downward) causal influence on them. The broader literature on emergence is discussed in Section 4.4. The chapter concludes by summarizing the methodological lessons that might be drawn from all this by economists (Section 4.5).

4.2 THE LIFE SCIENCES

The case for 'hierarchical reduction' in the life sciences has been presented with great force and clarity by Richard Dawkins. The similarities between his methodological stance and the microfoundations dogma in economics have been noted by several writers, including Wade Hands (2001, p. 385), Harold Kincaid (1997, Chapter 4) and Jeroen van den Bergh and John Gowdy (2003). Dawkins's position is strongly supported by many eminent biologists, some of whom contributed to the volume edited by two of his former students to celebrate the thirtieth anniversary of the publication of *The Selfish Gene* (Grafen and Ridley 2006; Dawkins 1976). But it remains deeply controversial, and its opponents have mounted a very strong case against micro-reduction, some of which is represented in the same volume.

They could draw support from an unexpected source. Steven Rose recounts an intriguing episode from 1986, when the octogenarian Karl Popper – 'the thinking scientist's favourite philosopher' – gave the first Medawar lecture in the elegant lecture hall of London's Royal Society in honour of his friend Peter Medawar, 'who had frequently argued that reductionism is not even second but first nature to scientists'. Popper's argument 'must have been galling to Medawar', who had been crippled by a stroke and sat in a wheelchair in the front row. Running out of time towards the end, Popper 'was forced to discard his text and summarize his take-home message on a hand-written overhead transparency, headed: "Eight reasons why biology cannot be reduced to physics"'. When he sat down, the Nobel laureate Sir Max Perutz asked him why biochemistry could not be reduced to chemistry. Not known for displaying courtesy to critics, Popper 'stood back, smiled sweetly and said simply: "Ah yes. I was surprised by that at first. But if you go away and think about it for an evening, you will see that I am right"' (Rose 2005, pp. 74–6).

Had Perutz read Popper's *Objective Knowledge* he would have found the answer to his question: emergent properties. As Hodgson explains, 'Popper and others rediscovered the idea of emergent properties some time after the Second World War' (Hodgson 2000, p. 114). Popper agreed with Perutz that chemistry might be reduced to physics, so that 'all the findings of chemistry can be fully explained (that is to say, deduced from) the principles of physics'. Although 'such a reduction would not be very surprising', he continued, 'it would be a very great scientific success. It would not only be an exercise in unification, but a real advance in understanding the world'. And it would give hope that 'we may also one day reduce all the biological sciences to physics'. And this would be 'a spectacular success, far greater than the reduction of chemistry to physics. Why? Because the kinds of things to which physics and chemistry apply are really very similar from the start' (Popper 1979, pp. 290–91).

Popper was convinced that this was a question of fact, not a matter of philosophical doctrine:

> If the situation is such that, on the one hand, living organisms may originate by a natural process from non-living systems, and that, on the other hand, there is no complete theoretical understanding of life possible in physical terms, then we might speak of life as an *emergent* property of physical bodies, or of matter.
>
> Now I want to make it quite clear that as a rationalist I wish and hope to understand the world and that I wish and hope for a reduction. At the same time,

> I think it quite likely that there may be no reduction possible; it is conceivable that life is an *emergent* property of physical bodies. (Ibid., pp. 291–2; original stress)

The principle of emergence is applicable, first of all, to the natural sciences. But similar considerations apply also to 'the emergence of consciousness' (ibid., p. 292) and to the inherently unpredictable course of human history, as Popper himself maintained in *The Poverty of Historicism* (ibid., pp. 296–8; cf. Popper 1957, pp. v–vii). In any particular branch of scientific inquiry, '[i]t may be that the field resists reduction … In this case we may have an example of genuine emergence' (Popper 1979, p. 295). This possibility should be vigorously pursued: 'So I would say: let us work out in every case the arguments for emergence in detail, *at any rate before attempting reduction*' (ibid., p. 294; original stress).

In their campaign against Dawkins's hierarchical reductionism, many practitioners of the life sciences were doing precisely that. Niles Eldredge, in his book *Reinventing Darwin*, argued that

> The implacable stability of species in the face of all that genetic ferment is a marvelous demonstration that large-scale systems exhibit behaviors that do not mirror exactly the events and processes taking place among their parts … Events and processes acting at any one level cannot possibly explain all phenomena at higher levels. (Eldredge 1995, p. 175, cited by Fodor 1997, p. 163 n7)

Similarly, in *Not in Our Genes*, Richard Lewontin, Steven Rose and Leon Kamin maintain that 'the relation between gene, environment, organism, and society is complex in a way not encompassed by simple reductionist argument'. In particular, 'we cannot think of any significant human behavior that is built into our genes in such a way that it cannot be modified and shaped by social conditioning' (Lewontin, Rose and Kamin 1984, pp. 266, 267). They emphasize the complexity of the relationship between an organism and its environment:

> Organisms do not simply adapt to previously existing, autonomous environments; they create, destroy, modify, and internally transform aspects of the external world by their own life activities to make this environment. Just as there is no organism without an environment, so there is no environment without an organism. Neither organism nor environment is a closed system; each is open to the other. (Ibid., p. 273)

Thus the relationship between organism and environment could best be described as a dialectical one.

The physiologist Denis Noble makes use of a striking metaphor – the gene as prisoner – to support a very similar conclusion:

> Where Dawkins talks of selfish genes, Noble talks of prisoner genes. Where Dawkins writes of genes, 'They are in you and me; they created us, body and mind; and their preservation is the ultimate rationale for our existence', Noble writes 'They are in you and me; we are the system that allows their code to be read; and their preservation is totally dependent on the joy we experience in reproducing ourselves (our joy, not theirs!). We are the ultimate rationale for their existence'. (Crace 2009, p. 30)

These critics had an ally in Stephen Jay Gould who, in a series of papers published in 1984–5, asserted the need to find a middle way between 'mechanists' and 'vitalists'. These were the two extremes that represent 'either advocates of an ultimate reduction to physics and chemistry (with no appreciation for the integrity of organisms) or supporters of a special force that gives life meaning (and modern mystics who would deny the potential unity of science)' (Gould 2007, p. 575). The 'vast majority of biologists', Gould claimed, hold to the middle position, which

> ... holds that life, as a result of its structural and functional complexity, cannot be taken apart into chemical constituents and explained in its entirety by physical and chemical laws working at the molecular level ... As levels of complexity mount along the hierarchy of atom, molecule, gene, cell, tissue, organism, and population, new properties arise as results of interactions and interconnections arising at each new level. A higher level cannot be fully explained by taking it apart into component elements and rendering their properties in the absence of these interactions. Thus, we need new, or 'emergent', principles to encompass life's complexity; these principles are additional to, and consistent with, the physics and chemistry of atoms and molecules. (Ibid., p. 576)

In addition to emergence, Gould also emphasizes the principle of downward causation. 'The material of biology', he maintains, is indeed 'ordered into a genealogical hierarchy of ever more inclusive objects: genes, bodies, demes (local populations of a species), species, and monophyletic clades of species'. Natural selection operates not only at the level of the gene, as Dawkins insists, but also at the level of the organism, the deme and the species; this has important implications for economics, as van den Bergh and Gowdy (2003) have shown. Now Dawkins argues, Gould continues, 'that genes are the only true causal agents and organisms merely their temporary receptacles. I strongly disagree with Dawkins, since I feel that he has confused bookkeeping (which may be done efficiently in terms of genes) with causality' (ibid., p. 226).

The philosopher Elliott Sober came to a very similar conclusion. Darwin, he notes, 'thought of evolution and natural selection in terms of organisms'. Subsequent progress in the biological sciences has expanded the conceptual possibilities in two directions: 'There is the group above and the gene below'. The importance of downward causation was now recognized by biologists, since 'the properties that are selected for and against may be causal factors in the survival and reproduction of genes and species, as well as of organisms' (Sober 1984, p. 368; see also Sober 1999, 2006).

Similarly Rose, while acknowledging 'the great reductionist triumphs of the nineteenth and early twentieth centuries: the elucidation of the basic chemistry of life' (Rose 2005, p. 81), is also a strong critic of Dawkins's reductionist programme. We saw in the previous chapter that he criticizes Dawkins's use of transportation metaphors. Taking a biological example, Rose maintains that an explanation of the muscle twitch of a jumping frog could not be reduced to biochemistry. The relevant fibres can be reconstituted as filaments in a test-tube and made to shorten, just as in a muscle contraction:

> But they do not thereby *become* a contracting muscle fibre. This requires a set of irreducible organizing relations, implicit in the physiology of the process but absent from either the biochemistry or chemistry, which define the *functions* of the muscle. This, I believe, is what Popper meant by the slogan that so outraged Perutz. (Ibid., p. 93)

Rose continues by invoking the fallacy of composition: 'It is also, I suppose, what might be conveyed by the well-known phrase that "the whole is more than the sum of its parts"', though in matters of biology this has regrettably 'become surrounded by a sort of mystic aura' (this is an allusion to the 'vitalism' that Gould had attacked):

> But what can be asserted, without retreating into hand-waving or New Age sloganeering, is that the key feature distinguishing a lower 'level' of the pyramid from those above it is that at each level new interactions and relationships appear between the component parts – relationships which cannot be inferred simply by taking the system to pieces. Furthermore, the claim makes an additional important assertion. Philosophical reductionism implies that, whatever higher-order properties emerge and however they do so, they are always somehow secondary to lower-order ones. The lower the order, the greater the primacy. Parts come before wholes. Yet, whatever the case may be for the properties of physical and chemical systems, the nature of evolutionary and development processes in biology means that there is no such necessary primacy. Wholes, emerging, may in themselves constrain or demand the appearance of parts. (Ibid., pp. 93–4)

Thus Rose concludes by explicitly endorsing the anti-reductionist principles of the fallacy of composition and downward causation that I am using in this book to criticize the microfoundations dogma in mainstream macroeconomics.

It should be stressed that the debate in the life sciences is a continuing one. As late as 2005, Rose could describe the fate of dissident anti-reductionists over several centuries in the following terms: 'their voices were *and still are* drowned out by an almost universal reductionist consensus' (Rose 2005, p. 79; stress added). Yet C. Kenneth Waters invoked 'the anti-reductionist consensus' in the title of a 1990 paper, and Sober himself began an article published at the end of the century with this claim: 'If there is now a received view among philosophers of mind and philosophers of biology about reductionism, it is that reductionism is mistaken' (Waters 1990; Sober 1999, p. 542). Huge issues are at stake in this debate, including the apparently very limited significance of purely genetic causes of common diseases (Manolio et al. 2009; Latham 2011) and the excessive reliance on pharmacology in the diagnosis and treatment of mental illness (Scull 2007).

4.3 METHODOLOGICAL INDIVIDUALISM

The first serious attempt to undertake micro-reduction in the social sciences came in the form of the doctrine of *methodological individualism*: Rajeev Bhargava (1992) and Lars Udehn (2001) provide substantial bibliographies. Scott Gordon traces the origins of the doctrine back to Thomas Hobbes (Gordon 1991, p. 72), and rather contentiously finds it central to both classical political economy (ibid., p. 206) and to Karl Marx and Friedrich Engels (ibid., p. 378). It certainly received an important stimulus after 1870 with the neoclassical or 'marginal' revolution in economics, which involved *inter alia* a shift in focus, from society and social class to the individual, and a corresponding shift in problem area, from production and distribution to consumption and exchange (Dobb 1973). Thus the principle of methodological individualism was, at least, implicit in the writings of William Stanley Jevons, Carl Menger and Léon Walras (and also, to a lesser extent, in Alfred Marshall). It appeared to fit especially neatly with the individualistic basis of Austrian economics, with its radical subjectivism and individualistic version of political liberalism, though as we shall see in Chapter 9 this connection is somewhat problematic.

The expression 'methodological individualism' originated in 1908 with the Austrian economist Joseph Schumpeter, and it was soon championed by the German sociologist Max Weber: 'the theoretical elaboration of the doctrine is due to Weber, and Schumpeter uses the term as a way of referring to the Weberian view' (Heath 2009, p. 2). Weber did not, however, consistently apply it in his own work (Gordon 1991, pp. 468–79). As John Davis has noted, Schumpeter himself repudiated the 'untenable' position that he described as 'sociological individualism', according to which 'all social phenomena resolve themselves into decisions and actions of individuals that need not or cannot be further analyzed in terms of supraindividual factors' (Schumpeter 1954, p. 36, cited by Davis 2003, p. 36). Thus he would probably have rejected reductionism and have denied 'the view that not only can one always in principle replace explanations of social entities by some individualist explanation, but one ought to do so whenever practically possible' (Davis 2003, p. 36).

In the 1950s there was a vigorous and prolonged debate on methodological individualism in the social sciences, with economics often being invoked but with no prominent economists being actively involved in the discussion. A very useful summary is provided by I.C. Jarvie (1972, pp. 173–8), and many of the key papers are reprinted – sometimes with significant revisions by their authors – in O'Neill (1973). It is not entirely clear why the question should have become important to social theorists at this time. It was much too early for a rebuttal of economics imperialism to be required; as late as the early 1960s Gary Becker was largely unknown, even to economists, outside Chicago. There was probably a political motivation, with methodological individualism being seen as an antidote to the collectivism and the potentially totalitarian Hegelian holism attributed to Marx and (with more justice) to some of his followers. A more narrowly academic motivation would have been supplied by the contemporary controversy between Marxists and Weberians on the nature and origins of bureaucracy, which was a very live issue in the early stages of the Cold War, with the analysis of Soviet society being a central ideological issue. Ironically, as already noted, Weber himself was not a consistent methodological individualist; sometimes he was as structuralist, or materialist, as Marx. The immediate inspiration for the debate seems to have been the philosophical writings of Karl Popper, which is not to say that Popper's own position on these matters was entirely consistent. Deborah Redman notes that he has often been accused of lack of clarity, and suggests that 'strict application of Popper's methodological individualism would eradicate modern macroeconomic theory', which is not a position that either he or his disciples would have welcomed (Redman 1991, p. 110; see also Hands 1993, pp. 69–73).

At all events, the case for methodological individualism was stated, in the opening round of the controversy, by Popper's disciple and LSE colleague J.W.N. Watkins. Since 'knowledge of the general characteristics of a social situation is always derivative knowledge', Watkins argued, 'pieced together from what is known of individuals' situations, then it is not possible to proceed *from* overall characteristics *towards* individuals' situations. The former is [*sic*] logically derivative from the latter'. Thus at the very outset Watkins states the two fundamental principles of micro-reduction: no fallacy of composition and no downward causation. He cites Weber in support, the great sociologist having chosen to 'abandon holistic ideal types and the impossible method associated with them, in favour of individualistic ideal types and the method of reconstructing historical phenomena with their aid' (Watkins 1952a, p. 27; original stress).

Economics is mentioned at several points in Watkins's article. He dismisses the notion that there is 'a long-term "wave" in economic life' which 'obeys its own laws' and 'must therefore be taken as a datum' (ibid., p. 28); there is a footnote reference to N.D. Kondratieff. He also cites Richard Stone, and thanks J.E. Meade and Lionel Robbins for providing economic examples to illustrate his own argument (ibid., pp. 28 n1; 30 n1; 31 n2). And there is a lengthy discussion of the neoclassical and Keynesian revolutions, which Watkins describes as 'the two most striking advances made in economics during the last century' (ibid., p. 34). He enlists not just Jevons, Menger and Walras but also Keynes as supporters of methodological individualism, citing the 'three fundamental psychological factors' – the propensity to consume, liquidity preference and the expected marginal efficiency of capital – as the 'ultimate independent variables' from which Keynes had deduced the macroeconomic principles governing the level of employment and the general price level (ibid., p. 35, citing Keynes 1936, pp. 246–7).

As we shall see in Chapter 5, this is not a defensible interpretation of Keynes. Watkins had also left himself open to another, much more damaging, objection: the principle of methodological individualism, as he defined it, proved to be vacuous. He could not avoid reference to the situations in which individual behaviour occurred. But, as Watkins's critics would soon point out, these were irreducibly *social* situations, so that 'methodological holism' had been let in through the back door. This becomes very clear in the 'Summary' that he provides at the end of his paper:

> We can apprehend an unobservable social system only by reconstructing it theoretically from what is known of individual dispositions, beliefs *and relationships*. Hence holistic ideal types, which would abstract essential traits from a social whole while ignoring individuals, are impossible; they always turn into individualistic ideal types. Individualistic ideal types of explanatory power are constructed by first discerning the form of typical, *socially significant*, dispositions, and then by demonstrating how, *in various typical situations*, these lead to certain principles of social behaviour (ibid., pp. 42–3; stress added).

'Relationships', 'socially significant dispositions', 'typical situations' – these point to a substantially diluted form of methodological individualism that all but the most dogmatic holists could happily live with.

Watkins soon reported having 'recently attended to a good deal of criticism' of the principle of methodological individualism (Watkins 1952b, p. 186; no details are given). The first published response came from the American philosopher May Brodbeck, who 'basically agree[d] with most of what Mr. Watkins says' (Brodbeck 1954, p. 154), but believed him to have over-stated his case. Her criticism of Watkins, however, goes much deeper than this suggests, since she proclaims the merits of 'methodological liberty'. Whether or not micro-reduction is possible or fruitful is a question of fact, Brodbeck suggests:

> since a group concept refers to a complex pattern of descriptive, empirical relations among individuals, there is no reason why the behavior of this complex should not itself be studied. Psychological laws may be ubiquitous, but social laws may be formulated without taking them into account. Psychological laws may have mass effects, making the behavior of institutions or crowds different from that of individuals. (Ibid., p. 153)

Even Hayek, a staunch defender of methodological individualism, had also identified the 'unintended consequences' of individual actions as 'the subject matter of social science' (ibid., p. 153). Brodbeck notes the 'growing interest by economists in collective rather than individualistic models', citing the Keynesian aggregate consumption function as an example of a hypothesis, 'of course, about a group and not about individuals' (ibid., p. 155). 'In some instances laws are closer at hand if the scientist sticks to the macroscopic level of the complex concept', Brodbeck concludes. 'From these laws he may construct theories. In other instances, the microscopic or psychological approach might be more fruitful; in still others, a combination of these approaches … This is not to recommend methodological licence, only methodological liberty for the social scientist to find his laws and explanations where he may' (ibid., p. 156).

An even more critical response came from the sociologist Maurice Mandelbaum, who did not refer to Watkins by name but must have had his argument in mind when he claimed that 'societal facts' were 'as ultimate' as 'are those facts which are "psychological" in character', that is to say, 'facts concerning the thoughts and actions of specific human beings' (Mandelbaum 1955, p. 307). To demonstrate 'the irreducibility of societal concepts', Mandelbaum cites the example of bank tellers, whose behaviour at work is entirely unintelligible except in the context of their status and roles. But 'the concepts of status and role are devoid of meaning unless one interprets them in terms of the organization of the society to which the individuals belong' (ibid., p. 308). In the following year Leon J. Goldstein did refer explicitly to Watkins in arguing that 'there are problems confronting social science that require solutions not amenable to individualistic analysis and yet are not holistic or historicist' (Goldstein 1956, p. 802). Historical explanation, he maintains, can often be provided 'only by a system of socio-cultural laws', and the fact that such laws are inconsistent with methodological individualism 'is hardly the ground for the rejection of a perfectly tenable program' (ibid., p. 811). Goldstein cites anthropology and also 'theoretical economics' in support of his position, since the latter 'provides a highly abstract account of economic behavior within economic and social institutions the existence of which is already assumed' (ibid., p. 802).

The philosopher Ernest Gellner also invoked anthropology and economics in his critique of 'Monadism-at-all-costs' (Gellner 1956, p. 176). It is necessary to distinguish three propositions, Gellner maintains, which are not incompatible:

> A generalisation is true only in virtue of the truth of singular propositions.
>
> A whole is made up of its parts.
>
> No *a priori* legislation is possible concerning the complexity of links in causal chains.
>
> The error of the individualist is to conclude from the first two propositions, which are analytic, to [*sic*] the falsity of the third, through the confused identification of the hierarchy of propositions in terms of generality with the hierarchy of things in terms of complexity and inclusiveness. (Ibid., p. 170)

Taking an example from anthropology, Gellner points to certain tribes that have maintained a segmentary patrilineal structure over time. Contrary to the claims of methodological individualists, it 'might very well be impossible to isolate anything in the characters and conduct of the individual tribesmen which *explains* how they come to maintain the system'. In more colloquial (but no less sexist) terms: 'History is *about* chaps. It does not follow that its explanations are always in terms of chaps' (ibid., p. 176; original stress).

The question of explanation and 'societal laws' is also central to Mandelbaum's second intervention in the debate, in which (agreeing with Goldstein) he argues that 'the simple dichotomy of methodological individualism and methodological holism' is false. It is possible to assert the truth of at least some 'irreducible laws governing the functional relationships of specific aspects or components in societal life' without accepting the doctrines of historical inevitability, holism or organicism (Mandelbaum 1957, p. 223–4). Goldstein soon stated his agreement with Mandelbaum, attributing a similar position to the great sociologist Émile Durkheim and raising, almost for the first time in the debate, the concept of emergence (though it is briefly mentioned by Brodbeck 1954, p. 154 and by Mandelbaum 1957, p. 216). 'When human beings live together', Goldstein notes, 'share common experiences, and so forth, there emerge common sentiments and modes of representation which would never have arisen apart from group life and which cannot be analysed into the bio-psychological characteristics of unsocialised individuals' (Goldstein 1958, p. 5).

Watkins replied to Brodbeck by claiming that methodological individualism was 'based on the metaphysical commonplace that social events are brought about by *people*'. He again invokes the authority of Keynes in support of this 'commonsensical' position, which 'hardly needed saying' (Watkins 1955, p. 58; original stress). But, as Brodbeck later complained, this confuses two quite different issues: language and explanation. 'One has to do with the nature of the *terms* or concepts of social science; the other with the nature of its *laws* and *theories* … The first issue is one of *meaning*, the second of *reduction*' (Brodbeck 1958, p. 1; original stress). Proponents of methodological individualism like Watkins have applied the term 'both to the view that there are no undefinable group concepts and to the view that the laws of the group sciences are in principle reducible to those about individuals', but 'descriptive emergence' needs to be carefully distinguished from 'explanatory emergence'. Only the former is the legitimate province of philosophers. 'The latter is a matter of fact' (ibid., p. 20), and depends entirely on the ability of the (social) scientist to identify the relevant 'composition laws'. In her concluding sentences Brodbeck reasserts her doubts on this score:

> If there be, as in principle there probably are, composition rules from which the behavior of groups may be predicted, these are most likely of such complexity and difficulty that it may well be the better part of wisdom for social scientists to look for whatever imperfect connections may exist among the group variables. These, in turn, may suggest the appropriate composition rules of individual behavior. But this is not for the philosopher to say. (Ibid., p. 22)

Watkins did not reply to Brodbeck's second paper, but he did respond to Goldstein with a series of brief comments that added little to his earlier articles but invoked the authority of Paul Samuelson at one point (Watkins 1958, p. 392). At another point Watkins refers contentiously to 'the practitioners of an individualistic method, from Adam Smith to Keynes' (Watkins 1959b, p. 243; cf. Watkins 1957, 1959a). It was left to Goldstein to reiterate Brodbeck's conclusion: 'Watkins's ontological thesis does not entail his methodological one' (Goldstein 1959, p. 241). In other words, one can agree that social entities *consist* only of human individuals without being forced to accept that their behaviour can be fully *explained* in terms of individuals.

Similar conclusions were drawn by Ernest Nagel in an authoritative text on the philosophy of science. 'Methodological individualism', he wrote, 'subscribes to what is often regarded as a factual thesis (although it is perhaps regarded as a program of research) concerning the *reducibility* of all statements about social phenomena to a special class of ('psychological') statements about individual human conduct' (Nagel 1961, pp. 541–2; original stress). It is necessary, Nagel continues, to distinguish 'the ontological thesis that "the ultimate constituents of the social world are individual people"' from 'the reductive thesis that statements about social phenomena are deducible from psychological statements about human individuals'. The two theses are separate: 'a commitment to the ontological thesis does not logically require a commitment to the reductive one' (ibid., p. 542). And Nagel was inclined to deny it, since 'no set of premises about the conduct of *individual* human beings might suffice for deducing some given statement about the actions of a *group* of men' (ibid., pp. 542–3; original stress).

He cites two cases: the difficulty of reducing thermodynamics to mechanics without invoking a statistical property of the ensemble of molecules, and the failure of microeconomics to account for macroeconomic phenomena, 'such as recurrent unemployment crises'. 'In consequence', he continues, 'without rejecting marginalist theory *in toto* in favor of an "institutional" or "historical" approach to economic problems, many students believe that the classical assumptions of the theory do not suffice to achieve the objectives for which the theory was devised, and require supplementation by additional ones' (ibid., p. 543). The most prominent of these students was J.M. Keynes, who added to 'psychological' assumptions about individuals 'assumptions concerning relations between large-scale *statistical aggregates* (such as national income, total national consumption, and total national savings)'. 'To be sure', Nagel concludes, 'no proof is available that these macroeconomic assumptions cannot be deduced from microeconomic ones. But there is also no proof that the deduction can be effected, and there is at least a presumption that it cannot be'. If, in fact, 'macroeconomic assumptions enable economists to account for aggregative phenomena no less adequately than do microeconomic postulates, the reduction of macroeconomics to microeconomics appears to offer no substantial scientific advantages'. Sociologists like Robert Merton (1957) had come to precisely the same conclusion.

In the same year the New Zealander K.J. Scott published a pithy note in which he accused Hayek, Popper and Watkins of hopeless confusion on this issue and declared the debate to be effectively at an end. 'Hayek and Popper have something important to say on methodological individualism', he concedes. 'I have been reading more recent writings on this subject, and I wish to report that the game's not worth the candle' (Scott 1961, p. 331). Again, economic examples proved fruitful: 'Most of Popper's examples of sociological laws contravene the principle of methodological individualism, for instance "You cannot have a centrally planned society with a price system that fulfils the main function of competitive prices" and "You cannot have full employment without inflation"' (ibid., p. 333).

According to another LSE philosopher, however, this was to miss the point. Joseph Agassi had already mounted a defence of 'institutionalistic individualism', which he considered 'to be Popper's great contribution to the philosophy of the social sciences' (Agassi 1960, p. 244). This position must be distinguished from both holism and 'psychologistic individualism':

> According to holism, society is a super-individual; according to psychologistic individualism society is the sum-total of individuals' interactions; according to institutionalistic-individualism society is the conventional means of co-ordination between individual actions ... Institutions are not just the reflection of the psychology of the majority of their participants. (Two identical groups of individuals in identical surroundings, but with somewhat different conventions or rules of behaviour, will develop very differently from each other not only socially but also psychologically.) As [Bertrand] Russell says, 'institutions mould character and character transforms institutions. Reform in both must march hand in hand'. (Ibid., pp. 264, 267; original stress deleted)

Here Agassi is referring to Russell (1956); no page number is cited. He himself is asserting the fallacy of composition and also admitting (through Russell) the principle of downward causation. As he wrote, fifteen years later, 'institutional individualism' is 'a *via media* between the two traditional views', holism and psychologism (Agassi 1975, p. 154). It is thus inconsistent with both macro-reduction and micro-reduction: 'we cannot reduce psychology into sociology and we cannot reduce sociology into psychology' (ibid., p. 152).

In very similar vein, J.O. Wisdom recognized the importance of emergent (social) properties and advocated the principle of 'transindividualism', which 'allows complete flexibility of explanation', with the causal focus being on individuals or on groups, depending on the facts of the situation: 'there is no *a priori* way of knowing without investigation which factor is the more significant in any given case' (Wisdom 1970a, p. 295; cf. R. Brown 1970; Wisdom 1970b; Miller 1978). A similar position was defended, two decades later, by Maarten Janssen, who argued in favour of a form of methodological individualism 'in which institutions are allowed as primitive terms in an explanation of social phenomena'. But these institutions need to be explained, rather than simply assumed to exist, as they are in the microfoundations literature: 'An equilibrium notion assumes the existence of a *coordinating device* at the aggregate level that coordinates individual actions' (Janssen 1993, p. 175; original stress). Thus Janssen concludes that 'studies in the microfoundations literature' are not consistent with the requirements of methodological individualism (ibid., p. 174).

Lars Udehn suggests that a distinction should be drawn between 'strong versions of methodological individualism, which suggest that all should be explained only in terms of individuals and their interaction, and weak versions of methodological individualism, which also assign an important role to social institutions and/or social structure in social science explanations' (Udehn 2002, p. 479). It is doubtful whether the weak version really qualifies as methodological individualism at all; it would certainly not satisfy those mainstream economists who demand microfoundations. Indeed, as one of the contributors to the debate noted, on this definition even Hegel might have claimed to be a methodological individualist.

The case against the strong version of methodological individualism has recently been restated by Geoff Hodgson (2007). I think it is a very convincing one, and it is rather surprising that it still needs to be made. One might have thought that the debate on methodological individualism was over by 1970, all the important points already having been made. In fact the doctrine seems to be a sort of ideological vampire, needing to be put back in its coffin every twenty years or so, like several propositions in mainstream economic theory (Quiggin 2010b). Thus Hodgson's critique echoes his own earlier objections, which the economics profession had ignored (Hodgson 1986) and which were very similar to those made by the philosopher Steven Lukes in a short paper in the *British Journal of Sociology* a generation earlier (Lukes 1968). Lukes defines methodological individualism as 'a prescription for explanations, asserting that no purported explanations of social (or individual) phenomena are to count as explanations, or (in Watkins's version) as rock-bottom explanations, unless they are couched wholly in terms of facts about individuals' (Lukes 1968, p. 121). He distinguishes four types of 'facts about individuals' or 'individual predicates'. Type (i) predicates 'are about human beings *qua* material objects and make no reference to and presuppose nothing about consciousness or any other feature of any social group or institution' ; examples include genetic make-up and brain states. Predicates of type (ii) 'presuppose consciousness but still make no reference to and presuppose nothing about any feature of any social group or institution'; they include aggression, gratification and stimulus-response. Type (iii) predicates 'do have a minimal social reference: they presuppose a social context in which certain actions, social relations and/or mental states are picked out and given a particular significance', for example co-operation, power and esteem (also utility maximization?). Finally, type (iv) predicates 'are maximally social, in that they presuppose and sometimes directly entail propositions about particular types of groups and institutions, for example cashing cheques, saluting and voting' (ibid., pp. 123–4).

Lukes's case against methodological individualism is that it is either incredible or innocuous:

> If the methodological individualist is saying that no explanations are possible (or rock-bottom) except those framed exclusively in terms of individual predicates of types, (i), (ii) and (iii), i.e. those not presupposing or entailing propositions about particular institutions and organizations, then he is arbitrarily ruling out (or denying finality to) most ordinarily acceptable explanations, as used in everyday life, but also by most sociologists and anthropologists for most of the time. If he is prepared to include individual predicates of type (iv), he seems to be proposing nothing more than a futile linguistic purism. Why should we be compelled to talk about the tribesman but not the tribe, the bank-teller but not the bank? (ibid., p. 125)

As Jutta Weldes puts it, 'the relevant social context is always built into seemingly individual-level predicates' (Weldes 1989, p. 362). Harold Kincaid concurs, criticizing Gary Becker's theories of discrimination and of the family on the grounds that

> Becker has to take as given the following: individual preferences for number of children and their 'quality', individual preferences for traits of spouses, relative wage and property shares of males versus females, the taste for discrimination, and the relative shares of capital owned by the races.
>
> All these 'exogenous' factors are precisely ones that we would expect to explain *holistically.* Attitudes about children, about sex roles, and about racial prejudice seemingly have their roots in larger social structures – the family; the media; peer, work, and ethnic groups; religious affiliation; and governmental and judicial institutions. Relative property and income shares also depend on social factors – historical factors like slavery, patriarchy, and so on. In short, the exogenous factors all seem to be social. So Becker's work seems to presuppose social explanations rather than reduce them. (Kincaid 1997, p. 21; original stress)

The few economists with an interest in methodology in the 1950s and 1960s kept out of the debate on methodological individualism, even when – as with Lionel Robbins – they were colleagues of Watkins and Popper at the LSE. When 'positivism' in economics was discussed, the term was used to refer to entirely different issues: the importance of predictive power and the supposed irrelevance of realistic assumptions in economic theory (Friedman 1953), or the case for a rigid separation between normative and non-normative propositions in matters of economic policy (Lipsey 1962). As Scott Gordon notes, 'Keynesian macroeconomics represents a significant breach in the principle of methodological individualism. Some critics of Keynesian theory contend that this breach is impermissible'. However, Gordon concludes, 'most economists value heuristic effectiveness and practicality more than the principle of methodological individualism, macroeconomics remains an established, though much troubled, branch of the discipline' (Gordon 1991, p. 588). (This last statement was already ceasing to be true when Gordon's book appeared). In the third quarter of the 20th century the great majority of orthodox economists would, if asked, have claimed to be methodological individualists, but (as we shall see in Chapter 5) they made very little of it, and seem to have had no inkling of the difficulties that Lukes and others had exposed. Still less did they show any awareness of the literature on the emergent properties of macro systems.

4.4 THE RE-EMERGENCE OF 'EMERGENCE'

I have taken the title of this sub-section from a paper by Byron Cunningham (2001), who used it to describe the literature in the philosophy of science in the 1990s. As we have seen, references to emergent properties can be found much earlier than this. Among the early 20th-century advocates of emergence were the maverick economists Thorstein Veblen and J.A. Hobson and the philosopher of biology C. Lloyd Morgan (Hodgson 2000, pp. 113–14). Durkheim argued that emergence was a central theme in theoretical sociology, and his position was supported by Talcott Parsons (1937, pp. 31–2, 738–43, 765, 773; see also Gordon 1991, pp. 442–3). Emergent properties were occasionally mentioned in the debate on methodological individualism, for example by Brodbeck, who suggested that 'it may be that even though group behavior is itself lawful there is no composition rule from which it can be predicted ... In any case, for whatever reason, the composition rule might break down, If it should, we have an instance of *explanatory* emergence'. This 'refers to laws of group behavior' that are 'not derivable from the laws, including whatever composition laws there are, about individual behavior'. She concluded that 'the group sciences are probably here to stay' (Brodbeck 1958, pp. 19–20; original stress). In similar vein, Laird Addis focused on the 'composition laws' that allow us to move from individuals, or small groups, to much larger groups or macro entities. If these laws break down, 'we have a case of what some call *explanatory emergence*' (Addis 1966, p. 326; original stress).

There is some controversy in the literature about the precise meaning of explanatory emergence. Mark Bedau distinguishes 'weak' and 'strong' versions, the latter requiring also *ontological* emergence, an example being the existence of the mental properties sometimes referred to as 'qualia'. Bedau rejects the strong version: 'There is no evidence that strong emergence plays any role in contemporary science ... Strong emergence starts where scientific explanation ends' (Bedau 2003 [2008], p. 159). He defends weak emergence, according to which emergent properties are '*ontologically* dependent on and reducible to micro phenomena', and also

> *causally* dependent on and reducible to their underlying phenomena ... At the same time, weakly emergent macro phenomena are autonomous in the sense that they can be derived only in a certain non-trivial way. In other words, they have *explanatory* autonomy and irreducibility, due to the complex way in which the iteration and aggregation of context-dependent micro interactions generate the macro phenomena. (Ibid., p. 160; original stress)

Bedau illustrates the point by means of (yet another) transport analogy: a strike by a city's public transport employees causes traffic jams. Here weak emergent phenomena have

> macro explanatory autonomy .... The traffic jam's ability to make everyone late is constituted by the ability of individual cars to block other cars. Aggregating the individual causal histories of each blocking car explains why everyone was late. However, the aggregate micro explanation obscures the fact that everyone would still have been late if the micro causal histories had been different. The transit strike raised the traffic density above a critical level. So, even if different individual cars had been on the highway, the traffic would still have been jammed and everyone still would have been late. The critical traffic density provides a macro explanation that is autonomous from any particular aggregate micro explanation. (Ibid., pp. 181–2)

A similar conclusion is drawn by William Bechtel and Robert C. Richardson, who take their examples from the biological and psychological sciences. In hierarchically organized systems, they argue,

> even though the processes at a particular level are constrained by the nature of the subsystems out of which they are constructed, the processes by which these subsystems interact are typically different from those occurring within the subsystems. The interactions *between* subsystems become increasingly important as the units engage in more complex modes of interaction ... Different models are needed to characterize the interactions between the components in a complexly organized system than are needed to characterize the behavior of the independent components. With emergent phenomena, it is the interactive organization, rather than the component behavior, that is the critical explanatory feature. (Bechtel and Richardson 1992, p. 285; original stress)

This relatively undemanding concept of emergence is closely related to the concept of downward causation, as Bernd-Olaf Küppers explains:

> The main idea behind these concepts can be summarized by the general claim that, if a material system reaches a certain level of complexity, manifested in a high relatedness of its components, then genuinely novel properties and processes may emerge, which cannot be explained by the material properties of the components themselves ... one can express the quintessence of the concepts of emergence and downward causation by two theses:
>
> 1. The whole is more than the sum of the parts.
> 2. The whole determines the behavior of its parts. (Küppers 1992, pp. 242–3)

Küppers's use of the word 'determines' is surely too strong here; 'significantly affects' would suffice.

Similarly, Jaegwon Kim distinguishes two sets of ideas about emergence. One is 'manifest in the statement that emergent properties are "novel" and "unpredictable" from knowledge of their lower-level bases, and that they are not "explainable" or "mechanistically reducible" in terms of their underlying properties'. The second set of ideas concerns 'claims about the causal powers of the emergents. Prominent among them is the claim that the emergents bring into the world new causal powers of their own, and, in particular, that they have powers to influence and control the direction of the lower-level processes from which they emerge' (Kim 1999 [2008], p. 129). As might be inferred from his use of inverted commas, Kim is highly critical of both emergence and downward causation. Küppers notes that, 'from the perspective of a scientist actually working in the borderline of physics and biology, both concepts remain rather vague and mysterious' (ibid., p. 243). Scott Gordon also suggests that, in natural science, '[t]here is a bit of mystery, perhaps even mysticism, about the idea of emergent properties. Nature is supposed, according to this, to have rather magical powers, and the true scientist is rather loath to accept this' (Gordon 1991, p. 48). Similarly, Cunningham (2001, p. S63) refers dismissively to 'the mythical vital properties' as unacceptable examples of ontological emergence, while Claus Emmeche, Simo Køppe and Frederik Stjernfelt (2000, p. 13) go further and also reject strong versions of downward causation on the grounds that they are 'in conflict with contemporary science'.

It is significant that these authors refer only to the natural sciences. There may indeed be, as Gordon has suggested, much more serious problems with the notion of emergence when it is applied to physical sciences, by comparison with social science, since:

> the individuals who compose a society are, in important respects, the products of a process of social enculturation. That is, they not only make up the society but are made by it. At this point the analogy between social and physical phenomena fails. It is true that new properties emerge when hydrogen and oxygen come together to form water, but no-one would claim that the properties of oxygen and hydrogen, considered by themselves, depend upon the properties of water. (Gordon 1991, pp. 49–50)

And again:

> whole-part relationships in social phenomena are not like those of the natural world. The characteristics of chemical elements are not dependent upon the compounds and other higher-level entities of which they are parts. Oxygen is oxygen, whether it is in a water molecule or a protein, a tree or a crocodile. But the human individual is different, in some important ways at least, in different

> social environments. To the degree that scientific explanation requires reduction of wholes to component parts, it poses difficulties in the domain of social phenomena which are much greater than those confronting the natural sciences. (Ibid., p. 54)

If micro-reduction is more difficult to accept in social science, the concepts of emergence and downward causation are correspondingly less problematical.

Now Kim's particular interest is the mind-body problem. The objections to emergence and to downward causation are most apparent here, since the age-old problems posed by mental causation of physical events, by consciousness and by intentional human agency seem to lead inexorably to an unacceptable Cartesian dualism, with separate and apparently unconnected 'physical' and 'mental' worlds. Emergence, Kim argues, 'is a form of what is now standardly called "nonreductive materialism", a doctrine that aspires to position itself as a compromise between physicalist reductionism and all-out dualisms'. He explains the rise of what he describes as 'emergentism' in terms of 'the nearly total collapse of positivistic reductionism and the ideal of a unified science which was well underway by the early 70s'. Hence it is 'no undue exaggeration to say that we have been under the reign of emergentism since the early 1970s'. Kim regards 'non-reductive physicalism' as 'an inherently unstable position', however, since it 'threatens to collapse into either reductionism or more serious forms of dualism' (Kim 1999 [2008], p. 128). Once it is accepted that 'any phenomenon of the world can be physically explained or it cannot be explained at all', Kim maintains, it follows that 'nonreductive materialism could not deliver on mental causation – any better than Cartesian dualism could. It could not explain, on its own terms, how mental phenomena, like belief, desire, feeling, and sensation, could causally affect the course of events in the physical world' (Kim 2005, pp. 150, 152). And so he denies that emergence offers a way out. Treating consciousness as an emergent property is to issue 'a promissory note that cannot be redeemed' (ibid., p. 158).

This may be true in this particular context, though it would be denied by many philosophers of mind, including Horst (2007) and Bhargava (1992). But Kim's objections have no clear relevance to the social sciences, or to economics in particular. While the treatment of emergence in the economics literature 'seems to be a rather motley collection of fragmentary and discordant concepts' (Harper and Endres 2011, p. 14), there is nothing 'mystical' or 'mysterious' in regarding 'the economy' as an emergent property, as Margaret Schabas proposes. She traces the concept of emergence in economics back to Friedrich List, to whom we 'owe the important insight that "the economy" has emergent properties, that it is more than the sum of its parts (households or individuals) ... J.S. Mill developed this further with his notion of "the economy of society"' (Schabas 2009, p. 12), while there are also intimations of emergence in 'Hayek's term "the Great Society"' (ibid., p. 13). 'Given this evident appeal to emergent properties', Schabas continues,

> it may be helpful to consider whether 'the economy' is a classic example of a Durkheimian social fact, or an 'institutional fact' as recently offered by John Searle (1995). I will suggest that both analytic tools are helpful and that this can help to enlighten us as to why economists have by and large avoided linking their discourse to this larger entity ... Searle helps to drive home the point that we cannot have a mere physical description of the economy; institutional facts must lie in a realm that attends to social (nonphysical) properties ... In sum, 'the economy' is a theoretical construct. (Ibid., pp. 13, 15)

Money, too, is an inevitably social phenomenon, which regulates the relations between individuals in society; Robinson Crusoe had no need of it (Smithin 2009, p. 61). As Joshua Epstein and Robert Axtell suggest, the distribution of wealth can be regarded as an example of emergence: 'we do not know what it would *mean* for an individual to have a wealth distribution: at a given time [*sic*], only groups can have distributions' (Epstein and Axtell 1996, p. 35).

More generally, David Harper and Anthony Endres (2011, p. 1) define emergence 'as occurring when wholes (combinations of things) produce structural or functional effects that are qualitatively different from what the parts can produce alone'. Two of their 'core characteristics' of an emergent system are:

> E6 – Unpredictability in principle: the first-time appearance of a new type of economic pattern cannot be predicted (i.e. logically deduced) through a rational procedure; E7 – Irreducibility: the systemic properties of the pattern do not follow from the properties of the system components in isolation or in simpler systems. (Ibid., p. 3)

They apply these definitions to economics by reference to the production of *novelty*, in the form of 'new routines, new capabilities, new firms, new networks, new markets and new institutions', and also extend the argument to capital: 'An emergent capital combination – such as a coupled system of a human driver and a motorcar – can make things happen that the capital goods cannot achieve separately' (ibid., pp. 2, 7) – as Richard Dawkins should have recognized. The 'coupled system' of humans and iPhones,

Harper and Endres suggest, provides an absorbing twenty-first century example (ibid., p. 8).

The analysis of complex systems may well lead to 'the radical remaking of economics', as Eric Beinhocker claims in the sub-title of a popular book on the subject. 'The ultimate accomplishment of Complexity Economics', he maintains,

> would be to develop a theory that takes us from theories of agents, networks, and evolution, all the way up to the macro patterns we see in real-world economies. Such a comprehensive theory does not yet exist, but we can begin to see glimmers of what it might look like. Such a theory would view macroeconomic patterns as *emergent* phenomena, that is, characteristics of the system that arise endogenously out of the actions of agents and their environment ... How can something be more than the sum of its parts? Or as the physicist Phil Anderson put it so well, 'Why is more different?' (Beinhocker 2006, p. 167)

Whether this will be the salvation of macroeconomics or its ultimate liquidation remains an open question:

> Our point of departure in agent-based modeling is the individual: we give agents rules of behaviour and then spin the system forward in time and see what macroscopic social structures emerge. This approach contrasts sharply with the highly aggregate perspective of macroeconomics, sociology, and certain subfields of political science, in which social aggregates like classes and states are posited *ab initio*. To that extent our work can be accurately characterized as 'methodologically individualist'. However, we part company with certain members of the individualist camp insofar as we believe that the collective structures, or 'institutions', that emerge can give feedback effects in the agent population, altering the behaviour of individuals. (Epstein and Axtell 1996, pp. 16–17)

'Why is more different?' Because of downward causation, at the very least, so that emergence is much more difficult to reconcile with methodological individualism than Epstein and Axtell are prepared to accept.

Precisely what emergence means for micro-reduction was, and remains, disputed. Küppers (1992, p. 242) describes emergence as having been invented by biologists and associated philosophers of science precisely 'in order to immunize themselves against the desperate picture of the world drawn by reductionism'. Similarly, in his book *The Possibility of Naturalism*, the sub-title of which is *A Philosophical Critique of the Contemporary Human Sciences*, Roy Bhaskar gives the following heading to one section of his chapter on agency: 'Emergent Powers and Materialism I: Against Reductionism' (Bhaskar 1998, p. 100). Bechtel and Richardson (1992,

p. 285), however, maintain that 'the multi-level, hierarchical picture developed here represents an alternative to both extreme reductionism and extreme holism and may capture much of what has led some biologists and psychologists to think of the phenomena they are investigating as emergent'. Herbert Simon took a rather similar position, defending only a 'weak interpretation of emergence', so that

> ... we can adhere (and I will adhere) to reductionism in principle even though it is not easy (often not even computationally feasible) to infer rigorously the properties of the whole from knowledge of the properties of the parts. In this pragmatic way, we can build *nearly independent theories* for each successive level of complexity, but at the same time, build bridging theories that show how each higher level can be accounted for in terms of the elements and relations of the next level below. This is, of course, the usual conception of the sciences as building upward from elementary particles, through atoms and molecules to cells, organs and organisms. The actual history, however, has unfolded, as often as not, in the opposite direction, from top down. (Simon 1996 [2008], p. 251; added stress)

Similarly, the solid-state physicist P.W. Anderson, who was quoted above by Beinhocker, defends both emergence, the hierarchy of science and '[r]eductionism, which I fully accept' (Anderson 1972 [2008], p. 223): 'it seems to me that one may array the sciences roughly linearly in a hierarchy, according to the idea: The elementary entities of science X obey the laws of science Y', where

X:	Y:
Many-body/solid state physics	Particle physics
Chemistry	Many-body physics
Molecular biology	Chemistry
Cell biology	Molecular biology
...	...
Psychology	Physiology
Social sciences	Psychology

On the surface, this seems very similar to Dawkins's hierarchical reductionism. 'But', Anderson continued, 'this hierarchy does not imply that science X is "just applied Y". At each stage entirely new laws, concepts, and generalizations are necessary, requiring inspiration and creativity to just as great a degree as in the previous one. Psychology is not applied biology, nor is biology applied chemistry' (ibid., p. 222). And macroeconomics, he might well have continued, is not applied microeconomics.

Thus Anderson criticized what he believed to be a mistaken application of reductionism:

> the reductionist hypothesis does not by any means imply a 'constructionist' one: The ability to reduce everything to simple fundamental laws does not imply the ability to start from those laws and reconstruct the universe. In fact, the more the elementary particle physicists tell us about the nature of the fundamental laws, the less relevance they seem to have to the very real problems of the rest of science, much less to those of society. (Ibid., p. 222)

A quarter of a century later the philosopher William Wimsatt also maintained that emergence was consistent with some versions of reductionism, but denied the traditional reductionist position that '[a]s science progresses, emergence claims will be seen as nothing more than temporary confessions of ignorance', a view that he attributed to Ernest Nagel (Wimsatt 1997 [2008], p. 99). A similar position had been defended by Carl Hempel and Paul Oppenheimer, for whom '[e]mergence of a characteristic is not an ontological trait inherent in some phenomena; rather it is indicative of the scope of our knowledge at a given time; thus it has no absolute, but a relative character; and what is emergent with respect to the theories available today may lose its emergent status tomorrow' (Hempel and Oppenheimer 1965 [2008], p. 64). It was important, they maintained, to eliminate from emergence 'the connotation of absolute unpredictability – a notion which is objectionable ... because ... it encourages an attitude of resignation which is stifling for scientific research' (ibid., p. 65).

For Wimsatt, this was not a serious problem. 'An emergent property', he maintained, 'is – roughly – a system property which is dependent on the mode of organization of the system's parts' (Wimsatt 1997 [2008], p. 101). This, he claimed, was consistent with a correctly formulated version of reductionism, and indeed offered

> a better understanding of the temptations of vulgar reductionism, '*Nothing but*'-isms and their fallacies. We regularly see statements such as 'genes are the only units of selection', 'the mind is nothing but neural activity', or 'social behavior is nothing more than the actions of individuals'. If total aggregativity is so rare, why are claims like this so common? These are particularly pervasive *functional localization fallacies* – moves from the power of a particular decomposition to claims that its entities, properties and forces are *all* that matters. (Ibid., p. 108; original stress)

Wimsatt does not refer directly to economics in his discussion of emergent properties, but the microfoundations dogma provides a telling example of his 'functional localization fallacy'.

4.5 CONCLUSION

Three broad conclusions can be drawn from the material presented in Part I. First, micro-reduction is an empirical question, not a methodological imperative, and there is little reason to regard it as a methodological virtue. Second, it has very largely failed in the natural sciences for empirical reasons, above all the existence of emergent properties and the importance of downward causation. Third, micro-reduction is very much a minority position in the other social sciences, despite the pretensions of economics imperialism. This is clear from the debate on methodological individualism that was summarized in this chapter, and it will be confirmed in Chapter 7, which looks at the way that social scientists have used the term 'micro-foundations'. As we shall see there, even those closest to mainstream economics (for example, the Chicago sociologist James Coleman) do not believe in it.

There are clear lessons for economics, or so one might have thought. But economists have remained almost willfully ignorant of all this. If anything, the economists' refusal to engage with the philosophy of science has become more complete in recent decades, as economic methodology has fallen into disrepute. Even the dissenters from the microfoundations dogma (many heterodox economists, and some dissident mainstream theorists) have mostly failed to draw on the micro-reduction literature, as we shall see in Part III. This is unfortunate, as it would have helped them clarify their ideas and would have strengthened their case. First, though, in Chapters 5–6 the long and tortuous post-1936 road that led the macroeconomists to 'microfoundations' will be mapped out; as we shall see, it did not proceed via the philosophy of science.

PART II

Microfoundations in the History of Economics and Other Social Sciences

5. 'Microfoundations' in the literature of economics, part I: 1936–1975

5.1 INTRODUCTION

In this chapter I trace the very chequered pre-history of the microfoundations dogma, down to 1975. It is a long and very complicated story, with many twists and turns. Part of it has been told by Teodoro Dario Togati (1998), in a sadly neglected book, and by Kevin Hoover (2010a); Hoover's account is, as will be seen, not entirely satisfactory.

The *term* 'microfoundations' was apparently invented by Sidney Weintraub in 1956, but the *concept* is somewhat older. My story begins in 1936, with the publication of the *General Theory*, and in Section 5.2 Keynes's scattered and indirect remarks on this question are assessed. Then, in Sections 5.3 and 5.4, I deal with the period from 1933 (just before the appearance of Keynes's great book) to the mid-1960s, proceeding chronologically and distinguishing three categories of authors: those who asserted the need for microfoundations, those who attempted to provide them without saying so, and those who did neither. In Section 5.5 I discuss the increasing use of the term in the macroeconomics literature of the late 1960s and early 1970s. The 1975 S'Agaro conference of the International Economic Association, which revealed continuing doubt and confusion on the question, is the subject of Section 5.6. The chapter concludes (in Section 5.7) by asking why the case for microfoundations had begun to resonate in the early 1970s (and not earlier), without yet achieving the canonical status that it would subsequently attain.

5.2 KEYNES AND MICROFOUNDATIONS

Despite his deep, lifelong interest in questions of philosophy, John Maynard Keynes wrote very little specifically on economic methodology. Possibly he was deterred by having a father who was the author of the standard text on the subject (J.N. Keynes 1890). At all events, the attitude of the younger

Keynes towards the relationship between macroeconomics and microeconomics is easily misunderstood. More than half a century ago the British philosopher J.W.N. Watkins, a disciple of Karl Popper, described him as a methodological individualist (Watkins 1952a, pp. 33, 35; above, pp. 53–4). Claudio Sardoni goes even further, arguing that 'Keynes indeed based his macroeconomic theory on microeconomic foundations that were essentially non-neoclassical' (Sardoni 2002, p. 5).

Most recently, Kevin Hoover has taken a more nuanced position. 'Taken together', Hoover suggests, 'Keynes's analysis of the fundamental components of aggregate demand and supply display a firm connection between microeconomic choices of firms and individuals and the macroeconomic outcomes. In every case, the causal mechanisms are driven by individual agents' (Hoover 2010b, pp. 17–18). Very true, but this 'firm connection' is a (much) weaker assertion than the microfoundations dogma, as Hoover himself almost immediately acknowledges: 'The outcomes for the economy as a whole clearly *emerge* out of individual behaviors ... *Emergence* is perhaps the most characteristic feature of Keynes's account of the relationship of microeconomic to macroeconomic behavior' (ibid., p. 18; original stress). But, as already noted, it is precisely the existence of emergent properties, in economics, sociology, the life sciences and the natural sciences more generally, which doom any micro-reduction project to inevitable failure. Hoover himself seems to recognize this, just a couple of pages later, in his discussion of J.R. Hicks, whose endorsement of the microfoundations dogma in all but name in *Value and Capital* is 'at least in part, a denial of Keynes's emergent properties of the economy as a whole' (ibid., p. 20).

What, then, did Keynes himself have to say on these matters? His first and perhaps most telling comment came in his 1926 obituary of Francis Ysidro Edgeworth, where he explained why economics could never become a mathematical science like physics:

> The atomic hypothesis which has worked so splendidly in Physics breaks down in Psychics. We are faced at every turn with the problem of Organic Unity, of Discreteness, of Discontinuity – *the whole is not equal to the sum of the parts*, comparisons of quantity fail us, small changes produce large effects, the assumptions of a uniform and homogeneous continuum are not satisfied. (Keynes 1926, p. 150; stress added)

'The whole is not the sum of the parts': this alone is enough to rule out the possibility of micro-reduction in economics. According to Rod O'Donnell (1989, p. 127–8), this principle had already been enunciated by G.E. Moore in the context of ethics, but there is no indication in the Edgeworth obituary that Keynes intends it to be restricted to ethical questions. He restates it in the *General Theory*, as might be expected, but not at the very beginning, as one might have hoped. Instead, Keynes invokes it at the end of Chapter 7 ('The Meaning of Saving and Investment'), where he describes what has come to be known as the 'paradox of thrift'. In the absence of an increase in investment spending, any increase in saving by an individual will reduce aggregate income and hence reduce the saving of others by an identical amount, so that aggregate saving is unchanged. While this can safely be ignored by any individual, it is 'nonsense to neglect it when we come to aggregate demand. This is the vital difference between the theory of the economic behaviour of the aggregate and the theory of the behaviour of the individual unit, in which we assume that changes in the individual's own demand do not affect his income' (Keynes 1936, p. 85).

Keynes does not return to this question until Chapter 19, on 'Changes in Money Wages', where he accuses classical theorists of begging the question of the effect of money wage reductions on the level of employment:

> For the demand schedules for particular industries can only be constructed on some fixed assumption as to the nature of the demand and supply schedules of other industries and as to the amount of the aggregate effective demand. It is invalid, therefore, to transfer the argument to industry as a whole unless we also transfer our assumption that the aggregate effective demand is fixed. Yet this assumption reduces the argument to an *ignoratio elenchi* … But if the classical theory is not allowed to extend by analogy its conclusions in respect of a particular industry to industry as a whole, it is wholly unable to answer the question what effect on employment a reduction in money-wages will have. (Ibid., pp. 259–60; cf. Coates 1996, p. 76)

An *ignoratio elenchi* 'refers to the fallacy of setting out to prove one proposition, proceeding to prove a different one, and then claiming that the original objective has been achieved' (Gordon 1991, p. 50). In Chapter 21 ('The Theory of Prices'), Keynes distinguishes the 'Theory of Value' from the 'Theory of Money and Prices', and complains that they appear to be entirely unrelated: 'we are lost in a haze where nothing is clear and everything is possible. We have all of us become used to finding ourselves sometimes on the one side of the moon and sometimes on the other, without knowing what route or journey connects them, related, apparently, after the fashion of our waking and our dreaming lives' (ibid., p. 292).

But this is a mystery of Keynes's own making, as his earlier discussion of individuals and aggregates should have suggested to him. His analysis of the means of 'escape from this double life' (ibid., p. 293) is also much less clear than it might have been, conflating in a single paragraph the micro-macro distinction (which at one point he seems to deny), the contrast between a stationary and a growing economy, and the difference between stationary and shifting equilibria (which he regards as equivalent to that between a monetary and a non-monetary economy). 'The right dichotomy', he suggests, 'is between the Theory of the Individual Industry or Firm and of the rewards and the distribution between different uses of a *given* quantity of resources on the one hand, and the Theory of Output and Employment *as a whole* on the other hand' (ibid., p. 293; original stress). But this is not a dichotomy at all: the opposite of 'whole' is 'part', not 'given' or 'constant'. The same lack of clarity is found in Keynes's (1936) prefaces to the German and Japanese editions of the *General Theory*, and it is not entirely absent from his restatement of 'The general theory of employment', published in the *Quarterly Journal of Economics* early in 1937, though it is striking just how often Keynes uses the phrase 'as a whole': three times in one paragraph in Chapter 21 (Keynes 1936, p. 293), and again three times in one paragraph of the *QJE* article (Keynes 1937, p. 219).

Not until the preface to the French edition, written in February 1939, does Keynes achieve the clarity of the Chapter 7 statement quoted above:

> I have called my theory a *general* theory. I mean by this that I am chiefly concerned with the behaviour of the economic system as a whole, – with aggregate incomes, aggregate profits, aggregate employment, aggregate investment, aggregate saving rather than with the incomes, profits, output, employment, investment and saving of particular industries, firms or individuals. And I argue that important mistakes have been made through extending to the system as a whole conclusions which have been correctly arrived at in respect of a part of it taken in isolation. (Keynes 1939, p. xxxii; original stress)

Here, at least, Keynes uses 'general' as synonymous with 'aggregate' (or 'macro'), in contrast to 'particular' (or 'micro'), and his denial of the possibility of micro-reduction in economics could hardly be more explicit. Elsewhere in the *General Theory* 'general' is taken to mean 'encompassing' and is contrasted with 'special', as in the preface to the English edition, where he defines his own analysis as 'a more general theory, which includes the classical theory with which we are familiar, as a special case' (Keynes 1936, p. vii). This is a quite different usage from that in the French preface.

Some authorities on Keynes have attributed his position on this question to a broader philosophical commitment on his part. Keynes was an organicist, they maintain, and therefore hostile to atomism, as his previously cited remarks in the Edgeworth obituary indicate; this is a constant theme in Togati's *Keynes and the Neoclassical Synthesis*, which includes an entire chapter on 'Keynes's anti-atomism' and refers repeatedly to 'Keynes's top-down strategy' for macroeconomics (Togati 1998, pp. 36–8, 154, 175–6, 303) and also alludes to his 'macrofoundations perspective' (ibid., pp. 33, 76–7, 238), which is analogous to the *Gestalt* theory of Jean Piaget and the related concept of 'emergent totalities' (ibid., p. 32). For Keynes, Togati suggests, expectations are 'inter-subjectively established, rather than simply reflecting individual psychology' (ibid., p. 232).

Other students of Keynes come to very similar conclusions. According to Anna Carabelli, pre-Keynesian or 'classical' theory relied on 'the premises of logical independence' derived from Newtonian physics, which allowed it 'to speak of economic individuals, of industries and of systems *in isolation* from each other'. Keynes, however, repudiated these premises: 'one of the leading methodological elements in Keynes's assault on the classical theory was provided by the concept of organic interdependence which grew directly from his approach to probability theory', and 'underlay his positive contribution to the study of the economy; it is the basic notion in the discipline of macroeconomics' (Carabelli 1994, p. 142; original stress). John Coates stresses the influence on Keynes of G.E. Moore, which Keynes himself acknowledged in his essay on 'My Early Beliefs':

> Moore thought that complex entities could be built up from simple objects, and that the meaning or value of these wholes is not simply the additive values of the constituent parts; in Keynes's words, 'their value depended, in accordance with the principle of organic unity, on the state of affairs as a whole which could not be usefully analysed into parts'. (Coates 1996, p. 74, citing Keynes 1972, p. 436)

Thus, as Ben Fine and Dimitris Milonakis suggest, Keynes's approach has 'a holistic and organicist outlook, both at odds with the individualistic overtones of neoclassical economics and more in line with some writers in the classical (in our sense of the word) tradition, and with the Historical Schools and American institutionalism' (Milonakis and Fine 2009, p. 275). Contrary to what Sardoni and (perhaps) also Hoover and Watkins believe, Keynes could never have accepted the dogma of microfoundations, whether they were of a neoclassical or a non-neoclassical variety. A slightly different interpretation is offered by O'Donnell, for whom Keynes's position was 'pluralist. The principle of atomism or methodological individualism was applicable in some situations, and the principle of organic unity in others' (O'Donnell 1989, p. 177). The atomist principle was – presumably – *not* applicable to macroeconomics.

5.3 THE FIRST TWO DECADES (1933–1953)

The story does not, however, begin with the *General Theory*. According to Hal Varian (1987), the first references to 'micro' and 'macro' in the economics literature come in a 1933 paper by Ragnar Frisch, who distinguished 'macrodynamic analysis' from 'microdynamic analysis'. This is not quite accurate, as Hoover notes: 'a discussion of the History of Economics Society's listserv indicated that Böhm-Bawerk referred to the *microcosm* and the *macrocosm* of a developed economy as early as 1891; while the earliest use of *macro-economic* (with the hyphen) recorded on the JSTOR journal archive is in an article by J.M. Fleming (1938)' (Hoover 2009, p. 406 n2). But Frisch, unlike Böhm-Bawerk, does seem to have been on the same wavelength as Keynes. In a 1932 radio broadcast on the grave economic situation facing his native Norway, Frisch argued that it was necessary to encourage consumer spending in order to stimulate output and employment. If instead society tried to save more, the result would be a fall in income and a *reduction* in saving. This was the 'paradox of thrift': a particularly clear statement of the fallacy of composition. The broadcast was recently recalled, approvingly, by another econometrician, the American Lawrence Klein (2006, p. 171).

Two of Frisch's papers from the early 1930s are also relevant. One was published in a *Festschrift* for Gustav Cassel (Frisch 1933) and the other, 'Some Problems in Economic Macrodynamics', was presented at the inaugural meeting of the Econometric Society in Leyden and summarized by Jakob Marschak (1934). There is no hint of microfoundations in either paper, as is acknowledged in the case of the 1933 paper, by Hoover (2010b, pp. 10–11). Twelve years earlier, Hoover had been much more emphatic on this point: 'Frisch's approach is wholly macroeconomic … His article does not hint at the desirability of microfoundations, even of the pseudo-microfoundations of the representative agent model: there is not an optimization model to be found' (Hartley, Hoover and Salyer 1998, p. 279). At all events, there is no indication that the question was raised in the discussion of Frisch's conference paper: 'Microdynamics are concerned with particular markets, enterprises, etc., while macrodynamics relate to the economic system as a whole' (Marschak 1934, p. 189); that is all. Questions from Tjalling Koopmans, Michał Kalecki, F. Divisia and Henry Schultz are briefly reported by Marschak (ibid., p. 192), but they have no bearing on the issue of microfoundations.

The next (non-) event came in 1936, a few months after the appearance (in February) of Keynes's *General Theory* (in which the words 'micro' and 'macro' are regrettably absent). This was the publication of James Meade's *Introduction to Economic Analysis and Policy*, which was the very first Keynesian textbook – or, more precisely, the first textbook with a Keynesian component. Part I, 'Unemployment', sets out a simplified version of the *General Theory*, with an emphasis on policy, while Section V, 'International problems', goes some way to filling the most significant gap in Keynes's own macroeconomic analysis by extending the arguments to the case of an open economy. In between, there are three sections on microeconomics, dealing with product markets, income distribution and the supply of the factors of production. If any single theorist might have been expected to advocate microfoundations it was surely Meade, a lifelong enthusiast for neoclassical economic theory, even when it was plainly wrong (as was the case with the theory of capital). Although macro and micro themes are interwoven throughout the book, there is no suggestion that one is foundational for the other. Significantly, in the chapter in Part I devoted to 'direct control of expenditure on consumption', Meade (1936, pp. 49–60) does not invoke utility maximization or any other aspect of the neoclassical theory of consumer behaviour. He remained a neoclassical Keynesian for the remainder of his very long and very productive life, without ever expressing –as far as I am aware – any opinion on the microfoundations dogma.

Three years later, another neoclassical Keynesian did precisely this. In *Value and Capital*, J.R. Hicks neatly begged the entire question in a passage in the chapter entitled 'The temporary equilibrium of the whole system' that deserves to be quoted in full:

> It is one of the most exciting characteristics of the method of analysis we are pursuing in this book that it enables us to pass over, with scarcely any transition, from the little problems involved in detailed study of the behaviour of a single firm, or single individual, to the great issues of the prosperity or adversity, even life or death, of a whole economic system. The transition is made by using *the simple principle*, already familiar to us in statics, *that the behaviour of a group of individuals, or group of firms, obeys the same laws as the behaviour of a single unit*. If a particular change in price (other prices being constant) can be shown to increase the demand for a certain commodity on the part of a representative individual, then it must increase the demand for that commodity on the part of all individuals similarly situated. (We have learnt to mark out, by our 'income effects', the differences in the situations of those persons who appear as buyers, and those who appear as sellers, in the relevant markets). The laws of market behaviour, which we have laboriously elaborated for those tenuous creatures, the representative individual and the representative firm, thus become revealed 'in their own dimensions like themselves' as laws of the behaviour of great groups

> of economic units, from which we can readily evolve the laws of their interconnexions [*sic*], the laws of the behaviour of prices, the laws of the working of the whole system. (Hicks 1939, p. 245; stress added)

This is not quite the origin of the term 'representative agent', but it is very close (a JSTOR search for the period 1900–1939 yielded very many 'representatives' and a very large number of 'agents', but no instance where the two words were used together). Hicks takes for granted the validity of his 'simple principle', which entails that the whole *is* the sum of the parts, and thereby rules out fallacies of composition, emergent properties – and any need for a 'theory of output as a whole'.

The book was reviewed by several eminent theorists, at least three of them sympathetic to Keynes: Kenneth Boulding (1939), Roy Harrod (1939), and Abba Lerner (1940). Fritz Machlup (1940, p. 277) described it as 'a great book', while Bernard F. Haley (1939, p. 560) asked 'How much of this is good for anything?', given that Hicks did not discuss applications of his theoretical analysis. Only one of the reviewers questioned the microfoundations aspect of Hicks's analysis. This was Oskar Morgenstern, who in an extended footnote to his 33-page review drew attention to the elimination of the concepts of 'income' and 'saving' from Hicks's discussion of economic dynamics. 'Among the paradoxical consequences of abolishing the notion of income', Morgenstern noted, 'would be that the entire multiplier analysis – so dear to modern economists – would break down, since there would be no income to split between consumption and saving. In the same manner there would be no room left for propensities to consume and to save. It is rather surprising that Cambridge has not yet protested against this implicit attack' (Morgenstern 1941, p. 392n; see also ibid., p. 393).

One early use of the term 'micro-economic' in conjunction with 'macro-economic' (both as adjectives, with hyphens), was by the Dutch econometrician P. de Wolff (1941) in a short note in the *Economic Journal.* As Varian observes, 'de Wolff's note is concerned with what we now call the "aggregation problem": – how to move from the theory of the individual consuming unit to the behaviour of aggregate consumption'. Five years later what came to be known as the 'aggregation debate' in econometrics began in earnest with a series of papers, and a book, by Lawrence Klein. In the first of his articles, Klein voiced what would later become a familiar complaint:

> Many of the newly-constructed mathematical models of economic systems, especially the business-cycle theories, are very loosely related to the behavior of

> individual households or firms which must form the basis of all theories of economic behavior .... These aggregative theories have often been criticized on the grounds that they mislead us by taking attention away from basic individual behavior. (Klein 1946, p. 93)

Klein's fifteen-page article is, however, devoted to a mathematical analysis of aggregation conditions, since 'the problem of bridging the gap between the traditional theories based on individual behavior and the theories based on community or class behavior is, to a large extent, a problem of proper measurement' (ibid., p. 93). Note that the metaphor ('bridging the gap') is now a horizontal and not a vertical one. Klein concludes as follows: 'It is only in models of macroeconomics that we can see through all the complex interrelationships of the economy in order to form intelligent judgments about such important magnitudes as aggregate employment, output, consumption, investment' (ibid., p. 108). There is no suggestion of microfoundations here.

In his book, *The Keynesian Revolution*, published in the following year, Klein does, however, advocate microfoundations in everything but name. He argues that Keynes's consumption function can be derived '[f]rom the accepted theories of consumer behavior' (Klein 1947, p. 58), while the investment function 'is based on the most classically accepted doctrine of profit maximization'. 'Again', Klein suggests, 'it seems best to develop a treatment from the behavior of an individual unit following an optimal principle, and then to derive the aggregative relationship for the economy as a whole' (ibid., p. 62; cf. ibid., pp. 68, 192–9). Looking back, almost half a century later, Klein showed himself now to be somewhat ambivalent about the case for microfoundations:

> There should be microeconomic foundations for macroeconomics, but important parts of macroeconomics have no counterpart in microeconomics, and it is not always possible to obtain satisfactory microeconomic foundations for every aspect of macroeconomics. It may not necessarily be a good research strategy to develop macroeconomics by a summation of microeconomic propositions. (Klein 1993, p. 35)

In 1947, however, he had been a strong supporter of this strategy.

So, too, was Tjalling Koopmans, whose famous attack on 'Measurement Without Theory', directed against institutional economists in general and Wesley Clair Mitchell in particular, included a complaint that their ultra-empiricism 'eliminates all benefits ... that might be received from economic theory – by which I mean in this context the theoretical analysis of the aggregate effects of assumed patterns of economic behavior of groups of individuals' (Koopmans 1947, p. 164). The young Ruttledge Vining came to Mitchell's defence, providing a vigorous assertion of the autonomy of the macroeconomic domain:

> I believe that in our discussions of trade fluctuations, national and international, we deal with the behavior of an entity that is not a simple aggregate of the economizing units of traditional theoretical economics. I think that we need not take for granted that the behavior and functioning of this entity can be exhaustively explained in terms of the motivational behavior of individuals who are particles of the whole. (Vining 1949a, p. 79)

In his reply Koopmans yielded some ground (Koopmans 1949, especially pp. 85–6), but Vining was left unmoved; 'There is more to the developing house than can be learned from the bricks' (Vining 1949b, p. 92). The controversy did Vining's career no good, and Koopmans's career no harm; Philip Mirowski (1989b) provides a gripping account of the rather dirty politics of the entire affair. It cannot be said that the aggregation controversy left a very deep imprint either on macroeconomic theory or on the practice of econometrics; it receives only a brief mention in Mary Morgan's well-received history of econometrics (Morgan 1990, pp. 202–5). Econometricians seem at this time to have suffered from an inferiority complex with respect to mainstream economic theorists (Qin 1993, pp. 183–8).

A decade later, Maurice Peston did launch a stinging attack on the very notion of microfoundations: 'The difficulty arises from the acceptance of the doctrine that micro-theory is fundamental theory and all other theory must be built up from it' (Peston 1959, p. 60). On the contrary, 'economic theory at any level of aggregation exists on a par with economic theory at any other level … macrotheory and microtheory are seen to be complements not substitutes' (ibid., pp. 59, 61). He concluded that the 'aggregation problem as understood at present … acts as a straightjacket on economic theory at all levels' (ibid., p. 63). Peston's paper seems to have had little or no impact. Five years after his article appeared, H.A. John Green's authoritative book on *Aggregation in Economic Analysis* was careful to focus on technical issues and steer clear of methodological controversy (Green 1964).

As we have seen, the aggregation debate began back in 1946, the same year in which the young Milton Friedman published a 19-page paper directing 'methodological criticisms' – the sub-title of the article – at Oskar Lange's *Price Flexibility and Employment* (Lange 1945). This would have been a perfect opportunity for Friedman to criticize Keynesian macroeconomics for its lack of microfoundations. But there is not the slightest hint of such a critique. Instead Friedman objects to Lange's 'casual empiricism, invalid use of inverse probability, introduction of factors external to the theoretical system, and the use of only some of the implications of a formal model that has others that are unrealistic'. Lange had attempted to 'escape the shackles of formalism' by resorting to 'illogical devices and specious reasoning' (Friedman 1946, p. 631). Friedman had earlier praised Jan Tinbergen's (1939) pioneering macroeconometric study of U.S. business cycles, again without querying the absence of microeconomics and even praising Wesley Mitchell (Friedman 1940).

In fact Friedman was never an enthusiast for the microfoundations dogma. His influential work on the consumption function, published as a book in 1957, did begin with an analysis of individual decision-making, yielding an inter-temporal utility-maximizing equation that he described as 'a cornerstone' of his permanent income theory of the consumption function (Friedman 1957, p. 14). ('*A* cornerstone', be it noted; most buildings have at least four). But he makes very little of its methodological implications, being interested instead in the theoretical and policy implications: the marginal propensity to consume was lower, the multiplier much smaller, and the capitalist economy much more stable, than Keynesians would expect (ibid., p. 238). The issue was the appropriate 'specification of the dynamic characteristics of the economic system itself' (Friedman and Becker 1957, p. 73), not the existence or otherwise of microfoundations.

Two decades later Friedman finally put his views on this issue beyond doubt when he listed four 'important empirical differences of judgement' in the theory of money. One he summarized as 'Build up or down':

> A second dichotomy ... is between the view that the best approach to analyzing aggregate change is from the top down – that is, analyzing the behaviour of aggregates *and then perhaps supplementing that analysis* with an examination of the determinants of how the aggregate is divided among components – or from the bottom up – that is, analyzing directly each component and constructing the aggregate as a sum of components ... Keynes, *like me*, was clearly in the top-down category. (Friedman 1976, p. 316; stress added)

This was entirely accurate, both as a statement about Keynes and as a reflection on his own past practice.

In economics the publishing event of 1947 was the appearance of Paul Samuelson's *Foundations*. Interviewed nearly half a century later about his early theoretical development, Samuelson claimed to have been 'worried about the micro foundations'. As he told David Colander and Harry Landreth, 'I worried most of all in my Chicago years and the first part of the time I was at Harvard. You know, I was like a tuna: the Keynesian system had to land me, and I was fighting every inch of the line' (Samuelson 1996, p. 161). But there is absolutely no evidence of this struggle in the *Foundations*, where the same sets of mathematical principles are applied first (and principally) to microeconomic questions and then (much more briefly) to macroeconomics, without any suggestion whatsoever that the former might be the foundation of the latter (see Samuelson 1947, pp. 276–83 on the Keynesian system, and pp. 335–42 on the business cycle). As Wade Hands has noted, in the context of the *Foundations*, 'there is no maximization (from individuals or any other "agents") going on anywhere in the Keynesian economics (or other "business cycle" models) of the 1940s' (Hands 2008, p. 472; see also Togati 1998, Chapter 8). As Samuelson subsequently wrote: 'No one associates a Keynesian system with a maximizing single mind or even to [*sic*] an as-if pretend maximizing system' (Samuelson 1998, p. 1384). He himself had, in fact, acknowledged this later in the interview with Colander and Landreth: 'I decided that life was more fruitful not worrying about it. You weren't making any progress on it. Moreover, the search today for micro foundations for macro does not have a rich set of results' (Samuelson 1996, p. 162). Yes, indeed.

Two years later James Duesenberry worried quite explicitly about the 'somewhat schizophrenic attitude' taken by economists toward the theory of consumption (Duesenberry 1949, p. 1). He is sometimes described as a pioneer in establishing microfoundations for the Keynesian consumption function, for example by J. Allan Hynes (1998, p. 39) and by Hoover (2010b, pp. 28–32). Duesenberry himself described the aggregate consumption function as 'a special case of the general theory of consumer behaviour' (Duesenberry 1949, p. 1). His first principle for empirical research was defined accordingly: 'every hypothesis ought to be stated in terms of the behavior of individual firms or households, even when we are only interested in aggregate results' (ibid., p. 75). But what he actually does is to use macroeconomic evidence – the long-run constancy of the average propensity to consume in the United States in the face of a substantial increase in real incomes – to *criticize* the established neoclassical theory of consumer behaviour and to advocate an alternative to it, in which relative (not absolute) income is crucial, and individual decisions are not reversible. This is a profoundly subversive exercise, as indicated by his approving references to Thorstein Veblen (ibid., pp. 14–15), and together with his equally subversive insistence on the interdependence of individual utility functions it probably explains why it never caught on, despite the considerable evidence in its favour (on which see Barba and Pivetti 2009). Whatever

Duesenberry's own intentions, his book is *not* consistent with the microfoundations dogma, which requires the uncritical use of neoclassical microeconomic theory to interpret macroeconomic reality. What he does, in fact, is the exact opposite of this.

One of his reviewers was Kenneth Arrow, whose Walrasian interests might have been expected to make him sympathize with the case for microfoundations. In fact Arrow's principal objection to Duesenberry is quite different: 'the most striking methodological deficiency in the entire work is its failure to set up explicitly a model of the economy against which to study the empirical data'. It is a *macroeconomic* model that Arrow has in mind, for he continues by complaining that 'nothing whatever is said about the other parts of the economy, such as the investment function and supply factors in general' (Arrow 1950, p. 910). In the following year, writing on 'mathematical models in the social sciences', Arrow took a different line, attacking Rutledge Vining's position in the aggregation controversy: 'As Koopmans points out, a full characterization of each individual's behavior logically implies a knowledge of group behavior; there is nothing left out ... one methodological principle emerges clearly: in order to have a useful theory of relations among aggregates, it is necessary that they be defined in a manner derived from the theory of individual behavior' (Arrow 1951a, pp. 133–4). But this is not really microfoundations, since the position attributed to Koopmans is tautological, and the question of the *definition* of aggregates does not go to the heart of the matter. Interestingly, these comments appeared in the same year that Arrow published his important book on *Social Choice and Individual Values* (Arrow 1951b), which demonstrated that it was not always possible to aggregate individual preferences to produce a coherent framework for social choice.

In any case, Arrow's endorsement of microfoundations for macroeconomics, if such it is, offers only 'in principle' support. In practice, he suggests:

> ... there is something to be said for at least the possibility of a collective basis for social theorizing, if not taken too literally. Much of our casual observation and much of our better statistical information relate to groups rather than individuals. We may therefore be led to generalize and form a theory whose subject is the total behavior of a group. So long as it is understood that such a theory is really a resultant of certain as yet unanalyzed laws of individual behavior, no harm will be done, and the greater convenience of empirical analysis on groups may be highly beneficial. (Arrow 1951a, p. 133)

In principle, then, Arrow advocated reduction in social theory, as the philosopher Alan Garfinkel noted: 'A full characterization of each individual's behavior logically implies a knowledge of group behavior; there is nothing left out. The rejection of the organism approach to social problems has been a fairly complete, and to my mind salutary, rejection of mysticism' (Arrow 1951a [1968], p. 641; cited by Garfinkel 1981 [1991], p. 445).

But Arrow was not entirely consistent on this question. Reviewing Paul Samuelson's collected papers, he complained that 'Samuelson has not addressed himself to one of the major scandals of price theory, the relation between microeconomics and macroeconomics' (Arrow 1967, p. 734). General equilibrium theory could be used to explain 'certain dramatic historical episodes', Arrow maintained, including the highly successful postwar recovery of the Western countries. 'On the other hand, the Great Depression and the problems of the developing countries remind us dramatically that something beyond, but including, neoclassical theory is needed' (ibid., p. 735). What this 'something' might be, Arrow does not say. In his 1994 Richard T. Ely lecture, however, he argued that information is 'an irreducibly social category in the explanatory apparatus of economics', and that 'individual behavior is always mediated by social relations. These are as much a part of the description of reality as is individual behavior' (Arrow 1994, pp. 1, 5; see also Arrow 1986). The interpretation of Keynes in Arrow and Hahn (1971) is briefly discussed in Section 5.5 below.

5.4 MODIGLIANI TO MACHLUP (1954–1963)

In 1954 Franco Modigliani published his life-cycle hypothesis, using 'the well developed tools of marginal utility analysis' to reconcile time-series and cross-sectional evidence on the relationship between consumption and income (Modigliani 1954, p. 389). 'The results of our labor', he concluded,

> basically confirm the propositions put forward by Keynes in *The General Theory*. At the same time, we take some satisfaction in having been able to tie this aspect of his analysis into the mainstream of economic theory by replacing his mysterious psychological law with the principle that men are disposed, as a rule and on the average, to be forward-looking animals. (Ibid., p. 430)

A tie, of course, is not a foundation. In his autobiography Modigliani does use the latter term, albeit with no 'micro' prefix (Modigliani 2001, p. 53). But there is also a hint of emergent properties, or perhaps a suggestion of the 'multiple realization' problem that has often engaged the attention of philosophers writing about micro-reduction (see above, pp. 68–70). Among the six 'main innovations' of the life-cycle hypothesis, he writes, is the fact that '[t]he national saving rate is not simply the result of the different thrift of its citizens, in the sense that different national saving rates are consistent with identical individual saving behavior during the life cycle' (ibid., pp. 80–81). Modigliani does not elaborate, but this statement would be very difficult to reconcile with any version of the microfoundations dogma.

The year 1956 is especially important in this story, since it was then that the term 'microeconomic foundations' made its first appearance in print (Hoover 2010b, p. 7). The culprit was Sidney Weintraub, who would soon become a pioneering Post Keynesian dissenter but was still in 1956 a respectable mainstream Keynesian. The term is not given a particularly prominent place. It appears once, in 'note 2' of the appendix to his article (on the macroeconomic theory of wages), in the context of an attempt to derive Keynes's *Z-N* function (the aggregate supply curve). Note that he is not dealing with individual consumers, or even individual firms: Weintraub's 'aggregation procedure' is one 'whereby industry supply concepts are transformed into notions of aggregate supply' (Weintraub 1956, p. 854). This, then, is not a microfoundations project at all in the post-1970, New Classical, sense. Weintraub is also responsible for the first recorded use of the term 'micro-foundations' (with hyphen), which appears in the title of a 1957 article, but nowhere else in this paper, where it is given no methodological significance whatsoever (Weintraub 1957). If Hicks, Klein and Modigliani had the concept of microfoundations without the word, Weintraub had the word, without the concept.

Also in 1956, Don Patinkin's influential *Money, Interest, and Prices* was published. This is sometimes regarded as a milestone in the development of the microfoundations dogma, again without the use of the word (e.g. by Hoover 2010b, p. 22). This interpretation is, however, very difficult to justify. In fact Patinkin seems rather to have anticipated the failure of the general equilibrium variant of the microfoundations project (on which see Shubik 1975, Kirman 1992, Togati 1998 and especially Rizvi 1994, and Chapter 6, Section 5, below). It is true that, in introducing his macroeconomic model, Patinkin claims that each of his aggregate demand and aggregate supply functions 'is built up from the individual demand and supply functions of the relevant individual goods' (Patinkin 1956, p. 199). Almost immediately, though, he makes an important concession: 'There is, however, no pretense of showing how this process of aggregation is actually carried out' (ibid., p. 200). Earlier in the book he hints at the problems posed by emergent properties, and the consequent danger of fallacies of composition, pointing to 'a clear lack of analogy between individual and market excess-demand functions … the effect of, say, an increase in the total wealth of the economy on the amount of market excess demand for a good cannot be determined until the distribution of this increase among the members of the economy is first specified' (ibid., p. 33; cf. pp. 181, 183). Three years later the decidedly non-Walrasian British economist George Richardson made a similar point, noting that while 'a sufficient condition for a group, or for a system as a whole, to be in equilibrium, is for all the component units individually to be in equilibrium', this was not necessary, 'for stability in the aggregates (e.g., levels of output,) by which we describe the system might be maintained without stability in the contributions of individual units' (Richardson 1959, p. 224). Earlier in his book, Patinkin had distinguished 'individual-experiments' from 'market-experiments', on the grounds that 'the unit of investigation is different' (Patinkin 1956, p. 12); there is no suggestion that any one such unit is the foundation of any other.

A much stronger claim to membership of the fledgling microfoundations club in the 1950s can be established for James Tobin, which is ironic given his subsequent opposition to the dogma and its anti-Keynesian implications. In 1958, however, Tobin was quite emphatic on the appropriate way to establish the liquidity preference (Keynesian money demand) schedule: 'This aggregative function must be derived from some assumption regarding the behavior of the decision making units of the economy' (Tobin 1958, p. 65), which he proceeds to do by modelling the decisions of individual investors in financial markets. While these individuals are not representative agents, since they differ in their attitudes towards risk and the 'critical' rate of interest at which they choose to hold their entire portfolio in cash, Togati (1998, pp. 175–6) correctly contrasts Tobin's 'bottom-up method' with Keynes's 'top-down approach'.

By 1970, however – before the microfoundations dogma had begun to take hold – Tobin was taking a different line: 'Macroeconomics concerns the determinants of the performance of entire economies', he wrote in an introductory textbook, and therefore deals in economy-wide aggregates. 'The basic assumption is that this can be done without much attention to the constituents of the aggregates, that is, to the behavior and fortunes of particular households, business firms, industries, or regions', even though 'the relationships among aggregate variables … are intended to be consistent with theoretical and empirical knowledge of the behavior of individual economic units and particular markets'. The aggregate consumption and production functions 'are intended to be consistent with', and 'should conform with', what is known about the behaviour of individual consumers and firms (Tobin 1970, pp. 44–5). Almost no-one would deny this; 'consistency' and 'conformity' between A and B are much weaker requirements than A's being 'derived from' B.

At a high-powered 1960 multi-disciplinary conference, the proceedings of which were published two years later, Arrow organized a 'symposium on macro- and microeconomics'. It was opened by Abba Lerner, who took an unusual line: 'the dichotomy of economics into micro- and macroeconomics is itself much too violent an oversimplification', he maintained:

> Rather than to classify different parts of economics as belonging to the one kingdom or the other, it is much more useful to arrange them according to the *degree* to which they abstract from parts of the economic system that are not under direct study. Instead of a dichotomy we then have a spectrum. (Lerner 1962, p. 475; original stress)

As an example, Lerner cited the relationship between money wages and employment, 'where the difficulties seem to stem from a bilateral over-concentration on the extreme cases instead of a consideration of the whole spectrum' (ibid., p. 480). At the microeconomic end, small money wage cuts will leave prices unaffected and lead to increased employment. 'The illegitimate application of this position to the macroeconomic end of the spectrum', where falling money wages would reduce the price level, could not be justified (ibid., p. 481). Unfortunately there is no record of the discussion of Lerner's paper, and therefore no way of knowing whether his treatment of the 'problem of integrating microeconomics with macroeconomics', which 'may very well lead to their ultimate synthesis', met with general approval. Kenneth Arrow was unable to remember any salient details, perhaps not surprisingly at a distance of half a century (personal communication, 30 April 2009).

It is possible that Lerner's paper influenced Gardner Ackley, whose very popular intermediate textbook appeared in the following year with an entire chapter devoted to 'Macroeconomics and Microeconomics'. 'The relationship between macroeconomics and theories of individual behavior', he suggested, 'is a two-way street. On the one hand, microeconomic theory should provide the building blocks for our aggregate theories. But macroeconomics may also contribute to microeconomic understanding'. The theorist may thus 'proceed in either direction' (Ackley 1961, p. 570). The metaphor – 'building blocks' – points to microfoundations, but this is evidently not where Ackley wishes to go.

In the same symposium in 1960 the Cambridge economist Richard Stone complained that macroeconomic theories 'tend to be relatively superficial and to ignore any optimizing principle which might be supposed to lie at the roots of human endeavor' (Stone 1962, p. 494). Alternatively put: 'In order to replace the *ad hoc* relationships which figure so largely in macroeconomics, the optimizing model tries to penetrate more deeply into the springs of human action' (ibid., p. 505). Stone's choice of metaphors is interesting: 'roots' and 'springs' are not 'foundations'. So is his choice of optimizing model, which is that of Ramsey (1928); as he notes, the Ramsey model has 'attracted remarkably little attention among economists' (ibid., p. 497). I confirmed this statement with a JSTOR search, which revealed only 17 references to Frank Ramsey in the economics journal literature between 1940 and 1960, not all of them to his 1928 paper and none of them very substantial (though an exception might be made for Samuelson and Solow (1956), which is devoted to capital theory and not to Keynesian macroeconomics). Stone notes that Ramsey's is a planning model, which he (Stone) uses to solve the problem posed by the Indian planner, P.C. Mahalanobis: what proportion of investment should be devoted to expanding capacity in the investment-goods industry? This is a *social* problem, and there is no suggestion in Stone's paper that the Ramsey model might have a bearing on individual behaviour, still less that it might become the microfoundations for the macroeconomic theory of an unplanned capitalist economy. Indeed, Stone concludes by suggesting that his analysis

> … should be enough to illustrate the unity of the social sciences. The limitations of pure economics as opposed to empirical economics are now becoming generally recognized, and it is high time economists took seriously the psychological and social postulates of their theory instead of squandering so much energy in preserving its purity, which beyond a certain age [stage?] is just another word for sterility. (Ibid., p. 505)

It was probably just as well that this was delivered at Stanford; even in 1960, it would not have gone down well in Chicago.

There was a small flurry of references to 'microfoundations' in the journals around this time, but almost all were bibliographical citations of Weintraub's 1957 article (Hoover 2010b, p. 7). Without using the word, however, Dale Jorgenson (1963) was beginning a lifelong project to provide neoclassical microfoundations for the theory of business investment, while Fritz Machlup was unique in defending the principle on explicitly methodological grounds. Number nine in Machlup's list of 'twenty main theses' governing the relations between 'macro- and micro-economics' was this:

'The decision to seek micro-economic explanations of macro-economic generalizations, that is, to search for the micro-theoretical foundations of macro-theoretical propositions, can be interpreted as a recognition of "methodological individualism" and of the methodological primacy of micro-theory' (Machlup 1963, p. 140). Earlier he had acknowledged that

> ... it is not a duty for every macro-theorist to search for the hidden micro-relations that lie at the root of the macro-relations. No-one is obliged to adapt his scientific curiosity to any methodological norm. To specialize in the construction of macro-models without worrying about the underlying micro-theories is neither unsound nor dishonorable. But to deny that all macro-theory requires a micro-theoretical underpinning, or to deride the efforts of those who do investigate it, would be unreasonable and obtuse. Fortunately such narrow-mindedness is becoming less frequent than it used to be. (Ibid., p. 109)

Machlup provides no evidence to support this final statement. But he can claim to have been the first in the economics literature to assert the need for microfoundations as a methodological principle.

5.5 FROM MACHLUP TO PHELPS, AND BEYOND (1963–1975)

I doubt whether Machlup's book was read by many macroeconomists, though it may have influenced the later complaints of his fellow Austrian émigré Oscar Morgenstern (1972, p. 1184) about the dangers of 'concentration on undifferentiated aggregates', a concern that he traced back to Richard Cantillon. It almost certainly had no impact on Robert Clower's celebrated attack on what he termed J.R. Hicks's 'Keynesian counter-revolution', presented at a conference in 1962 and first published in the following year in a German translation and only two years later in the original English version (Clower 1965 [1984], p. 34n). Clower concluded that 'orthodox price theory may be regarded as a special case of Keynesian economics, valid only in conditions of full employment' (ibid., p. 55). Hoover (2010b, pp. 22–3) discusses Clower's 1965 paper, but he overlooks a more relevant article that appeared two years later with the title, 'A Reconsideration of the Microfoundations of Monetary Theory'. (This, incidentally, illustrates the perils of computer-based literature searches. The paper was published in the *Western Economic Journal*, since renamed *Economic Inquiry*, which is not included in JSTOR). Here Clower argued (convincingly) that Walrasian general equilibrium theory was 'formally equivalent to the Classical conception of a barter economy', and claimed (less convincingly) to have proposed 'a reformulation of established micro-economic analysis suitable as a foundation for explicit analysis of the working of a money economy'. The latter, he conceded, was 'obviously unfinished' (Clower 1967, p. 8).

It was no nearer completion in 1971, when Arrow and Frank Hahn concluded their influential book on *General Competitive Analysis* with a chapter on 'The Keynesian Model'. Walrasian theory was not suited to the analysis of a monetary economy, they conceded. 'This chapter can be taken as no more than a beginning of taking seriously the Keynes of the chapters on expectations and the functions of money' (Arrow and Hahn 1971, p. 369). If there really was a general equilibrium variant of the micro-foundations project, as argued by Hoover (2010b, pp. 18–24), it had evidently not got very far by the early 1970s; as we shall see in Chapter 6, it made only a little more progress thereafter.

There were a couple of rather casual allusions to microfoundations in relatively obscure papers in 1966. Summarizing his doctoral thesis on the term structure of interest rates in one page in the *Journal of Finance*, Liang-Shing Fan (1966, p. 131) criticized 'the lack of proper micro-foundations' in existing interest rate theory. In a three-page article in the *American Economic Review*, P.A. Neher (1966, p. 855) commented on the 'extremely shaky' nature of 'the micro foundations [two words] of the agricultural sector's private investment function' in some contemporary theories of economic development. In the following year William R. Bryan and Willard T. Carleton published a paper in *Econometrica* modelling the behaviour of individual banks, 'with the purpose of improving the micro foundations of the theory of monetary dynamics' (Bryan and Carleton 1967, p. 321); the term appears in the abstract only, and nowhere in the body of the paper. These were leading journals, but the references to microfoundations were both insubstantial and devoid of any methodological discussion. The word was in the air, but not much more.

A significant landmark was established in 1969 with the publication of E.S. Phelps's paper, 'The New Microeconomics in Inflation and Employment Theory', which had been presented at the American Economic Association's meeting in the previous December. 'It is notorious', Phelps began, 'that the conventional neoclassical theory of the supply decisions of the household and of the firm are [*sic*] inconsistent with Keynesian employment models and with the post-Keynesian economics of inflation.' He ended the opening paragraph thus: 'It seems clear that macroeconomics needs a microeconomic foundation'. Although the article 'sticks doggedly to the neoclassical postulates of lifetime expected utility maximization and net worth maximization', Phelps's intention is 'to buttress Keynes' rather than to undermine him (Phelps 1969, p. 147). Again, there is some evidence of difficulty with metaphors: a buttress is *not* a foundation. Almost 40 years later, Phelps claimed only that his new microeconomics could be 'hooked up to' macroeconomic theory (Horn 2009, pp. 250–51). The remainder of the 1969 article is somewhat eclectic, citing Lange, Sidney Winter and even Sidney Weintraub (but not Ramsey). The evolutionary economist Winter was co-author with Phelps of a chapter in the edited book, *Microeconomic Foundations of Employment and Inflation Theory* for which Phelps's article was a sort of curtain-raiser. The book, too, was quite ecumenical, and has more to say about firms (and even unions) than about utility-maximizing individual consumers (Phelps et al. 1970).

Both Phelps's article and his book were widely read and frequently cited in the early 1970s, and there is some evidence that the term 'microfoundations' was being used more generally than it had been previously. One theorist who in the early 1970s seems to have been untouched by it was, rather surprisingly, Robert Lucas. There is no reference to microfoundations in the – admittedly very skimpy – index to his first volume of collected papers (Lucas 1981), and the term is absent from his major articles from the period 1969–1973. As late as 1973 he was unable even to remember the correct title of Phelps's book, to which he had contributed, missing out the crucial reference to 'foundations' and citing it as *Microeconomics of Inflation and Employment Theory* (Lucas 1973, p. 334). Lucas's concerns in the early 1970s seem to have been econometric, not methodological. But the monetarist Karl Brunner was already describing recent developments in portfolio analysis as having been 'exploited to provide a micro-foundation for monetary analysis' (Brunner 1971, p. 167), and the neoclassical economists Duncan Foley and Miguel Sidrauski felt obliged to apologize for not having provided any microfoundations in some sections of their text on monetary and fiscal policy and growth (Foley and Sidrauski 1971, p. 4). This apology, the significance of which was picked up by a perceptive reviewer (Hester 1972, p. 1186), was the very first of its kind; it would not be the last.

5.6 DISORDER AT THE BORDER: S'AGARO, 1975

An indication of the state of the debate on microfoundations in the mid-1970s, such as it was, can be inferred from the proceedings of the International Economic Association conference on 'The Microeconomic

Foundations of Macroeconomics', held in the Catalan resort town of S'Agaro in 1975. As Geoff Harcourt, the chair of the programme committee, reported, Hicks was the 'basic architect and guiding light of the conference' (Harcourt 1977, p. 2). It was a much more ecumenical affair than would be possible today. In addition to Harcourt and Hicks, the other four members of the programme committee were Takishi Negishi, a Walrasian; Luigi Spaventa, a Sraffian; Erich Streissler, an Austrian by nationality and by conviction; and the Old Keynesian, James Tobin. Participation was by invitation, and included Walrasians (Edmond Malinvaud and three of his associates); econometricians with an interest in aggregation problems (Green, Koopmans); Post Keynesians (Tom Asimakopulos, Paul Davidson); Sraffians and other radicals (Pierangelo Garegnani, Mario Nuti, Edward Nell); historians of economic thought (Susan Howson, Donald Moggridge); and an impressive collection of luminaries not otherwise classified (Charles Goodhart, Ursula Hicks, Axel Leijonhufvud, Michael Parkin, Austin Robinson, Martin Shubik, Joseph Stiglitz). Invited but not attending were Tobin, Jorgenson and Phelps; Hahn was not there, but he did send his paper (ibid., p. 1). The absence of Jorgenson and Phelps was especially unfortunate, given their strong support for microfoundations.

One remarkable omission is evident: no philosophers of science or economic methodologists were invited to S'Agaro, no papers were presented on the methodological issues raised by microfoundations, and (so far as I have been able to ascertain from the conference volume) no mention was made at any point of methodological individualism, emergent properties, micro-reduction or any other related philosophical concepts. The majority of the participants seem to have taken the desirability of microfoundations for granted, and when the dogma was challenged it was in an unsystematic, almost incidental, manner. What little consideration of methodological questions did take place seems to have come at the very end of the conference, in the 'final discussion session' (ibid., pp. 378–80, 391–4). An honourable exception should be made for Streissler, whose paper does refer to the 'contrast between individual design and social consequences', recognized by both Hayek and Marx, which makes it possible that 'macroeconomic consequences differ qualitatively and totally from what is planned microeconomically'. From this criticism of 'a naïve derivation of macroeconomic consequences from microeconomic phenomena', he draws the conclusion that 'it might be better to start out with a system analytically wholly macroeconomic from the very beginning' (ibid., p. 105). Towards the end of his paper Streissler invokes Occam's razor to cast further doubt on the need for microfoundations (ibid., pp. 123–4)

Apart from Streissler's contribution, Harcourt's description of Koopmans's paper as 'peripheral to the central objective of the conference' (ibid., p. 8) could be applied to most of them. It is small wonder that Harcourt himself drew attention to the 'air of general dissatisfaction that pervades the contributions to the final discussion session' (ibid., p. 21), in which Ursula Hicks commented that 'little progress had been made towards the objective of identifying the general relations between microeconomics and macroeconomics' (ibid., p. 395). It is difficult to agree with Harcourt's own, more optimistic, conclusion: 'views in the profession may now be converging together from very different starting points, at least in regard to analytical methods' (ibid., p. 22). There is very little evidence of this in the conference volume.

A second lesson of S'Agaro is that in 1975 'microfoundations' meant Walrasian general equilibrium theory, not representative agents with rational expectations maximizing lifetime utility and making bequests to grandchildren. Judging by the index, the only participant to refer to Frank Ramsey was Koopmans, in what Harcourt described as his 'peripheral' contribution (ibid., p. 150). Third, and perhaps most revealing, is the complete absence of party lines on the whole question. The need for microfoundations was explicitly endorsed by the Post Keynesian Davidson, though he insisted that they should be of a non-Walrasian nature (ibid., pp. 313, 391–2). It was explicitly denied by Nell, an eclectic radical with Post Keynesian affinities, who observed that the very title of the conference begged the question (ibid., p. 392); by the Walrasian, Yves Younès (ibid., pp. 378–9); and by the Sraffian, Spaventa, who referred (most unusually at this conference) to fallacies of composition (ibid., p. 137). Doubts were also expressed by Negishi, another Walrasian, who raised the prospect of providing macrofoundations for microeconomics (ibid., p. 142). At the end of the conference Negishi neatly – and perhaps unconsciously – subverted the foundational metaphor again by calling for the provision of 'a bridge or at least some stepping stones' between micro and macro theory (ibid., p. 380). (No-one but a lunatic would use stepping stones as a foundation for anything). Most of the participants, including the Post Keynesians Asimakopulos and Harcourt, and the quasi-Sraffian Nuti, simply ignored the methodological issues altogether.

5.7 CONCLUSION

The microfoundations dogma *could* have become established at any time after 1870, when the marginal revolution symbolized a shift in the focus of mainstream economics towards the study of individual behaviour and away from the macroeconomic questions of growth and distribution. In fact it did not emerge then, or indeed (as we have seen) for another century. This is a real historical puzzle. Why in the 1970s, and not very much earlier? Why then, and not in the late 1930s, in reaction to the *General Theory*?

As we have seen, some eminent neoclassical theorists were asserting the microfoundations dogma well before 1970, without using the term; the most obvious example is Hicks. Many others, who might have been expected to do so, did not: Meade, Samuelson, Patinkin and Friedman are cases in point. One or two notable economists who might have been expected *not* to sympathize with the case for microfoundations in fact did so, at least some of the time: Klein and Tobin are in this third category, along with Sidney Weintraub, who invented the term. It is difficult to see what can explain these differences, to which I shall return in Chapter 11.

There are, then, some perplexing questions for the period under review, to which I have no answers. And there is another – arguably much more important – question, which is why the microfoundations dogma should have triumphed so comprehensively, against all logic, in the quarter-century after 1975. This is the subject of the next chapter.

6. 'Microfoundations' in the literature of economics, part II: 1975–2012

6.1 INTRODUCTION

We saw in the previous chapter that there was no coherent, generally accepted microfoundations project in 1975, when the International Economic Association held its conference on the issue (Harcourt 1977). Within a decade all this had changed, and there were two such programmes, both apparently thriving. The first was the real business cycle project, which assumed continuous market-clearing (in product and labour markets), and drew its RARE (representative agents with rational expectations) microfoundations from Frank Ramsey's (1928) model of optimum saving in a socialist economy. The second was the New Keynesian project, which had the same RARE microfoundations but relied upon wage and price rigidities to rule out continuous market-clearing in the short run. Like the real business cycle theorists, however, the New Keynesians endorsed the Solow neoclassical growth model, which committed them to market-clearing in the long run.

The first real business cycle papers were published as journal articles in the early 1980s, though in some cases they had been circulated as National Bureau of Economic Research working papers since 1980, or slightly earlier. Thus 1982 is something of a milestone in the history of microfoundations. The first New Keynesian papers were published at the same time, or even a year or so earlier. The shared microfoundations principle of the two projects was very widely adopted, so much so that in 1987 Robert Lucas – who had by now abandoned business cycle theory in favour of research into the theory of economic growth – could proclaim the death of macroeconomics. Thus 1987 is a second important milestone. Within another decade it had become clear that what united the two projects was much more substantial than the points of disagreement between them, and a New Neoclassical Synthesis was being proclaimed. The third milestone is therefore 1997.

In this chapter I proceed in broadly chronological order. In Section 6.2 I return to the question of microfoundations in monetarist macroeconomics, before and after the 'rational expectations' revolution of Lucas and his colleagues. I then discuss the role of microfoundations in the two theoretical challenges to monetarism in the 1980s, real business cycle theory (Section 6.3) and New Keynesian macroeconomics (Section 6.4). The abortive attempt to provide microfoundations for macroeconomics through the development of a 'general disequilibrium' theory derived from the Walrasian tradition is outlined in Section 6.5. The emergence of the New Neoclassical Synthesis is the subject of Section 6.6, while in Section 6.7 I assess some justifications of the microfoundations dogma that were, belatedly, produced early in the 21st century. The chapter ends (in Section 6.8), with a brief coda on the status of microfoundations in mainstream macroeconomic theory in 2012.

6.2 THE FATE OF MONETARISM, MARK I AND MARK II

It will be recalled from the previous chapter that Milton Friedman had no time for the advocates of microfoundations. Equally significant, they had very little time for him, at least at the theoretical level (personal respect and political affinities are another matter). The original Monetarist challenge to the (Old) Neoclassical Synthesis was largely atheoretical, relying much more on empirical evidence and policy prescriptions than on a novel analytical perspective. This was often noted at the time, by critics and supporters alike. Thus Robert Lucas, looking back on his influential 1977 paper on business cycles ten years after its publication, acknowledged that he had drawn very heavily on Friedman's and Schwartz's *Monetary History* (1963) for facts: 'thoroughly disillusioned with standard macroeconomic theory, I appreciated the book's relatively atheoretical approach. From Friedman and Schwartz, it is a short and direct step back to the work of Wesley Mitchell (1913)' (Lucas 1987, p. 16). This is the same institutionalist Wesley Mitchell whom we encountered in the previous chapter, being attacked by Tjalling Koopmans in the 1940s for undertaking 'measurement without theory'.

Less appreciative of the Monetarists was the reviewer of David Laidler's *Monetarist Perspectives*. 'Laidler's evaluation', John Bryant complained, 'uses a style of analysis which is diametrically opposed to J.R. Hicks's position in his seminal paper, "A Suggestion for Simplifying the Theory of

Money" (1935)'. For Laidler, '[m]icrofoundations may be interesting in their own right, but from a macroeconomic perspective they are technical details which can safely be left for later. In contrast, it was Hicks's view, shared by this reviewer, that monetary theory is largely a waste of time until these microfoundation issues are addressed squarely' (Bryant 1985, pp. 122–3). This certainly was Hicks's view, in 1935, in *Value and Capital* (Hicks 1939) and also, or so the real business cycle theorists claimed, in his *Capital and Growth* (Hicks 1965). By 1979 his position had changed (see pp. 113, 176 below).

To the extent that Monetarism Mark I did have a firm theoretical basis, it was essentially macroeconomic rather than microeconomic in nature, stressing the link between aggregate expenditure and the quantity of money on the assumption that the velocity of circulation was relatively stable over time. The theoretical basis for this assumption was always very weak. Thus Philip Cagan's authoritative entry on 'Monetarism' for the *New Palgrave* dictionary of economics was almost entirely devoted to empirical evidence and policy issues and contained very little discussion of theoretical issues. The one paragraph on 'monetarist theory' stressed the stability of household demand for money, which 'depends on the volume of transactions, the fractions of income and of wealth the public wishes to hold in the form of money balances, and the opportunity costs of holding money rather than other income-producing assets' (Cagan 1987, pp. 494–5).

Similarly, Robert Lucas described his own work on business cycles as 'simply an attempt to understand and make more explicit the implicit model underlying the policy proposals of Henry Simons, Milton Friedman, and other critics of activist aggregative policy' (Lucas 1977 [1987], p. 234). His reference to 'the implicit model' is entirely justified, since Friedman always gave priority to empirical evidence and policy implications over considerations of theoretical rigour. Thus his influential 'Restatement' of the quantity theory contained only a brief, informal discussion of the microeconomics of money demand, for both individuals and firms, with no attempt to provide precise microfoundations (Friedman 1956 [1969], pp. 58–60). 'Almost every economist will accept the general lines of the preceding analysis', he claimed (ibid., p. 62); the difference of opinion between supporters and opponents on the quantity theory was essentially empirical. Fourteen years later, Friedman's widely-read 'Counter-Revolution in Monetary Theory' had no micro-theoretical content whatever (Friedman 1970 [1991], confirming his preference (shared with Keynes) to do economic theory 'top down, rather than bottom up' (see above, p. 85).

Thus it could not be claimed that Monetarist theory rested on secure, rigorous microfoundations, and so, when in the 1970s it was seen to fail both empirically and as a policy platform, the field was open for alternatives which could claim to have a rigorous analytical basis. As David Laidler has written:

> ... problems with the definition and measurement of money, long the Achilles' heel of that doctrine, reasserted their significance with a vengeance at that time. Financial innovations, some but not all of which were themselves responses to inflation, began to undermine the empirical stability of the demand for money function. On the policy front, this contributed to the difficulties that central banks encountered in ensuring a smooth end to inflation, and within academic monetary economics it contributed to an intellectual vacuum, which was soon to be filled, not least at the University of Chicago, by new classical economics. (Laidler 2010, p. 78)

Note that these theoretical developments preceded the failure of the Thatcher and Reagan experiments with monetarist policies.

By the early 1980s foundational metaphors were being used quite routinely in the titles of journal articles and books, by authors who showed no apparent awareness of the methodological minefields that they were tiptoeing around. Thus when the Italian Post Keynesian Mauro Baranzini edited a set of essays on *Advances in Economic Theory*, he entitled part two 'Micro-foundations of Macroeconomics' and part three 'Macro-foundations of Microeconomics', while the Old Keynesian Charles L. Schultze published a critical assessment of recent research on inflation in the United States under the title 'Some macro foundations for micro theory' (Baranzini 1982; Schultze 1981). In neither case was there any explicit discussion of the supposed foundations that were being supplied.

Some indication of the failure of microfoundations to penetrate the undergraduate curriculum can be obtained from Michael Parkin's 1982 textbook, *Modern Macroeconomics*. At this time Parkin was possibly the most prominent advocate of Monetarist ideas outside Chicago; with his colleague Laidler he had left Manchester for the University of Western Ontario in 1975 in a blaze of anti-Keynesian (and anti-Labour government) publicity. His 600-page intermediate text does give a reasonably balanced account of the Monetarist and Keynesian macro models, the latter in its IS-LM, 'neoclassical synthesis' version. The eight chapters of Part V deal with rational expectations models, which are described (rather surprisingly) as 'often regarded as being synonymous with Monetarism' (Parkin and Bade 1982, p. xx), though 'new classical' and 'new Keynesian' variants are subsequently distinguished (ibid., p. 378). The exposition of 'rational expectations models of income, employment, and the price level' makes extensive use of the Aggregate Supply-Aggregate Demand model developed earlier in the book. There is no mention of microfoundations, and indeed the only explicit discussion of methodology in the entire text (ibid., pp. 478–81) deals with entirely different matters: the distinctions between *ex ante* and *ex post* variables, and between equilibrium and disequilibrium methods of modelling economic activity. To some extent this reflects Parkin's professed 'aversion to methodological discussion in the abstract' (ibid., p. 478). But it also demonstrates just how remote the question of microfoundations was from the concerns even of a strongly anti-Keynesian macroeconomist like Parkin in the early 1980s.

The early New Classical models were distinctive essentially because they assumed agents to formulate rational expectations, rather than the adaptive expectations assumed by Friedman. In other respects the Lucas–Sargent–Wallace 'money supply surprise' model of the cycle 'seemed to have a great deal in common with Friedman's work: hence the "Monetarism Mark 2" label' (Laidler 2010, p. 78). It is surely significant that, as noted in the previous chapter, Robert Lucas himself made little or nothing of microfoundations in his major articles of the early to mid-1970s. Indeed, many of the problems with Monetarism Mark I were also soon encountered by Monetarism Mark II. As Fischer Black objected, these models seemed to 'depend on easily cured ignorance about the current state of the world and on inability to create simple securities' (Black 1987, p. 147 n7). By the end of the 1970s,

> Several weaknesses of the new classical equilibrium approach were becoming apparent. These deficiencies were mainly the consequence of utilizing the twin assumptions of continuous market clearing and imperfect information. Critics drew attention to aggregate price and money supply data readily available to agents at relatively low cost and questioned how this could be reconciled with the magnitude and length of actual business cycles supposedly caused by informational gaps. (Snowdon, Vane and Wynarczyk 1994, p. 215)

But 'with sticky prices ruled out on methodological grounds, new classical models were left without an acceptable explanation of business cycles involving money-to-output causality' (Snowdon and Vane 2002, p. 88). Neither was the empirical evidence at all convincing. In consequence, the monetary surprise model 'has been replaced since the early 1980s by new classical real business cycle models emphasizing technological shocks … new Keynesian models emphasizing monetary disturbances … and new neoclassical synthesis models combining insights from both approaches' (ibid., p. 88). In the process, as we shall soon see, they added the representative agent to the rational expectations assumption, creating the RARE microfoundations that are the subject of this book.

One final piece of the puzzle needs to be stressed. There was a methodological problem with the (Old) Neoclassical Synthesis, which was recognized by its Post Keynesian critics: the treatment of the short period and the long period was radically different. In the short period, the principle of effective demand applied, involuntary unemployment was the norm and fiscal policy was usually efficacious. In the long period, where the Solow growth model applied, continuous full employment (and full capacity utilization) was assumed, all markets always cleared, and fiscal policy was redundant or ineffective for macroeconomic stabilization. The Post Keynesians dealt with this inconsistency by rejecting market-clearing in the long period, or restricting it to highly improbable special cases: to Joan Robinson's (1956) mythical 'golden age', for example, or to the Harrod–Domar knife-edge with the actual, 'warranted' and 'natural' rates of growth all miraculously equal. Recognition of the importance of path-dependence made the dichotomy between a market-clearing long run and a short run with an excess supply of labour even less acceptable to those working in the Post Keynesian tradition (King 2002, Chapters 3, 9).

6.3 THE RISE OF REAL BUSINESS CYCLE THEORY

The real business cycle theorists took the opposite path. One great advantage of their RARE microfoundations was that continuous market-clearing could be assumed in both the short run and the long run. This permitted 'the breakdown of the short run-long run dichotomy in macroeconomic analysis by integrating the theory of growth with the theory of fluctuations' (Snowdon, Vane and Wynarczyk 1994, p. 245). This, they claimed, was the beauty of the Ramsey model. There seem to have been two intellectual reasons for the emergence of real business cycle theory in the early 1980s, quite apart from its political attractions. The first was the empirical failure of Monetarist models, even when combined with rational expectations. This is the explanation favoured by David Laidler (1990, p. 3). The other, emphasized by real business cycle theorists themselves at the time, was theoretical: a desire to place short-run and long-run (cycle and growth) theory on the same analytical footing. Its failure to do this was regarded as a major failing of the (Old) Neoclassical Synthesis.

There were some forerunners. As early as 1937, Gottfried Haberler was 'studying the decisions of a representative consumer ("Robinson Crusoe") who directly operates the production technology of the economy' (Dotsey and King 1987, p. 303); the reference is to his classic volume published by the League of Nations, *Prosperity and Depression* (Haberler 1937). And in 1974 the Chicago economists Merton Miller and Charles Upton published an undergraduate textbook whose central theme was the assumption of full employment, and continuous market-clearing, in the short run as well as in the long run. Miller and Upton began their 'Preface' by rejecting the idea that capitalist economies were essentially dysfunctional and required constant government intervention. 'We believe that the course in macroeconomics should emphasize rather that a market economy left to its own devices will settle into a full employment equilibrium' (Miller and Upton 1974, p. vii). Thus they focus on the neoclassical growth model and ignore such Keynesian irrelevances as effective demand, the multiplier, liquidity preference and IS-LM (ibid., p. ix). 'The *cognoscenti* will', however, 'detect the strong influence of that rapidly growing body of work in the field of finance under the heading of the "efficient markets hypothesis"' (ibid., p. x). 'Microeconomic foundations' appears in the titles of three chapters (4, on the aggregate saving and consumption functions; 9, on the demand for money; 16, on unemployment). Ramsey (1928) is one of eight pieces of reading recommended for Part 2 (on consumption and saving), along with Cass and Yaari (1966), while the bibliography for Part 4 (on money and the price level) offers six suggestions for reading on 'the microeconomic foundations of the demand-for-money function', from authors such as Robert Barro, William Baumol and James Tobin (ibid., pp. 144, 316).

David Cass and Menahem Yaari were not (quite) the first to rediscover the Ramsey model. In the previous year Cass (writing alone), E.S. Phelps and J.R. Hicks had cited Ramsey in their work on the theory of economic growth. The contents of Phelps's *Golden Rules of Economic Growth* are accurately summarized in the sub-title: 'studies of efficient and optimal investment'. One chapter deals with 'the Ramsey problem and the golden rule of accumulation'. Here Phelps introduces 'the social utility function' (Phelps 1965, pp. 69, 102) and discusses the problems involved in using it 'for policy purposes' (ibid., p. 103). There is no suggestion that it might be put to any other use, and certainly no attempt is made to invoke it as a microfoundation for positive (as opposed to normative) macroeconomic theory. The same is true of the paper by Cass, in which 'a centralized, closed economy is postulated' (Cass 1965, p. 233), and the problem to be solved is the maximization of social welfare by the central planning authority; it has nothing to do with the operation of an unplanned capitalist economy. The position with Hicks is slightly more complicated. Although mainly devoted to 'intertemporal Optimum theory' (Hicks 1965, p. 264), *Capital and Growth* does contain a – rather cryptic – chapter entitled 'Keynes after growth theory', in which 'we are back in Pure Positive Economics' (the capital letters are Hicks's). But his concern here is with 'what might have happened if the monetary system had been the only obstacle to optimum growth' (ibid., p. 288); Hicks does not claim to be reconstructing Keynesian macroeconomics in its entirety on the basis of Ramsey-type microfoundations.

This did not prevent the real business cycle theorists from claiming him as a forerunner. An early reference to Ramsey in the macroeconomics literature was that of Robert Hall (1971), in whose 'intertemporal competitive equilibrium' model of the effects of changes in fiscal policy 'there are a large number of identical individuals, each seeking to maxmimise an intertemporal utility function of the Ramsey form'. 'Throughout', he explained, 'we use the term equilibrium in its Walrasian sense, to indicate that all markets clear. In every case, we calculate the full general equilibrium in the economy, over all time periods and all markets' (Hall 1971, pp. 229–30). This, however, was not a business cycle model, the first published versions of which, based on RARE microfoundations derived from the Ramsey model, came from Robert Lucas (1975, 1977). Very soon thereafter there was a flurry of articles on real business cycles, beginning with that of Finn Kydland and Edward Prescott, whose 'approach integrates growth and business cycle theory' in order to eliminate the inconsistency between short-run and long-run theorizing in the (neoclassical) Keynesian tradition. 'Like standard growth theory, a representative infinitely-lived household is assumed' (Kydland and Prescott 1982, p. 1345).

In the following year the influential paper by John Long and Charles Plosser bore the simple title, 'Real business cycles'. Their 'model economy … is populated by a single infinite-lived individual (or a constant number of identical individuals) with given initial resources, production possibilities, and tastes' (Long and Plosser 1983, p. 43). These agents are assumed to change their labour supply decisions over time so as to smooth out their consumption possibilities in the face of 'exogenous output shocks'. The model also assumes rational expectations, complete information, no frictions or adjustment costs, no long-lived commodities, no money and no government (ibid., pp. 40–41). The resulting real business cycles are the equilibrium outcomes of efficient decision-making by the representative agent, and are explicitly not to be regarded as 'welfare-reducing deviations from the "natural rate" paths of an ideally efficient Walrasian economy' (ibid., p. 42).

The real business cycle literature expanded rapidly in the next few years. Plosser teamed up with Robert King to integrate 'monetary services' into the model, and made an early use of the term 'dynamic, stochastic general equilibrium models' based on 'the planning problem for a representative agent' (King and Plosser 1984, p. 366). None of these early real business cycle models listed Ramsey in their references, but their debt to him was always evident, sometimes crassly so, as in this 1989 statement: 'The standard neoclassical analysis focuses on optimal quantities chosen by a "social planner" or representative agent' (King, Plosser and Rebello 1988, p. 200). It did not occur to these authors to ask in what sense the decisions of a social(ist) planner might provide microfoundations for a capitalist economy. They simply repeated the mantra that '[t]he essential flaw in the Keynesian interpretation of macroeconomic phenomena was the absence of a consistent foundation based on the choice theoretic framework of microeconomics' (Plosser 1989, p. 51). For the real business cycle theorists, the neoclassical growth model of Solow, Koopmans and Cass was 'the benchmark model for our understanding of economic fluctuations as well as growth' (ibid., p. 54).

We shall see in Chapter 9 that Robert Solow was dismayed by the way in which his theory had been misused, while the leading general equilibrium theorist Frank Hahn concluded his review of Lucas's (1987) *Models of Business Cycles* with the statement that 'I was much irritated by what is here on offer' (Hahn 1988, p. 284). There was another, more improbable, dissident. The financial economist Fischer Black viewed the assimilation of growth and business cycle theories as a mistake, and the real business cycle models of Lucas and his colleagues as far too aggregated (Black 1987). As his biographer explains:

> In a nutshell, Fischer's view is that the return on capital fluctuates so much because future income values are so uncertain, and future income values are so uncertain because the details matter. Firms know that people in the future will want food and housing, and transportation services, but they don't know exactly what kind. Firms must make investment and production decisions without knowing the details that they would have to know in order to be sure they were doing the right thing. (Mehrling 2005, p. 208)

Black rejected Keynesian models on the grounds that they 'assume that people act against their own interests in systematic and massive ways' (cited in ibid., p. 211). His was an equilibrium model of a real business cycle, but his microfoundations were not of the RARE variety, and his work was rejected by the leading journals (ibid., p. 208).

6.4 THE NEW KEYNESIAN CHALLENGE

The earliest New Keynesian models were contemporary with, or perhaps even slightly ahead of, the first real business cycle models (Dotsey and King 1987). In his 1990 survey article the veteran Keynesian Robert J. Gordon (1990, p. 1115) cited early papers by Stanley Fischer and by E.S. Phelps and John Taylor, both claiming to have reconciled rational expectations with the Keynesian position on the effectiveness of counter-cyclical monetary policy. Neither of them provided RARE microfoundations for this proposition, which they justified by reference to the widespread use of contracts that entailed a degree of (downward) nominal wage and price rigidity. Fischer stated explicitly that his paper 'does not provide a microeconomic basis for the existence of long-term nominal contracts', while Phelps and Taylor invoked 'the ancient and honourable tradition of Keynesians past' in assuming that 'there are disadvantages from too-frequent or too-precipitate revisions of price lists and wage schedules', but conceded that 'we do not pretend to have a rigorous understanding of these considerations at this time' (Fischer 1977, p. 194; Phelps and Taylor 1977, p. 166). Neither paper cited the Ramsey saving model or made any reference to a representative consumer, focusing instead on the behaviour of firms and, in the case of Phelps and Taylor, a hypothetical auctioneer. Evidently Phelps did not at this stage regard his recent rediscovery of the Ramsey model as being at all relevant to questions of macroeconomic policy.

In his own comparative analysis of 'seven schools of macroeconomic thought', published just over a decade later, Phelps himself did, however, describe the central role of microfoundations in the emergence of New Keynesian theory as an alternative to New Classical economics:

> Those Keynesians not comfortable about dispensing with the rational-expectations specification and even those merely curious to see whether Keynesian doctrine could coexist somehow with rational expectations were therefore interested in continuing the exploration. The New Keynesian models represent a second army … in the continuing push to establish microfoundations for the Keynesian tenets: the persistence of slumps from a permanent demand shock, and the 'effectiveness' of monetary stabilization policy. (Phelps 1990, p. 52)

A very early member of this second army was Takashi Negishi, whose 1979 book bore the title *Microeconomic Foundations of Keynesian Macroeconomics* (see Bronfenbrenner 1981). Drawing his inspiration from Hicks (1974), Negishi states his intention to 'construct a non-Walrasian microeconomics that can explain a Keynesian fixprice equilibrium with a general glut' (Negishi 1979, p. 2). This requires explicit consideration of 'a process of monetary exchange' that is 'justified only if we assume away perfect information' (ibid., pp. 10–11). Negishi claims to have provided microfoundations not only for involuntary unemployment but also for the foreign trade multiplier, 'by explaining, rather than assuming, rigid prices' (ibid., p. 158). But he is not an exponent of RARE microfoundations. For one thing, he does not rely on the Ramsey consumption model, defining microeconomics as 'theories of rational behavior of individual consumers *and firms*' (ibid., p. 195; stress added), and making explicit use of the concept of the representative firm. For another, while urging the need 'to integrate microeconomics and macroeconomics', he also insists that 'Micro and macro remain two distinct theories and the propositions in the latter are not derivable from those of the former' (ibid., p. 247). This is an (almost) explicit statement of the fallacy of composition.

Another early statement of New Keynesian theory, which asserted the same principle, came from Peter A. Diamond in his 1982 Wicksell lectures, published two years later as *A Search-Equilibrium Approach to the Micro Foundations of Macroeconomics.* Right at the start of lecture 1, Diamond acknowledges the problem with his title:

> The name is somewhat misleading. If macroeconomics is to acquire a firm microeconomic basis, we will at the same time have changed microeconomics to incorporate the macro reality of cyclical unemployment, which is now missing in general equilibrium micro models. Thus, a better title for my two lectures would be *A Search-Equilibrium Approach to the Integration of Micro- and Macroeconomics.* (Diamond 1984, p. 1)

This is the principle of downward causation, in everything but name. But Diamond continues to use foundational metaphors throughout the lectures. Explaining the defects of his 'strawman Keynesian model', with fixed prices and wages and an unexplained rationing mechanism, he states his belief that 'the model can be improved by reconstruction from a micro foundation' that recognizes the importance of repeated transactions in the markets for consumer goods, intermediate products and labour (ibid., pp. 52–3). This, Diamond continues, is the justification for his 'attempt to construct the micro foundation for Keynesian macro out of implicit contracts' (ibid., p. 54), which establishes the possibility of 'multiple natural rates of unemployment' (ibid., p. 63) and thus a case for Keynesian demand management policies. The initial criticism of the concept of microfoundations and the validity of the metaphor is not sustained.

Very similar ambivalence can be found in the slightly later work of another prominent New Keynesian, Peter Howitt (1986, 1987). Howitt's reservations were sufficiently strong to justify his inclusion among the 'mainstream dissenters' whose views are considered in Chapter 9.

By the end of the decade there was less self-questioning by New Keynesians on the centrality of microfoundations to their project. In their best-selling graduate text, Olivier Blanchard and Stanley Fischer described Keynesian macroeconomics as being 'in theoretical crisis', and defended their choice of 'a neoclassical benchmark' model, with 'optimizing individuals and competitive markets' on the grounds that no more realistic alternative to it had yet been developed (Blanchard and Fischer 1989, p. 27). They regretted the Keynesian reliance on 'shortcuts' instead of 'a model based on first principles', but saw this as an inevitable, if imperfect, basis for policy advice in the absence of such a model; the alternative was 'a harmful utopia that leaves the real world to charlatans' (ibid., p. 28). Thus they devote an entire chapter to 'some useful models', including IS-LM and the Mundell–Fleming model, which they regard as 'the workhorses of applied macroeconomics' (ibid., p. 506). This was an uncomfortable, eclectic position: 'It would clearly be better for economists to have an all-purpose model, derived explicitly from microfoundations and embodying all relevant imperfections, to analyze all issues in macroeconomics (or perhaps all issues in economics). We're not quite there yet' (ibid., p. 505).

In similar vein, Robert Gordon began by describing New Keynesian theory as 'an outpouring of research within the Keynesian tradition that attempts to build the microeconomic foundations of wage and price stickiness'. This distinguished the New Keynesian project from 'its arch-opposite, the new-classical approach' (Gordon 1990, p. 1115). Joseph Stiglitz agreed: 'There is now a general consensus that good macroeconomics must be built upon solid microfoundations'. But this does not entail acceptance of RARE microfoundations. Economics is 'a behavioural social science', and macroeconomics needs microfoundations that embody 'a more thorough understanding of how informational considerations affect the functioning of labour, capital, and product markets'. Rational expectations is not a sensible assumption, Stiglitz maintains. 'And one cannot develop an understanding of how those markets function from models based on representative individuals, no matter how complicated are the dynamic programmes they might be solving' (Stiglitz 1992, pp. 42–3). As Togati suggests, this left Stiglitz, rather like Frank Hahn, in 'an uncomfortable conceptual middle ground', accepting the need for microfoundations, rejecting the RARE variety, but having nothing with comparable simplicity and rigour to put in its place (Togati 1998, p. xxix; cf. ibid., pp. 245–6, 248–9).

David Romer's position was no more comfortable. Central to his account of 'the new Keynesian synthesis' was the need to provide a 'microeconomic basis for the failure of the classical dichotomy' (Romer 1993, p. 7). The New Keynesians' 'recent progress in understanding the microeconomic foundations of the real impact of aggregate demand disturbances' (ibid., p. 8) came from models which demonstrate how nominal frictions that seemed small at the level of individual households and firms could have large macroeconomic consequences. Thus the new classical claim that nominal rigidity is 'inconsistent with any defensible microeconomic assumptions' has 'been refuted' (ibid., p. 19). However, Romer concludes, a purely microeconomic approach 'is unlikely to be enough', since '[u]nderstanding how microeconomic properties give rise to observed macroeconomic phenomena is a realistic goal. But uniting microeconomics and macroeconomics may not be: the simplifications that are useful in understanding most microeconomic phenomena may be fatal to attempts to understand macroeconomic fluctuations'. This statement hints at the fallacy of composition and the non-inferability of macro phenomena from micro, but does not quite get there. Neither does Romer's endorsement of continuing research into 'the macroeconomic evidence concerning the effects of monetary and other aggregate demand disturbances' (ibid., p. 20). It does seem safe to conclude that Romer's microfoundations project did not involve micro-reduction.

For reasons that I do not claim fully to understand, these early New Keynesian reservations about the microfoundations dogma were soon to evaporate. Five years after Romer's paper was published, Roy Rotheim edited a set of papers that offered a critical comparison between New Keynesian and Post Keynesian theories, from the perspective of the latter. As a perceptive reviewer noted, the (predominantly Post Keynesian) contributors agreed that the New Keynesians 'overemphasise the importance of the microfoundations of macroeconomics with respect to Keynes's idea of an "independent" level of macroeconomic analysis', rendering New Keynesian economics 'theoretically uninteresting and harmful for policy purposes' (Tamborini 1999, p. F792). As if to reinforce the point, another edited volume that appeared in the same year, Marcello Messori's *Financial Constraints and Market Failures*, bore the sub-title 'the microfoundations of the new Keynesian macroeconomics'. The sub-title was an accurate reflection of the contents of the book, which contains no discussion of the case for microfoundations but simply takes it for granted (Messori 1999).

What is really striking in all of this is the more or less complete absence of any attempt to provide a justification of the case for microfoundations, which seems generally to have been regarded as self-evident. Thus Olivier Blanchard was quite right to complain about 'the quasi-religious insistence on micro foundations' (1992, p. 126). In the 1990s such complaints were frequent (see, for example, Dixon 1994, Hoover 1995a, pp. 729–31 and Backhouse 2000). This criticism applies even to a methodologically aware scholar like E. Roy Weintraub, whose influential survey article, and subsequent book, both have 'microfoundations' in the title. His book was the first (other than the S'Agaro conference volume) to be devoted entirely to the question; he had provided a summary of the arguments two years earlier in an article in the *Journal of Economic Literature* (Weintraub 1977, 1979). The rebellious son of the early Post Keynesian Sidney Weintraub (see Weintraub 2002), Roy Weintraub was an accomplished mathematical economist who was just beginning a protracted change of career path that would take him from general equilibrium theory to the history of economic thought, and from Lakatos to postmodernism. In the late 1970s, however, this trajectory lay ahead of him, and Weintraub was still firmly in the Arrow–Debreu–Hahn – or, more precisely, the Clower–Leijonhufvud – tradition. Like Hahn, he simply took it for granted that the quest for microfoundations was a legitimate one, although it was unlikely to be successful any time soon. There is no discussion in either the book or the article of the issues surrounding inter-theoretic reduction that were discussed in Chapter 3, and Weintraub makes no reference to any of the abundant literature pre-1979 that is cited there.

Instead, as noted by Hartley (1997, pp. 123–4) he begs the question in a breathtaking manner: 'The preceding pages have suggested that the question of *appropriate* microeconomic foundations for macroeconomics is still an open one' (Weintraub 1977, p. 19; original stress). Weintraub conceded that Walrasian general equilibrium theorists had, thus far, failed to provide such foundations. 'At a minimum', however, 'general equilibrium theorists have demonstrated quite convincingly that Keynesian macroeconomics cannot be derived from any simple Walrasian microsystem' (ibid., p. 18). So much the worse for Walras, Mark Blaug might have responded. But Weintraub takes a quite different line: 'There should be little argument about the proposition that some form of revivified, reconstituted general equilibrium theory is the only logically possible general link between microeconomics and macroeconomics' (ibid., p. 19). It did not seem to occur to him that a link is not a foundation. Weintraub's attempt to close down the argument in this way was never going to succeed, even though it was endorsed by Hahn as 'a useful, well-written account of the many efforts in the last ten years to build some kind of bridge between Walrasian general equilibrium analysis and Keynesian theory' (Hahn 1980, p. 187). In fact Weintraub soon came under attack for his highly questionable methodology (see Dow 1981, 1983; Weintraub 1982–3; below, pp. 166–7). He was unfortunate to be writing at precisely that moment in time when mainstream macroeconomists were giving up on general equilibrium theory and adopting the RARE microfoundations, based on a synthesis of Ramsey and Lucas, with which this book is principally concerned, while dissident voices inside and outside the mainstream were beginning to take issue with the whole microfoundations dogma.

One reviewer, however, was not himself yet ready to take either of these positions. John Hicks, now inclined to distinguish himself from the younger J.R. Hicks and distinctly sympathetic to Post Keynesian critiques of the mainstream (see Hicks 1980–81), pointed to a 'pedagogic problem' that Weintraub himself had identified: 'The student goes to "micro" lectures on Mondays and to "macro" lectures on Thursdays; and they just don't fit … The trouble is that the approach is different, the Monday lectures being in some sense classical, the Thursday lectures being Keynesian'. The problem, Hicks suggests, is that there were two lines of division, not one, and they had got mixed up. 'Once they are separated, we should have four sets of lectures, not two: macro-classical on Tuesdays, micro-Keynesian on Wednesdays, as well as the two that were already being given' (Hicks 1979, p. 1452). This, he claims, might help to build a 'bridge' – note the horizontal metaphor – between micro and macro. Hicks states 'what I think should go into those Wednesday lectures. Monetary institutions, certainly, but also a look at other markets, labor markets, and product markets, to see how they really work, and can work' (ibid., p. 1543). Though he does not use the term, Hicks is here, in effect, advocating a New Keynesian approach to microfoundations.

6.5 MICROFOUNDATIONS IN GENERAL DISEQUILIBRIUM

One alternative to both New Classical and New Keynesian theory was the general disequilibrium approach of Robert Clower, Axel Leijonhufvud and Edmond Malinvaud (Rizvi 1994). It had long been recognized that Walrasian general equilibrium theory was very difficult to reconcile with Keynes's *General Theory*. The problem was beautifully summarized in the long title of a 1975 paper by the Yale theorist Martin Shubik: 'The general equilibrium model is incomplete and not adequate for the reconciliation of micro and macroeconomic theory'. As we saw in the previous chapter, a similar conclusion had been reached, rather tentatively, by Kenneth Arrow and Frank Hahn, who ended the chapter on 'The Keynesian model' in their influential treatise on the Walrasian model with a disclaimer: 'This chapter can be taken as no more than a beginning of taking seriously the Keynes of the chapters on expectations and the functions of money' (Arrow and Hahn 1971, p. 369).

The seemingly insuperable obstacles that confront anyone attempting to reconcile Walras and Keynes are well described by Shubik: 'When a system is in equilibrium and there is no uncertainty most of the reasons for money and financial institutions disappear. Thus to start with a general equilibrium framework to study the role of money and financial institutions is to throw most of the problem away' (Shubik 1975, p. 552). General equilibrium theorists assume complete futures markets and unlimited trust between traders. 'By contrast', Shubik observes, 'in the actual world few futures markets exist; moreover money and ownership claims are used heavily to substitute for the need for trust' (ibid., p. 555). Thus Walrasian models can shed very little light on the actual working of real-life capitalist economies.

Neither Arrow nor Hahn ever felt able to go quite this far in renouncing what they always regarded as a magnificent intellectual achievement. Nonetheless, Arrow was sceptical about the microfoundations project, on the grounds that '"atomistic" assumptions concerning individual households and firms are not sufficient to establish the existence of equilibrium: "global" assumptions are also needed ... [so that] a limit is set to the tendency implicit in price theory, particularly in its mathematical versions, to deduce all properties of aggregate behaviour from assumptions about individual economic agents' (Arrow 1968, p. 382, cited by Rizvi 1994, p. 358). Hahn was no less ambivalent (Togati 1998, pp. 253–5). In his 1974 inaugural lecture, he admitted that 'it is absolutely correct to maintain that every feature of an actual economy which Keynes regarded as important is missing in Debreu'. 'But it is also true', he continues, 'that Debreu and others have made a significant contribution to the understanding of Keynesian economics just by describing so precisely what would have to be the case if there were to be no Keynesian problem' (Hahn 1974 [1984], p. 65). However, what appears to be a substantial concession to the autonomy of macroeconomics is almost immediately retracted, when Hahn criticizes Keynes's use of the Marshallian representative firm as 'a drastic short cut' that might well lead to 'significant errors' (ibid., p. 65) and then makes the following affirmation: 'I do not deal with the view that macroeconomics is in some sense essentially different from other kinds of economics in dealing with relations which are not deducible from the actions of agents, *since it is rather obviously false*' (ibid., p. 66; stress added).

This was an unusually explicit denial of the fallacy of composition, which Hahn often repeated in other contexts. Here are three examples:

> This leaves at least one important matter undiscussed. That is, of course, macroeconomics, which we think of as an essentially Keynesian invention. The reason for not discussing it is that I have nothing to say. Certainly, macroeconomics serves as a good 'simple' model which many economists feel is what we need. It also no doubt helps in [T]reasuries. But how one is to give it a theoretical foundation I do not know ... Whether, for instance, in discussing investment behaviour one is to think of some 'representative' investor or some particular statistical average seems unresolved. *The law of large numbers is perhaps not as applicable to social as to physical* phenomena ... It is pretty clear that usable economics will have to be of some sort of macro character. But what sort? (Hahn 1977 [1984], p. 193; stress added)

> 'Macroeconomics is different from microeconomics'. If it is then I for one do not know what it is...In our present state of knowledge, macroeconomics is simply the project of deducing something about the behaviour of such aggregates as income and employment from the micro-theory which we have. The whole enterprise of giving microeconomic foundations to macroeconomics is therefore misnamed. If macroeconomics before this enterprise was innocent of microeconomics it is not easy to see that it was anything at all. (Hahn 1982, p. 311)

> I start in praise of Lucas. He not only realized that it was impossible to believe that there are two separate subjects called macroeconomics and microeconomics, but he acted on this realization. This is not the project of providing microeconomic foundations for macroeconomics. Such a project is absurd – What exactly are we asked to provide foundations for? If we are interested in the behaviour of aggregates, then we must use economic theory to help us, and *the only theory we have is one of rational and self-seeking agents*. On this matter, then, three cheers for Lucas. (Hahn 1983, p. 223; stress added)

It is hard to imagine a more forthright denial of the fallacy of composition than those contained in these three statements.

Where Hahn parted company with Lucas was in the latter's 'view that we can treat the world as if it were in continuous Walrasian equilibrium' (ibid., p. 224). Hahn, then, was a firm adherent to the general disequilibrium approach to microfoundations, even if he often denied the validity of the foundational metaphor and rejected the claim that 'equilibrium' entailed market clearing. As Edmund Phelps would soon explain, 'economic equilibrium is not defined in the same terms as physical equilibrium', that is, in terms of states of rest. Rather it hinges on the assumption of 'correct expectations, that appears to be the essential property of equilibrium at least in the orthodox use of the term' (Phelps 1987, p. 177).

Malinvaud's 1976 Yrjö Jahnsson lectures, published in the following year in book form as *The Theory of Unemployment Reconsidered*, provide a detailed and widely read account of the general disequilibrium approach. At the outset he claims to be supplying 'clear foundations' for the theory of unemployment, but significantly he nowhere uses the term 'microfoundations' (Malinvaud 1977, pp. vii, viii). His discussion of unemployment and medium-term economic policy is distinctly non-reductive, with emphasis being placed on the 'autonomous demand for goods' as one of 'two main sources of peturbation'. As the principal components of autonomous demand, he distinguishes private fixed investment, voluntary inventory accumulation, foreign demand, public spending and taxation receipts, none of them provided with any microfoundation (ibid., p. 95). The paradox of saving makes a somewhat veiled appearance later in the same chapter, where Malinvaud notes that 'People cannot always earn as much as they want, or consume as much as they would like to; firms cannot always recruit or sell as much as they had planned; but no-one can ever be directly forced to save less than he decides' (ibid., p. 115).

While it enjoyed considerable critical acclaim in the late 1970s and early 1980s, it soon became apparent that the general disequilibrium alternative had failed to replace the RARE microfoundations programme as the most favoured position in mainstream macroeconomic theory. Arguably it had fallen between two stools, as the previously cited passage from Malinvaud suggests, being neither reliably Keynesian nor succeeding in providing acceptable microfoundations for the anti-Keynesians. There was, moreover, a nasty technical problem for any variant of the theory that did not assume representative agents. This was posed by the Debreu–Mantel–Sonnenschein theorem, according to which:

> ... in an economy in which every individual has a well-behaved excess demand function, the only restrictions on the aggregate excess demand functions are that it is continuous, homogenous of degree zero in prices, and satisfies Walras's Law. *Nothing* else can be inferred. Any completely arbitrary function satisfying those three properties can be an excess demand function for an economy of well-behaved individuals. Having an economy in which every single agent obeys standard microeconomic rules of behavior tells us virtually nothing about the aggregate economy. (Hartley, Hoover and Salyer 1998, pp. 12–13; original stress)

For this reason general equilibrium models were falling out of favour with microeconomists at precisely the time that they were being rediscovered by macroeconomists.

Finally, and almost certainly less important than it should have been, was the inability of both general equilibrium and general disequilibrium theorists to make any sense of the use of money by the agents in their models. 'Up to now', George McCandless and Neil Wallace frankly confessed in 1991, 'no-one has formulated a model of transaction difficulties that has won wide assent. We have no widely accepted model of monetary exchange' that explains why people should hold 'some intrinsically useless stuff that the government has issued and calls money', especially 'when there coexist assets in the economy that give higher real rates of return than money does' (McCandless and Wallace 1991, pp. 257, 258). And there is an additional problem: in their overlapping generations model, money is used once in a lifetime, not every day. 'Despite these weaknesses', they conclude, 'some useful insights can be gained from using an overlapping generations model for fiat money. Moreover, there is currently no other way to model a monetary economy that is clearly superior' (ibid., p. 258).

Fourteen years earlier, Paul Davidson had argued that these problems were insoluble. There was no possible role for money, Davidson maintained, either in Walrasian general equilibrium or in Clower–Leijonhufvud general disequilibrium:

> Unfortunately Clower's construction ... does not get to the essence of the underemployment problem of monetary economies ... The possibility of insufficiency of effective demand at any level of employment in Keynes's system is a result of his definition of money and its essential properties, where money 'cannot be readily produced:– labour cannot be turned on at will by entrepreneurs to produce money' (Keynes, 1936, p. 230), nor is any other producible good a gross substitute for money as either a means of settling contractual obligations or as a time machine (see Davidson, 1978, ch. 9). Since all Walras's

> Law systems and even Clower's model ultimately require the gross substitutability of excess demand, such models are incapable of introducing money into their framework. (Davidson 1977 [1991], p. 205)

To repeat: for Davidson, this conclusion holds for general equilibrium (GE) and general disequilibrium models alike: 'the schism between GE and monetary analysis is as deep and irreparable as the difference between Euclidian and non-Euclidian geometry', so that 'to speak of monetary GE models is a contradiction in terms' (ibid., pp. 211, 214). The same objection applies also to Jean Michel Grandmont's price rigidity/market imperfection version of the theory (ibid., pp. 210–11), and presumably also to the Malinvaud variant, though this is not explicitly stated. Davidson concludes that Clower's use of 'an *ad hoc* revision of GE systems to achieve "Keynesian results" ... is suggestive of a degenerate research program *à la* Lakatos' (ibid., p. 209). Degenerative or not, the general disequilibrium project had certainly foundered by the mid-1980s.

6.6 THE EMERGENCE OF THE NEW NEOCLASSICAL SYNTHESIS

By 1990, in fact, the dividing lines between the different schools of thought in mainstream macroeconomics were becoming increasingly blurred, so that Harry Garretsen (1992, p. 54) could claim quite correctly that 'many new-Keynesian models are better characterized as classical rather than Keynesian'. Microfoundations played an important role in this process. By the mid-1990s the case for RARE microfoundations was so widely accepted among mainstream macroeconomists of all schools that detailed and authoritative rebuttals were routinely ignored. The distinguished general equilibrium theorist Alan Kirman first declared of 'modern economic theory' that 'the emperor has no clothes' – this is the sub-title of Kirman (1989) – and then published a robust critique of the use of representative agent models in macroeconomics which begins by acknowledging the fallacy of composition:

> First, whatever the objective of the modeler, there is no plausible formal justification for the assumption that the aggregate of individuals, even maximizers, acts itself like an individual maximizer. Individual maximization does *not* engender collective rationality, nor does the fact that the collectivity exhibits a certain rationality necessarily imply that the individuals act rationally. There is simply no direct relation between individual and collective behavior. (Kirman 1992, p. 118)

Kirman concludes that 'the assumption of a representative individual is far from innocent; it is the fiction by which macroeconomists can justify equilibrium analysis and provide pseudo-microfoundations' (ibid., p. 125). The reference to 'pseudo-microfoundations' suggests that Kirman was not opposed to the quest for non-RARE microfoundations, and indeed he did point to the 'alternative and attractive approach' offered by 'game theory, where the interaction between heterogeneous individuals with conflicting interests is seriously taken into account' and no assumption of omniscience is required (ibid., p. 131). In more recent work, however, he has expressed strong opposition to the microfoundations dogma (Kirman 2011a, 2011b).

Two important books should also be mentioned in this context. As we saw in Chapter 3, Harold Kincaid's *Individualism and the Unity of Science* made a powerful case against micro-reduction in both the natural and the social sciences, using biology and economics as case studies in the empirical failures of reductionism (Kincaid 1997). It drew warm praise from Mark Blaug (1999), but this was the only review of the book by an economist, and it appeared in the *Manchester School*, which was not a leading mainstream journal; there was also a long and enthusiastic review by the philosopher Michael Bradie (2000) and shorter, unfriendly notices by two anthropologists (Penn and Gudemann 1999) and a sociologist (Van den Berghe 1998). Admittedly, Kincaid's book was the work of a philosopher.

In the same year the economist James Hartley published a perceptive critique of representative agent modelling, criticizing both Walrasian and New Classical economists for begging the question when they asserted, without any supporting evidence, that micro relationships were more stable and more predictable than macro relationships when the reverse was often the case (Hartley 1997, pp. 120–27). New Classical microfoundations are in any case spurious, he maintains: 'Models with firms are purely *ad hoc*; they are not grounded in individual optimization', while money itself is 'a purely aggregate phenomenon', of no use whatever to Robinson Crusoe (ibid., pp. 185, 187). As for the admittedly serious difficulties involved in aggregation, Hartley argues, RARE models evade the problem rather than solving it (ibid., p. 146). Walrasian models offer no solution; it had been known for twenty years that the Sonnenschein–Mantel–Debreu theorem leads to the 'depressing conclusion' that 'very little can be inferred about the aggregate economy from a general equilibrium model' (ibid., p. 185).

Hartley concludes that the use of the representative agent in macroeconomic theory was nothing but 'a restatement of the fallacy of composition', as Paul Samuelson had recognized half a century previously in the first edition of his famous introductory textbook: 'What is true for each is not necessarily true for all; and conversely, what is true for all may be quite false for each individual' (Samuelson 1948, p. 9, cited by Hartley 1997, p. 174). Hartley returns to this question in the next chapter, on 'the myth of microfoundations', citing James Coleman on the importance of emergent properties and on the significance of downward causation:

> Not only do the actions of microeconomic agents combine to create macroeconomic phenomena, but these macroeconomic relationships influence microeconomic agents. Coleman (1990) calls these relationships the micro-to-macro and the macro-to-micro transitions and notes that good social science makes both transitions correctly. (Ibid., p. 188)

While the microfoundations dogma is 'a myth', Hartley concludes (ibid., p. 194), 'the return to macroeconomics *qua* macroeconomics is already taking place' in the work of the New Keynesians (ibid., p. 204).

While his optimism was profoundly misplaced, as we saw in a previous section, Hartley's critique of microfoundations in general, and RARE microfoundations in particular, was a powerful one. But it was very largely ignored. There were only two reviews, a rather lukewarm but broadly positive piece by David Colander (1998) in the *Journal of Economic Literature* and a very favourable review by Frank Schohl in the *Journal of Evolutionary Economics*. Schohl's only substantive criticism is that Hartley omitted to mention Joseph Schumpeter, whose stress on innovation necessarily involves a variety of heterogeneous agents (Schohl 1998, p. 19; see also Schohl 1999). I have found no evidence that mainstream macroeconomists are aware of the existence of Hartley's book; certainly none of them has ever attempted to refute it. And Dario Togati's excellent *Keynes and the Neoclassical Synthesis*, published in the following year (Togati 1998), was not reviewed in any academic journal.

The books by Hartley and Kincaid appeared in the very same year – 1997 – in which a new consensus in macroeconomics was being proclaimed. The phrase 'new neoclassical consensus' seems to have originated with Marvin Goodfriend and Robert King (1997, p. 232), who stressed its reliance on 'the systematic application of intertemporal optimization and rational expectations'. The same point was made, in slightly different terms, by most of the participants in the session at the January 1997 meeting of the American Economic Association on the theme 'Is there a core of usable macroeconomics that we should all believe in?' (Blanchard 1997; Blinder 1997; Taylor 1997; Solow 1997). Shortly afterwards, in July 1997, the *Economic Journal* published a symposium on the microfoundations of monetary economics, in which none of the contributors took issue with the concept, not even David Laidler, whose reservations have already been noted (Laidler 1997).

In late 1996 and early 1997 Carlos Usabiaga Ibáñez interviewed a number of leading macroeconomists, asking them about the relationship between micro and macro. Their answers were nearly all in broad agreement. Thus Costas Azariadis, asked if there was still a frontier between micro and macroeconomic, replied thus:

> If you took a beginning graduate macroeconomics course, 17 or 18 years ago, it lasted 14 weeks. One week in it was devoted to 'the microfoundations'. But now the microfoundations are all the weeks of all courses [*laughter*]. There's still a frontier between micro and macro, but it's of a different kind from the frontier we used to have 20 years ago. Twenty years ago we used to have specialized tools to deal with macroeconomic issues, especially with short-run business cycles and money. Now the tools are more similar, but the issues remain different ... But in terms of doing general equilibrium, and writing down consistent laws and market clearing expectations, we have become quite similar. (Ibáñez 1999, pp. 22–3).

Christopher Pissarides replied that 'The frontier is becoming blurred ... the distinction is more in terms of the questions that we ask rather than the techniques that we use' (ibid., p. 212). And Dennis Snower, though unwilling to rely on representative agent models in all circumstances, replied that for him 'microfoundations provide an important discipline without any of the serious disadvantages that previous macroeconomic research suffered from' (ibid., p. 262).

Ibáñez asked Lawrence J. Christiano whether it was still possible to distinguish between micro and macroeconomics. While noting that the 'set of questions' asked by macroeconomists remained distinctive, and acknowledging that some macroeconomists continued to use the IS-LM model, Christiano also stressed the newly established similarity in method: 'Some time ago, another important distinction between macroeconomics and microeconomics lay in the conceptual framework used ... Now, the distinction in conceptual framework has largely disappeared, in favour of the microeconomic tradition' (ibid., p. 91). Martin Eichenbaum was even more definite: 'No [*laughter*]. And that's a good thing. That was the whole plan and it succeeded. Keynes had the view that macro was somehow a fundamentally different subject than micro. He was wrong and the profession now recognizes it' (ibid., p. 130).

The response of the New Keynesian Robert Gordon to the same question was only slightly more nuanced: 'Yes, but less than in the past ... There is a strong desire for microfoundations' (ibid., p. 174). And Thomas Sargent invoked a new metaphor. 'It's increasingly difficult to differentiate between micro and macroeconomics', Sargent replied, 'because macroeconomics imports ideas very rapidly from micro. For example, the equilibrium concept we use' (ibid., p. 250). Only Charles Bean expressed strong opposition to the use of representative agent models, which 'loses a lot of what are the key features of macrodynamics, which we associate with the fact that agents ... are different, very heterogeneous, and that they have different bits of information' (ibid., p. 40). His was really the sole dissenting voice.

With hindsight, it is clear that agreement on the adoption of RARE microfoundations was what made the New Neoclassical Synthesis possible. Pedro Duarte notes that there was 'no Kuhnian substitution of one paradigm by another via revolutions, but rather a merging of previously rival paradigms and a "steady accumulation of knowledge"' (Duarte 2010, p. 4, citing Blanchard 2000, p. 1375). The New Classicals and real business cycle theorists brought with them their rational expectations, while New Keynesians came with their nominal rigidities and market failures. As Duarte explains, it was a successful marriage from the very start:

> Therefore, despite the major points of disagreement among the new classical and RBC macroeconomists, on the one hand, and the new Keynesians on the other, these two camps shared significant methodological and theoretical grounds: they all adopt the rational expectations hypothesis, favor general equilibrium models, and have in their benchmark models a representative agent in an environment of complete markets. (Duarte 2010, p. 11)

Thus both parties agreed on the need to explain cyclical fluctuations 'in terms of a dynamic stochastic general equilibrium model of a representative agent' (ibid., p. 22). As the new millennium dawned, Michael Woodford, one of the most prominent advocates of the New Neoclassical consensus, could proclaim the

> ... resolution of the schism between the 'micro' and the 'macro' branches of economics, that has so characterized the pedagogy of the past several decades. In principle, the grounds for reunification of the subject would seem to be largely in place. Macroeconomics no longer claims that the study of aggregate phenomena requires a distinct methodology; instead, modern macroeconomic models are intertemporal general equilibrium models, derived from the same foundations of optimizing behavior on the part of households and firms as are employed in other branches of economics. (Woodford 1999, p. 31)

He would soon provide a monument to the new synthesis in his magisterial *Interest and Prices* (Woodford 2003).

6.7 THE CASE FOR THE DEFENCE

At long last, in the twenty-first century, some advocates of RARE micro-foundations did begin to offer justifications for the procedure, pretty well for the first time since Fritz Machlup had done so in 1963 (above, pp. 92–3). The first was Ralph Bailey, in a critical review of Kevin Hoover's *Causality in Macroeconomics* (Hoover 2001b). Bailey took issue with Hoover's defence of the autonomy of macroeconomics:

> The attractions of microfoundations are substantial: relative model parsimony, a plausible account of expectation, a criterion for favouring some equations and model variables over others. Agents are indeed heterogeneous: nonetheless they react in broadly similar ways to such a stimulus as a rise in the interest rate. Thus representative-agent models seem a good way to capture certain aspects of aggregate behaviour. (Bailey 2002, p. F585)

This is a rather weak defence. Rational expectations are not plausible and, as will shortly be seen, the use of the representative agent requires a rather strong *ad hoc* assumption about agents' preferences. Precisely how micro-foundations encourage 'relative model parsimony' is not explained, and the nature of the criterion that is used to 'favour some equations and model variables over others' remains unclear.

In the same year Partha Dasgupta offered a more elaborate defence. 'At a practical level', Dasgupta asks, 'does it matter that a macro model lacks an adequate microfoundation? After all, if the model works well, why worry that it lacks foundation?' Note the elision from 'microfoundations' to 'foundations', as if there could in principle be no foundation other than a microeconomic one. 'There are four reasons why one must worry', Dasgupta continues:

> First, it is difficult to judge if a macro model works well (e.g. if it provides good forecasts). Even the many ingenious tests that have been devised by econometricians cannot clinch matters. Microfoundations provide a needed discipline in the design of macro models; they serve as an anchor. The second, related, reason is that there may be several macro models that interpret the macro facts, such as they are, equally well. Microfoundations could enable us to choose among them. The third reason is purely intellectual. Even if we have constructed a sound macro model by some holistic leap of the imagination, we would still want to know what accounts for its soundness. The fourth reason is prudence: a macro model which currently works well will almost certainly not continue to work well. In other words, macro relationships should be expected to undergo changes over time. Good microfoundations would enable us to know how to adapt the model to changing conditions. (Dasgupta 2002, p. 74)

None of these four reasons is very convincing. The first, though it does offer a new metaphor (microfoundations as an 'anchor'), is question-begging. The second is highly speculative: *if* two contrasting macroeconomic models give the same (empirical?) results, then there might well be a case for invoking microeconomics to choose between them, but it is a very big 'if' (and Dasgupta gives no examples). The third 'reason' is again question-begging, while the fourth makes the unobjectionable, but very weak, claim that microeconomics can inform macroeconomics. The reverse is also true, as we have seen in the context of the principle of downward causation, so that this (again) is not a strong argument for micro-reduction in economics.

In the preface to their textbook on *Recursive Macroeconomic Theory,* Lars Ljungkvist and Thomas Sargent provide an extensive discussion of the case for microfoundations, and attempt to rebut some opposing arguments. This is sufficiently unusual to be worth quoting at length:

> This book is about micro foundations for macroeconomics. Browning, Hansen, and Heckman (2000) identify two possible justifications for putting microfoundations underneath macroeconomic models. The first is aesthetic and preempirical: models with micro foundations are by construction coherent and explicit. And because they contain descriptions of agents' purposes, they allow us to analyze policy interventions using standard methods of welfare economics. Lucas (1987) gives a distinct second reason: a model with micro foundations broadens the sources of empirical evidence that can be used to assign numerical values to the model's parameters. Lucas endorses Kydland and Prescott's (1982) procedure of borrowing parameter values from micro studies. Browning, Hansen, and Heckman (2000) describe some challenges to Lucas's recommendation for an empirical strategy. Most seriously, they point out that in many contexts the specifications underlying the microeconomic studies cited by a calibrator conflict with those of the macroeconomic model being 'calibrated'. It is typically not obvious how to transfer parameter values from one data set and model specification to another data set, especially if the theoretical and econometric specification differs.
>
> Although we take seriously the doubts about Lucas's justification for microeconomic foundations that Browning, Hansen, and Heckman raise, we remain strongly attached to micro foundations. For us, it remains enough to appeal to the first justification mentioned, the coherence provided by micro foundations and the virtues that come from having the ability to 'see the agents' in the artificial economy. We see Browning, Hansen, and Heckman as raising many legitimate questions about empirical strategies for implementing macro models with micro foundations. We don't think that the clock will soon be turned back to a time when macroeconomics was done without micro foundations. (Ljungkvist and Sargent 2004, pp. xxvi–xxvii)

The supposed 'aesthetic and preempirical' advantages of microfoundations, also described by Ljungkvist and Sargent as the benefits of 'coherence', raise all the familiar problems of scientific realism that were outlined in Chapter 3. Models with RARE microfoundations, the only type that these authors are prepared to contemplate, fail the minimal test of 'realisticness' (above, p. 25), confusing beauty with truth and thereby making 'seeing the agents' a most unlikely outcome (Krugman 2009). It should also be noted that Ljungkvist and Sargent consider only the narrow empirical objections of Browning, Hansen and Heckman, and make no attempt to rebut the broader methodological case against micro-reduction that was summarized in Part I.

Finally, in his monumental text on the neoclassical theory of economic growth, Daron Acemoglu provides a detailed defence of the standard assumption of 'the representative household' (Acemoglu 2009, pp. 149–55). 'The major convenience of the representative household assumption', he claims, 'is that rather than modeling the preference side of the economy as resulting from the equilibrium interactions of many heterogeneous households, it allows us to model it as a solution to a single maximization problem' (ibid., p. 149). He begins by discussing the 'as if' assumption involved, given that households are not in fact identical, and defends it from the Debreu–Mantel–Sonnenschein theorem, which results from 'strong income effects'. 'Special but approximately realistic preference functions', Acemoglu maintains, 'as well as restrictions on the distribution of income across households, enable us to rule out arbitrary excess demand functions' (ibid., p. 151). These are known in the literature as 'Gorman preferences' after the econometrician Terence Gorman. This assumption leads to linear Engel curves (p. 151) and permits 'a *strong representative household*' assumption, in which changes in the distribution of income and endowments do not affect 'the demand side' (ibid., p. 152; original stress). This is a specific, technical response to a particular theorem in the general equilibrium literature, which again – whatever its merits – does not begin to come to grips with the broader philosophical issues raised by microfoundations. Acemoglu does not justify the claim that Gorman preferences are 'approximately realistic'. If they are not, he is vulnerable to the objection that, in models with heterogeneous agents, aggregation is in general impossible (Forni and Lippi 1997; see also Hartley 1999).

In the final analysis, though, empirical evidence plays only a small role in the mainstream case for microfoundations. This point is made with distressing clarity by Simon Wren-Lewis, an intelligent and self-critical advocate of the new neoclassical consensus in macroeconomics who was involved in the construction of the DSGE model now used by the Bank of England, when he contrasts two 'methodological approaches':

> The pre-microfoundations approach puts the stress on data consistency: models that are not consistent with the data (in an econometric sense) should be rejected. In contrast, the Bank of England's new model embodies a quite different approach. Internal consistency is vital, because only then can we be sure that relationships are consistent with the axioms of microeconomic theory. Econometric consistency is not essential (it is 'handled' via ad hoc, non-core relationships), but instead is a pointer to future theoretical development. (Wren-Lewis 2007, pp. 47–8)

Thus contact with reality ('data consistency') has a lower priority than internal theoretical consistency. In a recent reconsideration of these issues, Wren-Lewis criticizes not this fundamental principle but only the inability of New Keynesian models of price rigidity to provide the necessary internal consistency (Wren-Lewis 2011).

6.8 CODA

What, then, can be said in conclusion about microfoundations in 2012? Despite its status as the defining characteristic of 'modern macroeconomics', it is clear that the microfoundations dogma remains a source of controversy and not a little confusion. A representative example (sorry!) can be taken from a set of articles that I read in late 2010, when I was in the early stages of writing this book. *Agenda* is an Australian journal specializing in economic policy, published at the Australian National University from an essentially mainstream perspective. In its first issue for 2010 there was a symposium on Paul Krugman's (2009) interpretation of the global financial crisis and his defence of an 'Old Keynesian' IS-LM macroeconomic model as the basis for monetary and fiscal policy. Three of the papers were strongly critical of mainstream macroeconomics. Two of them argue that it needs *better* (that is, non-RARE) microfoundations, while the third invokes the fallacy of composition and thus (implicitly, at least) rejects the microfoundations dogma altogether.

Ian McDonald's principal objection to Krugman's critique of mainstream macroeconomics is that 'it offers no clues about the microeconomic foundation that would support the sustained impact on activity of the decline in aggregate demand'. He continues, 'This absence of a microeconomic foundation for macroeconomics', is a recurrent problem in Krugman's work (McDonald 2010, p. 90). McDonald does not favour RARE micro-foundations; on the contrary, he is a strong advocate of a quite different, behavioural microeconomics derived from the work of Daniel Kahneman and Amos Tversky. If their 'prospect theory' had 'been around in the 1960s', McDonald argues, 'when Keynes' influence was stronger, then the micro-foundations revolution may have avoided an excessive reliance on *Homo economicus*'. But McDonald regards Krugman's 'lack of micro-foundations' as at best 'a stop-gap or temporary solution ... as a programme for macroeconomics it is unsatisfactory' (ibid., p. 91).

Similarly, John Quiggin combines harsh criticism of the unrealistic nature of DGE models with strong support for the microfoundations dogma. 'First', he writes, given the failure of DGE as a progressive scientific research programme, 'the [replacement] programme needs more realistic micro-foundations. As Akerlof and Shiller (2009) observe, we need to look at how people actually behave, and how this behaviour contributes to the performance of the economy as a whole' (Quiggin 2010a, p. 116; an extended version of this argument can be found in Quiggin 2010b).

Finally, in this issue of *Agenda*, David Vines invokes the Bagehot–Dow 'paradox of liquidity', in all but name: 'Everybody – well, almost everybody – thought that financial institutions could diversify away their risks by holding a mixture of assets. Few economists understood the way in which a sale of assets by some institutions could mean that all institutions end up having to sell assets, leading to a generalized fire sale, and causing a crisis' (Vines 2010, p. 110). Although Vines does not himself draw this conclusion, it is difficult to see how the 'domino effects' that he correctly sees as being intimately involved in the crisis are consistent with any version of the microfoundations dogma, RARE or otherwise.

These examples illustrate just how often the question of micro-foundations continues to crop up in the literature of macroeconomics, and just how confused economists are about it – even those on the outer fringes of orthodoxy like McDonald and Quiggin. The *Agenda* symposium is especially revealing since it proves to be Vines, probably the least heterodox of the three contributors, who is also the least sympathetic to micro-foundations. Quiggin's book, *Zombie Economics*, reveals him to be a strong critic of RARE microfoundations but also inconsistent on the other crucial issue: is he opposed to the whole project, or does he simply want RARE microfoundations replaced by what I have termed the HABOR variety (heterogeneous agents with bounded rationality)?

'The appealing idea that macroeconomics should develop naturally from standard microeconomic foundations has turned out to be a distraction', he writes, suggesting that he will take the first and not the second position (Quiggin 2010b, p. 83). Later he seems to endorse the principle of downward causation, noting that 'the economy is not a simple machine for aggregating consumer preferences and allocating resources accordingly. The economy is embedded in a complex social structure, and there is a continuous interaction between the economic system and society as a whole' (ibid., p. 124). Finally, Quiggin acknowledges that '[p]henomena like animal spirits, social trust, and business confidence can't be reduced to individual psychology. They arise from economic and social interactions between people' (ibid., p. 129). So far, so good. 'If the micro-foundations approach underlying DSGE is of little use in understanding the macroeconomy', he asks, 'where should we turn?' (ibid., p. 123). 'We must model a world where people display multiple and substantial violations of the rationality assumptions of microeconomic theory and where markets depend not only on prices, preferences, and profits but on complicated and poorly understood phenomena like trust and perceived fairness. First, the program needs more realistic micro-foundations' (ibid., pp. 123–4). And his next sub-heading is: 'Better Micro-foundations' (ibid., p. 124). All but the first of these quotations are taken from a five-page section of the same chapter.

Quiggin's confusion is shared with very many authors on these matters, including (as we shall see in Chapter 8) many heterodox economists, whose attitude towards mainstream economics is very much more critical than his. First, though, we need to consider what has been made of microfoundations by practitioners of the other social sciences.

7. Crossing the border: 'microfoundations' in the other social sciences

7.1 INTRODUCTION

The term 'microfoundations' has been taken up by many sociologists, political scientists and theoretically minded historians, in what appears at first glance to be yet another striking example of successful economics imperialism (Fine and Milonakis 2009). In this chapter I trace the eruption of the microfoundations dogma into the literature of several other social sciences. The story that I have to tell is again a complicated one. As we have seen, economists have been very careless in their employment of metaphors, and very largely ignorant of the methodological minefield(s) that they were traversing. I had not anticipated that similar criticisms might apply to their colleagues in the disciplines of sociology, political science or history, but in fact they do, albeit to a lesser degree. In the event, the economists' attempts to colonize the other social sciences proved to be largely unsuccessful. Thus the microfoundations dogma provides a very informative historical case study in the use – and misuse – of metaphors in social science, and in the failure of economics imperialism. I begin by considering the use of both the term and the concept of microfoundations in sociology (Section 7.2), in political science (Section 7.3) and in historiography (Section 7.4). Then I discuss its application to Analytical Marxism, which straddles all three of these academic disciplines (Section 7.5), before drawing some tentative conclusions (in Section 7.6).

7.2 THE SOCIOLOGISTS

Social scientists have always been more methodologically aware than economists. Debates between individualists and anti-individualists go back a very long way, and have involved many leading social thinkers (see, for example, the papers collected in O'Neill 1973, and above, pp. 52–62). By the 1980s the age-old principle of methodological individualism was being re-branded as a requirement for microfoundations, and in sociology it proved highly contentious. Randall Collins's influential article 'on the microfoundations of macrosociology' may have borrowed the term from economics, but it described a very different project. It originated in the ethnomethodological research of Harold Garfinkel and other 'radical microsociologists', who had studied 'real-life interaction in second-by-second detail' (Collins 1981, p. 984). One product of this new field of 'social phenomenology' was 'its discovery that actual everyday-life micro-behavior does *not* follow rationalist models of cognition and decision-making' (p. 985; stress added), which should therefore be discarded. Collins concluded that it had given

> ... a strong impetus toward translating all macrophenomena into combinations of micro-events. A micro-translation strategy reveals the empirical realities of social structures as patterns of repetitive micro-interaction. Microtranslation thus gives us a picture of the complex levels of abstraction involved in causal explanations. (p. 985)

Evidently these 'translations' do not amount to microfoundations as understood by mainstream macroeconomists, who have no time for 'complex levels of abstraction' and would not be impressed either by Collins's references to 'interaction ritual chains' or by his claim that the 'result of microtranslating all social structure into such interaction ritual chains should be to make microsociology an important tool in explaining both the inertia and the dynamics of macro structure' (ibid., p. 985; original stress deleted). 'Chains' are not foundations at all, and neither is an 'important tool' also a foundation. Even these rather muted claims by Collins aroused the ire of Gary Alan Fine, who objected that 'Macrosociological presuppositions inherent in microsociology concern physical realities, social structure, institutional connections, organizational power, history, and tradition. These presuppositions, *implicit* in writings of microsociologists, are too often ignored in the service of an oppositional perspective' (Fine 1991, p. 161, original stress; see also Huber 1990 for a militantly feminist statement of this position).

Another landmark in the debate among sociologists on microfoundations was the publication of a volume edited by Michael Hechter (1983) with the same title as Collins's article. The book brought together a number of papers presented at the University of Washington Seminar in Macrosociology in 1979–1982, dealing with problems as diverse as career choices by American academics, the cohesion of the Japanese family, French political regionalism, and the worker's decision to go on strike. All employed rational choice models of one sort or another, but none of them claimed to have reduced social behaviour to individual decision-making. 'There seemed to be no reason why an appreciation of the role of structural factors in social life could not be combined with a concern for individual action', Hechter explained. 'Whereas the resulting synthesis could be labeled as individualistic', however, 'it represents a structural rather than atomistic kind of individualism', as advocated by the French sociologist Raymond Boudon (1979):

> In such an approach the structure first determines, to a greater or lesser extent, the constraints under which individuals act. While these constraints define the limits of the individual's possible action, they are insufficient to determine his or her behavior. *In no way does this imply that individual attributes should be given greater weight than structural constraints*; it merely asserts that social phenomena cannot be understood without taking the intentions and consequences of individual action into account. (Hechter 1983, p. 8; stress added)

Boudon's 'structural individualism' brings to mind the 'institutionalistic individualism' defended by Joseph Agassi (1960) in the debate on methodological individualism of the 1950s and early 1960s (above, pp. 59–60). This was (in my view quite rightly) dismissed by his critics as not being individualism at all (Lukes 1968). It would certainly not be acceptable to macroeconomists committed to the dogma of microfoundations, and it may be significant that Hechter himself seems not to use the term 'microfoundations' anywhere in his Introduction (in the absence of an index, it is impossible to be absolutely sure).

Hechter's book was reviewed in all the leading sociological journals. One reviewer noted that contributors claimed that 'rational choice models are useful for the explanation of macrosociological phenomena' (Cohn 1985, p. 221), and offer 'a fruitful guide for conducting empirical research' (Opp 1985, p. 362). But the claims that the sociologists were making for their microfoundations were much less ambitious than those of the economists, as Shirley Dex pointed out:

> It is not entirely clear ... whether we are being asked to regard rational choice theories as merely complementary to structural or normative social theories (p. 8), or stand-alone and 'better explanations of key macrosociological problems' (p. 10). Hechter waivers between these two positions and stops a long way short of views like those of Chicago economist Gary Becker. Becker claims that the method of economics ... explains any and every aspect of social and economic behaviour, and eliminates the need for other theories therefore. (Dex 1985, p. 301)

Similarly, Karl-Dieter Opp concluded that the claims of the economists were unwarranted: 'rational choice explanations may incorporate many sociological variables as specific preferences and constraints. Thus, the approach chosen by the authors does not lead to the abandoning of sociology' (Opp 1985, p. 362). This criticism has not, however, prevented Opp himself from being broadly supportive of micro-reduction in sociological theory (Udehn 2001, pp. 196–8).

Charles Tilly was equally sceptical concerning the prospects for microfoundations in sociology. An individualistic 'rational choice' theory of strike action, for example,

> ... provides no guide to aggregating individual decisions, especially where utility schedules and subjective estimates of the probability of success vary. It avoids the free-rider problem. It ignores the fact that strikes always involve the interdependent decisions of at least two groups. It relegates to the analytic periphery the relative power of the parties, the likelihood of state intervention, the condition of the labour market, the internal organization of the workforce ... It claims much more than it delivers. In varying degrees, similar difficulties beset all the individualistic rational action explanations actually proposed in *Microfoundations*. (Tilly 1985, p. 1096)

Of the reviewers, only Randall Collins (1985) and George Homans endorsed the attempt to '[explain] social phenomena by general propositions about the behaviour of individuals as members of the human species ... Horrible as this may seem to many, the theory is inherently reductionistic: it reduces the social to the individual' (Homans 1984, p. 877). Not that Homans would bring much comfort to mainstream economists, for he was an opponent of maximizing models and favoured replacing the label 'rational choice theory' with the more accurate tag of 'behavioral-cognitive psychology' (ibid., p. 879); his version of microfoundations was thus much closer to Herbert Simon than to Gary Becker.

Homans was, in any case, part of a fairly small minority. More typical were the participants in a conference sponsored by the theory sections of the German and American Sociological Associations in 1984 on 'The Micro-Macro Link'. Several US heavyweights took part, including Peter Blau, James Coleman, Randall Collins and Neil Smelser. The 12-page index to the conference volume (Alexander et al. 1987) has no entry for 'microfoundations', and the prevailing metaphors ('links', 'bridges' and 'connections') tend to be horizontal rather than vertical. The only contributor to use the term 'microfoundations' was Coleman, a friend and colleague of Gary Becker's at Chicago, whose position on the issue is important (and complex) enough to deserve separate treatment, later in this section. Among the others, Bernhard Giesen entitled his paper 'Beyond Reductionism', Richard Münch concluded his by affirming that the 'relationship between micro-interaction and macrostructures is that of interpenetration' (Münch 1987, p. 335), and Dean Gerstein insisted that 'micro and macro are general, mutually correlative terms, which may be usefully instantiated in many different ways' (Gerstein 1987, p. 90).

Collins reflected the position of most participants in concluding that macrosociologists could legitimately 'go on studying the world system, the structure of the state, or any other macrotopic without using micro research methods or invoking microtheory' (Collins 1987, p. 194). Nonetheless, he suggests, 'the effort to connect micro- and macrotheories is worth making ... the power of explanatory theory on either level will be enhanced if we can show their mutual penetration in a fairly precise way' (ibid., p. 195). Summarizing the proceedings of the conference, Münch and Smelser refer to 'complicated interrelations ... between micro and macro levels' that constitute 'a complex and contingent order'. Repeating Münch's earlier statement, they end the volume thus: 'The relationship between micro-interaction and macrostructures is that of interpenetration' (Münch 1987, p. 335). This is not microfoundations.

Even Coleman, who might have been expected to view the concept of microfoundations in a more favourable light, turns out not to have done so (Udehn 2001, pp. 292–306). Citing both Weber's theory linking the Protestant ethic to the rise of capitalism, and more recent 'frustration theories' of social revolution, Coleman objects that

> In both instances the micro-to-macro transition is made simply by aggregation of individual orientations, attitudes or beliefs. If the theoretical problem is, however, a problem involving the functioning of a social *system*, as it is in the case of explaining the rise of a capitalist economy, or in explaining the occurrence of a revolution, then it should be obvious that the appropriate transition cannot involve the simple aggregation of individual behavior. (Coleman 1987, p. 157; original stress)

He proceeds to criticize neoclassical economists for neglecting 'the social assumptions' behind their models of general equilibrium (ibid., p. 158).

Coleman made similar comments in his contribution to a symposium in the *Journal of Business* in the previous year: 'both in the microfoundations and in the apparatus for moving from individual to system-level behavior', he argues,

> ... there is more structure than is assumed in neoclassical economic theory ... markets function differently and give different equilibrium prices, depending on

> the institutions through which exchanges are organized … Social institutions and social networks – which are not completely, but are largely, ignored in neoclassical theory – can make differences in outcomes without any change at all in the model of rational action. (Coleman 1986, pp. S368–S369)

Evidently Coleman's use of the term 'microfoundations' is quite different from the usage favoured by the economists that he is attacking, and similar points are made repeatedly in his influential treatise, *Foundations of Social Theory* (Coleman 1990, pp. 28, 197, 330–31, cited by Hartley 1997, pp. 171, 186, 188; see also Liska 1990; Smelser 1990; Frank, 1992, pp. 148, 154, 157–8; Baron and Hannan 1994, pp. 1114–15; and Hechter and Kanazawa 1997).

By the mid-1990s, most sociologists would have agreed with Geoffrey Ingham that

> … sociology differs from mainstream economics in the following ways:
>
> (i) social and economic structures have properties that cannot be reduced to those of individuals taken singly;
>
> (ii) social and economic action has 'meaning' that cannot be reduced to the calculus of want satisfaction or utility maximization;
>
> (iii) social and economic life is based upon power (and associated) 'asymmetries' and inherent uncertainty. (Ingham 1996, p. 252)

It would be surprising if this were not so, given the classical position inspired by Émile Durkheim, which 'holds that an argument is sociological only if it *cannot* be reduced analytically to arguments about individual action' (Baron and Hannan 1994, p. 1116; stress added). Nicos Mouzelis invoked 'Durkheim's rule that social facts must be explained by other social facts' to argue that '"macro facts" must in the first instance be explained by other "macro facts"', although this 'does not mean, of course, that establishing macro-micro linkages and providing micro foundations is a useless activity' (Mouzelis 1995, p. 27).

There seems to be less discussion of the 'microfoundations of sociology' in the 21st century than there was in the 1980s and early 1990s. Where they do still refer to microfoundations, sociologists seem to be making much less ambitious claims, methodologically speaking, than the economists. Thus Fine and Brooke Harrington (2004) treat small groups not only as 'the microfoundations of civil society' but also as 'a cause, context, *and consequence* of civic engagement' (Fine and Harrington 2004, p. 352; stress added). This is a clear and unsurprising recognition of the principle of downward causation. The philosopher Mario Bunge proposes 'systemism' as 'the alternative to individualism and holism' in social science, specifically criticizing the 'obsolete individualism of … the neoclassical microeconomists' (Bunge 2000, p. 147). 'Individualism is deficient', he argues, 'because it underrates or even overlooks the bonds among people, and holism because it plays down or even enslaves individual action. By contrast, systemism makes room for both agency and structure' (ibid., pp. 156–7; see also Bunge 1996, pp. 145, 277–81; Bunge 1998, pp. 72–9, 102–7; and, on agency and structure, Fernández-Huerga 2008 and McKenna and Zannoni 2012).

Similarly, Karen Cook (2000, p. 685) uses the term 'microfoundations' to encompass 'theoretical perspectives developed at the micro level that link in different ways to more macro levels of sociological analysis … [and] highlight the linkages between individual behaviour and social structure emphasizing interdependence and the social context of interaction'. But these are not microfoundations in the economists' sense of that term, and it is significant that the vertical metaphor has once again dissolved into a horizontal one: 'linkages' are not foundations. As Michael Ryan concludes: 'there have been a number of attempts to integrate the micro- and macro-levels of theory and the work of their representative theorists since the early 1980s … recent theorists have sought to show how both levels merit attention but that the greatest level of focus should be on the ways in which they interact with each other' (Ryan 2005, p. 503).

7.3 THE POLITICAL THEORISTS

In politics the most prominent advocates of microfoundations have been the Analytical Marxists, who are the subject of a later section. The question seems to have insinuated itself into mainstream political science via attempts to apply rational choice theory to the analysis of political behaviour (Amadae and Bueno de Mesquita 1997; Achen 2002). In this context Donald Green and Ian Shapiro (1994, p. 7) identify 'three classic texts': Kenneth Arrow's *Social Choice and Individual Values* (1951b), Anthony Downs's *An Economic Theory of Democracy* (1957) and Mancur Olson's *The Logic of Collective Action* (1965). Almost half a century after the publication of Arrow's book, Green and Shapiro concluded that much less had been achieved than the advocates of rational choice models liked to claim, though this did not prevent them from using the term 'microfoundations' uncritically in their opening chapter (Green and Shapiro 1994, pp. 3, 4).

At all events, the political scientists arrived at the problem of microfoundations rather earlier than the sociologists. As early as 1978 Ronald Rogowski was offering a survey of what he termed 'rationalist theory', which he regarded as 'the most promising avenue in the recent history of political inquiry' (Rogowski 1978, p. 323). It is, he notes, 'focused exclusively on the individual', and asserted the principle 'that explanation must be tied to individual behavior and not to some reified system' (ibid., p. 304). Thus 'the premise of rational choice applies solely to *individuals*. Statements of the form, "The nation-state seeks always to maximize its power", are not rationalist, unless they are derived by strict logic from rationalist premises about individual behavior' (ibid., p. 300; original stress). Despite his sympathy for the project, Rogowski's 'midterm report' on its progress to date is not favourable. It developed largely as a consequence of 'the theoretical faddishness of the discipline', he maintains. Rationalist theory has often been 'trivialized' by its exponents (ibid., p. 313), so that the 'scientific consequences' are 'almost wholly bad' (ibid., pp. 305, 306). In fact, many of the political scientists whose work Rogowski discusses were not providing microfoundations at all: 'Rationalist theories of *institutions* – parties, governments, bureaucracies, legislatures – have tended to draw on the economics of the firm, and of oligopolistic competition or monopoly'. Some even used 'the revisionist view of the firm taken by Cyert and March' (ibid., p. 302). But firms are not individuals.

Neither, of course, are the nation-states that act as agents in rational choice theories of international relations (Morrow 1988). It might be thought that this problem could be evaded by postulating a single foreign policy dictator in each state, rather like the Beckerian family with its dominant (male) head. In his influential book *The War Trap*, Bruce Bueno de Mesquita made precisely this assumption in applying neoclassical economic theory to a problem of immense significance for humankind: 'I have assumed that a single foreign policy decision maker has final authority for all war-and-peace decisions. That policymaker was assumed to be a rational expected-utility maximizer' (Bueno de Mesquita 1981, p. 45). This allows him to escape from Arrow's voting paradox. Nonetheless:

> That is not to say that international relations must be or should be studied from the perspective of individuals. Although nations, alliances, and systems are not themselves purposive actors, they are entities endowed with attributes that may constrain the possible courses of action open to the individuals responsible for guiding their policy. By understanding how such attributes as the level of industrialization, urbanization, and mobilization of national resources (or the degree of commitment among allies or antipathy between foes) affect the

> feasibility of various possibilities, we may learn a great deal about the options that particular decision makers in particular places at particular times can or cannot choose. (Ibid., p. 17)

This conclusion is very similar to that of Michael Hechter, as reported in the previous section. Structural constraints on choice appear to rule out any possibility of explaining the behaviour of states entirely in terms of the decisions of powerful individuals.

Rather similar difficulties were detected by one reviewer of Michael Taylor's (1988) edited volume on rational choice models of revolution:

> Though none of the authors views structural variables as wrong, each sees structural-determinist models as incomplete without satisfactory microfoundations that make the actions of revolutionary participants intelligible or rational ... A recurring theme in most of these essays is that structural-determinist models should be *complemented* , not replaced, by rational-choice explanations. (Downing 1990, pp. 679–80; original stress)

Again, these are not microfoundations as mainstream economists would understand them.

Taylor himself took a nuanced view of the relationship between individual and structural explanations in his contribution to another collective volume, entitled *Politics and Rationality*:

> ... neither facts about individuals nor facts about social structures provide 'rock-bottom' or 'ultimate' explanations of social change. I am therefore rejecting both one-sided methodological individualism or 'voluntarism' and any approach to explaining social change that sees individuals – their actions, desires, and beliefs, and even their very identities – as explicable solely in terms of their locations in social structures or that tries to explain, in some cases without reference to individual action at all, structural and other sorts of change in terms of facts about structures. (Taylor 1993, p. 91)

In the same volume, Peter Lange and George Tsebelis claimed to provide microfoundations for the analysis of strikes over wages in neocorporatist economies. 'By microfoundations', they explain, 'we mean that the theory should be consistent with fully rational and strategic behavior on the part of the individual *and collective* actors involved', which include unions. 'Labor and Capital negotiate over the division of the economic output through negotiations at the level of the factory, the branch, *or the whole country*' (Lange and Tsebelis 1993, pp. 140, 143; stress added). The editors' definition of microfoundations was equally accommodating. Rational choice theory depends on methodological individualism, they note, and this 'amounts to the position that explanation must at some point go through the individual' (Booth, James and Meadwell 1993a, p. 1). It is difficult to see who would disagree with this bland statement, especially when it is followed by the recognition that 'rational choice theorists do not conceive of persons as atomized, self-sufficient monads. Rather, persons are thought of as embedded in networks, contexts, and institutions' (ibid., p. 2).

Another political scientist, Daniel Little, though sympathetic enough to Analytical Marxism that he uses the term 'microfoundations' in the title of his book, makes the modest claim that a 'macro-explanation is insufficient unless it is accompanied by an analysis at the level of individual activity – a micro-analysis – which reveals the mechanisms which give rise to the pattern to be explained'. Thus 'an assertion of an explanatory relationship at the social level (causal, functional, structural), must be supplemented by' micro explanations (Little 1998, pp. 7, 10; see also Sørensen 1999). This rather innocuous statement is, however, immediately followed by a 'stronger version':

> ... we must have at least an approximate idea of the underlying mechanisms at the individual level if we are to have a credible hypothesis about explanatory social regularities at all. A putative explanation couched at the level of high-level social factors whose underlying individual-level mechanisms are entirely unknown is no explanation at all. (Ibid., p. 10)

But Little proceeds to use both horizontal and vertical metaphors: micro and macro phenomena are 'linked together' (p. 12), with 'a bridge' between them (p. 23), and the macro is 'accompanied by' (p. 7), 'supported by' (p. 10), 'bolstered' (p. 12), 'based on' and 'grounded in' the micro (p. 13). At one point he concedes that 'there may be legitimate forms of macro-explanations in social science which are not subject to these specific criticisms; and in that case microfoundational arguments would be silent' (p. 13). In later work Little has come out strongly against both micro-reduction and excessive reliance on rational action, which he regards as 'now only a relatively small part of individual explanation' (Little 2009, p. 164). But he continues to use the term 'microfoundations' (ibid., pp. 165–6, 169).

7.4 THE HISTORIANS

In historical scholarship, too, there has been some discussion of 'the micro-macro link', or 'the microfoundations of macrotheory'. While historians are aware of the debates over microfoundations in economics and sociology, they have been generally unwilling to follow the lead of the economists. 'In new microhistory the link between micro and macro levels is not a simple reduction or aggregation. The movement from one level or sphere to another is qualitative, and generates new information' (Peltonen 2001, p. 357). 'Words like "link", "nexus" or "foundation"' (p. 359) are often used by historians, indicating some confusion in the use of vertical and horizontal metaphors. When the historian 'crosses over boundaries' between micro and macro, there is often 'a double bind' (p. 357), since if the micro is either typical or exceptional no new information is generated. Matti Peltonen concludes that 'historical study is, at least in methodological questions, an independent and original mode of research' (p. 359).

The eminent Italian historian Carlo Ginzburg traces the origins of the term 'microhistory' to the American scholar George R. Stewart, who in 1959 wrote over 300 pages on the minute details of the battle of Gettysburg, while in the 1970s a Mexican historian, Luis González, used the term as a synonym for 'local history'. In 1958–60, Ginzburg recalls, the great *Annales* historian Fernand Braudel gave '*microhistoire*' 'a precise but negative connotation', denoting traditional narrative history 'dominated by protagonists who resembled orchestra directors'. The term was 'obviously modeled on *microeconomics* and *microsociology*' (Ginzburg 1993, p. 13; original stress). In the Italian literature, the term *microstoria* could also be dated to the late 1960s, soon losing its negative connotations. Ginzburg himself took up this form of narration by reference to *War and Peace*, inspired by 'Tolstoy's conviction that a historical phenomenon can become comprehensible only by reconstructing the activities of *all* the persons who participated in it' (ibid., p. 24; original stress). But Ginzburg steps back from this position when he reviews the work of the historian Siegfried Kracauer, who 'recognizes that certain phenomena can only be grasped by means of a macroscopic perspective. This suggests', Ginzburg continues, 'that the reconciliation between macro- and microhistory is not at all taken for granted (as Toynbee wrongly believed). It needs to be pursued' (ibid., p. 27. There needs to be 'a constant back and forth between micro- and macrohistory, between close-ups and extreme long-shots', since 'the results obtained in a microscopic sphere cannot be automatically transferred to a macroscopic sphere (and vice versa)' (ibid., pp. 27, 33). This is essentially the same as the conclusion reached at this time by sociologists with an interest in comparative history (see, for example, Knapp 1990).

These questions continued to resonate in the historiographical literature in the early years of the new century, in journals as diverse as *History and*

Theory (Norkus 2005) and *Journal of the Early Republic* (Lamoreaux 2006). Writing about 'macrohistory and micromechanisms' in the Chinese revolution, Tang Tsou may have been the first historian to use the term 'microfoundations' (a JSTOR search did not throw up an earlier usage in an historical journal):

> ... we need nothing less than a theory of human choices – rational, nonrational, and irrational – while taking full account of both structural constraints and historical accidents. This theory should enable us to provide microfoundations to macrohistory while allowing macrohistory to throw light on the significance of the various micromechanisms, individually and in different combinations and permutations. (Tsou 2000, p. 209)

This is much less than a call for micro-reduction, and Tsou's hoped-for microfoundations are evidently not RARE ones. In any case, he did not expect them to be forthcoming: 'Unfortunately, such a theory does not exist and perhaps never will' (ibid., p. 209), even though 'direct and readily observable micromechanisms' could be identified that helped to explain the transformation of the Chinese political system (ibid., p. 211).

Three years later, the Icelandic historian Sigurđur Gylfi Magnússon discovered the same themes in the work of an Italian scholar. Gianna Pomata, he reports, 'argues that by a macrohistorical approach we miss the opportunity to handle information which might be important. But then she adds an extremely interesting further observation: "But so does micro-history, because macroscopic realities do not entirely correspond to the sum of microrealities that make them up"' (Magnússon 2003, p. 719, citing Pomata 2000, p. 115). Pomata invokes the fallacy of composition in all but name:

> No conclusion reached at the microlevel can be transferred whole to the macrolevel. So even the integration of all possible microhistories – Tolstoj's dream of 'a history of everybody' – would not allow us to capture the whole of historical reality. The historical record includes connections that are visible only at the macrolevel. Therefore, general history is useful, and indeed necessary. (Magnússon 2003, p. 719, citing Pomata 2000, p. 115)

Magnússon himself seems to disapprove of her conclusion, which is that micro- and macrohistory must be regarded as being very largely autonomous disciplines; macrohistory should instead be 'connected with micro-historical findings' (ibid., p. 719). This, again, falls far short of a case for micro-reduction, as does Richard Brown's conclusion, based on his analysis of the microhistory and the 'postmodern challenge': 'notwithstanding my brief for microhistory, let us continue along our various paths. Not only do we continue to need syntheses, we continue to need monographs of all sorts. Microhistory is *one* way, not the *only* way' (Brown 2003, p. 19; original stress).

7.5 THE ANALYTICAL MARXISTS

By its nature Marxism is a multi-disciplinary enterprise, and it is therefore not surprising that the scholars who define themselves as 'Analytical Marxists' have a background in philosophy, sociology, political theory or history, rather than economics. However, all of them are familiar with both Marxian and mainstream economic theory, and one of them – John Roemer – is adept in and an enthusiastic advocate of both Walrasian general equilibrium modelling and game theory. In the 1980s several of the Analytical Marxists attempted to apply the principle of methodological individualism to the Marxian theory of history, and to Marxian political economy in particular. Roemer (1979) seems to have been the first to use the term 'microfoundations' in the title of a paper. It was followed by a flurry of books and articles in the early to mid-1980s, some early critical articles (Howard and King 1989; Weldes 1989), book-length critiques by Tom Mayer (1994) and Marcus Roberts (1996) and, most recently, a comprehensive and very well documented survey article by Roberto Veneziani (2012).

As Veneziani notes, the broader Analytical Marxism project needs to be distinguished from the sub-school that came to be known as Rational Choice Marxism. Reacting against the often cloudy language and sometimes muddled thinking of mid-twentieth century Hegelian Marxism, the Analytical Marxists reject the 'antique, and bad, metaphysics, which saturate parts of Marx's corpus' and the writings of many of his followers (Booth 1993, p. 80). Instead they reveal 'a concern for rigour and clarity to a degree unusual in Marxian theory … Great attention has been paid to the exact meaning of concepts, the process of deduction by which concepts are derived, and how far these concepts can sustain traditional Marxian propositions' (Howard and King 1992, p. 335). The Analytical Marxists drew their inspiration from Georgy Plekhanov, Nikolai Bukharin, Evgeny Preobrazhensky, Oskar Lange and Michał Kalecki rather than from the more popular icons of the New Left like Louis Althussser, Antonio Gramsci, George Lukacs and Jean-Paul Sartre. Analytical Marxism is 'consistent with an antireductionist perspective that emphasizes the importance of social structures and the role of culture, social norms, endogenous preferences, and non-instrumental rationality' (Veneziani 2012, p. 3), while Rational Choice Marxism embraces methodological individualism and its corollary, the application of rational (individual) choice theory to all the central problems of Marxian theory. As Veneziani demonstrates, the broader Analytical Marxism project continues to thrive, while Rational Choice Marxism 'has been abandoned by all its most prominent practitioners' (ibid., p. 3).

For a while, though, very ambitious claims were made by some of its advocates. Thus Roemer's influential *Analytical Foundations of Marxian Economic Theory* begins by defining the microfoundations approach, which 'consists in deriving the aggregate behavior of the economy as a consequence of the actions of individuals, who are postulated to behave in some specified way. I have taken this approach throughout the book'. He continues by giving an important example. In his discussion of the falling rate of profit, it is postulated that 'a technical innovation is introduced only if it increases profits for a capitalist ... one is not allowed to postulate an increasing organic composition of capital unless one can show what individual entrepreneurial mechanism leads to it'. Similarly, Roemer regards references to the class identity of capitalists as question-begging. 'That individuals behave as members of a class, rather than as individuals, should be a theorem in Marxian economics, not a postulate' (Roemer 1981, p. 7).

Jon Elster went even further, explicitly stating the reductionist nature of his approach to Marxian social theory:

> By [methodological individualism] I mean the doctrine that all social phenomena – their structure and their change – are in principle explicable in ways that only involve individuals – their properties, their goals, their beliefs and their actions. Methodological individualism thus conceived is a form of reductionism. To go from social institutions and aggregate patterns of behavior to individuals is the same kind of operation as going from cells to molecules. (Elster 1985, p. 5)

The 'rationale for reductionism', Elster continues, is 'to reduce the time-span between explanans and explanandum' in scientific laws (ibid., p. 5). He endorses Roemer's use of this principle, 'generating class relations and the capital relationship from exchanges between differently endowed individuals in a competitive setting' (ibid., p. 7). Elster goes on to apply the microfoundations approach both to criticize Marx's theories of value and crisis and to attempt an individualist explanation of class consciousness, class struggle and the emergence of ideologies. Perhaps the most important conclusion drawn by the Rational Choice Marxists is that Marxian 'class analysis requires microfoundations at the level of the individual to explain why and when classes are the relevant unit of analysis' (Roemer 1982, p. 513). The same principle was subsequently extended to the explanation of banditry, peasant revolutions and other forms of social change (Taylor 1988), and also to questions of personal identity (Little 1998).

The precise implications of this emphasis on microfoundations were, however, never entirely free from ambiguity. It has often been noted in the literature on Analytical Marxism that neither Roemer nor Elster were entirely consistent in their approach to microfoundations (see, for example, Howard and King 1989, pp. 405–7, Fisk 1991 and Udehn 2001, pp. 312–13, 315–16 on Elster; Udehn 2001, p. 317 on Roemer). As Heath notes, 'Elster's move from methodological individualism to the instrumental conception of rationality is based upon a *non sequitur*' (Heath 2009, p. 11). Roemer's original statement of the case for microfoundations seems to require only consistency between micro and macro, and not the reduction of the latter to the former. Elster himself devotes a significant part of an earlier book to analysing the fallacy of composition, 'whose importance for the social sciences has often been casually acknowledged, but never – as far as I know – been the object of a systematic analysis' (Elster 1978, p. 96). He defines the conditions necessary for the absence of the fallacy very clearly: 'what is possible for any single individual must be possible for them all simultaneously' (ibid., p. 99), and even cites the Kaleckian paradox of costs (p. 97, where it is wrongly attributed to 'one of Keynes's radical pupils', who is not named). By 1985, when he published *Making Sense of Marx*, Elster seems to have forgotten all about the fallacy of composition (see also Philp and Young 2002). Twenty years later, Zenonas Norkus described 'the now already extinct Rational Choice Marxism' as being '[a]mong many theories that have disappointed Elster' (Norkus 2005, pp. 352, 353).

Further complications had already been introduced by Erik Olin Wright, Andrew Levine and Elliott Sober, who defended the quest for microfoundations but rejected Elster's methodological individualism. In Chapter 8 we shall discover that a similar conclusion was drawn by some Post Keynesian economists, on the grounds that the capitalist firm is not an individual. But the argument of these three Analytical Marxists is quite different. 'This may seem like a paradoxical stance', they admit; 'how can one be simultaneously committed to the irreducibility of social explanations to individual-level explanations and to the importance of elaborating microfoundations?' (Wright, Levine and Sober 1992, pp. 115–16). The resolution of the apparent paradox was as follows: it is necessary to distinguish between tokens and types, that is, between particular instances and the characteristics that tokens may have in common. Thus 'being rich is a type of which Rockefeller is a token' (ibid., p. 116). They conclude that 'the reductionist program of methodological individualism fails because science has explanatory projects beyond the explanation of token events' (ibid., p. 120). I suspect that the substantially shrunken domain of microfoundations in this version would not satisfy the 1985 Elster, perhaps not Roemer, and most certainly not the mainstream macroeconomists. The waters are further muddied by the authors' use of bridge metaphors: 'linkages between micro and macro', and 'micro-mediations' (ibid., p. 121).

All this suggests that the Rational Choice Marxists themselves had not thought through the reductive implications of microfoundations, and at the very least that they might have been well advised to avoid the term. (In Chapters 8 and 9 I shall have something very similar to say about the use of 'microfoundations' by many heterodox economists of other theoretical persuasions). In any case, as I have already noted, the Rational Choice variant of Analytical Marxism is now effectively dead. Its influence lingers, however, with radical-Marxian economists who have little or no time for Elster or Roemer but nevertheless use the same language. Thus Jonathan Goldstein's 'introduction to a unified heterodox macroeconomics', with the aim of integrating Marxian and Keynesian ideas, includes both 'macrofoundations' and 'microfoundations'. Goldstein even claims to endorse in-principle micro-reduction: 'while a preference exists for rational choice models to achieve micro reductions, in no way is this an absolute priority. Such micro reductions simply may not be feasible'. This statement is very difficult to reconcile with the recognition, earlier on the same page, of the importance of reciprocal causation between micro and macro phenomena: 'individual behavior is conditionally/conjuncturally determined by the macrofoundations discussed above. In turn, individual or group behavior alters the social and economic environment with important feedback effects to micro behavior' (Goldstein 2009, p. 41).

In the same volume, another contributor declares his support for non-RARE microfoundations. Agent-based modelling with bounded rationality is able both to avoid the problems of aggregation and to generate emergent macroeconomic properties, Bill Gibson argues. 'The microfoundations afforded by the agent-based approach', he maintains, provide 'a link between [the] previously disembodied macroeconomic framework of analysis and the underlying heterogeneous, and boundedly rational agents that populate the system' (Gibson 2009, p. 95). But in the 21st century this is very much a minority position among Marxian and other radical political economists.

7.6 CONCLUSION

We may conclude that mainstream economists have largely failed to convince other social scientists of the merits of their crusade for microfoundations, as Edgar Kiser has shown in a slightly different context. While acknowledging that many sociologists have borrowed 'agency theory' from economics, Kiser denies that this is a success story for economics imperialism: 'The way agency theory has been used in political science and sociology is much different from its use in economics, indicating that the "economic imperialism" metaphor is not a good description of the intellectual diffusion process in this case' (Kiser 1999, p. 147). And there has also been a process of reverse colonization. 'Some economic agency theorists are now incorporating aspects of social and organizational structure, multiple agents, and even heterogeneous microfoundations' (ibid., p. 166). In an interesting variant on the trade metaphors that were briefly discussed in Chapter 2, Kiser concludes that '[s]ociologists should not be taking a protectionist stance towards foreign imports – it is becoming increasingly clear that free trade in ideas benefits all parties, since most intellectual progress is taking place in the intersections of the disciplines' (p. 167). This does not, however, prevent him from using the term 'microfoundations' twice on the final page of his paper.

This concludes the discussion of the tortuous path by which the microfoundations dogma became established in mainstream economics and (as we have seen in this chapter) failed to take over the other social sciences. One lesson from this failure is that some sociologists, political scientists and historians have been rather careless in their use of spatial metaphors. As we shall see in Part III, the same criticism can be made of many heterodox economists.

PART III

Dissenting Voices

8. The dissenters, part I: the Post Keynesians

8.1 INTRODUCTION

Of all the various schools of heterodox economics, the Post Keynesians might have been expected to take a clear and highly critical position on the microfoundations dogma. First and most obviously, their theoretical allegiance to Keynes and/or Kalecki, supplemented in many cases by Marx and Sraffa, should have rendered them immune to the doctrines of methodological individualism and micro-reduction and made them profoundly suspicious of any project that envisaged the elimination of macroeconomics as an autonomous scientific discipline. Second, Post Keynesians have always tended to take a much greater interest in questions of methodology than their mainstream opponents, many of them endorsing the Critical Realist position of Roy Bhaskar and Tony Lawson, which (as we shall see in Chapter 10) cannot be reconciled with any version of microfoundations. Finally, their systematic and sustained hostility to mainstream economic theory should have made them very suspicious of the (admittedly often tacit or poorly formulated) philosophical basis of the New Neoclassical Synthesis.

However, as I shall demonstrate in this chapter, it has not worked out like this. The disagreements, uncertainties and ambiguities of the Post Keynesians on this fundamental issue testify again to the ability of the microfoundations metaphor to generate confusion and to mislead people who really should have known better. I have to include myself in this category. Several of the Post Keynesians with whom I had conversations in 1992–3 referred approvingly to microfoundations without being challenged, and I myself criticized the neoclassical nature of Keynes's supposed microfoundations in the *General Theory* in my introduction to the book in which these conversations appeared (King 1995, p. 3).

It is possible to distinguish three (or, just possibly, four) categories of Post Keynesians on this issue. First, there are the unambiguous and explicit supporters of microfoundations, a position that is almost always accompanied by the claim that 'ours are better than yours'. Second are the unambiguous and explicit critics of microfoundations, with or without an assertion of the need for macrofoundations of microeconomics. Third, and probably the largest group, are those Post Keynesians whose position is ambiguous, ambivalent, inconsistent or unclear. Many Post Keynesians can, indeed, fairly be accused of using the word 'microfoundations' much too loosely. I myself was in this category for far too long. Fourth, there are some who simply ignore the whole question: a recent example is provided by Elgar's authoritative *Handbook of Alternative Monetary Economics* (Arestis and Sawyer 2006), a 524-page volume with 29 contributions, only one of which makes any reference to the issue. This is Roy Rotheim's piece on credit rationing, which dismisses the need to provide microfoundations for it (Rotheim 2006, p. 325). Some Post Keynesians do not fit comfortably into any of these categories: Nicholas Kaldor, for example, straddled the second and third of them, while Claudio Sardoni would be at home in either the first (where I have put him) or the third.

In what follows I shall deal with the first three categories in turn (in Sections 8.2, 8.3 and 8.4). I was tempted to present the individual authors in alphabetical order, since the absence of any substantial or sustained debate on microfoundations between Post Keynesians makes it difficult to justify a chronological treatment. After some reflection I have decided that this would be even more confusing, but it is important to note that to a regrettably large extent the Post Keynesians whose views on microfoundations are outlined in this chapter have been talking across each other and not to each other. Section 8.5 is devoted to the monetary theorist and methodologist Sheila Dow, who has had more to say on the question of microfoundations than any other Post Keynesian author and has almost always taken the correct line, without always being quite as clear as she might have been. In the final section, I discuss the damage that might have been done to Post Keynesianism by its lack of clarity on these questions.

8.2 THE SUPPORTERS

Paul Davidson has always claimed that Post Keynesians are able to supply microfoundations for macroeconomic theory that are superior to those of the mainstream. He was quite explicit on this at the 1975 S'Agaro conference. Apart from the Austrian economist Erich Streissler, it was in fact Davidson who provided the clearest endorsement of microfoundations at the conference (Harcourt 1977, pp. 313–14, 391–2). He insisted that 'Marshall-Keynes microeconomic theory' had in fact already supplied the necessary microfoundations for Post Keynesian macroeconomics (ibid., p. 314), a claim repeated in many subsequent writings. Most recently, in the second edition of his *Post Keynesian Macroeconomic Theory*, Davidson repeatedly criticizes the neoclassical and neo-Walrasian microfoundations that New Keynesian economists rely on. He concludes by defending 'the properties of a system of microeconomic demand and supply functions that has thrown out the axioms of ergodicity, ubiquitous gross substitution and non-neutral money' as the basis for a genuinely new Keynesian macroeconomics (Davidson 2011, pp. 333–4).

Writing from a rather different perspective, George Feiwel, in the first intellectual biography of Michał Kalecki, suggests that Kalecki himself was concerned to provide microfoundations:

> Kalecki's model represents a more useful microeconomic account of output and distribution as a whole [than that of the mainstream]. Macroeconomic models require a microeconomic foundation. While it is not at all reprehensible to concentrate on building macroeconomic models without paying much attention to the underlying microrelations, the efforts of those who attempt to provide such an underpinning are particularly commendable. (Feiwel 1975, p. 93)

There is more than an echo here of Fritz Machlup (1963). Several Kalecki scholars have followed Feiwel on this issue. Thus Alberto Chilosi regards Kalecki as having provided superior microfoundations. Kalecki, he writes, deals with 'the issue of how the microeconomic behaviour of firms brings about the macroeconomic outcomes of his theory ... the issue of the microeconomic foundations of macroeconomic models in a non-perfectly competitive framework is very modern and is still the focus of attention of economic theorists' (1989, p. 103). Chilosi cites Kalecki's 1936 review of the *General Theory*, which is 'very modern ... because of its focus on the microeconomic foundations of macroeconomic aggregates in an imperfectly competitive framework' (ibid., p. 109). His article concludes with an allusion to New Keynesian theory: 'Finally, Kalecki's quest for the microeconomic foundations of non-perfectly competitive macroeconomic models makes him a real, and instructive, antecedent of a very interesting modern line of research' (ibid., p. 117).

In similar vein Jerry Courvisanos, in his book on investment cycles in capitalist economies, writes that 'The *microfoundations* ... have been developed by Kaleckian and related post-Keynesian authors' (Courvisanos 1996, p. 26; original stress). He cites Kalecki's mark-up pricing hypothesis and its elaboration by Tom Asimakopulos (1975), Alfred Eichner (1976), Geoff Harcourt and Peter Kenyon (1976) and Adrian Wood (1975). More recently Malcolm Sawyer, in section three of a survey paper on 'crises and paradigms in macroeconomics', uses the heading 'micro-economic foundations and human behaviour' (Sawyer 2010, pp. 291–6). 'The lines of argument pursued here are that the microeconomic foundations claimed by the mainstream macroeconomists are a major weakness and that a macroeconomic analysis based on those micro foundations has not been established. Further, heterodox macroeconomics has always had microeconomic foundations, but the nature of those foundations have [*sic*] differed between authors' (ibid., p. 291).

Sawyer is, however, a strong critic of RARE microfoundations, 'since the conditions for aggregation have not been established, and a reliance on the representative agent approach precludes differences between individuals and groups' (ibid., p. 293). Keynes and Kalecki, on the other hand, 'clearly had microeconomic foundations for their macroeconomic analysis', although 'the microeconomic foundations which they provided were different' (ibid., p. 294). They are also superior to those of the mainstream in two ways. First, they concentrate on the firm rather than on the household, and thus on investment rather than on consumption. Second, they are not simple, and certainly not RARE. 'Heterodox macroeconomics has not and would not wish to bring forward a universal set of microfoundations comparable to the manner in which the mainstream economists proceed. Heterodox macroeconomics has to grapple with the heterogeneity of behaviour and actions at the individual and organizational levels and with that behaviour in the context of fundamental uncertainty' (ibid., p 294).

Jan Toporowski is another Kaleckian who takes a very similar line to Sawyer. He attributes support for microfoundations also to Hyman Minsky: 'In his view [Richard] Goodwin's models in particular suffer from an absence of foundation in "the behavior of business firms"' (Toporowski 2008, citing Minsky 1954 [2004], pp. 2–3). Minsky uses a form of '[c]ore-supplementary model disaggregation' that is superficially similar to that used by the Bank of England in its recent macroeconomic modelling. 'Minsky's core-supplementary model determination', however, 'is designed to give his theory microeconomic foundations in market process, whereas the Bank of England's models preclude such foundations'. Moreover, Minsky's treatment of 'economic agents' is greatly superior to that of mainstream macroeconomics: 'For Minsky the essence of capitalism was its domination by firms rather than households' (Toporowski 2008, p. 728).

Toporowski makes an interesting distinction, not often found in the literature, between methodological individualism, which he rejects, and microfoundations, which he endorses. The confusion of microfoundations with methodological individualism can be avoided, he maintains, if (like Marx, Kalecki and Minsky) one takes the capitalist firm rather than the individual as the determining microeconomic agent. This position would almost certainly have been endorsed by Alfred Eichner, who believed that his own model of oligopoly pricing and investment behaviour by the 'megacorp' supplied the 'micro foundations of the corporate economy' (the title of Chapter 2 of Eichner 1985), and thus of his entire macrodynamic analysis. In an early Post Keynesian textbook, Philip Arestis (1992, p. 139) explicitly adopted the Eichner model of the oligopolistic corporation as 'our micro-foundations of Post-Keynesian economics'.

I offer two more twenty-first century examples. The first is Claudio Sardoni who, in his contribution to a *Festschrift* for Victoria Chick, reveals his position through his choice of title, 'On the microeconomic foundations of macroeconomics: a Keynesian perspective'. Sardoni begins with this unequivocal statement:

> All strands of contemporary mainstream macroeconomics share the strong belief that macroeconomic theory must be based on sound microfoundations, which is generally interpreted as macroeconomics being based on neoclassical microeconomic foundations. In other words, macroeconomic analysis must be consistent with the fundamental features of the neoclassical model of the economy. In this chapter, I argue that macroeconomics must indeed be based on rigorous microeconomic foundations, but this does not imply that the microfoundations of macroeconomics must be neoclassical. (Sardoni 2002, p. 4)

He criticizes the New Keynesians Bruce Greenwald and Joseph Stiglitz (1987, pp. 127–31) for suggesting that Keynes was inconsistent on this question. While they accept that Keynes (correctly) had microfoundations, Greenwald and Stiglitz claim that they were 'essentially traditional and incompatible with his vision of the working of the macroeconomy'. They cite Chapter 18 of the *General Theory*, Sardoni notes, which Post Keynesians regard as 'one of the chapters where the innovative character of Keynes's economics appears most clearly'(Sardoni 2002, p. 12 n5). Sardoni's own position is that 'Keynes indeed based his macroeconomic theory on microeconomic foundations that were essentially non-neoclassical' (ibid., p. 5), especially with respect to entrepreneurial investment decisions.

Even Sardoni, in places, weakens his commitment to microfoundations: 'the observed macro-phenomena are the outcome of individual decisions and actions; therefore a satisfactory analysis of the working of the macroeconomy requires that individual behavior be analyzed' (ibid., p. 6); this is not a statement of the case for micro-reduction. And again: 'Although I share the conviction that the behavior of individuals is conditioned by macroeconomic factors, I also believe that this should not imply that the development of macroeconomic analysis can be carried out by *ignoring* microeconomic issues. It cannot be ignored that aggregate outcomes derive, *though in a non-simplistic way*, from individual decisions and actions' (p. 11; stress added).

My second example of a Post Keynesian supporter of microfoundations is Tae-Hee Jo, who gave his 2007 University of Missouri-Kansas City PhD thesis the title 'Microfoundations of Effective Demand' (UMKC 2007). As he writes in an article summarizing his thesis, Jo's stress is on the 'social provisioning process', which 'means that all the economic activities are occurring in a social context – cultural values, class/power relations, norms, ideologies, and ecological system' (Jo 2011, p. 1098). He claims not to be an individualist, since 'both methodological individualism and methodological holism become irrelevant to the explanation of the social provisioning process ... it is the genuine interaction between social agency and/structures that are [*sic*] to be understood and explained' Thus 'heterodox microfoundations begins [*sic*] with active human agency embedded in the social provisioning process' (ibid., pp. 1101–2). The third of Jo's four-point conclusion is: '(3) The conventional micro-macro dichotomy is to be rejected. The account of social provisioning requires microfoundations of macroeconomics beyond fallacious neoclassical microfoundations by focusing on embedded behaviors and on the in-depth analysis of the historical provisioning process' (ibid., p. 1110).

8.3 THE OPPONENTS

Despite the claims of some of their interpreters, I think that it is clear that the founding fathers of Post Keynesian macroeconomics would have had no truck with the microfoundations dogma. As demonstrated in Chapter 5, Keynes was an implicit critic of microfoundations; his repeated assertion of the need to provide a 'theory of Output and Employment *as a whole*' (Keynes 1936, p. 293; original stress) really cannot be interpreted in any other way. The same is true of Kalecki, as Peter Kriesler maintains. As we saw in Chapter 3, Kriesler argues that, for Kalecki, 'the micro and the macro analyses ... lie side by side interdependently, that is, on an equal footing' (Kriesler 1989, p. 136). Kriesler concludes by suggesting

> ... a return to the classical method of analysis ... once again emphasizing the similarity in method between Kalecki and the classical economists. That is, one first considers (say) the microanalysis, holding output constant. At the next stage the level of profits can be considered, with pricing and distribution held constant. These, together, then determine the level of output, which is then used to modify the previous analysis of pricing and distribution. The *iterative process* will continue until either the system's solutions result in stable outcomes for all the processes or some dynamic can be determined. (Ibid., p. 138; stress added)

Kriesler concludes by citing the Sraffa scholar Alessandro Roncaglia (1978, p. 22) on the implications of the classical method.

As Heinz Kurz has recently noted, Piero Sraffa himself was a strong critic of neoclassical theory on precisely this issue. His study of early 20th-century developments in the natural sciences led Sraffa to

> ... the question of whether the parts should be seen as constitutive of the whole, or vice versa. Marginalist economics, starting from methodological individualism, advocated the former view. Sraffa implicitly rejected this position by developing his analysis not from given individual agents but [from] a 'given system of production'. (Kurz 2008, p. 71)

To the best of my knowledge Joan Robinson, who was Sraffa's friend and tireless advocate, never wrote anything explicitly on the issue of microfoundations, though she would certainly also have regarded the notion that macroeconomics could be reduced to microeconomics as absurd. Robinson did touch on the matter in her last major paper, 'What are the questions?' In mainstream theory, she wrote:

> The analysis of markets is treated under the heading of micro theory, but it cannot be understood without some indication of the macro setting in which it operates. A prisoner-of-war camp, a village fair, and the shopping center of a modern city cannot all be treated in exactly the same terms. The macro setting of the analysis of 'scarce means with alternative uses' is very vaguely sketched [by orthodox theorists]. It appears to rely upon Say's Law, for the scarce means are always fully employed. (Robinson 1977, p. 1320)

In a footnote to this passage she comments sardonically on the assumption that excess supply of any commodity leads inexorably to a zero price. In the case of labour, this means a zero wage: 'presumably the workers must have died long ago' (ibid., p. 1320, n. 3)

Like Robinson, Nicholas Kaldor did not make any direct statement on the question of microfoundations. However, as we saw in Chapter 3 he defended his macroeconomic theory of income distribution against the criticisms of neoclassical Keynesians like Samuelson and Modigliani on the explicitly macroeconomic grounds that parameter values that he had chosen were not arbitrary, but were a necessary condition for the survival of the capitalist system (above, pp. 41–2). Moreover, as Ramesh Chandra and Roger Sandilands (2010) have noted, Kaldor's subsequent emphasis on increasing returns to scale, derived from Adam Smith and Allyn Young, was also explicitly macroeconomic. Costs in any particular (manufacturing) industry are a decreasing function of the rate of growth of (manufacturing) output as a whole, they maintain, which suggests that an important element of downward causation is at work in Kaldor's later growth theory. In his widely read lecture on the causes of the slow growth rate in post-war Britain, Kaldor makes this point explicitly, describing dynamic increasing returns to scale as a 'macro-phenomenon', since each industry benefitted from the expansion not just of its own output but also of output as a whole (Kaldor 1966, p. 9).

But Kaldor also offers a salutary example of the difficulties caused by confusing microfoundations with what I defined in Chapter 3 as the social and philosophical foundations of macroeconomics. In the final years of his life he became convinced that the New Keynesian economist Martin Weitzman had

> demonstrated that constant returns to scale, strictly interpreted, are a sufficient condition for the absence of involuntary unemployment. The latter arises because a worker who is not offered a job cannot turn himself into his own employer (in the manner originally suggested by Wicksell) since he cannot compete effectively with firms organised for large-scale production. (Kaldor 1983, p. 12)

Kaldor agreed with Weitzman that Keynesian macroeconomics, which hinged on the principle of effective demand, was inconsistent with Keynes's own assumption of perfect competition. 'There is a sense therefore in which the natural habitat of effective demand macroeconomics is a monopolistically competitive micro-economy. Analogously, perfect competition and classical macroeconomics are natural counterparts' (Weitzman 1982, p. 801, cited by Kaldor 1983, p. 13). I suspect that Kaldor never referred to microfoundations in so many words but that, if pressed, he might not have rejected the notion.

Now Kaldor was quite clearly wrong, on two levels. First, there is the fatal slide from 'perfect competition' to 'long-run equilibrium in perfect competition', which is all the more surprising since it came from someone who had become a strident opponent of any form of equilibrium theorizing in economics. Outside long-run equilibrium, there is absolutely no reason why a perfectly competitive firm should not operate with excess capacity. The neoclassical firm will remain in operation so long as price exceeds average variable cost; in a recession this will normally involve a profit-maximizing (loss-minimizing) output lower than the level that would minimize average total cost. Thus it could increase output without an increase in average cost, which is a sufficient condition for the existence of excess capacity. Second, and more important, there is a neglect of capitalist reality. The reason why the unemployed cannot (all) employ themselves has nothing to do with the shape of the firm's demand or cost curves, and everything to do with their lack of capital. To take an historical example: the mid-nineteenth century British cotton industry was probably as close to the textbook case of perfect competition as any manufacturing industry before or since, with a near-homogeneous product, free entry and exit, and a minimum-cost scale of output that was small relative to the industry's output. Yet the suggestion that with a little more ambition or initiative the many unemployed cotton operatives could have become self-employed would have been treated with derision in (say) 1842 or 1878, and rightly so. They did not have the capital. Otherwise they would have been capitalists, not (unemployed) workers; and if they had all become capitalists there would have been no wage labourers, and therefore no capitalists either. Kaldor seems to have believed (wrongly) that he needed microfoundations, yet it was his unfortunate neglect of social and philosophical foundations that led him astray.

Luigi Pasinetti is a strong critic of the microfoundations dogma, and claims that his position was shared not only by Kaldor but also by Robinson, Sraffa and two other prominent 'Cambridge Keynesians', Richard Goodwin and Richard Kahn:

> The Cambridge School proposed an analysis in which the macroeconomic dimension always came first with respect to the microeconomic dimension. The theoretical propositions of each member of the School always avoided starting from subjective behaviour (or preferences) and from the study of single individuals ... This does *not* mean a denial of the role of microeconomics as a field of economic investigation, but it *does* mean the impossibility of explaining crucial economic phenomena on the sole basis of microeconomic behaviour. (Pasinetti 2005, p. 843; original stress)

This is an accurate summary of the views of the five theorists under discussion (though Kaldor, as we have just seen, was not entirely consistent on this issue).

Pasinetti might have added Wynn Godley to his list. Interviewed by the sociologist Robert Evans in the mid-1990s, and asked specifically about microfoundations, Godley replied: 'Well, … when people speak of microfoundations they tend to mean by that a very special thing, which is it's all deducible in terms of the optimizing behaviour of individual rational agents, and I don't accept that as an appropriate concept' (Evans 1997, p. 436, cited by Mata 2011, p. 20). In his book on the Cambridge Post Keynesians, Pasinetti makes it very clear that he himself rejects the need for microfoundations, explicitly denying the possibility of micro-reduction in economics by reference to the fallacy of composition and to emergent macroeconomic properties (Pasinetti 2007, pp. 277–9). In Pasinetti's own theoretical system, the crucial equation 13, which establishes the conditions that are necessary for full employment and 'full expenditure', is 'a single truly macroeconomic relation' (ibid., p. 285).

In an influential radical assessment of Post Keynesian economics at the beginning of the 1980s, the radical American theorist James Crotty had already emphasized their denial of the microfoundations dogma as one of the principal contributions of the Cambridge Keynesians:

> Unexplained preferences of isolated individuals with respect to consumption matters over time have been removed from center stage. Capital accumulation is seen as an autonomous, self-sustaining process … Once it has taken hold in an era, it tends to *create* the micro conditions necessary for its reproduction. Thus, the standard logical relation between microeconomics and macroeconomics is reversed and Marx's question is posed once again: *What is the macro foundation of microeconomics*? (Crotty 1980, p. 23, original stress)

He has developed his critique of the microfoundations dogma in subsequent work (Crotty 1994, 1996).

Another theorist with Post Keynesian sympathies who was explicitly critical of microfoundations was George Shackle, whose work forms something of a bridge between Keynes and Austrian economics. Shackle is very clear that order at the macro level might very well co-exist with a lack of order at the micro level. This is implied by the law of large numbers, he maintains, and is entirely consistent with an emphasis on the individual's freedom to choose:

> There is, on the one hand, the objective aggregative mechanical predictive dynamics sought by the econometricians, and on the other the subjective private

> descriptive dynamics of the individual ... it may be permissible and convenient to have a short-term predictive dynamics of the economy as a whole even when, by assuming individual free will, we preclude ourselves from a predictive dynamics of the individual. (Shackle 1954, p. 747)

There is nothing wrong with the econometrician treating the economy 'as a machine whose future behaviour, in the absence of shocks from outside itself, is fully determined by its history over some stretch of the past, so that this future behaviour is in principle predictable'. This would allow the production of an 'objective' theory of the economy:

> This theory concerns the total results of what is done by large numbers of people all taken together, and is thus 'aggregative'. It treats this mass of people as though they constituted a machine with a stable, knowable structure whose manifested result is capable of being described by differential equations or at any rate by integro-differential equations. Thus the theory can be called 'mechanical'. (Ibid., p. 748)

The study of individual choice, Shackle continues, is quite different. It is 'descriptive and not predictive', 'private and subjective and not public and objective' (ibid., p. 749).

To repeat: both types of theory, for Shackle, are both 'permissible and convenient', a position recently endorsed in very similar terms by Alan Kirman (2011a, 2011b).

Another critic of microfoundations who was also a Post Keynesian of sorts was the eclectic Austrian economist Kurt Rothschild. His position is particularly interesting, as his celebrated early paper on price theory and oligopoly (Rothschild 1947) is sometimes seen as an early exercise in Post Keynesian microfoundations; this is how Geoff Harcourt described it to me in our 1992 conversation (King 1995, p. 181). Forty years later, however, Rothschild had become a forceful critic of the microfoundations dogma. His case against microfoundations is based on the virtues of methodological pluralism in a complex and uncertain world:

> A freedom from narrow methodological prescriptions has often proved to be an essential precondition for new insights and the birth of new theories; and this is no less true for the natural sciences than for the social sciences. The greater the complexity of a phenomenon and its interrelated elements, the greater the importance of attacking the problem from different angles and with a variety of methods. (Rothschild 1988, p. 17)

Rothschild is unconvinced by mainstream accusations of 'ad hocery', which, he argues (citing the philosopher Paul Feyerabend), 'is not a theoretical weakness but can be … a necessary element in the difficult stages of developing new theories or extending old ones' (ibid., p. 17). In his last book, published in the year before his death, Rothschild begins his discussion of Keynes with an attack on the microfoundations dogma, and he comes back to it on two subsequent occasions (Bürger and Rothschild 2009, pp. 28, 142, 146).

There are many more twenty-first century examples of Post Keynesian hostility to the microfoundations dogma. Paul Ormerod, for example, invokes complexity theory to make a sharp criticism of RARE microfoundations in the context of the Global Financial Crisis of 2007–08. 'In the brave new world of DSGE', he writes, 'the possibility of a systemic collapse, of a cascade of defaults across the system, was never envisaged at all. Modern complexity theory', however, 'and specifically network theory, tells us that in an interconnected system, the *same* initial shock can, if we could replay history many times, lead to dramatically different outcomes' (Ormerod 2009, p. 11; original stress). Ormerod's principal criticisms are directed against the 'rational expectations' component of the RARE acronym, but the principle of 'increasing connectedness between financial institutions' that he emphasizes (ibid., p. 14) points also to the fallacy of composition and to the rejection of microfoundations.

The Kaleckians, Eckhard Hein and Till van Treeck, identify three growth regimes, two of them characterized by fallacies of composition: the 'paradox of accumulation' in finance-led growth regimes, and the 'paradox of profits' in contractive regimes. In the first case, 'at the micro level, firms restrict capital accumulation in order to increase the rate of profit, but at the macro level the conditions are such that the rate of capital accumulation increases together with the rate of profit', while in the second case 'at the micro level, firms reduce capital accumulation in order to increase the rate of profit, but at the macro level this leads to a falling rate of accumulation and a falling rate of profit, too' (Hein and van Treeck 2010, p. 229). Everything depends on the values of the relevant parameters. Only in the third, 'profits without investment', regime is there no danger of a fallacy of composition. Similar models are developed by several of the contributors to Hein and Stockhammer (2011).

Finally, there are two authors who emphasize the importance of money as a reason for rejecting the microfoundations dogma. One is Sergio Rossi, who, in a paper entitled 'Financial stability requires macroeconomic foundations of macroeconomics', argues that that there is an *a priori* case for rejecting microfoundations where money is the subject of analysis: 'The macroeconomic foundations of macroeconomics are not empirical laws, derived from constant series of events and influenced by the agents' forms of behaviour. *Independently of individual or collective behaviour*, the macrofoundations stem from the flow nature of money and concern *the logical structure* of payments relating to production and exchange' (Rossi 2010, p. 68; stress added). Equally, John Smithin is concerned to defend the autonomy of monetary macroeconomics, since '[t]he example of money is, in fact, the very model of a social fact or social institution. It contains each of the three elements described above, collective intentionality, the assignment of function, and a constitutive rule (e.g. the statement that the note is legal tender)' (Smithin 2009, p. 50). Money is in fact a *prerequisite* for private property, markets and capitalist profit; without it, there are no individual economic agents to engage in transactions with each other.

Writing about the original Post Keynesians – he cites Keynes, Kalecki, Kaldor, Robinson, Abba Lerner, Sidney Weintraub and (more contentiously) Davidson – Smithin notes that 'their aggregative functions were not usually based on putative microeconomic assumptions, but plausible conjectures or hypotheses as to the behavior of the system as a whole' (Smithin 2004, p. 57). It is possible to 'work backwards, as it were, and specify particular functional forms for utility functions, maximands and constraints, which in combination will yield the originally hypothesized [macro] results ... The important point which should be made, however, is that this laborious discovery does not actually add anything in terms of discoveries about how the economy works' (ibid., p. 58). But there is 'no need to posit any kind of group mind or collective consciousness to explain the evolution of social institutions'. In this context Smithin invokes the support of Marx (Smithin 2009, p. 52), who wrote, in a well-known passage in *The Eighteenth Brumaire of Louis Bonaparte*: 'Men make their own history, but they do not make it just as they please; they do not make it under circumstances chosen by themselves, but under circumstances directly encountered, given and transmitted from the past' (Marx 1852, p. 247).

8.4 THE UNCERTAIN

Between the Post Keynesian supporters and the critics of microfoundations, there is a substantial intermediate category: those who have been unclear, ambivalent or plain careless in their use of the word. As we shall see, it includes some of the very best Post Keynesian theorists. In roughly chronological order, in this section I implicate Sidney Weintraub, Geoff Harcourt, John Cornwall, Victoria Chick, Alessandro Vercelli, Amitava Dutt and

Giuseppe Fontana. One of the Post Keynesians who has written on economic methodology, Jesper Jespersen, also belongs in this category, but his views will be considered in the chapter that follows, on the methodologists (pp. 212–13 below).

As we saw in Chapter 5, the term 'microfoundations' was invented by Sidney Weintraub, the father of Post Keynesian economics in the United States. But it is a simple matter to demonstrate that he did not really mean it. As Jan Kregel has shown,

> [T]he two levels of Weintraub's analysis are the obverse of one another, the demand-outlay analysis providing the microfoundations of the aggregate demand curve and the aggregate supply and demand curves providing the macrofoundations for the microeconomic demand for labor curve. The aggregate supply curve supports the actual or market aggregate demand curve in precisely the same way as the micro labor demand curve supports the actual or market labor supply path. (Kregel 1985, p. 552)

Thus, for Weintraub, 'involuntary unemployment depends on the *macro*foundations of labor demand, and not on conditions in the labor market alone' (ibid., p. 554; original stress), though Weintraub does not use the term 'macrofoundations'. Kregel himself is a firm advocate of 'macrofoundations for microeconomics', which he regards as a necessary consequence of a non-ergodic economic universe, in which

> … individual actions are constrained by the actions of other individuals which cannot be predicted with certainty and thus when taken together form an aggregate or global or macroeconomic constraint which is not the simple, linear, and therefore predictable summation of individual behaviour. Thus it is not macroeconomics that has to be brought into closer touch with microeconomics, but rather one must try to formulate a macrofoundation for uncertain individual decisions. (Kregel 1987, p. 528)

Here Kregel takes a stronger line against microfoundations than the position that he attributes to Weintraub.

Geoff Harcourt was co-organizer of the 1975 S'Agaro conference, and edited the conference volume. However, like two of the other Post Keynesians who took part (Tom Asimakopulos and Mario Nuti), Harcourt did not address the issue of microfoundations. At the annual meeting of the American Economic Association five years later he defended the Post Keynesians from Lorie Tarshis's (1980) criticism of their microfoundations, which Tarshis regarded as insufficiently realistic. Harcourt cited his own work with Peter Kenyon on pricing and the investment decision (Harcourt and Kenyon 1976). In the same brief comment, he 'heartily endorse[d]' James Crotty's 'reference to Marx's view that it is macro-economic processes which tend to create required micro-economic structures' (Harcourt 1980, p. 27). Harcourt told me, in our 1993 conversation, that 'the microfoundations of macroeconomics ha[s] been my most sustained interest all my life' (King 1995, p. 181). And yet, in his valedictory lecture upon his retirement from Cambridge in 2010, Harcourt criticized modern mainstream economics for rejecting any role for 'the fallacy of composition, a vital strand of the economics of Keynes'. This meant that the mainstream has rejected the 'core Keynesian insight that the whole is often greater than the sum of the parts' (Harcourt 2010, p. 48).

John Cornwall provided an ambiguous statement concerning microfoundations in his important book on *Modern Capitalism*:

> [T]he fact that the present study will not explicitly derive the micro-underpinnings of the model does not in any way imply that such an extension is not possible. If the arguments to follow are at all convincing, then the analysis should be suggestive of means to extend micro-theory in ways that takes accounts [*sic*] of the constraints on the form of rational behaviour introduced by the numerous types of frictions and imperfections accounted for here. (Cornwall 1977, p. 41)

Despite the reference to 'under-pinnings', this could be interpreted as an early statement of the importance of downward causation. In later work, however, he drew on institutionalist ideas like those of Geoff Hodgson (below, pp. 193–4), to argue that institutions 'enable action, by prescribing behaviour when it is impossible to identify an optimal response to a situation … institutions provide relatively enduring macrofoundations for economic behaviour; they act as a quasi-inert "operating system" within which the income-generating process functions, producing protracted periods of either better or worse macroeconomic performance depending on the degree of "institutional fitness"' (Setterfield and Thirlwall 2010, p. 489; cf. Cornwall and Cornwall 2001).

Victoria Chick did not devote a specific chapter, or part of a chapter, to economic methodology in her influential *Macroeconomics after Keynes*. One reviewer interpreted her overall position as one of hostility to microfoundations, since she 'argues that Keynes thought in a "holistic" manner, in sharp contrast to the reductionist approach of much of subsequent Keynesian analysis. She reminds us that Keynes regarded the macroeconomic approach as distinctive, dealing with aggregative behaviour where the whole is not the sum of the parts. Macroeconomics is seen not as simply a matter of aggregating up from micro-foundations' (Foster 1984, p. 361). Against this interpretation, it should be noted that Chapter 5 is entitled 'The microfoundations of aggregate supply'. Here Chick seems to argue that Say's Law was a logical consequence of the neglect of micro-foundations by Ricardo and his contemporaries: 'On the face of it, ignoring demand seems absurd, but it arises from viewing the aggregate functions as originating or having validity at the aggregate level directly, instead of being derived from microeconomic behaviour' (Chick 1983, p. 82). Chick does not elaborate, but in the following chapter she refers to the large body of theoretical and empirical work on consumption and investment that had been accomplished since Keynes: 'almost all that work is entirely rooted in microeconomic behaviour (indeed plans and decisions must be formulated at that level), though in the case of investment in particular, not rooted in any sound microeconomic principles (for good reason), and not orientated towards re-integration with macroeconomics' (ibid., p. 103). The metaphors are ambiguous: 'integration' and 'rooting' point to very different relationships between micro and macro, and there are earlier references to 'the link' between them (ibid., p. 83).

Chick's position became a little clearer twenty years later, when she argued that 'consistency between a theory of decision making (microeconomics) and the overall outcome of decisions (macroeconomics) cannot, in general, be achieved. Some "slippage", some compromise of internal consistency, is bound to arise' (Chick 2002, p. 55). Keynes's theory of investment, she concludes, is precisely such a compromise; it 'favours his macroeconomics, allowing him to determine the properties of equilibrium in his system while giving a result for disequilibrium also' (ibid., pp. 66–7). She therefore rejects the possibility of 'impeccably logical micro-foundations', which could be provided only at the expense of 'the logic of the whole' (ibid., p. 55). This seems quite close to the 'in principle reductionist, in practice anti-reductionist' position of Herbert Simon (see above pp. 35, 69).

In his book on the *Methodological Foundations of Macroeconomics*, Alessandro Vercelli is severely critical of New Classical macroeconomics and defends Keynes against Robert Lucas and his allies. In the concluding chapter, though, Vercelli appears to endorse the micro-foundations dogma. He is (correctly) keen 'to defend the autonomy of macroeconomics', which was threatened by the New Classicals. However,

> This does not imply that we should give up making serious efforts to provide rigorous micro-foundations for our macroeconomic statements, if that means

> searching for greater consistency between the two disciplines. In other words we should continue to pursue a full synthesis between microeconomics and macroeconomics. Many things have been learned from past attempts, unsuccessful as they were, and many others may be understood through further efforts. (Vercelli 2008, p. 236)

This is a very confusing passage. Providing *micro-foundations* is not the same thing as ensuring *greater consistency*, which is in any case a much less ambitious project than achieving a *full synthesis*. Elsewhere in the book Vercelli does seem to acknowledge the problems that arise with the quest for microfoundations. He is, for example, unimpressed by the principle of methodological individualism (ibid., pp. 102, 113), and cites the important passage from Keynes's *Essays in Biography* in which Keynes suggests that, in the social sciences, the atomic hypothesis breaks down and 'the whole is not the sum of the parts' (ibid., p. 224 n10, citing Keynes 1926, p. 150). This alone, as we have seen, is enough to bury the notion of microfoundations (above, p. 76). But it comes in a footnote, and it really should have been placed in the text and given much more emphasis. Vercelli is also (justifiably) hostile to inter-theoretic reductionism: 'the only known way to reduce biology to chemistry is murder' (ibid., p. 236). Yet he refuses to draw the appropriate conclusions from his own argument.

In a paper that is as yet unpublished, Amitava Dutt 'argues that microfoundations are indeed important for heterodox macroeconomics and makes the case for an analysis of the economy that privileges neither the micro nor the macro side' (Dutt 2006, p. 1). 'Neglect of the individual can lead to various problems with heterodox macroeconomic analysis', he maintains, including the use of 'mark-up pricing models and Marxian crisis models that generate great instability but ignore the appropriate mechanisms, based on individual decisions', that are involved (ibid., pp. 20, 22). Dutt concludes by affirming the importance of achieving consistency between the micro and macro aspects of economics'. This is 'an approach that cuts the Gordian knot at neither micro nor macro but somewhere between them, (although I would hesitate to call it meso, given its ambiguities), and reaches towards the extremes from that middle … [it] follows a methodology distinct from the neoclassical one, using accounting identities and empirically-based behavioural identities, while eschewing the optimizing individual' (ibid., pp. 23, 24).

Finally, Giuseppe Fontana notes that 'Post Keynesian economists are well known for their critical views of recent developments in economics. In particular, they have been on the front line in arguing against the modern

New Keynesian search for the microeconomic foundations of macro-economics ... They argue that, if anything, it is microeconomics that is in urgent need of macroeconomic foundations' (Fontana 2009, p. 61); he cites the 1980 paper by James Crotty at this point. Fontana thus 'supports the Post Keynesian claim that the obsessive search in modern economics for the microeconomic foundations of macroeconomics is fallacious because, if anything, it is microeconomics that is in urgent need of macroeconomic foundations. The microeconomic foundations of macroeconomics must thus be complemented by the macroeconomic foundations of micro-economics' (ibid., p. 70). And here, as if to complete the circle, Fontana cites Geoff Harcourt (Harcourt 2006, p. 3).

8.5 A SPECIAL CASE: SHEILA DOW

For more than three decades Sheila Dow has been the most influential Post Keynesian writer on methodological questions. Her first incursion into the debate on microfoundations came in 1981, in an extended review article of E. Roy Weintraub's (1979) *Microfoundations*, an important text that was discussed in Chapter 6 (above, pp. 112–13). She is best known, however, for her *Methodology of Macroeconomic Thought* (1985b, 1996), a substantial comparative study of Austrian, Marxian, neoclassical and Post Keynesian macroeconomics from the perspective of a methodologist, and for *Economic Methodology: An Inquiry* (2002). Dow has also published many articles on similar themes.

In her critique of Weintraub, Dow is principally concerned to attack the 'neo-Walrasian microfoundations' that he is uncritically defending and to deny his contention that 'some sort of revivified, reconstituted general equilibrium theory is the only logically possible general link between microeconomics and macroeconomics' (Weintraub 1979, p. 161, cited by Dow 1981, p. 329). She intends instead to promote the virtues of a very different (Post) Keynesian microeconomics derived from the behavioural theory of the firm, in which both human institutions and 'market imperfections' such as money wage rigidity are to be welcomed as major sources of macroeconomic stability. The microfoundations dogma is tangential to Dow's argument, though she does at this early stage in the controversy identify the principal problem with RARE microfoundations. There is an inconsistency at the heart of the argument, she suggests: 'the micro-foundations literature is essentially reductionist; for consistency and completeness, reductionism should go down to the level of individual human behavior; for reductionists, the "representative firm" and "representative household" should be meaningless concepts' (Dow 1981, p. 334).

At one point, too, Dow poses the central question, which she surprisingly attributes to Weintraub himself: 'can neoclassical microeconomics be made compatible with neoclassical macroeconomics? In other words, can the two paradigms be fused, and does the fallacy of composition – or any other consideration – preclude the fusion of two levels of aggregation?' (ibid., p. 330). But she does not comment on the relationship between inter-theoretic *fusion* and inter-theoretic *reduction*, which are very different operations. Dow does not offer an answer of her own to Weintraub's question, though she does invoke the fallacy of composition for a second time in her discussion of the connection between Keynesian micro-economics and Keynesian macroeconomics:

> There may be inconsistencies between the two levels of theory arising from the fallacy of composition (e.g. of the widow's cruse variety). But as part of a paradigm (the post Keynesian paradigm), they are perfectly consistent. Indeed, the cross-fertilization is particularly fruitful in the area of cost-plus theories of firms' pricing behavior and their central role in theories of inflation. (Ibid., p. 331)

(The 'widow's cruse' refers to an Old Testament parable cited by Keynes in the *Treatise on Money* in a striking anticipation of Kalecki's theory of profits: 'capitalists get what they spend', just as the biblical widow found her jar of cooking oil miraculously replenished each morning by exactly the amount that she had taken out to cook the previous evening's meal). It is, of course, the *reduction* of macro to micro that is ruled out by the fallacy of composition, not any possibility of *consistency* or *cross-fertilization* between them; Dow's language could have been a little clearer, as she now acknowledges.

Roy Weintraub's reaction to her criticisms can be inferred from the title of his reply: 'Substantive Mountains and Methodological Molehills'. The neo-Walrasian and Post Keynesian research programmes, he claims in Lakatosian vein, are 'only incidentally different in method' but have fundamental differences in their theoretical 'hard core', above all in their treatment of equilibrium outcomes (if any) and the role (if any) of institutional change (Weintraub 1982–3, p. 301). There is no reference to micro-foundations in his nine-page paper, other than to the title of his book. In her rejoinder Dow took a significant methodological step backwards, objecting only to the neo-Walrasian nature of Weintraub's microfoundations and not to the microfoundations dogma as such. Indeed, she recommends her book

Money Matters, co-authored with Peter Earl, 'for a treatment of monetary economics with post Keynesian microfoundations' (Dow 1982–3, p. 306). There is now no mention of the complications that might be posed by the fallacy of composition.

Chapter 14 of *Money Matters* includes a section headed 'Monetarist Microfoundations', without any consideration of the methodological issues involved (Dow and Earl 1982, pp. 185–92), while the authors' own 'disequilibrium behavioural microeconomics ... as a starting point' is in effect presented as their alternative, anti-monetarist microfoundation: the concept without the word (ibid., p. 173). But there is also a brief and very critical discussion of 'reductionist theories' that treat 'individual components ... as if they are microcosmic representations of the aggregate features' (ibid., p. 178). 'One interpretation of the message of the *General Theory*', with which they evidently sympathize, 'shifted attention away from the relative price concerns so central to reductionist theory and focused on aggregates of income and expenditure' (ibid., p. 179). However, the tension between advocating microfoundations and resisting reductionism is not satisfactorily resolved.

Dow devotes a full chapter of her *Methodology of Macroeconomic Thought* to 'The Micro-foundations of Macroeconomics'. Here she restates her 1981 position: 'The fallacy of composition is a central feature of any discussion of microfoundations; according to this fallacy, individual actions, if common to a large number of individuals, will generate an outcome different from what was intended by each' (Dow 1996, p. 85; see also p. 99) – and, more importantly, she might have added, different from what might have been inferred by an independent observer from the actions of each. The four schools of macroeconomic thought take quite different positions on this question, she maintains:

> At one extreme, neo-Austrians avoid the problem by arguing that there is no macroeconomic knowledge other than that generated by micro-foundations. The polar version of Marxian theory suggests that there is no microeconomic knowledge other than what derives from the macro, or class, level. (Ibid., p. 108)

(This is probably a little too strong in both cases, as we shall see in the case of the Austrians in Chapter 9). The great majority of mainstream macroeconomists, Dow continues, believe that the Hicksian 'programme for resolving the micro-foundations issue has been successful' – so successful, in fact, that 'the issue is now (with a few exceptions, such as Janssen (1993), seldom raised' (ibid., p. 108).

Dow's discussion of the question in Post Keynesian thought again emphasizes the need for consistency between micro and macro theory, and she rather confusingly describes this also as a requirement for 'holism'. 'Keynes', she writes, 'can be interpreted also as having taken a holistic approach in the sense that the *General Theory* was a logically consistent combination of micro and macro analysis, but the micro-foundations were not equivalent to neo-classical micro-foundations' (ibid., p. 98). The Post Keynesian approach, she concludes, 'is also a holistic approach which attempts to avoid any logical micro-macro inconsistency' (ibid., p. 108). Given the misunderstanding that 'holism' often engenders, it is probably a term better avoided in this context. More important, Dow provides no real discussion of reductionism in this chapter, and her references to Post Keynesian microfoundations (e.g. ibid., p. 98) sit rather uneasily with the recognition that in Post Keynesian theory 'the unit of analysis is frequently groups, on the grounds that this provides macro-foundations for micro-economic behaviour' (ibid., p. 109). In this sense, Dow notes, citing Crotty (1980), 'it is the aggregate which governs the individual, rather than the other way round' (ibid., p. 99). She took a stronger line in the earlier (article) version of this chapter, published in the *Eastern Economic Journal*, which includes the following, unambiguous statement: 'The Keynesian method is not reductionist, and thus does not require the derivation of all theory from the behavior of individuals' (Dow 1985a, p. 350). It is unfortunate that nothing quite as clear as this can be found in either edition of her *Methodology of Macroeconomic Thought*.

In *Economic Methodology: An Inquiry* there are two brief allusions to microfoundations. One comes in Dow's analysis of postmodernist philosophy, which encourages a shift in attention 'from the general to the particular'. An example in economics, in recent decades, has been 'a gradual project to build up the microfoundations of macroeconomics, that is, to express aggregate outcomes as the results of rational individual behaviour' (Dow 2002, p. 123). I suspect, though, that any postmodernist influence on the microfoundations dogma must have been both indirect and unconscious. Roy Weintraub is briefly referred to in this context, but it is hard to think of any proponent of RARE microfoundations, the Ramsey model and the monolithic mathematical majesty of 'modern macroeconomics' in the Wickens (2008) mode who would give a postmodern philosopher the time of day. Earlier in the book Dow makes another brief allusion to microfoundations, this time in the context of Post Keynesian analyses of credit rationing and Hyman Minsky's financial instability hypothesis:

> Both the credit-rationing case and the financial instability hypothesis are relatively straightforward in their translation from the micro-level to the macro-level, because each deals with systematic changes which can be expected to apply across the economy. The Minsky approach, however, suggests that it is not only macro-events like monetary policy action which can impinge on the micro-level; confidence in expectations may not be best analysed at the individual level, but rather as responding to developments at the macro-level. (Ibid., p. 30)

But that is all.

Not until 2010 did Dow provide a vigorous critique of the microfoundations dogma as a whole when, in a paper on Keynes's approach to knowledge, expectations and rationality, she identifies a 'paradox of liquidity, whereby the attempt to make portfolios more liquid reduces liquidity in the system' as a whole. Dow continues by attacking Robert Lucas's unsuccessful attempt to 'subvert any fallacy of composition' (Dow 2010, pp. 4, 16). This, she explains, is why 'Keynes' general theory did not take the form of a single large model, including formal microfoundations ... Only if social conventions can be derived deductively from optimizing individual behaviour can they be incorporated in a bottom-up microfoundations framework'. Dow expresses some sympathy with the feminist economist Julie Nelson's suggestion 'that individual behaviour instead needs to be expressed in relation to macrofoundations, to capture the macro influences on the individual' (ibid., p. 20). On balance, though, Dow rejects this formulation, since 'danger lies, from a Keynesian perspective, in retaining the idea of the macro and micro levels as conceptually distinct, with one foundational to the other. How the reality is segmented for analytical purposes within a pluralist framework is a matter of judgment, and different partial analyses can focus on different directions of influence between the micro and macro levels' (ibid., pp. 20–21).

8.6 CONCLUSION

Why, then, did so many Post Keynesians come to endorse the microfoundations dogma, with or without reservations and hesitations, and why have relatively few of them explicitly denounced it? I have already conceded *mea culpa* in this regard, and as we saw in Sections 8.2 and 8.4 I have been in very good company. In the early days of Post Keynesianism, I suspect, the appeal of microfoundations was so great because it appeared to offer an additional, powerful weapon with which to attack the mainstream:

'our microfoundations are better than yours'; 'oligopoly is easier to reconcile with the principle of effective demand than perfect competition'. This analytical confidence and self-assertion is very clear in Davidson's contributions to the 1975 S'Agora debates. The worries expressed more recently by Dutt, Jo and others suggest that this confidence was misplaced. The continuing Post Keynesian quest for microfoundations is now, I suspect, much more of a defensive reaction to an increasingly aggressive and dogmatic economics profession. Microfoundations seem to have become essential if Post Keynesians are to engage the mainstream, and to be able to publish in the leading journals. In an era of increasingly damaging research assessment exercises, this is becoming a career-determining, and potentially career-terminating, issue. As Smithin notes, the mainstream requirement for microfoundations has been imposed without any serious methodological discussion. While Hayek and others argue that methodological individualism is a necessary condition for human freedom, 'at the sharp end of academic trench warfare, involving editorial decisions at academic journals, hiring, tenure and promotion decisions, and the allocation of research funding, it is sometimes difficult to believe that any such philosophical reflection is going on' (Smithin 2009, p. 43).

However, given the relatively underdeveloped state of their microeconomics, Post Keynesians have also put themselves at a real competitive disadvantage with respect to the mainstream on this question. They find it very difficult to rebut the mainstream accusation that their own, Post Keynesian microfoundations are simply not up to the job, on all three criteria (above, p. 28). This is certainly true as regards *solidity*: fundamental and apparently irreconcilable differences continue to exist between the adherents of Davidson's 'Marshall–Keynes microeconomics', for example, and supporters of the Kalecki–Eichner 'oligopoly-administered pricing' alternative. There is no single, generally accepted version of Post Keynesian microeconomics, and (arguably) agreement is further away now than it was half a century ago. Neither is Post Keynesian microeconomics as *extensive* as its neoclassical rival – it is not even close. The Kalecki–Eichner approach to pricing and investment under oligopoly is probably its strong point (I am revealing my own preferences here), but other areas of microeconomics are still much less well developed. There has been some interesting work on the labour market, for example, but there is still no clear, comprehensive alternative to mainstream labour economics. The same can be said of consumer theory, which has in turn prevented the emergence of a distinctively Post Keynesian welfare economics (Jo 2012): how *should* economic goods be valued if the neoclassical notion of consumer surplus is repudiated? And this is not a purely academic problem. There have been some perceptive heterodox critiques of the Stern Report, but what, precisely, is the *positive* Post Keynesian alternative to mainstream policy prescriptions on global warming or on environmental issues more generally (Mearman 2009)?

Foundations, to repeat, *must come first*. The constitutive nature of the foundational metaphor is most evident, and most damaging, here (above, p. 14). It suggests that if you have no microfoundations your macroeconomics are necessarily flimsy and unsafe; in order to construct them, you must concentrate your energies on microeconomics. Probably the great majority of Post Keynesian macroeconomists would reject this conclusion, but it seems to follow inescapably if the microfoundations metaphor is accepted. Thus Post Keynesians would be well advised to shift their rhetoric from the vertical to the horizontal plane. And the same is true, as we shall see in the following chapter, for many heterodox economists of other persuasions.

9. The dissenters, part II: mainstreamers, Austrians and institutionalists

9.1 INTRODUCTION

As we saw in Chapters 5–6, there have always been economists who have doubted the microfoundations dogma. In Chapter 8 the opposition of many Post Keynesians was documented. In this chapter I distinguish three further categories of dissidents: mainstream economists, usually but not invariably of an Old Keynesian disposition, and Austrians and institutionalists from the heterodox camp. They are a very motley crew. As will become apparent in Section 9.2, the mainstream dissenters are united by a broad sympathy for Keynes, but not by very much else. One might expect the Austrians to be strong supporters of microfoundations on explicitly methodological grounds, since methodological individualism has always been a core Austrian principle. But they are also strongly opposed to neoclassical models of profit and utility maximization, and in practice, Austrian macroeconomics reveals clear pre-Keynesian (Wicksellian) roots. This is a complicated story, which is told in Section 9.3. The institutionalists are the subject of Section 9.4. While they tend to draw their macroeconomics, such as it is, from the Post Keynesians, the institutionalists also have some distinctive ideas on the relations between the social and the individual, and on the emergence of social properties, which are directly relevant to the relationship between micro and macroeconomic theory. In Section 9.5 I draw some general conclusions about the nature of dissent from the microfoundations dogma.

9.2 MAINSTREAM DISSENTERS

Support for the microfoundations dogma was pretty well unanimous among New Classical economists, and there was very substantial agreement too among New Keynesians. As we saw in Chapter 6, New Classical and New Keynesian theorists discovered the supposed virtues of providing 'rigorous microfoundations' for their macroeconomic analysis at approximately the same time, in the late 1970s and early 1980s. Even those New Keynesians who were unconvinced by the RARE microfoundations adopted by the great majority, such as Joseph Stiglitz, generally stated their opposition by asserting that 'ours are better than yours'. In Stiglitz's case, the crucial assumption was the existence of asymmetric information, which he claims to involve a much greater degree of realism than the majority position, eliminating the representative agent and casting doubt on the prevalence of rational expectations. As he wrote in 2006: 'Today, there is no disagreement that good macro-models must be based on microeconomic principles. But there is disagreement over what this entails ... not surprisingly, macro-economic analyses based on flawed micro-foundations are themselves flawed' (Stiglitz et al. 2006, p. 161).

Stiglitz made the same claims fifteen years earlier: 'There is now a general consensus that good macroeconomics must be built upon solid micro-foundations' (Stiglitz 1991, p. 8; see also Stiglitz 1992). He had no quarrel with this proposition, though he did note that, 'like all doctrinal positions, the contention that all macroeconomic work should begin with a specification of the microeconomic foundations can be carried too far' (Stiglitz 1991, p. 9). Stiglitz's main objection, however, is to the confusion between the general principle that microfoundations are necessary and the 'argument that there is a particular set of micro-foundations upon which it should be built: namely, competitive environments with rational agents operating with rational expectations in environments in which adverse selection and incentive (moral hazard) problems are largely absent' (ibid., p. 8). He repeated these propositions in a joint paper with Bruce Greenwald, and – most unusually for either New Classical or New Keynesian theorists – attempted to provide a rationale for microfoundations. 'The insistence on micro-foundations enhances the ability of economists to distinguish among alternative theories, and helps to set the research agenda ... the micro-foundations from which the aggregate behavior is derived can often be tested directly. A rejection of the underlying hypotheses should suffice to cast doubt on the validity of the derived macro-theory' (Greenwald and Stiglitz 1993, p. 24). This was Keynes's own position, they maintain: 'In fact, we would argue that Keynes did the best he could with the micro-foundations which were available at the time' (ibid., p. 25 n3).

Despite Stiglitz's claims to the contrary, however, there certainly was 'some disagreement' with the microfoundations dogma among mainstream economists. It came, first and foremost, from self-proclaimed Old Keynesians, and from the occasional Monetarist. A notable example of the former is William Baumol, who describes himself as a 'Keynesian' (with no qualifying adjective) and the *General Theory* as 'a work of genius'. 'Macroeconomics', Baumol argues, 'can be interpreted as the most effective simplifying breakthrough in the history of economic ideas'. While Keynesian macroeconomics might stand in need of substantial alterations, 'the one thing the work evidently does *not* need is complication for its own sake or for the sake of enhanced realism ... I have little sympathy for efforts to provide extensive microeconomic foundations for macroeconomic analysis' (Baumol 2009, p. 308; original stress). This does not mean that micro and macro had nothing to learn from each other. On the contrary, '[f]ull partnership with microeconomists is indispensable' (ibid., p. 314).

Prominent among the Monetarist dissenters is David Laidler, whose account of pre-Keynesian macroeconomics in *Fabricating the Keynesian Revolution* claims that the fallacy of composition had been acknowledged before 1936 by 'classical' theorists such as Frederick Lavington, A.C. Pigou and Ralph Hawtrey (Laidler 1999, pp. 84, 87, 126). In an earlier book, Laidler defended the autonomy of macroeconomics. 'Microfoundations may be interesting in their own right', as one critic summarized Laidler's position, 'but from a macroeconomic perspective they are technical details which can safely be left for later' (Bryant 1985, pp. 122–3, reviewing Laidler 1982). This was a little too generous to Laidler, who in subsequent work criticizes the microfoundations metaphor as an example of the 'Cartesian Fallacy' (Laidler 1992, p. 104) but also uses it without any explicit reservations. 'From the very outset', he writes in a very favourable review of a book of essays by Robert Clower, 'he has been concerned with the microeconomic foundations of monetary theory', and had succeeded in showing that 'monetary theory based on Walrasian foundations is inevitably trivial to the point of emptiness'. It is necessary to accomplish Clower's attempted revolution, Laidler concludes; this would involve 'some alternative general equilibrium notion' – but evidently not the abandonment of microfoundations in any form (Laidler 1986, p. 548).

Laidler's doubts were more evident in a 1988 conference paper, a sort of obituary for Monetarism, in which he tries to 'show how the search for sound microfoundations for monetarist propositions ended up undermining them' (Laidler 1990, p. 97). 'In the process of acquiring market-theoretic microfoundations', he suggests, macroeconomics has 'lost its separate identity' (ibid., p. 102). Unlike Robert Lucas (see Chapter 6), Laidler apparently does not regard this as a good thing. But he continues to use the term without explicit criticism (e.g. in a 1986 essay reprinted in the same volume: ibid., p. 61; see also Laidler 1999, pp. 339–40), and never decisively clarified his own position on whether the problem was *Walrasian* microfoundations, which 'trivialised money in the first place' (Laidler 2008, p. 16), or microfoundations of any variety, on the grounds that they were inconsistent with the necessary autonomy of macroeconomics. If Bryant's assessment was a little too kind to Laidler it was less than generous to Hicks (Bryant 1985, p. 123). The confident neoclassical synthesizer of *Value and Capital* shifted his ground towards the end of his life, leading Paul Davidson, an unyielding critic of all versions of mainstream macroeconomics, to welcome him as a late convert to the Post Keynesian camp (Davidson 1980) and to publish his 'explanation' of IS-LM – in effect a recantation – in the *Journal of Post Keynesian Economics* (Hicks 1980–81). As we saw in Chapter 6, Hicks's views on microfoundations were by 1980 much more nuanced than Bryant suggests (above, p. 113).

James Tobin, too, was beginning to have second thoughts on the issue of microfoundations. Tobin's (partial) recantation was all the more significant because, as noted in Chapter 5, his early efforts to provide microfoundations for the demand for money and for the firm's investment decisions marks him out as a pioneer of the dogma that, late in life, he came to doubt. As late as 1993, writing as a self-proclaimed 'unreconstructed old Keynesian', Tobin described the New Keynesian 'program to develop improved microeconomic foundations for imperfectly flexible prices' as 'certainly laudable objectives' that will 'make Keynes more palatable to theorists' (Tobin 1993, p. 47). Interestingly, the only explicit statements of his reservations about microfoundations that I have been able to trace come in two published interviews, with Brian Snowdon and Howard Vane in the same year (1993), and with David Colander in 1997. 'How important do you think it is for macroeconomics to have neoclassical choice-theoretic foundations?', Snowdon and Vane asked Tobin. His reply is worth quoting in full:

> Well, I think it's important for the behavioural equations of a macroeconomic model not to contradict choice-theoretic considerations, to be in principle consistent with them. But I think the stronger version of 'microfoundations' is a methodological mistake, one that has produced a tremendous amount of mischief. I refer to the now orthodox requirement of postulating representative agents whose optimizations generate 'macroeconomic' behavioural equations. That is a considerable sacrifice of the essence of much of macroeconomics. Suppose you have a lot of different types of agents, who are all maximizing. Then it's their aggregation into a behavioural equation that you want for a macro model. That aggregation won't necessarily be the solution for any single agent. To insist that it must be seems to me to be very wrong-headed. It has put us on the

> wrong track in macroeconomics or what passes for macroeconomics. (Snowdon and Vane 1999, p. 96)

When Colander asked how he explained the attraction of New Classical economics to younger theorists, Tobin noted that 'the idea that you should have microfoundations of everything you do, everything you say is going on in the economy, including short-run behavior, has a surface plausibility' but 'not much possible content' in a macroeconomic world that is characterized by 'what is obviously to me, disequilibrium behavior ... what it means is that you can't do any *macro*economics'. The result, Tobin continues, is a 'schism between abstract academic theory and practical macroeconomics' as carried out by government economists and central bankers who, Tobin contentiously implies, find little or no use for the supposedly micro-founded academic theory (Colander 1999, p. 125; original stress).

These conversations revealed doubts about microfoundations on the part of several of the interviewees. When Snowdon and Vane posed their standard question to Milton Friedman, he revealed his usual lack of enthusiasm (see Chapter 2):

> It is less important for macroeconomic models to have choice-theoretic microfoundations than it is for them to have empirical implications that can be subjected to refutation. Choice-theoretic microfoundations may provide hypotheses for improving macroeconomic models, but the key macroeconomic models have been of long standing and have had a great deal of success without the more recent emphasis on choice-theoretic microfoundations. (Snowdon and Vane 1999, p. 136)

The New Keynesian theorist N. Gregory Mankiw was equally sceptical:

> I am not sure that all macroeconomics necessarily has to start off with microeconomic building blocks. To give an analogy, all of biology is in some sense the aggregate of particle physics, because all biological creatures are made up of particles. That doesn't mean that the natural place to start in building biology is to start with particle physics and aggregate up. Instead I would probably start with theory at the level of the organism or the cell, not the level of the sub-atomic particle. We have a lot of models like the IS-LM model in macroeconomics that are very useful in studying the macroeconomy, even though those models don't start off with the individual unit and build up from there. (Ibid., p. 107)

Later in the conversation Mankiw was asked how successful research had been in recent years in 'providing a more substantial microfoundation for Keynesian economics'. He replied, in similar vein to Friedman, that this was an empirical matter. 'The jury is still out on that one. There is a small empirical literature, but I can probably count the number of empirical papers on the fingers of two hands. I hope it is a growth area, but so far the literature has not been as empirically oriented as I would like' (ibid., p. 120).

Even Robert Lucas denied that it was 'crucial' for macroeconomics to have choice-theoretic microfoundations. 'It depends on the purposes you want the model to serve'. Short-term forecasting models could do without them, but for the appraisal of major policy changes microfoundations were indispensable (Snowdon and Vane 1999, p. 158). Unfortunately Snowdon and Vane did not ask this question of the majority of their interviewees; it would have been useful to read the replies of Robert Clower, John Taylor, Olivier Blanchard, Franco Modigliani, Edward Prescott and Paul Romer. David Colander's own response is discussed below (pp. 185–6).

When Colander asked Tobin's colleague Robert Shiller whether there should be different methodologies for micro and macro, his reply was no less nuanced:

> The terms macro and micro represent schools of thought as much as different subject matter. The terms suggest that macro is an aggregation of micro but in fact the differences between these schools of thought are perhaps as much in terms of method as of subject matter. The difference is a bit analogous to calculus and geometry in math. Geometry naturally seems to lend itself toward [*sic*] axiomatization, but calculus is rarely presented to students as an axiomatized system. I think that macro can be, in this sense, more like calculus. We start from some intuitive feeling; we build little models but they're not complete models; they don't work from first principles and so there's often been more willingness to introduce real-world complexity in human behavior in macro than in micro. (Colander 1999, p. 138)

Perhaps, as Colander suggests, this interpretation reflects a distinctive 'Yale tradition' in macroeconomics (ibid., pp. 116–17).

Probably the most forthright and consistent Old Keynesian opponent of the microfoundations dogma, at least in its RARE version, has been Robert Solow. This is somewhat ironic, given the important role of the Solow growth model in the emergence of RARE microfoundations in the early 1980s (see Chapter 6). Solow first expressed his reservations in 1979: 'If we need good micro-foundations for macroeconomics, we are equally in need of good macro-foundations for microeconomics. Cant phrases about optimizing behaviour lead nowhere without a reasonable specification of what is being maximized and what constraints are perceived' (Solow 1979, pp. 353–4). Seven years later he advocated a pragmatic approach:

> Macroeconomics can hardly just tread water while more realistic micro-foundations are being worked out, taught and tested. In the meanwhile, the older rough-and-ready approach may be the best we can do, and not intolerable. I mean the informal micro-rationalization of macroeconomic relationships with all of its infuriating reliance on stylized facts, partial econometric analysis, appeals to common sense and even amateur sociology. (Solow 1986, p. 197; cited by Togati 1998, p. 248)

A decade later, when his Federico Caffé lectures were published, Solow seemed to be claiming that this problem had now been solved, since 'explicit modeling of imperfect competition' meant that 'macroeconomics can be built on more realistic micro-foundations' (Solow 1998, pp. 3–4).

But there was still a certain ambivalence about Solow's position. In addition to repeated claims that New Keynesian theorists had now set out the correct micro-foundations (ibid., pp. 9–10, 12–14, 52, 74), he now distinguished strong and weak versions of the dogma. 'One possible methodological decision is to insist that a valid macro model must be an exact aggregation of the corresponding micro-economy'; this led to the RARE micro-foundations that Solow had always opposed (ibid., p. 32). 'As an alternative, I would be quite content with a macro model that could be described as "loosely abstracted" from particular micro assumptions' (ibid., pp. 32–3). The macro theory would then 'correspond to' the micro assumptions, and would benefit from 'embedding it' in 'a more realistic micro context' (ibid., pp. 33, 51). These metaphors are much weaker than 'foundational' metaphors, which have been used 'literally, too literally in my opinion' (ibid., p. 10; cf. Solow 1999, p. 660).

If anything, Solow's position on this question has hardened over time. By 2007 he was objecting that 'the macro community has perpetrated a rhetorical swindle on itself, and on its students', since:

> If you pick up any 'modern macro' paper it tells you it will exhibit a 'micro-founded model' that will then be used to study this or that problem. When the model turns up, it is, of course, the representative-agent, infinite-horizon, intertemporal-optimization-with-conventional-constraints story with its various etceteras. This model has no valid claim, except by reiteration, to be 'micro-founded'. Basic microtheory tells you no such thing. The analogy I use is that it is as if my diet consisted entirely of carrots and, when asked why, I reply grandly that I am a vegetarian. Being a vegetarian is no excuse for choosing and, worse, promoting a ridiculously restricted menu among the thousands that are available. (Solow 2007, p. 235)

Use of the Ramsey model as the microfoundation of 'modern macro' is 'tendentious and misleading' (Solow 2008, p. 244). Some economics students seem to recognize that they have been swindled, Solow suggests, even if their teachers could not:

> It is a puzzle how this happened to macroeconomics ... I do not have a pat answer. No doubt there were flaws in the 'hydraulic Keynesianism' that preceded 'modern macro'. That would provide an initial impetus to any 'new' approach that could claim to correct old errors. But that would not explain why the macro community bought so incontinently into an alternative model that seems to lack all credibility as applied to quarter-to-quarter or year-to-year events. (Solow 2007, p. 236)

These are harsh criticisms, though in this passage Solow appears to concede the legitimacy of RARE microfoundations for long-run analysis, and it could be argued that they are implicit in his own growth model. He himself denies this:

> I deliberately avoided recourse to the optimizing representative agent and instead used as building blocks only aggregative relationships that are in principle observable [and] I immediately warned the reader of the possibility of aggregative short- to medium-run supply-demand imbalances that would not fit into the model. I feel guilty about some things, but not about 'modern macro'. (Solow 2008, p. 244)

At all events, to use his own analogy, a fully carnivorous macroeconomics without any microfoundations at all might prove too hard for Solow to digest.

It would be wrong to suggest that resistance to the microfoundations dogma was confined to Monetarists and Old Keynesians, since some prominent New Keynesians were also – intermittently – sceptical. In 1987 Alan Blinder criticized Robert Lucas on precisely this question: 'Must we be restricted to microfoundations that preclude the colossal market failures that created macroeconomics as a subdiscipline?', Blinder asked. 'This is a judgment call', he concluded,

> [B]ut I judge the Keynesian approach more scientific. First, good science need not always be built up from solid microfoundations. Thermodynamics and chemistry, for example, have done pretty well without much micro theory. Boyle's Law applies directly to aggregates, much like the marginal propensity to consume. And the microfoundations of medicine are often very poor; yet much of it works. Empirical regularities that are formulated and tested directly at the macro level *do* have a place in science. (Blinder 1987, p. 135; original stress)

However, Blinder had changed his mind on this issue, since in an earlier paper he had actually included 'microfoundations' in the title (Blinder 1982).

In a 1986 article on 'Keynes after Lucas', Blinder pointed to the mounting empirical evidence against the life-cycle/permanent income hypothesis as indicative of the failure of microfoundations: 'it seems unlikely to me that stricter adherence to narrow-minded conceptions of maximizing behavior will play major roles in the rehabilitation of the consumption function' (Blinder 1986, p. 216). Earlier in this paper, however, Blinder takes a rather different position: 'Closely connected to the puzzling popularity of market-clearing models was a revival – I might almost say a fundamentalist revival – of the search for microfoundations for macroeconomic models. *This is always a worthy cause*; but the NCE [New Classical Economics] school pushed it to incredible extremes' (ibid., p. 212; stress added). And again: 'The renewed search for microfoundations was welcome, but the insistence on neoclassical purity did macroeconomics little good' (ibid., p. 214). Thus Blinder raises no objection in principle to the quest for 'impure' (presumably non-RARE) microfoundations.

Peter Howitt was equally inconsistent, endorsing the need for microfoundations in a 1986 paper on 'The Keynesian recovery' and even – bizarrely – interpreting Keynes's theory of effective demand as the Cambridge economist's own 'alternative micro-foundation' (Howitt 1986, p. 628). In his *New Palgrave* entry on 'Macroeconomics: relations with microeconomics', however, Howitt takes a quite different line:

> Thus the quest for microfoundations has been a mainspring of development in macro theory. However, this does not mean that macro has been developing into a branch of applied micro. The forces tending to make macro theory conform more closely with micro principles have been opposed by equally important forces requiring those principles to be modified radically before being applied to macro questions.
>
> More specifically, what has restrained the urge to apply micro principles is a widespread recognition that some of the most important phenomena manifest defects in the economic system that standard micro theory rules out with its basic assumption of equilibrium. (Howitt 1987, p. 273)

Howitt's conclusion is optimistic:

> The disunity between micro and macro that has motivated so many contributors is shrinking rapidly on the frontiers of research where micro theory is being transformed by the explicit consideration of informational problems like those so often adduced by macroeconomists and where macroeconomics without

> specific reference to individual transactors, their decision problems and conditions of equilibrium is becoming increasingly rare. (Ibid., p. 275)

There is no foundational metaphor here. However, Howitt has subsequently used the term 'microfoundations' in the title of at least one paper (Howitt 2006). In his contribution to the *Festschrift* for Axel Leijonhufvud, Howitt recommends agent-based modelling on the grounds that 'the approach assumes simple behavioural rules and allows a coordinated equilibrium to be a possible emergent property of the system itself' (Howitt 2008, p. 157). As we saw in Chapter 4, however, emergent properties are difficult to reconcile with any convincing version of micro-reduction (above, pp. 68–70).

In Chapter 5 of a technical book on the aggregation problem Ekkehart Schlicht denounces the microfoundations dogma:

> This chapter sets out to argue that there is nothing particularly disreputable in doing macroeconomic analysis even if no explicit microeconomic foundation is available. It will be argued, in fact, that macroeconomic laws might possess a certain degree of independence from their microeconomic underpinnings, and that analogies between microeconomic and macroeconomic laws might be misleading. (Schlicht 1985, p. 63)

Schlicht invokes the example of thermodynamics, in which there is also 'a possible difference in quality' between molecule movement and heat. 'Incidentally', he suggests, 'our shopping behaviour might be a macro-phenomenon in this sense' (ibid., p. 63).

He emphasizes 'the context dependency of macro relations' (ibid., p. 78), and relates it to the distinction between internal relations and external relations in philosophy, citing Bertrand Russell in support (ibid., p. 79 n19).

Schlicht also hints at the fallacy of composition: 'Furthermore, closed aggregation might lead to macroeconomic laws which have no qualitative counterpart in any of the underlying microeconomic relations, they might appear quite different. This is due to what might be denoted the *system effect*' (ibid., p. 80; original stress). In a section headed 'Macroeconomic order and microeconomic chaos' (ibid., pp. 94–7), he again alludes to the principle of non-inferability:

> If there is a true micro model *f* which is stable, i.e. which remains unchanging over time, the associated macro model is stable. If the micro model changes … however, this microeconomic instability does not carry over to the macro model. Hence the macro model is not only more general, but more stable than the underlying micro model. (Ibid., p. 95)

'Micro chaos and macro order might coexist', Schlicht concludes, citing Hayek in support (ibid., p. 96). Finally, in a section headed 'structural causality' (pp. 100), he defends 'this holistic view', 'that micro relations are "determined" by macro relations' (ibid., p. 98), and invokes the support of Charles Darwin and Karl Marx, together with structuralist and functionalist sociology.

In the 1980s repeated expressions of doubt concerning the microfoundations dogma could be found in the writings of well-known mainstream economists. One of the better-known was Olivier Blanchard, whose widely used postgraduate textbook *Lectures on Macroeconomics*, co-authored with Stanley Fischer, took 'a pragmatic position' on the question. In a passage cited earlier (above, p. 110), they wrote:

> It would clearly be better for economists to have an all-purpose model, derived explicitly from microfoundations and embodying all relevant imperfections, to analyze all issues in macroeconomics (or perhaps all issues in economics). We are not quite there yet. And if we ever were, we would in all likelihood have little understanding of the mechanisms at work behind the results of simulations. Thus we have no choice but to be eclectic. (Blanchard and Fischer 1989, p. 505)

But this is not an 'in principle' repudiation of microfoundations. It is necessary to weigh '[t]he costs and benefits of deriving a model from first principles', Blanchard and Fischer explain in a footnote (ibid., p. 558 n2). Their decision to 'introduce the workhorses of applied macroeconomics such as the IS-LM and Mundell–Fleming models' (ibid., p. 506), which have no such derivation, is to be interpreted in this light. Although Blanchard soon complained about 'the quasi-religious insistence on micro foundations' that had too often been adopted as one of the 'methodological ukases' of New Classical economics (Blanchard 1992, p. 126), this did not prevent him, much later, from vigorously defending mainstream macroeconomics, microfoundations and all (Blanchard 2008; Blanchard, Dell'Arica and Mauro 2010).

By the early 1990s dissatisfaction of sorts with the microfoundations dogma was quite widespread. Reviewing M.C.W. Janssen's *Microfoundations: A Critical Inquiry*, the British macroeconomist Huw Dixon showed an unusual awareness of the methodological problems that it posed. 'The search for microfoundations for macroeconomics is an interesting case study' in the application of methodological individualism (MI), he suggests (Dixon 1994, p. 947). 'This seems an unnecessary and fruitless task … individuals always make choices situated in a particular historical position, within a world of customs, conventions, and institutions. MI seeks to explain all this from an imaginary and hypothetical "original position" without such social institutions'. This he finds unconvincing: 'all we can say as economists is that individual choices and social institutions are mutually consistent' (ibid., p. 948).

Dixon's review appeared in the *Economic Journal*, and other dissenters began to find outlets in the most important mainstream journals. Thus the *American Economic Review* published an important article by the MIT economist Ricardo Caballero entitled 'A fallacy of composition'. In fact the title was slightly misleading, as Caballero identifies several such fallacies, all resulting from 'the fact that direct microeconomic arguments do not consider the strong restrictions that probability theory puts on the joint behavior of many units that are less than fully synchronized' (Caballero 1992, p. 1279). One example is the observation that the price level is more rigid downwards than upwards, a finding that could not be derived from asymmetries at the level of the individual firm. Neither did asymmetric factor adjustment costs at the firm level entail asymmetric responses of the aggregate capital stock and the level of employment to positive and negative shocks (ibid., pp. 1279–80). Caballero italicizes his conclusions: 'Thus, *in the absence of aggregate fluctuations, the size of the flows in and out of employment has nothing to do with the microeconomic asymmetry*' (ibid., p. 1283). And again: '*direct application of microeconomic explanations to aggregate data can be seriously misleading, since they typically do not consider the natural probability forces that tend to undo such explanations*' (ibid., p. 1291).

Caballero does not, however, make any explicit reference to microfoundations, and denies that his paper represents 'an argument for the irrelevance of microeconomic stories as explanations of aggregate behavior. Underlying any cross-sectional story there has to be a microeconomic story' (ibid., p. 1291). His paper was not often cited, and seems to have had almost no impact on mainstream macroeconomics, though earlier versions were cited by Mohammed Dore in his extended critique of the New Keynesian approach to business cycle theory (Dore 1993, pp. 125–6; see also Dore 2002). Caballero himself has not followed it up, and indeed has continued to take a highly orthodox position in subsequent published work.

Alan Kirman's critique of representative agent models was much more frequently cited, if in the end no more influential. It appeared in the *Journal of Economic Perspectives*, a non-mathematical sister journal to the *AER* distributed with it but intended for a broader, less specialized readership. Kirman's conclusions came with all the authority of a leading general equilibrium theorist:

> Given the arguments presented here – that well-behaved individuals need not produce a well-behaved representative agent; that the reaction of a representative agent to change need not reflect how the individuals of the economy would respond to change; that the preferences of a representative agent over choices may be diametrically opposed to those of society as a whole – it is clear that the representative agent should have no future. Indeed, contrary to what current macroeconomic practice would seem to suggest, requiring heterogeneity of agents within the competitive general equilibrium model may help to recover aggregate properties which may be useful for macroeconomic analysis. (Kirman 1992, p. 134).

Kirman advocates an alternative approach to macroeconomic theory, based on interactions between diverse individuals who operate only in a limited subset of the economy (see Kirman 1999b for an extended discussion). 'Within such models', he notes, there can and should be considerable aggregate regularity. However, the fact that behavior at the macroeconomic level exhibits regularities does not mean that it is useful or appropriate to treat the economy as a maximizing representative individual'. Kirman was pessimistic – correctly, as it transpired – about the prospect that his approach might overcome 'the stultifying influence of the representative agent' (Kirman 1992, p. 134). Unlike Caballero's, Kirman's arguments were widely read and often cited, but they, too, were rarely acted upon (see also Kirman 2011a, 2011b).

For a brief period at the end of the 1990s it seemed possible that David Colander's 'Post-Walrasian economics' might prove attractive to mainstream theorists who were dissatisfied with RARE microfoundations. At this stage in his career Colander, already well known for his trenchant criticisms of graduate training in economics in Ivy League universities (Klamer and Colander 1989), was equally forthright in his opposition to any form of microfoundations, insisting instead on the need for macrofoundations for microeconomics (Colander 1994, 1996). Subsequently he became much less critical both of the PhD coursework curriculum and of mainstream macroeconomic theory (Colander 2007). Like Blanchard's and Blinder's, however, Colander's verdict on the microfoundations dogma has been distinctly unstable over time. Thus he and his co-author Casey Rothschild criticize Paul Krugman for defending 'good models' with microfoundations while continuing to advocate the use of 'simple *ad hoc* undergraduate models' on pragmatic grounds. 'Our argument is stronger', they claim; 'while we agree with these practical considerations, we go further and argue that in many cases the microfoundations approach is demonstrably *worse* for describing the world and for prescribing policy. We also question the conventional wisdom that graduate models are even *theoretically* more sound'. It is common practice in the natural sciences, they note, to use macro models without providing microfoundations, and with good reason: 'in intrinsically complex systems like the macro economy, it is not clear that models built from the micro-level up – *however* firm their foundations – are theoretically more satisfactory than models built around "high-level" emergent macro-properties' (Colander and Rothschild 2009, p. 119; original stress).

But this sits uncomfortably both with Colander's repeated advice to macroeconomists not to concern themselves with methodology and with his call for them to 'rethink the concept of micro foundations' since 'an *appropriate micro foundation* is needed'. In this vein he 'acknowledges the importance of empirically based micro foundations' (Colander et al. 2009, p. 9; original stress). This statement comes in a paper on 'The financial crisis and the systemic failure of academic economics' co-authored with Kirman and with one American, three German and two Danish critics. The authors note, without apparent irony, that '[t]he representative agent appeared without methodological discussion' (ibid., p. 7 n5). But this is a discussion that Colander himself has been keen to discourage: 'worry less about methodology', he advises heterodox economists (Colander 2009, p. 67), as if the problems posed by the microfoundations dogma were somehow methodologically neutral.

We may conclude from this section that, while the microfoundations dogma has provoked some dissent within mainstream economics, the dissidents have not always been consistent in their opposition to it, and they have seldom taken their criticisms beyond the weaknesses of RARE microfoundations to consider the broader methodological issues raised by any attempt to reduce macro to micro in economics. A particularly striking confirmation of this judgement was provided in 2008 by the critique of Dynamic Stochastic General Equilibrium (DSGE) models by five prominent mainstream macroeconomists, three of whom (David Colander, Peter Howitt and Alan Kirman) have already featured in this chapter (the other two co-authors are Axel Leijonhufvud and Perry Mehrling). Critics of DSGE models, they suggest, 'recognize that the behavior of the aggregate need not correspond to the behavior of the components, and that it generally cannot be derived from a consideration of the latter alone' (Colander et al. 2009, p. 236–7). This being the case, 'what makes macroeconomics a separate field of study is the complex properties of aggregate behavior that emerge from the interaction among agents', behaviour which 'cannot be deduced from an analysis of individuals alone' (ibid., p. 236); 'the fallacy of composition exists, and must be dealt with' (ibid., p. 237).

But this does not lead these eminent critics consistently to repudiate the microfoundations dogma in its entirety. On the one hand, recent work in 'full agent model equilibria … offers the possibility of jettisoning all micro foundations' (ibid., p. 238). On the other hand, the New Classical efforts to formulate microfoundations 'rightfully challenged the rigor of the previous work' (ibid., p. 237). Moreover, 'macroeconomists must acknowledge that micro foundations are a choice variable of theorists. The appropriate choice cannot be determined a priori; it needs to be made in reference to empirical data and educated common sense in a way that will lead to useful macro models' (ibid., p. 236). Serious methodological error or 'choice variable'? The microfoundations dogma surely cannot be both.

9.3 AUSTRIAN DISSENTERS

Have Austrian economists performed any better than this? It might be thought that they would have been happy to accept the microfoundations dogma, welcoming it as a belated acceptance by the mainstream of a principle that they themselves have defended from the outset. Certainly some form of methodological individualism has always been prominent in Austrian economics (Hodgson 1986). Towards the end of the nineteenth century, Eugen von Böhm-Bawerk maintained that '[w]e must not weary of studying the microcosm if we wish rightly to understand the macrocosm of a developed economic order' (Böhm-Bawerk 1891, p. 21). Ludwig von Mises went further, denouncing (in a memorable passage that I have already quoted) 'the doctrines of universalism, conceptual realism, holism, collectivism, and some forms of *Gestaltpsychologie*', according to which 'society is an entity living its own life, independent of and separate from the lives of the various individuals, acting on its own behalf and aiming at its own ends which are different from the ends sought by the individuals' (von Mises 1949, p. 145). Thus, for Mises, 'all of economics is microeconomics' (Hands 2001, p. 43).

Also a stern critic of holism and all forms of collectivism, Friedrich von Hayek was strongly opposed to Keynesian macroeconomics on methodological grounds. His disagreement with Keynes

> … did not refer so much to any detail of the analysis as to the general approach followed in the whole work. The real issue was the validity of what we now call macroanalysis, and I feel now that in a long-run perspective the chief significance of the *General Theory* will appear that more than any other single work it

> decisively furthered the ascendancy of macroeconomics and the temporary decline of microeconomic theory. (Hayek 1966 [1995], p. 241)

This was a recurrent theme in Hayek's critique of the social sciences as a whole, which he believed to have made the 'mistake of treating as definite objects "wholes" that are no more than constructions, and that can have no properties except those which follow from the way in which we have constructed them from the elements' (Hayek 1955, p. 57; cf. Hartley 1997, pp. 114–15). Keynes was not the originator of this fallacy, which Hayek traced back to Auguste Comte (ibid., p. 58; cf. Hayek 1963 [1995], pp. 60–61), but Keynes was largely responsible for the increased prominence of a 'pseudo-scientific economics of averages' (Hayek 1972, p. 20).

Ludwig Lachmann was also a strong defender of methodological individualism as the only consistent basis for subjectivism in economics. It 'means simply that we shall not be satisfied with any type of explanation of social phenomena which does not lead us ultimately to a human plan' (Lachmann 1969, p. 94). He wrote a lengthy pamphlet, published by the neoliberal Institute of Economic Affairs, on *Macro-economic Thinking and the Market Economy*, giving it the sub-title 'An essay on the neglect of the micro-foundations and its consequences'. Macroeconomic equilibrium, he claimed, was 'a more problematical concept than market equilibrium' (Lachmann 1973, p. 15). Although 'macro-equilibria require causal explanation in terms of human choice and decision', this important principle was neglected by mainstream macroeconomic theorists, for whom '[s]tereotypes play the part of economic agents' (ibid., p. 19). Thus 'only lip-service is paid to the micro-economic foundations' (ibid., p. 30), and 'these perfunctory affirmations are of no significance' (ibid., p. 31).

Lachmann claims that even 'Böhm-Bawerk's model, being essentially macroeconomic, does not provide an adequate basis for a capital theory that could properly be called Austrian'. Such a theory, 'starting at the ground level, that is, at the microlevel where production plans are made and carried out', would avoid the 'arid macroeconomic formalism' to which both neoclassical and neo-Ricardian capital theorists had succumbed. They had all been engaged in a 'controversy about a fictitious macroeconomic magnitude' (Lachmann 1976a, pp. 145, 146, 147). Lachman therefore welcomed the 'evolution towards subjectivism by means of the disaggregation of macroaggregates' that had taken place in recent decades (Lachman 1978, p. 9), while the editor of the volume in which this statement appeared went even further, opposing demands for the 'coordination' of macroeconomics and microeconomics on the grounds that the 'subordination' of macro to micro was the correct methodological demand (Spadaro 1978, p. 220).

It seems probable that Lachmann, like Böhm-Bawerk, Mises and Hayek, would have agreed with a twenty-first century statement of methodological principle by Peter Boettke and Peter Leeson:

> The Austrian position with regard to macroeconomic theory can be summed up as follows: while there may indeed be macroeconomic problems (unemployment, inflation, business cycles), there are only microeconomic explanations and solutions. There are no aggregate relationships unmoored to individual choices that matter for economic analysis. (Boettke and Leeson 2003, p. 450)

As Edwin Dolan had written, many years earlier, 'Austrian writers are characteristically critical of the use of macroeconomic aggregates, especially when these appear as arguments in mathematical formulations that imply functional and/or causal relationships between aggregates' (Dolan 1976, p. 6). Even 'the currently fashionable mathematical models that feature efficient markets and rational expectations' fail to satisfy modern Austrians, but testify instead to the irrationality of mainstream macroeconomic theorists (Steele 2007, p. 3; see also O'Driscoll and Shenoy 1976; Garretsen 1992, pp. 86–7).

And yet, and yet. Hayek almost certainly never used the term 'microfoundations', and regarded even 'microeconomics' with great suspicion, owing to its links with the anti-Austrian notion of constrained optimization. Moreover, he 'does not mention methodological individualism after the 1950s. Indeed, the role that evolutionary explanations come to play in his later work implies a tacit retraction of his commitment to the doctrine' (Heath 2009, p. 7). Thus Andy Denis regards Hayek as a holist, who maintains that 'individuals are merely the *foci* in the network of relationships' (Denis 2009, p. 3). Denis includes Hayek, with Adam Smith, Dugald Stewart, the early Malthus, Marx and Keynes as advocates of 'the holistic, or "organicist" approach, seeing macro level entities as an organism or a system' (Denis 2009, p. 8). In similar vein Marek Hudík maintains that Hayek's concept of spontaneous order is independent of any theory of individual behaviour and suggests that Hayek would have been forced to agree that 'there are problems of social sciences, which are not problems of behaviour *and are irreducible to them*' (Hudík 2011, pp. 147–8; stress added). And, in their recent survey of Austrian capital theory, Anthony Endres and David Harper (2011) demonstrate that Hayek was much less consistent than either Menger or Lachmann in his rejection of capital aggregates.

Austrians certainly are consistent in their strong objections to RARE microfoundations (Horwitz 2010). An emphasis on the personal idiosyncrasies of real individuals and their diverse and unpredictable reactions to a fundamentally uncertain economic environment is essential to the Austrian concept of 'market process'. This is enough to make them automatically hostile to the (neoclassical) representative agent, and is usually taken to be inconsistent with any formal analysis of market equilibrium, with or without rational expectations. Lars Udehn has noted the inconsistencies in Hayek's position on this issue, which include an acceptance of the principle of group (not individual, still less gene) selection (Udehn 2001, pp. 282–5; cf. Hands 2001, pp. 45–8). As Denis has argued, the profoundly Austrian focus on the unintended social consequences of individual actions also points to a holist rather than an individualist methodology, for all Hayek's protestations to the contrary:

> The method of the social sciences is said to be 'individualist' because it 'starts' with individuals. But when we recall that these individuals are not considered *qua* individuals, but as vehicles of specific socially inculcated beliefs, as nodes in networks of social relations, the aptness of the designation seems questionable. Methodologically what Hayek describes is entirely holist. (Denis 2010, p. 5; see also Hartley 1997, p. 171)

Even Mises, Denis suggests, sometimes expresses 'a clearly holistic social ontology' (ibid., p. 14).

To the best of my knowledge, however, the only Austrian economist to have explicitly recognized the difficulties that microfoundations pose for Austrian theory is David Levy. While it is true that 'only individuals make choices', Levy suggests, 'wherever knowledge is imperfect the theorist cannot dispense with collective terms' in the analysis of individuals' knowledge and beliefs (Levy 1985, pp. 102, 103). This is inherent in the very nature of decentralized knowledge, 'where only specialists in technical areas know how to reduce some collective term to its individual components' (ibid., p. 105). Non-economists are simply unable to reduce technical terms such as 'GDP' or 'the Consumer Price Index' in this way. Hence they 'are methodological collectivists for the sensible reason that methodological individualism is a very costly way of looking at the world' (ibid., pp. 107–8). Levy concludes that Austrians need to acknowledge a rather disconcerting implication: the existence of microfoundations for macroeconomics does not rule out the existence of macrofoundations for microeconomics.

Thus it comes as no surprise that when Austrians come to write about real macroeconomic problems, rather than criticizing the very concept of macroeconomic theory, they find themselves forced to abandon the dogma of microfoundations and fall back on a pre-Keynesian but nonetheless genuinely macroeconomic analysis. Thus in 1978 Roger Garrison declared that his diagrammatic exposition of Austrian macroeconomics was 'consistent with the methodological individualism so characteristic of Austrian theory' (Garrison 1978, p. 168). But his discussion is replete with (non-reduced) macroeconomic terms like 'employment', 'full employment', 'real income', 'aggregate production time' (this to replace the problematical Böhm-Bawerkian term 'average period of production'), 'the [natural] rate of interest', the 'quantity of capital', 'voluntary saving', 'the price level', 'investment', 'the real level of consumption' and 'the supply of money'. Garrison's Figure 13, which summarizes his model (ibid., p. 195), is expressly designed to permit comparison with the mainstream IS-LM model. The entire analysis has a distinctly Wicksellian flavour, and indeed Garrison cites Wicksell favourably at one point (ibid., p. 192). 'Because of its focus on the co-ordination problem', he maintains, 'there is no *sharp* distinction between Austrian macroeconomics and Austrian micro-economics' (ibid., p. 169; original stress). By the same token, the former has not been reduced to the latter.

Two decades later Garrison took issue with those Austrian theorists like Israel Kirzner and Karen Vaughn, who reject the legitimacy of macro-economics as such. His own 'capital-based model' is 'intended to help put capital back in macro and help put macro back in modern Austrian economics' (Garrison 2001, p. 13). There is only one reference to micro-foundations in the index, to a paragraph in which Garrison strongly criticizes the RARE microfoundations of New Classical economics, since it 'affected form more than substance' and offered only 'the illusion' of real individuals making choices and forming expectations (ibid., p. 21). 'If an economy could be usefully modeled as the market for a single service provided by a representative supplier', Garrison concludes, 'there would not likely be any issues that would give macroeconomics a distinct subject matter' (ibid., p. 25).

A second important Austrian macroeconomist is Steven Horwitz, who describes his own thinking as 'post-Wicksellian' (Horwitz 2000, p. 9). Although the title of his most important book is *Microfoundations and Macroeconomics*, and while he repeatedly refers to the requirement for microfoundations that are superior to the RARE ones supplied by New Classical economists, Horwitz's brand of Austrian macroeconomic theory appears to me to fail his own test. Thus he refers at one point to the microeconomic effects of macroeconomic properties, acknowledging that

> … downward price rigidities, whether derived from state intervention, institutional conditions or social conventions in the market, do have important and adverse microeconomic consequences. If prices are unable to fall with significant speed in the face of an excess demand for money, resource misallocation and general economic decline will ensue. This is one example of the way in which a macroeconomic problem (an excess demand for money) reveals itself in the microeconomic process. (Ibid., p. 27)

There is no suggestion that this 'excess demand for money' can be reduced to statements about individuals, and the reference to 'social conventions' as a potential source of price rigidity seems to rule out any possibility of providing microfoundations for this important phenomenon. Instead Garrison is inadvertently confirming Levy's point about the inescapability of *macro*foundations. Later he refers, without any irony, to Hayek's criticism of the Keynesian

> … misunderstanding of the relationship between the demand for consumer goods and the demand for production goods (capital). Hayek's complaint is that those who believe that by stimulating the final demand for goods and services we can therefore stimulate the demand for the production goods needed to produce them ('derived demand') *are guilty of a fallacy of composition.* The doctrine of derived demand (i.e., that an increased demand for a particular good will increase the demand for its inputs) applies only at the level of individual goods. *It cannot be applied in the aggregate.* (Ibid., p. 59; stress added)

Further comment on this passage would be superfluous.

9.4 INSTITUTIONALIST DISSENTERS

Problems of definition are more substantial in the case of institutionalism than with other heterodox schools of thought. The 'New Institutionalism' of Douglass North and Oliver Williamson is best regarded as a slightly off-centre variant of mainstream economic theory, and will not be considered here. Instead attention will be paid to the self-identified (Old) institutionalists in the tradition of Thorsten Veblen, John R. Commons and Wesley Clair Mitchell, who are associated with the *Journal of Economic Issues* and the *Journal of Institutional Economics*, and to advocates of the 'evolutionary' or 'Schumpeterian' approach to economic dynamics. One problem appears immediately, since it was Joseph Schumpeter, himself a strong admirer of Walras, who coined the term 'methodological individualism', even if he did not consistently employ the principle in his own theoretical work (Udehn 2001, pp. 104–7).

It would be wrong to look too hard for sharp definitions in this context, since heterodox schools of thought in economics have fuzzy boundaries with a considerable degree of inter-penetration, and this is evidently the case with institutionalism. Closely related ideas have also been defended by economists who would possibly not self-identify as institutionalists, like Roger Sandilands, a tireless exponent of the ideas of Allyn Young, himself a disciple of Adam Smith; the historians of economic thought Robert Heilbroner and William Milgate, who have affinities with radical and Marxian political economy and also with Post Keynesianism; and Lance Taylor, who describes himself as a 'structuralist' macroeconomist. Others, like Alfred Eichner, had at least one foot in the Post Keynesian camp, but also considerable sympathy with (and influence on) institutionalism. The central issue that is directly relevant to the microfoundations dogma concerns the way in which the relationship between the individual and the social should be conceived, and on this question several of these theorists – notably Sandilands, Heilbroner and Milgate, and Taylor – are in broad agreement with the institutionalists.

The crucial arguments have been set out most clearly by Geoff Hodgson, who makes the central points about the fallacy of composition, downward causation, the importance of emergent properties and the case for a relatively autonomous macroeconomics with great clarity (Hodgson 2000). He is unequivocally an (Old) institutionalist and is thus a long-term critic of the doctrine of methodological individualism, as noted briefly in Chapter 4 (Hodgson 1986, 2007; above, pp. 60–61). For Hodgson the essential principle is that 'a socially determined individual cannot provide the ultimate explanatory bedrock that methodological individualism requires' (Hodgson 2002, p. 159). Causation runs downwards, from the macro to the micro, no less than upwards, from the micro to the macro. Thus 'institutionalism in the tradition of Veblen, Commons and Mitchell' asserts the following important proposition:

> The social structure stands above individuals in a hierarchical arrangement, and the causal powers associated with the higher level may not simply impede or constrain behaviour but may also affect and alter fundamental properties, powers and propensities of individuals. When an upper hierarchical level affects components at a lower level in this manner, this may be seen as a special and stronger case of 'downward causation' that we may term as *reconstitutive downward*

> *causation*. Those particular social structures that have the capacity for substantial, enduring and widespread reconstitutive downward causation upon individuals are termed *institutions*. (Ibid., p. 175)

One consequence of this proposition concerns the formation of individual preferences, which are not a 'rock bottom explanation' of anything but are themselves created through learning mechanisms that are conditioned by relations of social power (ibid., pp. 175–8).

Hodgson does not discuss the implications for the microfoundations dogma, but he might well have done. 'Surely the recognition of the inextricably social roots of all behavior leads to the view that macrofoundations must precede microbehavior, not the other way round, as modern economic thought perceives the issue' (Heilbroner and Milgate 1995, p. 8). More precisely, '"micro" and "macro" merge, in that microbehavior cannot be understood without taking cognizance of its social origins, and social forces remain empty abstractions unless they enter into the motivational concreteness of one or more individuals' (ibid., p. 87). The 'income' that the rational individual is supposed by mainstream economists to allocate between competing demands according to the precepts of rationality is 'intrinsically a social concept' (Heilbroner 1988, p. 190). Thus New Classical economics is fundamentally mistaken, since it involves 'a denial of the sociality not only of governments but of all economic agents and the markets in which they interact', and ignores questions of 'power, commitment and values' (Heilbroner and Milgate 1995, pp. 83, 84).

Taylor makes a slightly different but entirely compatible point about the fluidity of the social:

> The economy rests on changing social relations – all attempts to describe it in terms of timeless constructs like Newton's laws, Einstein's field equations, or Feynman's diagrams are bound to fail. Stochastic but rational expectations built upon a nonexistent 'true' model correspondingly have no content. (Taylor 2004, p. 202)

Hodgson would certainly agree with this, since he has always insisted on the need for historical specificity in economic theory. 'A historically grounded economics', he suggests in a book entitled *How Economics Forgot History* that is critical of Keynes's supposed neglect of this question, 'can make much use of ... Keynesian macroeconomics. A key difference is that attempts to place these theories on universal microfoundations are rebutted and these insights are based on an understanding of historically specific institutions' (Hogson 2001, p. 354).

The evolutionary economists Kurt Dopfer and Jason Potts come to rather similar conclusions by a different route. In their 'micro meso macro framework', a population of heterogeneous agents creates a variety of rules, which are then diffused among the population in a set of processes of de-coordination and re-coordination. From this perspective methodological individualism is not wrong but insufficient, and due to its complexity the macroeconomic system cannot be described as a linear aggregation of its parts. The microfoundations dogma 'is at best autistic, and at worst dangerously irrelevant', since

> … the global macroeconomy is quite possibly the most complex system in the known universe, and certainly at least as complex as the human brain or the global ecosystem. Yet although no neuroscientist would describe the mind as a simple neuron-to-behavior aggregation, and no ecologist would describe the ecosystem as a simple gene-to-ecosystem aggregation, the current mainstream paradigm of economic analysis is analogously that, namely the supposition that micro operations sum to aggregate economy. (Dopfer and Potts 2008, p. 24)

Walrasian economics is question-begging, they argue, since the necessary theory of economic co-ordination is simply assumed at the outset. Keynesian macroeconomics, at the other extreme, 'collapsed the generic dimension to a crude caricature of generic rules, dispensing entirely with social and technical rules of organization and allowing only some behavioral rules relating to marginal savings and investment propensities' (ibid., p. 86). A truly general theory would link the micro, meso and macro levels, with causation operating in both directions, upwards and downwards.

This neo-Schumpeterian framework is quite distinct from, but broadly consistent with, Sandilands's Smithian reading of Allyn Young, who focused on the dynamic increasing returns to scale generated by the 'increasingly complex nexus of specialized undertakings' in communications, transport, research and advertising, which provide continuous reductions in costs as the size of the market grows (Sandilands 2009, p. 294). Again there is a Post Keynesian connection, since Young's ideas exercised a long-term influence over the growth theories of Nicholas Kaldor, his teenage student at the London School of Economics. For all his inconsistency on these issues, Kaldor would almost certainly have agreed with Sandilands's conclusion:

> While modern growth theory focuses on the microeconomic foundations of neoclassical growth theory by noting how entrepreneurs allocate resources to innovation according to a profit-maximizing balancing of private costs and

> benefits that may also yield external benefits, Young's more classical approach stresses the macro foundations of microeconomics. (Ibid., p. 301)

Or, as I would prefer the point to be put: downward causation, from macro to micro, is no less important than upward causation, from micro to macro.

This point is made explicitly by Jeroen van den Bergh and John Gowdy, who draw extensively on the literature in evolutionary biology in advocating an unusual variant of the 'hierarchical approach' to scientific explanation. This approach

> ... can resolve the "which degree of reduction" debate by understanding or explaining systems on multiple levels rather than reducing all phenomena to a single level, whether micro, macro or meso. In a hierarchical system, entities and processes at one level can be made dependent on those at higher or lower levels. This leads to a system with upward and downward causation. (Van den Bergh and Gowdy 2003, p. 76)

There are clear implications for the microfoundations dogma: 'it is futile to search for a definite and unique microfoundation for macroeconomic relationships. Microeconomic and macroeconomic theories and models should be regarded as complementary' (ibid., p. 67). Van den Bergh and Gowdy make only passing reference to emergent properties. Harper and Endres, however, argue that '[e]mergence is ubiquitous in evolutionary economic processes. Emergence occurs every time there is an appearance of a qualitatively new good, technology, design, routine, organizational capability, firm, network, market or industry. Accordingly, emergence is one of the "big ideas" at the heart of both evolutionary-institutional economics and complexity research' (Harper and Endres 2011, p. 14). As we saw in Chapter 4, they argue that emergence is fundamentally incompatible with (micro-) reduction (above, pp. 67–8).

These methodological conclusions are reflected in substantive institutionalist theory, but somewhat erratically, as is the case with the – very much more substantial – Post Keynesian literature that was discussed in the previous section. Gardiner Means's 1947 manuscript, *A Monetary Theory of Employment*, not published until 1994, is one of the few attempts to develop an institutionalist alternative to (Old) Keynesian macroeconomics, emphasizing price and wage rigidities in a predominantly oligopolistic and partly unionized economy. Although his non-Marshallian microeconomic model is quite different from that of Keynes, Means is very clear that no foundational analogies are implied. On the contrary:

> Optimum employment is not used to mean optimum use of resources. It has to do with the amount of employment, not the direction of employment ... This discrimination rests on two beliefs: (1) that the two sets of problems, optimum employment and optimum use, are reasonably separable; and (2) that the first has to be close to solution before the second can be effectively tackled ... the central problem of optimum employment *has to be tackled for the economy as a whole as a single integrated problem*, whereas the problem of optimum use can be tackled piecemeal, with improvement first in one area and then in another. (Means 1947 [1994], pp. 5–6; stress added)

This is not, though, a distinctively institutionalist position; an almost identical statement can be found in a contemporary text by the impeccably neoclassical Keynesian, Tibor Scitovsky (1952, p. 9), and as we have seen it was a commonplace among the post-1936 generation of 'Cambridge Keynesians' (above, pp. 42–3).

By 1976 Alfred Eichner was using the term 'micro foundations' in the sub-title of his first major book on macroeconomic theory. 'One of the most striking aspects of present economic theory', he wrote, 'is its disjointed nature. The two major bodies of theory, micro and macro, have only a slight relationship to one another ... Micro and macro theory, then, stand as two separate bodies of analysis, with little in the way of a common perspective or a common set of variables to bind them together' (Eichner 1976, p. 189). His use of the metaphor 'bind together' suggests that Eichner was not engaged in a micro-reduction project, and this impression is reinforced by subsequent references to the need for a 'common bond' between his own micro model of oligopoly and Post Keynesian macroeconomic theory, 'which will at the same time be more congenial to the Keynesian aggregate analysis and better able to explain the post World War II inflation'. He continues, 'Yet merely to establish this common bond is not enough. The two bodies of theory must be made truly compatible so that the implications to be derived from the one are not inconsistent with the deductions made from the other' (ibid., p. 190). Eichner continued to use the foundational metaphor, which he came to describe as Kaleckian in inspiration (Eichner 1985, pp. 28–9, 124).

Ambiguity and confusion continue to be found in institutionalist writing on macroeconomic themes. Thus a subsequent institutionalist writer, Theodore Rosenof, invokes the authority of George Feiwel, whose rather misleading characterization of Kalecki's attitude on this question has already been noted (above, p. 151), to argue that 'an institutionalist microeconomics would have complemented and completed Keynesian macroeconomics, giving it a more valid and appropriate microeconomic foundation than that provided by outdated Marshallian assumptions' (Rosenof 1997, p. 27, paraphrasing Feiwel 1989). This, Rosenof argues, would have reinvigorated institutionalism, which had remained 'very much on the sidelines until the problem of inflation flickered in the 1950s and then enveloped the economy in the 1970s' (ibid., p. 71). It was 'Eichner's basic objective', he claims, 'to breach [*sic*: bridge?] the gap between macroeconomics and microeconomics, to provide Keynesianism with structurally based microfoundations', thereby completing 'the aborted Keynesian revolution' (ibid., p. 141, citing Eichner 1983, p. 218).

One further example: in response to the recent global financial crisis, Philip Mirowski offers 'a structural theory of the crisis, informed by Institutionalist themes'. This 'alternative to a neoclassical macroeconomics' involves 'possible alternative heterodox microfoundations' inspired by the work of Hyman Minsky (Mirowski 2010, p. 415; the term is repeated on pp. 418 – as a section heading – 419, 424 and 441). Again, though, Mirowski's is not a micro-reduction project: 'the Minskian categories', he writes, would need to be supplemented with a microeconomic theory of market evolution', which would provide it with 'a deeper grounding' (ibid., p. 421). And at one point he criticizes the micro perspective, not of mainstream economists but of market players: 'It is characteristic of the dynamic of economic development that human participants, from their individual parochial vantage points, attribute any observed "failure" to a particular localized market, whereas from an analytical point of view, it should more appropriately be attributed instead to the entire network architecture' (ibid., p. 434).

It is apparent from this that the same array of metaphors that bedevils the Post Keynesian discussion of the microfoundations dogma – 'binding', 'bonds', 'congeniality', 'consistency', 'bridges', 'grounding' – is also found in the institutionalist literature. And many institutionalists have found it no easier than the Post Keynesians to avoid the term 'microfoundations', when micro-reduction is clearly not what they intend to endorse.

9.5 CONCLUSION

Like the Post Keynesians whose views were discussed in Chapter 8, the Austrians and institutionalists have also been uncertain, unclear and divided on the question of microfoundations. In their defence, it might be argued that this reflects the complexity of the issues that are involved, and in particular the difficulty of ensuring that intentional human agency is not swallowed up by the structural macroeconomic determinants of individual behaviour (on which, see McKenna and Zannoni 2012). As for the mainstream dissenters from the microfoundations dogma, they are a motley crew, and their dissidence seems to have been derived much more from sound instincts (not always maintained, as we have seen in the cases of Blanchard and Blinder) than from any clear position on the issues of micro-reduction and emergent properties that have concerned philosophers of science. Whether specialists in economic methodology have done any better will be discussed in the following chapter.

10. The economic methodologists and microfoundations

10.1 INTRODUCTION

As we saw in Chapters 5–6, in their discussion of microfoundations mainstream economists have rarely referred either to the philosophy of science or to its application to the methodology of their own subject. Almost all would pay lip-service to methodological individualism, but they would do so without any serious consideration of its implications, or its problems. This lack of engagement with methodological questions has become more obvious in recent decades, and it has a clear parallel in the increasing neglect of the history of economic thought. Earlier generations of mainstream economists were generally much better informed, with Milton Friedman (1912–2006) and Paul Samuelson (1915–2009), for example, publishing important papers on methodological issues (Friedman 1953; Samuelson 1963). Despite the neglect, often verging on contempt, of the bulk of the profession, economic methodology has flourished as a branch or sub-discipline of economics, with its own professional society, the International Network on Economic Method, and several specialist journals. Most, though not all, of its practitioners are trained in economics and continue to practice as economists, so that they have a thorough knowledge of the literature, including that on the relationship between macroeconomics and microeconomics. Their opinions (or absence of opinions) on the microfoundations dogma are thus of considerable interest.

The substantial modern literature on economic methodology is well surveyed by John Pheby (1987) and by Marcel Boumans and John Davis (2010). It began in 1934 with Lionel Robbins's *Nature and Significance of Economic Science*, which took a very strong rationalist, deductivist line, emphasizing the *a priori* nature of economic knowledge and the importance of individual intuition and minimizing the role of empirical research and the collection of factual evidence (Robbins 1934). In reaction to Robbins, many economic methodologists defended the broadly positivist position associated with Karl Popper, who argued that science could progress only when theoretical conjectures were subjected to empirical testing in an attempt to falsify them. Two writers in this broad tradition, Lawrence Boland and Terence Hutchison, are discussed in Section 10.2. A variant of Popper's ideas was developed by Imre Lakatos, who drew on the work of Thomas Kuhn to propose his own 'methodology of scientific research programmes', according to which the only genuinely progressive scientific paradigms were those that generated 'novel facts'. Lakatos's most consistent advocate among economists has been Mark Blaug, whose views on microfoundations are the subject of Section 10.3.

A very different approach, strongly influenced by postmodernist philosophy, is represented by the 'social studies of science' school, which is considered in Section 10.4 through the work of D. Wade Hands. The Critical Realist ideas of Roy Bhaskar and Tony Lawson, which are widely supported by Post Keynesian economists, are discussed in Section 10.5, while several methodologists with no clear affiliation to any of these schools form the subject of Section 10.6. Finally, since Kevin Hoover has written so much on the methodological issues that surround microfoundations, he deserves a separate section (10.7) to himself. It will be evident by this point that the economic methodologists have not been as clear or as consistent as they might have been in their criticism of the microfoundations dogma.

10.2 THE POPPERIANS

The Canadian methodologist Larry Boland is a dedicated follower of Karl Popper (Boland 1996). The sub-title of his *Foundations of Economic Method* is 'A Popperian Perspective'. Popper himself never expressed an opinion on the microfoundations dogma. Born in 1902, he had pretty well made up his mind on all the most important issues in the methodology of science by the middle of the twentieth century, and although he held up economics as a model for the other social sciences this did not commit him to any specific position on any particular question in dispute, or even to any detailed interpretation of the principle of methodological individualism, which he did support. Moreover, as already noted, Popper was a firm critic of reductionism, at least when applied to the life sciences. An additional problem in interpreting Boland's own position on microfoundations is a distinct lack of clarity in his writing. As Mark Blaug rather unkindly observed in reviewing a volume of Boland's collected essays, there was good reason for the author to complain (as he did) of being misunderstood, since 'to this day it is difficult to find two economists who agree about what it is that Boland said in these papers' (Blaug 1997, p. 1945).

The first edition of *Foundations of Economic Method* had a chapter with the title 'On the "Necessity" of Microfoundations for Macroeconomics'. While he deserves credit for recognizing the methodological significance of this question as early as 1982, Boland's treatment of it fully confirms Blaug's judgement as to the difficulty that readers have had in interpreting him. The title itself is provocative, and yet Boland never explains why he has placed 'necessity' in inverted commas. The chapter begins with a long passage from Arthur Okun on the need for 'a solid bridge' between macroeconomics and microeconomics. Keynes's bridge, Okun suggests, was 'defective', since 'none of the explanations flowed directly from the implications of optimization by individual agents or from a specific institutional constraint' (Okun 1981, pp. 817–19, cited by Boland 1982, p. 79). There is a second, slightly less lengthy, epigram in which Robert Clower repeats his familiar claim that Keynes was a disequilibrium theorist.

The first words by Boland himself beg a series of questions:

> There is virtually no discussion among economists of a need for macrofoundations for microeconomics, except, perhaps implicitly, in the writings of some institutionalists. In contrast, the demonstration of the existence of microfoundations for macrotheories is considered essential by many leading economists. The reason is the same for both and is easy to find. Demonstrating the dependence of all macroeconomics on microeconomic principles is essential for the fulfillment of the (methodological) individualist requirements of neoclassical economics. However – and this is not widely pointed out – this 'necessity' presumes that microeconomic theory, in the form of general equilibrium theory, is a successful individualist program. (Boland 1982, p. 80)

If microfoundations are indeed entailed by methodological individualism, which of the many sub-species of methodological individualism identified in Chapter 3 above does Boland advocate? Why is 'necessity' (again) in inverted commas? Is the virtual absence of discussion about macrofoundations to be welcomed or regretted? If (Walrasian) general equilibrium theory fails as an 'individualist program', does this mean that the microfoundations project is bound to fail? Or does the Ramsey model provide a satisfactory alternative?

After repeated forays into the remainder of Boland's brief (15-page) chapter, I am still unable to answer any of these questions, other than the first (as the approving reference in the Okun epigram to 'a specific institutional constraint' might suggest, Boland favours Joseph Agassi's 'institutional individualism'). His treatment of Keynes is certainly not enlightening. Boland cites a long, familiar passage from Keynes's 'general theory of employment' article on the need for 'a theory of demand and supply of output *as a whole*' (Keynes 1937, pp. 219–20, cited Boland 1982, p. 83; original stress), but his interpretation is contentious. 'It is easy to conclude from these fragments of Keynes' own view of his departure' from (neo-)classical theory, Boland suggests, 'that he was not arguing that macroeconomics lacked microfoundations. Rather, he was arguing that the traditional (micro) theory lacked necessary macrofoundations!' (Boland 1982, p. 83).

Whether the exclamation mark is an expression of agreement or disgust is not obvious. A second exclamation mark is provided in the next paragraph:

> In effect, by denying the adequacy of the macrofoundations of traditional theory, Keynes was simply arguing that microeconomic theory is *false*! Presumably, it is false because it is not logically consistent with all macrophenomena – such as persistent disequilibria – and thus, by *modus tollens*, at least one of the assumptions of microtheory is false and hence microtheory as a whole is false. If this is granted, why is there a concern for the microfoundations of macrotheory? (ibid., pp. 83–4)

Why indeed! Of course, many scholars would deny that Keynes regarded neoclassical microeconomics as false, since he stated very clearly in a well-known passage in the *General Theory* that 'the [neo]classical theory comes into its own again' once full employment is attained (Keynes 1936, p. 378; for Kaleckians and Sraffians this represents a powerful *criticism* of Keynes). Many would also dispute Boland's claim that 'Keynes accepted both the psychologism and the Inductivism upon which neoclassical theory is founded' (ibid., p. 94). But the relevance of all this to the microfoundations dogma, and to Keynes's own (inferred) attitude towards it, is never made clear.

If Boland's interpretation of Keynes is somewhat obscure, his own position – firm support in principle for microfoundations – does soon emerge. 'But the failure to provide microfoundations today', he continues, 'does not mean that they are impossible to provide. The critics would be better off taking the bull by the horns and trying to prove that it is impossible to provide them in the future'. Were the critics to fail, and if 'a successful microeconomic theory does exist, then the only uncertainty might be about how long it might take to solve the problem of microfoundations' (ibid., p. 85). And again: 'It must be agreed (first) that (to be consistent with individualism) neoclassical macroeconomics must be not more than an aggregation of microeconomics' (ibid., p. 90).

There is, Boland concedes, an alternative:

> The other way is to compartmentalize the discipline, giving each competitor its own department. ... However, this second way is only a temporary measure whenever competitors deal with the same phenomena. Unless they are shown to be logically equivalent, there remains the possibility that the economics profession could be destroyed by a life-or-death struggle caused by those economists who think that neoclassical microtheory is applicable to all economic phenomena and thus think that there is no need for a separate macrotheory. (Ibid., p. 89)

This is a very unsatisfactory passage (Hartley 1997, pp. 125–6). What is meant in this context by 'the same phenomena', and how they might legitimately be considered 'logically equivalent', are precisely the issues at stake in the controversy concerning microfoundations, but Boland has nothing to say on either question. Why should it be 'the economics profession' that might be destroyed in the course of the controversy, and not the 'separate department' or 'compartment' of (Keynesian) macroeconomics? Again, Boland does not explain.

In the second, substantially rewritten, edition of *Foundations of Economic Method* the chapter devoted to microfoundations has disappeared, but the issues receive attention in Chapter 2, 'The Explanatory Problem of Individualism'; in Chapter 9, 'From Macroeconomics to Evolutionary Game Theory'; and (briefly) in Chapter 17, 'Individualism and Social Knowledge'. In Chapter 2, Boland criticizes Mark Blaug (1992) for 'giving up methodological individualism rather than macroeconomics. I suspect that he only has psychologistic individualism in mind, since, contrary to what Blaug says, Popper's methodological individualism does not have to be a narrow reductionist program; only the special version, psychologistic individualism, does' (Boland 2003, p. 35). Boland himself again defends 'the Popper-Agassi alternative' of 'institutional individualism', according to which '[i]nstitutions are to be included among the explanatory variables along with the aims of individuals ... Unlike psychologistic individualism, institutional individualism is not necessarily a reductionist research program' (ibid., p. 38). As we have seen, this form of methodological individualism is full of problems; it would certainly not satisfy the advocates of microfoundations among twenty-first century neoclassical macroeconomists.

Rather strangely, Boland does not use the term 'microfoundations' anywhere in this early chapter. It does however appear, somewhat elliptically, in Chapter 9, which repeats large parts of the first edition's Chapter 5 but now includes a discussion of agent-based models, in the form of evolutionary game theory. 'I now wish to raise a new question', Boland writes:

> Given that evolutionary game theory does not presume the existence of a general equilibrium but does deal with a whole economy, and given that … it considers simultaneously processes of experimenting and groping by individual players, can evolutionary game theory be a plausible alternative to macroeconomic theory and thus render macroeconomic theory irrelevant? … I will try to determine whether evolutionary game theory is a worthy competitor or just an alternative microfoundation for macroeconomic theory. (Ibid., p. 141)

Boland's answer to this important question is, yet again, difficult to interpret. He claims that 'the evolutionary economics promoted by Nelson and Winter [1974; 1982] in effect, amounts to a different microfoundation for a different macroeconomics', rather than a replacement for any form of macroeconomics (ibid., p. 156). This would seem to rule it out as a 'worthy competitor'.

On the previous page, though, Boland seems to take a quite different line: 'If economic theory needs both micro- and macrofoundations, perhaps the distinction was a false one from the beginning' (ibid., p. 155). The 'perhaps' here is intriguing, or perhaps I should say infuriating; it is not explained. In Chapter 17, close to the end of the book, Boland does endorse macrofoundations, more or less: 'following on from the discussion in Chapter 9', he writes, 'it could easily be argued that theorists such as Richardson [1959] and Arrow [1986; 1994] are in effect arguing for macrofoundations for microeconomics'. (We have already encountered George Richardson and Kenneth Arrow: see pp. 88, 90 above). Boland seems to agree. This does not entail approval of 'some sort of neo-Marxian "Holism"', he maintains:

> Holism is simply the view that wholes (such as Nations, Clans, Tribes, or Social Classes) determine how individuals in society behave. For example, you may think that you are making a free choice but you may be naively unaware that your tastes are determined by your social position. For the most part, it can be argued, most people in the same social position behave the same way and thus make the same kind of choices. But the demand for macrofoundations does not necessarily make this holist type of argument.
>
> Macrofoundations in a general methodological-individualist context only intends to recognize that any individual's decision-making relies on knowledge of macro variables. The existence of a market system itself is a social phenomenon that is more than the behavior of one individual. (Ibid., p. 279)

Where does this leave the microfoundations dogma, and in particular the two critical questions of non-inferability and emergence? Boland's own position on these two critical questions remains profoundly obscure.

Much greater clarity was provided by Terence W. Hutchison, the doyen of twentieth-century British writers on economic methodology, with a publishing career that spanned eight decades. Politically, Hutchison was a consistent and outspoken classical liberal, and he might therefore be expected to have sympathized with the individualism that underpinned the microfoundations project. But he was also an unrelenting critic of neoclassical economic theory, on the grounds that it had always placed far too much emphasis on analytical rigour and far too little on empirical relevance. This theme runs through all his writings on methodology, from the logical positivism of his first book, *The Significance and Basic Postulates of Economic Theory* (Hutchison 1938) to the historical essays in his *On the Methodology of Economics and the Formalist Revolution* (Hutchison 2000). One chapter in the latter book has the title, 'Ultra-deductivism from Nassau Senior to Lionel Robbins to Daniel Hausman', though in fact Hutchison traces the origins of the ultra-deductivist vice – and he is in no doubt that it *is* a vice – even further back, to David Ricardo (ibid., pp. 257–60; see also Hutchison 1994, Chapters 3–5).

No great friend of Keynes, and a resolute enemy of the Cambridge Keynesians, Hutchison was nevertheless sympathetic to macroeconomics and severely critical of attempts to reduce it to microeconomics. As he wrote in 1995:

> Some economists would consider, especially among those most concerned with real-world policy making, that, in the twentieth century, it is the development of monetary and macroeconomics, especially on the empirical and statistical side, where much the most practically important progress has been achieved. It seems, however, that some philosophers of science seek to banish macroeconomics from the subject, because, inevitably, a preponderantly inductive method is required, while microeconomics, as cultivated academically, has remained predominantly deductive, with little improvement of its predictive content, in spite of much ingenious refinement and filigree. It may be, even, that just because macroeconomic prediction seems still, at the end of the twentieth century, so pathetically more inaccurate and unreliable than many of the predictions of physics, it is not realized that the very important *empirical* improvement achieved by macroeconomics, since Keynes, may well have brought about at least a slight but vitally important reduction in inaccuracy, allowance being made for a perhaps considerable increase, in recent decades, in the instabilities, discontinuities, interdependencies, and unpredictabilities of the politico-socio-economic world. (Hutchison 2000, pp. 44–5; original stress; cf. ibid., pp. 181, 265–76)

This is what my mother would have called a back-handed compliment, and it should be read in conjunction with Hutchison's earlier argument that empirically relevant general theories are even more difficult to discover in macroeconomics than in microeconomics.

He makes no explicit reference, here or elsewhere, to New Classical theory, but he would almost certainly have acknowledged that his strictures applied to it no less than to all versions of Keynesianism. As early as 1938 he had been severely critical of the assumption of 'perfect expectation' in neoclassical microeconomics (Hutchison 1938 [1960], pp. 94–104; cf. Hutchison 1981, Chapter 8). And the New Classicals, in turn, would have been dismayed by Hutchison's verdict on William Stanley Jevons, whose 'emphatically empirical and inductive ... pioneering contributions' to macroeconomics were much more valuable than his deductive work in the theory of value (ibid., p. 266).

10.3 THE LAKATOSIAN

Mark Blaug was possibly the most important historian of economic thought in the second half of the twentieth century. Author of the highly influential *Economic Theory in Retrospect*, first published in 1962 and still in print in its fifth (1996) edition, Blaug was also the author of *The Methodology of Economics* (1980; second edition 1992). This is a broadly Lakatosian interpretation of mainstream economics that is highly critical of the discipline's failure to subject its 'protective belt' of 'non-core' propositions to empirical testing. In the earlier book Blaug dealt at some length with the emergence of Keynesian theory, and could thus hardly avoid at least touching on the question of microfoundations. 'Classical economic theory', he notes in the opening chapter, 'was almost wholly macroeconomics; neoclassical theory was nothing but microeconomics; macroeconomics came back into its own with Keynes and for a decade or so virtually replaced microeconomics' (Blaug 1968, p. 4). 'In modern macroeconomics', he wrote in the chapter on neoclassical theory, 'we simply posit an aggregate outcome of individual choices in accordance with a definite global rule: Keynes's consumption function, for example, is not built up from individual maximizing behaviour' (ibid., p. 302). There is no indication that Blaug regards this as a bad thing. On the contrary: in the later chapter on the Keynesian Revolution Blaug endorses it, because of its empirical content:

> The contribution of the *General Theory* to modern economics was not simply to replace the conventional concentration upon firms and households with an emphasis on aggregates, nor even to place income and employment at the centre of macroeconomics instead of money and price levels, but to formulate theory in terms of a model whose key variables were specified in such a way as to be capable of quantitative measurement and testing. In retrospect *the* Keynesian revolution was the stimulus which the *General Theory* gave to the construction of testable models of economic behaviour. (Ibid., p. 663; original stress)

Some of this survived to reappear in the fourth (1985) edition; despite the publication of the Lucas critique and the rise of New Classical macroeconomics, there are only slight modifications to these two passages (Blaug 1985, pp. 297, 678). And there is a new 'Methodological Postscript', reinforcing the point about testability. Neoclassical models, Blaug now complains, invoke variables that are 'frequently incapable of being observed, even in principle', and are 'useless for predictive purposes'. 'Furthermore, the microeconomic character of the analysis made testing difficult in view of the fact that most available statistical data were of an aggregate nature: the problem of deducing macroeconomic theorems from microeconomic propositions was not faced squarely until Keynes's work showed that there was a problem' (ibid., p. 669). This somewhat enigmatic statement is not followed up with any criticism of the microfoundations dogma, or indeed by any attempt to compare the methodology of Keynes with that of the New Classicals. In the fifth edition of *Economic Theory in Retrospect*, which was published at a time when Keynesian theory had long ceased to be regarded by the mainstream as 'modern macroeconomics', the entire issue has disappeared. All that remains, in a more than 700-page book, is a single sentence repeating the point about Keynes's consumption function not being derived from individual maximizing behaviour (Blaug 1996, p. 280).

In *The Methodology of Economics* Blaug makes a rather broader attack on the principle of methodological individualism. What would it imply for economics, he asks?

> In effect, it would rule out all macroeconomic propositions that cannot be reduced to microeconomic ones, and since few have yet been so reduced, this amounts in turn to saying goodbye to the whole of received macroeconomics. There must be something wrong with a methodological principle that has such devastating implications. (Blaug 1980, p. 51)

Yet Karl Popper held up economics as a methodological model for the other social sciences. After quoting Popper on this point, Blaug concludes as follows:

> Let us, by all means, commend methodological individualism as a heuristic postulate: in principle, it is highly desirable to define all holistic concepts, macroscopic factors, aggregate variables, or whatever they are called, in terms of individual behaviour if and when this is possible. But when it is not possible, let us not lapse into silence on the grounds that we may not defy the principle of methodological individualism. (Blaug 1980, p. 51)

All this is repeated, verbatim, in the second edition (Blaug 1992, p. 46), in which Blaug also – prematurely – announces the 'terminal decline' of New Classical macroeconomics and 'a simply amazing resurgence of a new Keynesian economics in the spirit rather than the letter of Keynes' (ibid., p. 198). He does not use the term 'microfoundations' or discuss the contemporary controversies surrounding it, and ends with a very questionable assessment of the driving force behind macroeconomic debate since Keynes: 'To sum up 56 years of macroeconomics in one bold generalization is no doubt presumptuous but I remain convinced that the driving force in this long saga was the pursuit of empirical validation' (ibid., p. 205).

Blaug soon became much more sceptical concerning the empirical achievements of mainstream economic theory, but he seems to have returned to the question of microfoundations as a major source of methodological weakness only once. This is in a very favourable review of Harold Kincaid's *Individualism and the Unity of Science,* in which he endorses Kincaid's argument that:

> … all these microeconomic and macroeconomic theories with their alleged microfoundations actually let holistic considerations in by the back door. Either they treat socially determined individual preferences as exogenous, and hence assign the bulk of their explanatory power to social structures that they never investigate, or they appeal to socially determined norms, rules and conventions, as in the use of backward induction and "trembling hand equilibria" in game theory, while claiming to be practising methodological individualism. (Blaug 1999, pp. 249–50)

This is, in essence, the same (correct) point made by many earlier critics of methodological individualism (above, pp. 61–2).

10.4 SOCIAL STUDIES OF SCIENCE

D. Wade Hands is the most prominent advocate among economic methodologists of the constructivist, 'science studies' or 'sociology of scientific knowledge' school of thought. In his collection of essays, *Testing, Rationality, and Progress*, he has nothing explicit to say about microfoundations, but he does endorse Mark Blaug's position on Keynesian macroeconomics: 'There can be little doubt that Keynesian economics is a best gambit in economics if anything is' (Hands 1993, p. 46). Eight years later, in *Reflection without Rules*, Hands noted that the strong version of methodological individualism advocated by Lionel Robbins and Ludwig von Mises would eliminate macroeconomics. For them, 'all of economics is microeconomics, and although macroeconomic regularities might sometimes be of interest to economists and policy makers, macroeconomic constructs such as the consumption function are devoid of any real explanatory power' (Hands 2001, p. 43). Hands is sympathetic neither to this position nor to micro-reduction in other sciences. He comments favourably on the 'relatively new and rapidly growing literature on evolutionary economics that does not take the standard microreductionist strict-Darwinian approach to evolutionary change' but instead 'grounds its evolutionary economics in macro-oriented evolutionary biology such as the punctuated equilibrium theory of Stephen Jay Gould, Niles Eldredge, and others' (ibid., p. 385; cf. pp. 49–50 above).

Hands also rejects the 'eliminative materialism' proposed by some philosophers of mind, who argue that 'since beliefs can not be reduced to physiological processes in the brain, they should be eliminated'. For Hands this claim is refuted by the existence of multiple realizations, and the related concept of supervenience:

> If two people had identical brains, identical in every single physical and chemical way, it seems reasonable to say that they would have the same thoughts (mental activity), but just because two people have the same thought, say hunger or lust, it need not imply that their brains are physically and chemically in exactly the same state. (Ibid., p. 170)

He concludes that the 'supervenience of the mental on the physical allows one to maintain a commitment to a materialist ontology without requiring the reduction of mental kinds to physical kinds', though he acknowledges that this 'is a debate that remains a long way from closure' (ibid., p. 170).

The implications for economics are very important:

> If the social supervenes on the individual (or the sum of the individuals), then the same individual behavior would produce the same social behavior, but social behavior could not necessarily be reduced to the behavior of individual agents. In other words 'same individual' implies 'same social', but 'same social' need not imply 'same individual'.

And this, Hands continues, is directly relevant to the question of microfoundations:

> Similarly, supervenience also provides a different way of thinking about the relationship between micro- and macroeconomics. The standard way of thinking about 'microfoundations' is reductionist – the macro needs to be reduced to the micro (usually a specific form of micro) and if it can not be reduced to micro then it needs to be eliminated – but if the macro simply supervenes on the micro, then it is possible to maintain that micro behavior is in some sense more basic (same micro implies same macro) but not require that macroeconomic features be reduced to microeconomic behavior (same macro need not imply same micro). (Ibid., p. 171)

Thus Hands, too, is an opponent of micro-reduction in economics.

10.5 THE CRITICAL REALISTS

There are very clear affinities between the Critical Realist approach to the philosophy of science and the anti-reductionist position on microfoundations. Critical Realists reject atomistic thinking in favour of holism (a rather dangerous concept, as we have seen). They prefer organic metaphors to mechanical, spatial and constructional metaphors, and, most important, advocate 'open system' rather than 'closed system' thinking and are very critical of the deductive modes of reasoning employed by mainstream economists. As we saw earlier (above, pp. 68–9), the founding father of Critical Realism, Roy Bhaskar, is a strong critic of micro-reduction. He explicitly endorses the principle of downward causation and stresses the importance of 'emergent causality (viz. that reference to an element at the higher-order level may be a contingently necessary condition for the explanation of what happens at the lower-order level)' (Bhaskar 1998, p. 100). Thus he emphasizes the 'causal irreducibility' of higher-level (or macro) phenomena in social science (Brown 2012, p. 122).

Bhaskar's disciple, Tony Lawson, goes even further, arguing that the deductive method *requires* (micro-) reduction. To reject the former is to repudiate the latter (Smithin 2009, p. 66, citing Lawson 1997, pp. 98–9). In his own defence of macroeconomics as a relatively autonomous discipline,

John Smithin also invokes Critical Realism: 'Acceptance of the critical realist account of social reality would seem to make possible a macroeconomics which is not completely hamstrung, as is contemporary orthodoxy, by obeisance to the axiomatic-deductive *microfoundations* project' (Smithin 2004, p. 56). Smithin sees critical realism as offering the prospect of a revitalization of macroeconomic theory as traditionally conceived, since it recognizes the autonomous existence of social structures and does not require them to be reduced to statements about individuals (Smithin 2009, Chapter 3).

And yet Critical Realism is not enough to render its proponents immune to the microfoundations dogma. This is evident in the case of the Danish Post Keynesian, Jesper Jespersen, who has written a thorough and penetrating analysis of the important methodological issues that arise in macroeconomic theory, from a broadly Critical Realist perspective and drawing on much of the relevant literature, including Dow (1985b, 1996) and Hartley (1997). Throughout his *Macroeconomic Methodology*, Jespersen repeatedly identifies the reasons why the microfoundations project was doomed to failure, and even devotes the whole of Chapter 7 to 'The Fallacy of Composition'. Earlier, in a chapter entitled 'Uncertainty and "The Economy as a Whole"', he explains that 'The fallacy of composition occurs when incorrect macroeconomic conclusions are drawn from a misplaced analogy between macro-behaviour and microeconomic behaviour' (Jespersen 2009, p. 142). He invokes the paradox of thrift and the paradox of costs to illustrate the problem, here and in Chapter 7 (see especially ibid., pp. 189–93).

In his concluding chapter Jespersen defends 'seven theses with relevance for a realistic macro-analysis', the second and third of which are directly linked to the question of microfoundations. Thesis no. 2 connects an open social ontology to the existence of fundamental uncertainty: 'Volatile microeconomic expectations lie behind the aggregate macroeconomic behaviour, which at the very same time become[s] both cause and effect'. This is a very clear recognition of downward causation. 'This micro-macro interdependency', he continues, 'rules out by its nature that the future can be known with certainty'. According to the third thesis, '[t]he analytical road leading from micro to macro is not just a matter of simple aggregation'. This is because, as the Critical Realists would put it:

> Only the surface of the macroeconomic landscape is directly observable. Structures in the 'deeper' strata are assumed to make an impact on how 'the economy as a whole' changes through historical time. Therefore, one cannot make a

> one-way deduction from observed microeconomic behaviour to macroeconomic tendencies. (Ibid., p. 227)

Once again, downward causation – from macro to micro – features prominently in Jespersen's analysis.

This is a powerful argument, but it sits uneasily beside one section of Chapter 7. Jespersen begins this section by quoting Keynes:

> Though an individual whose transactions are small in relation to the market can safely neglect the fact that demand is not a one-sided transaction, it makes nonsense to neglect it when we come to aggregate demand. This is the vital difference between the theory of the economic behaviour of the aggregate and the theory of the behaviour of the individual unit. (Keynes 1936, p. 85, cited by Jespersen 2009, pp. 184–5)

Unaccountably this is immediately followed by Jespersen's own statement, which directly contradicts it:

> It is not the [a?] question of whether a microeconomic foundation is relevant for macroeconomic theory that divides neoclassical and post-Keynesian macroeconomic analysis. *On the contrary, it is how a relevant microeconomic foundation can be formulated* and whether it can be incorporated into an analytical macroeconomic model that describes an open and structured landscape. (Jespersen 2009, p. 185; stress added)

The section in which this observation appears has the title, 'Keynes's Microeconomic Foundation Characterized by Uncertainty'. Thus Jespersen is asserting two inconsistent propositions: (i) microfoundations are in principle impossible, due to the fallacy of composition (which is also the only reasonable interpretation of the two sentences from Keynes that have just been quoted); and (ii) Keynes and the Post Keynesians have succeeded in providing microfoundations for their macroeconomic theory, while neoclassical efforts to do so for theirs are doomed to failure. As we saw in Chapter 8, many other Post Keynesian writers with no great interest in questions of methodology have also attempted to straddle this extremely uncomfortable fence.

10.6 THE ECLECTICS

In this section I consider the views on microfoundations expressed by several economic methodologists who do not fit neatly into any of the categories used in the previous sections. I begin with *Rational Economic*

Man, a widely read book in which the British philosopher Martin Hollis and the American radical economist Edward J. Nell mount a relentless and at the time well-received attack on 'positivism' in economics, instead defending a realist ontology with strong Marxian roots and occasionally also invoking 'Conceptual Pragmatism'. Unsurprisingly, in a book published in 1975, they make no explicit reference to microfoundations, but their position on the underlying philosophical issues is very clear. 'Neo-Classical Economic Man is a sovereign individual with utilitarian forebears', they write, 'and is first to be studied in isolation from his fellows and from the institutions surrounding him. The behaviour of social molecules, according to this view, is the effect of combining social atoms' (Hollis and Nell 1975, p. 264). This principle was established very clearly by John Stuart Mill, who wrote, in his *System of Logic* that 'Human beings in society have no properties but those which are derived from, and may be resolved into, the laws of the nature of the individual man. In social phenomena the Composition of Causes is the universal law' (cited ibid., p. 264). Against this position Hollis and Nell direct their own 'Classical and Marxian rumblings', since 'We believe neither that economic man can be defined apart from his social setting nor that the social setting is, even in theory, created by the combined work of individual wills' (ibid., p. 265).

Earlier in the book this anti-atomism is applied directly to the question of microfoundations:

> ... micro-economics is often introduced to students, as if it were more basic than macro-economics. The economic world is composed of economies, composed of firms and markets, composed of individuals. So it seems natural to start with atoms and work up to more complex structures. This strategy accords well with Positivist epistemology, since all empirical knowledge is thought of as a hierarchy in which each level is supported from below until a foundation of simple observation statements is reached ... So it would be not only natural but also obligatory to reduce macro to micro. Conceptual Pragmatism simply removes the pillars of the temple. Micro is not more basic than macro and, unless there are pedagogic gains, there is no reason to start with it. The only question is what produces the most elegant and convenient whole. (Ibid., p. 155)

This statement is commendably clear and direct (though, as we saw in Chapter 2, it does not do justice to those positivists, like Otto Neurath, who opposed hierarchical reductionism; see above, pp. 34–5). It seems, however, to have been overlooked in the heated controversies that followed the publication of *Rational Economic Man*, which focused on the other, quite different, issues raised in the book.

Five years after the publication of *Rational Economic Man*, Homa Katouzian, in his book *Ideology and Method in Economics*, took a position very similar to that of Terence Hutchison. In the words of one reviewer, Katouzian criticizes neoclassical microeconomics for being 'devoid of empirical implications' and the academic economists for concentrating on 'insignificant and unrealistic "puzzles" rather than substantial problems of actual social concern' (Green 1981, p. 1582; in this review Edward Green endorses Daniel Hausman's defence of mainstream economics against these charges). Katouzian takes no great interest in the question of microfoundations, and there are no references in the index to this term, to (methodological) individualism, or to micro and macro. There is, however, a brief and brutal passage in which he dismisses the positivist claim that 'all science (including social science) can be reduced to physics. This view', Katouzian continues, 'may be described as *substantial reductionism*. The positivist claim that *the method* of all sciences can be reduced to *the method* of physics is the methodological analogue to that discredited view; it may be described as *methodological reductionism* (Katouzian 1980, p. 74; original stress). Katouzian's hostility to both claims is evident; he does not apply it to the relationship between microeconomics and macroeconomics, however, but rather to demonstrate that Popper was not (on these criteria) a logical positivist. In the present context his book must be regarded as a missed opportunity.

As Green suggests, Daniel Hausman has consistently defended mainstream economics from methodological critics like Blaug, Hutchison and Katouzian, arguing that economists have for the most part done the best that they could in very difficult circumstances. As the title of his book *The Inexact and Separate Science of Economics* suggests, Hausman insists that 'sciences are not all alike, and that philosophers and methodologists must be sensitive to the details of the disciplines they study' (Hausman 1992, p. 319). Economics is, perhaps, more like chemistry than physics, but 'it is a social science. As such, one might question whether it should be modeled after *any* of the natural sciences' (ibid., p. 320; original stress). In the same spirit, Hausman rejects any dogmatic insistence on methodological individualism in economics: 'If unfamiliar forms of explanations can be well tested and can command empirical support, they should be pursued. Economic theory has not been successful enough to justify theoretical or methodological purism' (ibid., p. 99).

Hausman has very little to say about macroeconomics, for which there is no entry in the index. There is a brief and rather inconclusive reference in the Appendix, which provides an introduction to the philosophy of science.

Here Hausman notes the 'special difficulties' of providing explanations in the social sciences, and offers a rather more favourable verdict on methodological individualism. 'The stricter formulation of methodological individualism calling for the elimination of all non-individualistic terms is untenable', he concludes, 'but weaker versions are plausible. Methodological individualism is accepted by many economists and is sometimes used as a basis to criticize macroeconomic theories' (ibid., p. 322). Whether Hausman himself agrees with such criticism is not clear.

Don Ross evidently does not. Reviewing the third edition of Hausman's (2008) anthology *The Philosophy of Economics*, Ross comments favourably on Kevin Hoover's chapter 'on the extent to which macroeconomics should be regarded as a dubious enterprise if it cannot be given microfoundations. I agree with Hoover that this widespread belief among economists is not well supported, and unnecessarily restricts degrees of freedom in the discipline' (Ross 2009, p. 175, citing Hoover 2001a [2008], pp. 57–89). As we shall see in the following section, Hoover himself has not been entirely consistent on these questions.

I conclude this section by referring to two recent publications by economic methodologists. The first is by Roger Backhouse, a prominent historian of economic thought who has also published widely on methodological questions (see, for example, the essays in Backhouse 1998). Before 2010, however, his only detailed reference to microfoundations came in a book review, in which he gave a broadly favourable assessment of Harold Kincaid's *Individualism and the Unity of Science* (Kincaid 1997):

> Kincaid's main argument, which seems entirely justified, is that neoclassical economics (loosely, the economics found in standard modern micro and macro textbooks) cannot be justified by a general philosophical appeal to individualism. The argument that macro theories *must* be reducible to micro theories is a type of reductionism which holds in neither biology and psychology (where behaviour is not necessarily reducible to biochemistry) nor in economics. Appeals to methodological individualism are not enough. Economic theories may draw on lower level theories but that does not thereby make them superior to theories that do not. They need to be tested. (Backhouse 2000, p. F194; original stress)

Thus Backhouse is – or in 2000 was – a strong critic of the microfoundations dogma. It must be said, however, that he has not applied these criticisms in any of his subsequent writing on the history of mainstream macroeconomic theory. In a recent book-length discussion of the relationship between science and ideology in the recent history of mainstream economics, Backhouse notes the role of microfoundations as a major component of 'the quest for rigorous macroeconomics'. While he is critical of the use of general equilibrium modelling in macroeconomics, however, and writes favourably of the objections raised by Arrow, Clower and Leijonhufvud, he expresses no opinion on the legitimacy of the microfoundations dogma as such (Backhouse 2010, pp. 121–4).

Finally, in their recent authoritative text on economic methodology, Marcel Boumans and John Davis (2010) criticize reductionism and defend a variety of pluralist positions, including 'epistemological pluralism' (p. 154), 'triangulation' (p. 156) and 'methodological pluralism' (p. 156). Triangulation is 'the idea that the best way to produce reliable results is to come at problems from quite different points of view using different methods and perhaps data, and then focus on those results upon which these different points of view separately arrive' (p. 156). This shades into methodological pluralism: 'According to Warren Samuels, this is the view that absent "meta-criteria" by which one methodology can be shown unequivocally to be superior to all others, analyses should not be rejected solely on the basis of methodological considerations. From this it follows that reductionism is wrong and that there are inescapably different kinds of knowledge implying the methodological policy recommendation that we ought to promote different kinds of knowledge in order to advance science as a whole' (p. 156).

On the previous page, Boumans and Davis define a 'version of reductionism in economics' as 'the claim that macroeconomics needs to have microfoundations, and should thereby be reduced to microeconomics. However, were one to argue that not only do macroeconomic relationships depend on microeconomic ones, but also microeconomic relationships depends [*sic*] on macroeconomic ones, one would be abandoning reductionism in favor of an epistemologically pluralist understanding of the two parts of economics' (p. 155). This is one justification for epistemological pluralism; the other is the division of labour, a risk-averse notion that promoting different research strategies will increase the growth of knowledge since 'some of them will be successful' (p. 155), but we do not know in advance which.

10.7 KEVIN HOOVER: A SPECIAL CASE

Kevin Hoover is an econometrician who turned to methodology because of his dissatisfaction with New Classical macroeconomics. As he notes in *New Classical Macroeconomics: A Sceptical Inquiry*:

> Methodology is indeed unavoidable. What Keynes (1936, p. 383) thought about the relationship between economists and politicians is *mutatis mutandis* also true of the relationship between economists and methodologists: Practical economists, who believe themselves to be quite exempt from any methodological influences, are usually slaves of some defunct methodologist. (1988, p. 733)

Hoover has written at some length on the methodology of macroeconomics over almost a quarter of a century in books, papers in economics journals, and also articles in leading philosophy journals (*The Monist* and *Erkenntnis*). Always opposed to the microfoundations dogma, Hoover has sharpened his criticism over the years. But he has also shifted his ground, and he has been less than entirely consistent in his opposition to it. His is an instructive case study in how the question of microfoundations can generate some confusion even among the best of its adversaries.

In *New Classical Macroeconomics* Hoover describes how the 'Keynesian dominance of macroeconomics' came to an end for two reasons, one practical (it had little to say about inflation) and one theoretical: the absence of microfoundations (1988, p. 3–4). He is very clear on the intentions of the New Classicals: 'The ultimate goal of the new classical economics is the euthanasia of macroeconomics' (p. 87), while '[Eugene] Fama's attack on the problem of integrating monetary theory and value theory is radical: he simply abolishes monetary theory' (p. 95). Hoover himself is evidently not sympathetic to this project, but he does not yet provide a clear, explicit attack on microfoundations, and in references to the neoclassical synthesis and its Keynesian critics he appears to accept its legitimacy. Thus he writes that 'Hahn and Clower offer direct criticisms of the microfoundations of Patinkin's system … Gurley and Shaw's analysis is aggregative. It is, nevertheless, based implicitly on a microeconomic foundation quite close to that of Patinkin' (p. 92). The book was reviewed by Leonard Rapping, who in 1969 published a celebrated paper with Robert Lucas on microfoundations in the labour market but who was now a radical economist who had moved a long way from his former co-author in political terms. While Rapping is generally sympathetic to Hoover's position, he regards the triumph of the microfoundations dogma as inescapable: 'economists now view macro models without microfoundations as cars without engines … Methodologically speaking, we are all Lucasians now' (Rapping 1990, p. 73).

Seven years later, in a review article dealing with texts on economic methodology by Blaug, Boland, Hausman and Alexander Rosenberg, Hoover attacked Rosenberg, who 'stigmatises aggregate economics without microeconomic theory as mere curve-fitting', and 'claims that the history of science supports the "rational expectationist" view of the necessity of microfoundations for macro-phenomena' (1995a, pp. 728, 729); the references are to Rosenberg (1992), p. 132, 129. Rosenberg offers no argument for microfoundations, Hoover objects, other than drawing parallels with procedures in the natural sciences. He disputes Rosenberg's interpretation: 'On the contrary, to take an example from physics, it was the increasingly accurate account of the actual (aggregate or macro) behaviour of gases – the ideal gas law and deviations from it – that supported the advancement and refinement of the microphysical theory of molecular behaviour, not the other way round' (Hoover 1995a, pp. 729–30). This is also true of social science, Hoover maintains: the law of large numbers is used by insurance companies, who do not need to know much about the characteristics of individuals. 'Rosenberg should have drawn a different conclusion', he suggests; 'the intentional character of economic behaviour, because it limits the precision of prediction and explanation at the individual level, demonstrates the microfoundations of macroeconomics – construed as direct reduction of aggregate to individual behaviour – is *impossible*; *macroeconomics is autonomous* and must seek improvements through its own development'. Inadvertently, the New Classical economists themselves acknowledged this through their reliance on the representative agent: 'This is not microfoundations' (ibid., p. 730; stress added).

However, in his introduction to his edited volume *Macroeconometrics*, published in the same year, Hoover took a rather different position. 'Keynes had already provided informal microeconomic rationales for consumption, investment, and portfolio behaviour in *The General Theory*', he observes, and cites later work by Klein, Baumol, Tobin, Modigliani and Brumberg, Friedman and Lipsey: 'Each of these was an attempt to provide microfoundations for a part of the Keynesian model, and each was to some degree successful theoretically and empirically' (Hoover 1995b, p. 3). Evidently their quest for microfoundations was not, after all, 'impossible'. 'The decisive break with the piecemeal approach to microfoundations', Hoover continues, 'was Clower's (1965) article "The Keynesian Counter-revolution" … After Clower, macroeconomics could go two ways: give up the search for Keynesian features and adopt wholeheartedly the implications of the Walrasian model, which is essentially the new classical approach, or attempt to provide microfoundations for the impediments to smooth price adjustment that would justify Keynesian features, which became the new Keynesian approach', while '[t]he macroeconometric models in widespread use in commercial forecasting and government policy analysis circa 1970 were an uneasy compromise between the drive for deep microfoundations and the exigencies of empirical reality' (ibid., p. 4). There is no suggestion here that New Classical Economics had no microfoundations: on the contrary, 'the important thing about Muth's hypothesis was that it modelled expectations as part of the scheme of general-equilibrium microfoundations' (ibid., p. 5). The general theme of Hoover's introduction is that the microfoundations project is a good one, that both the New Classicals and the New Keynesians had provided microfoundations for their macroeconomics, but that they were *different* microfoundations.

In the same year, in an article published in *The Monist* with the title 'Is macroeconomics for real?', Hoover argued 'that ontological reduction of macroeconomics to microeconomics is *untenable*. Thus, while the program of microfoundations may illuminate macroeconomics in various ways, it cannot succeed in its goal of replacing macroeconomics' (Hoover 1995c, p. 235; stress added). He invokes Uskali Mäki's realist ontology to argue 'that macroeconomic aggregates exist *externally* (i.e., independently of any individual human mind) and *objectively* (i.e., unconstituted by the representations of macroeconomic theory)' (ibid., p. 236; original stress). Hoover claims that methodological individualism in economics 'appears to be based on an instinctive belief in *ontological individualism*: the doctrine that all that exists fundamentally for the economy are individual economic actors' (p. 237; original stress). He cites both Blaug (who claims that ontological individualism is 'trivially true') and Hayek to support this interpretation (ibid., pp. 238–9, citing Blaug 1992, p. 45).

Section 3 of Hoover's paper is entitled 'The Supervenience of Macroeconomics on Microeconomics' (ibid., pp. 246–50). Hoover cites Jaegwon Kim and Alexander Rosenberg, who use the notion of supervenience to justify micro-reduction, and (against them) David Levy (1985): 'What Levy's argument demonstrates is that Hayek is mistaken, that how people theorize about the macroeconomy *is* constitutive of macroeconomic phenomena' (p. 249). Hoover is, again, strongly critical of representative agent models:

> Empirically, far from isolating a microeconomic core, real-business-cycle models, as with other representative-agent models, use macro-economic aggregates for their testing and estimation. Thus, to the degree that such models are successful in explaining empirical phenomena, they point to the ontological centrality of macroeconomic and not microeconomic entities … they are but the simulacrum of microeconomics. (Ibid., p. 253)

(The *Concise Oxford Dictionary* defines 'simulacrum' as 'Image of something; shadowy likeness, deceptive substitute, mere pretence'; 'deceptive substitute' seems to be what Hoover has in mind). This was the first time that Hoover used ontological arguments and the concept of supervenience to attack the microfoundations dogma, but as we shall see he was soon to repudiate them both.

In his brief book *The Methodology of Empirical Macroeconomics*, which consists of lectures delivered at the University of Nijmegen in 1997, lecture 3 is entitled 'Does Macroeconomics need Microfoundations?' Here Hoover repeats his criticism of ontological individualism and of representative agent models, which 'are just as aggregative as old-fashioned Keynesian macroeconometric models. They do not solve the problem of aggregation: rather they assume that it can be ignored' (Hoover 2001a [2008], p. 82). 'This is the simulacrum of microeconomics, not the genuine article' (ibid., p. 93). Hoover employs physical examples to press the point: the reduction of the ideal gas laws to Newtonian mechanics 'is not micro all the way down. In addition to Newton's laws, the kinetic theory relies on a statistical assumption – that is, an implicitly macro assumption'.

And Hoover now refers to emergence for the first time: 'The phenomena of temperature and pressure can be thought of as *emergent properties* of the aggregation of molecules' (ibid., p. 67; original stress). He again invokes supervenience, which 'guarantees the autonomy of the macro level in the sense that it ensures that one can rationally use an independent language and categories to describe the macro level and that one should not expect to find unique deductions from the micro to the macro' (ibid., p. 68; see Reiss 2004 for strong criticism of this part of the book). Hoover concludes thus: 'It shall remain necessary for the serious economist to switch back and forth between microeconomics and *a relatively autonomous macroeconomics*, depending upon the problem at hand' (p. 86; stress added). He makes similar points in the introduction to a co-edited anthology of articles on real business cycle theory. Contrary to the 'rhetorical argument' of these theorists, their reliance on the representative agent means that 'they do not provide genuine microfoundations'. This conclusion is reinforced by the Sonnenschein–Mantel–Debreu results (discussed in Chapter 6 above). 'Starting with first principles, or general equilibrium theory, only, we can derive all sorts of macroeconomics. Some form of *aggregate* structure must be provided' (Hartley, Hoover and Salyer 1998, p. 12; original stress).

In his book *Causality in Macroeconomics* Hoover again stresses the importance of ontology and suggests that ontological individualism has traditionally been the basis for economists' belief in methodological individualism (Hoover 2001b, pp. 109–11). Section 3 of Chapter 5 is entitled 'The Supervenience of Macroeconomics on Microeconomics' (pp. 119–24), and here Hoover takes a very similar line to that of his *Monist* article: 'the nature of the relationship through which the elements of macroeconomics supervene on the elements of microeconomics precludes direct reduction of the macroeconomic to the microeconomic, *even in principle*' (p. 124; stress added). Two of his reviewers agreed (a third reviewer, Ralph Bailey (2002) demurred, offering a (rare) methodological defence of microfoundations; see above, p. 123). James Holmes endorses Hoover's argument that 'the holding of money requires an individual to conceive of some measure of the price level, an index, which he terms a *synthetic* aggregate in counter-distinction to a *natural* aggregate such as the prices of a good'. Holmes concurs with Hoover that, 'because macroeconomics involves money, it must involve concepts that are fundamentally not microeconomic' (Holmes 2003, p. 593) As we have seen, the Post Keynesian theorist John Smithin takes a very similar position on the irreducibly macroeconomic nature of money (above, p. 161). And in his review the econometrician David Hendry came up with a telling analogy: 'A timepiece is much more than the sum of its parts – knowing everything about all the micro components (in the extreme, at a quantum level) would be of little help in explaining how a watch "told the time"'. So, too, with the supposed microfoundations of macroeconomics (Hendry 2003, p. 376).

But Hoover himself qualifies this conclusion in the following chapter of *Causality in Macroeconomics*, where he relies on the complexity of the world to argue (in effect) that while microfoundations are possible in principle the project is unlikely to succeed in practice: 'This [real-world complexity] does not suggest that no reduction in the direction of microeconomics is possible, but it does give another reason to think that such a reduction will necessarily be incomplete and that there is probably some optimal level of reduction, which nonetheless involves considerable aggregation' (ibid., p. 131; original stress). Finally, in the concluding Chapter 11, Hoover brings in emergent properties to support a very different conclusion: 'reduction of macro to micro is *not possible*. The macroeconomic aggregates have emergent properties that, of their nature, cannot belong to microeconomic entities. These properties give the aggregates an external, objective existence – they are independent of individual human minds and of the representations of economic theory. And genuine causal relationships worthy of scientific study connect them' (ibid., p. 285; stress added). This is the final sentence of the penultimate page of the book; it is very difficult indeed to reconcile with the statement on p. 131 that was quoted immediately above it.

There is a brief discussion of microfoundations in Hoover's chapter 'A history of postwar monetary economics and macroeconomics' in the Blackwell *Companion to the History of Economic Thought* (Hoover 2003, pp. 416–19). Here he takes broadly the same line as in his *Macroeconometrics* book (Hoover 1995b), describing Klein as a pioneer in 'securing the microfoundational underpinnings' of the Keynesian consumption and investment functions (Hoover 2003, p. 416); there is no suggestion that this was in principle an impossible project. Hoover again attacks the representative agent approach: 'With no serious account of how to construct economy-wide aggregates from the choices of individual agents, this move was a serious retreat from the original goal of the microfoundational program' (ibid., p. 419) – a goal which, by implication, is a sensible one.

By 2006, however, Hoover was taking a much harder line against the microfoundations dogma than he had ever done before:

> The appeal of microfoundations is largely ontological: everyone agrees that the economy is composed of individuals making choices subject to constraints. The operative question, however, is can the aggregate outcomes be inferred from detailed knowledge of individuals? The practical answer is clearly no. *No one has proposed an analysis of macroeconomic aggregates that truly begins with individuals.* Who would know how? Is this because the problem is just too difficult? Or is it because it cannot be done in principle? The advocate of the representative agent model implicitly believes the former. I have argued elsewhere that macroeconomic aggregates are emergent phenomena that belong to categories different than even similarly named microeconomic concepts, and that, in principle, one cannot reduce the macro to the micro. (Hoover 2006, p. 249; stress added)

Here he refers to Hoover (2001a, Chapter 5). In 2009 he described the microfoundations dogma as an ideology:

> ... both in the neutral sense of a more or less coherent set of beliefs guiding the collective activity of macroeconomic research and in its pejorative sense of false consciousness – a collective illusion shared by macroeconomists. My contention is that, even in its neutral sense, the ideology of microfoundations rests on a mistake about the ontology of the social world; whereas, in its pejorative sense, it shares the characteristic, common to political ideologies, of serving as a tool of persecution and intellectual repression. The ideologue searches for intellectual purity. Since the consciousness is false, ideology in this sense is bound to be a muddle – but a deeply pernicious muddle. (Hoover 2009, p. 388)

He again invokes emergent properties, citing the philosopher Hilary Putnam, who correctly 'argues that many physical explanations work only at a macro level' (ibid., p. 395).

In a very significant change of tack Hoover also cites another philosopher, John Searle, who allows for collective as well as individual intentionality:

> Searle's (1995) account of social facts as a background of constitutive rules created through collective intentionality and constraining the actions of individuals provides a rich understanding of the independence of super-individual economic structures from particular economic agents while preserving channels through which the beliefs, intentions, choices, and actions of individuals influence the behaviour of macroeconomic aggregates. (Ibid., p. 405)

These are the first references that I have been able to trace in Hoover's writings on microfoundations to the critical issue of downward causation that I emphasized in earlier chapters (above, pp. 9, 40). There is also a rare reference to the fallacy of composition: 'The focus of early macroeconomists on fallacies of composition is warranted by the recognition that the collective intentionality generates a set of causal structures that is systematically distinct from the underlying individuals' (ibid., p. 400). But Hoover now repudiates his earlier reliance on the notion of supervenience, which 'may be too weak to support the status of macroeconomics. It may mistake an epistemological problem for an ontological one' (ibid., p. 393).

This is a very important concession, and I think that it marks a significant change in Hoover's position. His conclusion is forceful:

> The irony of the program of microfoundations is that, in the name of preserving the importance of individual intentional states and preserving the individual economic agent as the foundation of economics, it fails to provide any intelligible connection between the individual and the aggregate. Instead, it embraces the representative agent, which is as close to an untethered Hegelian World (or Macroeconomic) Spirit as one might fear in the microfoundationalist's worst nightmare. (Ibid., p. 405)

Yet, in two more recent papers, Hoover seems to have had second thoughts. We saw in Chapter 5 above how his treatment of microfoundations in the history of economic thought conceded too much, with his contentious identification of 'three microfoundational programs', two of which aimed to provide 'non-eliminative' microfoundations for macroeconomic theory (Hoover 2010b, p. 7; cf. above, pp. 76, 79).

And, in a paper published in the journal *Erkenntnis*, Hoover again takes issue with representative agent models. Here he distinguishes 'three distinct theses' that 'march under the microfoundational banner'. The first is the 'weak ontological claim' that 'without individuals there would be no aggregates'. This he now regards as 'uncontroversial'. The second thesis is that 'How individuals behave affects or conditions how aggregates behave'. Keynes accepted this, Hoover correctly suggests, and so it seems does Hoover himself, and pretty well everyone else. Third, and much more controversial, is the claim that 'Aggregates are nothing else but the addition of individual behavior'. This is 'the dominant view in economics today' (Hoover 2010a, p. 331). So far, so good. But while the representative agent model is 'the most popular way of implementing the reduction of macroeconomics to microeconomics' (ibid., p. 332), Hoover continues, it is not the only one. Blanchard and Fischer (1989) offer alternatives, relying on 'idealizations' (in particular, monopolistic competition). If these models had succeeded, Hoover suggests, they *would* have provided 'successful microfoundations' (ibid., p. 337).

And so it seems, for Hoover, the microfoundations project *is* possible in principle. In practice, however, he accepts that Blanchard and Fischer's 'idealizations' have not succeeded, and so in practice their version of microfoundations has failed. This sees Hoover returning to something very similar to his 2001 conclusion – microfoundations are possible in principle but not in practice – and it is very difficult indeed to square with the position that he took in 2009.

10.8 CONCLUSION

Three conclusions may be drawn from the material presented in this chapter. First, the economic methodologists did not speak with one voice on the question of microfoundations, and several prominent authors have themselves been ambivalent, to a greater or lesser extent, about the important issues that it raised. Second, the majority of the methodologists were nevertheless hostile to the dogma, and they did refer to some of the critical literature in the philosophy of science that was outlined in Part I above. This literature, as we saw in Part II and in the first two chapters of Part III, remained a closed book to almost all of the mainstream economists who endorsed microfoundations, and also to many of their heterodox opponents. Third, this was to their detriment: they had neglected economic methodology at their peril.

11. Conclusion

11.1 INTRODUCTION

I began this book with an account of what would happen if the microfoundations dogma were to prevail: the death of macroeconomics as a separate discipline and its reduction to a mere branch, or application, of neoclassical microeconomics. Then, in Part I, I drew on the literature on metaphors, and on the philosophy of science, to argue that it was unlikely to succeed, not least because it had already failed both in biology and in the other social sciences. In defence of the relative autonomy of macroeconomic theory I set out the two principles of the fallacy of composition and downward causation. The emergent properties of macroeconomic systems, I suggested, made their reduction to microeconomics impossible. In Part II, I mapped the road to microfoundations in economics since 1936, and a very rocky, uneven and circuitous road it proved to be, though it did get there in the end. In the other social sciences the road had the same name but a quite different destination. Finally, in Part III, I looked at the dissenters who refused to take the road to microfoundations. These were mainly heterodox economists, but there were also some prominent mainstream dissidents and a good (but not unanimous) majority of the economic methodologists.

In this final chapter I want to consider some of the issues that have arisen, but have not been properly addressed, in Parts I–III. First, in Section 11.2, I ask why the microfoundations dogma emerged when it did, and not before, and why it eventually triumphed in the 1980s. Then, in Section 11.3, I pose Jerry Fodor's crucial question: 'So, then, *why is there anything except physics*?' (Fodor 1997, p. 161; original stress). That is to say, I ponder the reasons for the continued existence of the 'special sciences', and what this might imply for economics. In Section 11.4 I speculate on the future of a relatively autonomous, but not wholly independent, discipline of macroeconomics. Finally, in the very brief Section 11.5, I suggest four important lessons that we might all learn from the sorry example of the microfoundations delusion.

11.2 SOME EXPLANATIONS

So why did the microfoundations dogma take over mainstream macroeconomics? Why did it triumph in the early 1980s, but not before? Why not very much before? Andy Denis (2009), for example, traces the origins of methodological individualism back two whole centuries to Jeremy Bentham, while the marginalist revolution in economic theory in the 1870s placed the individual agent very firmly at the centre of orthodox economic theory. Why, then, were there so few advocates of microfoundations before the 1970s? The obvious answer is the simple one: it is a very bad idea. So how are we to explain its extraordinary success?

Recently, Robert Solow asked himself precisely this question:

> So I am left with a puzzle, or even a challenge. What accounts for the ability of 'modern macro' to win hearts and minds among bright and enterprising academic economists? I have no easy answer. Probably these fashions have no single explanation, but depend on the random (or nonrandom) combination of favourable factors.
>
> There has always been a purist streak in economics that wants everything to follow neatly from greed, rationality, and equilibrium, with no ifs, ands, and buts. Most of us have felt that tug. Here is a theory that gives you just that, and this time 'everything' means everything: macro, not micro. Moreover it is practically guaranteed to give laissez-faire-type advice, which happens to fit nicely with the general turn to the political right that began in the 1970s and may or may not be coming to an end.
>
> One can imagine how this style of macroeconomics would appeal to some economists with a certain sort of temperament, especially as they are following the example of excellent and charismatic protagonists. The relaxed approach to empirical validity may simply reflect what Melvin Reder once called 'tight-prior-economics' in describing an earlier Chicago School. Add some active proselytizing and heresy hunting. Is that enough to account for the current state of macro-theory? I don't rightly know. But I do think it is important that a few other, more eclectic, more data-sensitive approaches to macro-theory should remain in the profession's gene pool. (Solow 2008, p. 245)

Here Solow suggests two explanations, which are not mutually exclusive and probably reinforce each other: physics envy and politics. He dismisses a third – empirical evidence – and does not even consider a fourth: methodological considerations.

The first, and perhaps most plausible, explanation is indeed physics envy. What Solow terms 'the purist streak' leads intellectual historians like Roy Weintraub to tell the story of 'how economics became a mathematical science' (this is the sub-title of Weintraub 2002); critics have long complained about 'beauty mistaken for truth'. But formal models, using highly advanced mathematics, do offer a degree of rigour that is unavailable to those who reject RARE microfoundations. They also permit the theorist, or so it is claimed, to avoid the 'ad hoc assumptions' that were dismissed by Michael Wickens (above, p. 1). Lance Taylor adds a twist to this argument, inadvertently citing the title of the popular British TV police series, *New Tricks*: 'The new tricks included ... extensive new classical use of the deterministic and stochastic optimal control methodologies being perfected by applied mathematicians in the 1960s. The notion that there is a "true model" of the economy may have come from this source' (Taylor 2004, p. 201). In addition to beauty, there was an additional attraction: the prospect of exporting the models to the other social sciences, thereby promoting economics imperialism. It is certainly true that modelling a genuinely Keynesian world with non-ergodicity and fundamental uncertainty is a very difficult enterprise. Some Critical Realists claim that it simply cannot be done (Brown 2012). At all events, the temptation to slide from the intractable real world into tractable fantasy worlds is very difficult to resist.

In practice, of course, the purists were unable to deliver, and the new tricks involve the 'modern macroeconomists' in *ad hoc* assumptions of their own that are at least as objectionable as the Keynesian macroeconomic generalizations that Wickens objected to. We have already encountered one example, the 'Gorman preferences' needed to make the representative agent at least minimally plausible (above, p. 125). Two others are equally incredible. The first is the 'no-bankruptcies' assumption in Walrasian models and the related 'No Ponzi' condition that is imposed on DSGE models. This eliminates the possibility of default, and hence the fear of default (since these are agents with rational expectations, who know the correct model, and hence know that there is no possibility of default), and hence the need for money, since if your promise to pay is 'as good as gold', it would be pointless for me to demand gold (or any other form of money) from you. Money would be at most a unit of account, but never a store of value. The second is the unobtrusive postulate of 'complete financial markets', smuggled into Michael Woodford's *Interest and Prices* (Woodford 2003, p. 64), which means that all possible future states of the world are known, probabilistically, and can be insured against: this eliminates uncertainty, and hence the need for finance. It does, however, pose a question that Plato might have recognized: not 'who will guard the guardians?', but 'who will insure the insurance companies?' (The AIG bailout in 2008 supplied the answer: the state, as insurer of last resort). As Yanis Varoufakis, Joseph Halevi and Nicholas Theocarakis (2011) have shown, in economic theory it is a simple matter to have either complexity or truth, but it is difficult (if not impossible) to have both.

At all events, physics envy surely is a major part of the explanation for the attraction of microfoundations. As the French students complained in their short-lived revolt against the graduate curriculum in 2000, mainstream economics has lost touch with reality; it has quite literally become autistic (Fullbrook 2003). But this is not the whole story, and it leaves a great deal unexplained. Paul Samuelson was possibly the best mathematician of all those whom I have cited in this book, but the need for rigour did not push him very far towards microfoundations. And the same could be said of Alan Kirman, and a number of others.

The second explanation is politics, which must also have helped to make the microfoundations dogma attractive. As Solow notes, 'modern macro' is 'practically guaranteed to give laissez-faire-style advice' on questions of macroeconomic policy, and in the age of neoliberalism the urge to establish policy ineffectiveness propositions must have been a strong incentive for the pursuit of the microfoundations project. There is no doubt that the 'small government' implications of Real Business Cycle models were a big attraction to many of their protagonists. Denis also stresses the political implications of methodological individualism, criticizing

> [t]he Panglossian consequences of the adoption of a reductionistic ontology. If the macro is just the aggregate of micro behaviours, then individual rationality implies a socially rational outcome. Any apparent macro pathology, such as [un]employment, can be ascribed to micro level decisions – which are either rational, in which case the apparent unemployment can be safely regarded as voluntary, a species of leisure, or they are the consequence of micro-level errors – pricing oneself out of a job – which cannot be rectified by collective action. A reductionist ontology creates a strong default policy prescription of *laissez-faire*. (Denis 2009, p. 14)

And political undertones can be detected a long way from economics. The anti-reductionist biologists Steven Jay Gould, Richard Lewontin, Steven Rose and Elliot Sober have something else in common: they are all Marxists of sorts, members of the British and American New Left. We encountered Sober in Chapter 7 as a cautious defender of Analytical Marxism (above, p. 143), and Lewontin has discussed the political implications of modern biology at some length (Lewontin 1993).

Can it be a coincidence that all these critics of reductionism in the life sciences share a common political stance? The answer seems to be: yes and no. In the wrong hands, Dawkins's genetic determinism can very easily degenerate into the worst type of Social Darwinism, celebrating the triumph of the genetically superior upper classes and higher races. The ideological objections to sociobiology and other variants of biological determinism are cogently stated in the book by Lewontin, Rose and Leon J. Kamin (1984), to which they gave the telling title, *Not in Our Genes*. But Dawkins's supporters are not (for the most part) fascist beasts, and the doggedly anti-Marxist Popper was, as we have seen, no friend of the biological reductionists. The latter could, in any case, mount a convincing case that recognition of the biological constraints on human behaviour and social organization is a necessary safeguard against the over-ambitious and sometimes unpleasantly authoritarian dreams of unrealistic romantic revolutionaries (see Pinker 2005, Chapter 16).

Thus it seems that politics and the philosophy of science are not always connected, at least not in any obvious or simple way. The same is true of economic ideology, even though the need to establish policy ineffectiveness certainly was a factor in the methodological position taken in the late 1970s by the New Classicals. But the pro-reductionist Lawrence Klein was a Marxist in the late 1940s, and the anti-reductionist Milton Friedman was a classical liberal, yet on microfoundations they took the exact opposite of the positions that one would have predicted for them. There is not even a clear link between a theorist's attitude to Keynes and his position on microfoundations. Compare James Meade with James Tobin, loyal Keynesians both: Meade never espoused microfoundations, while Tobin (before his change of mind) was a vigorous early advocate. Self-proclaimed New Keynesians continue to deny the policy ineffectiveness propositions of the New Classicals, which are only defensible on the assumption of RARE microfoundations but evaporate if either element in the acronym is rejected. In particular, the rational expectations (RE) component is needed to establish that 'the price is right', so that regulation is unnecessary, or worse. Without rational expectations, a strong case for government intervention is easy to construct, even by supporters of (non-RARE) microfoundations (Quiggin 2010b).

One final point needs to be made about the political implications of microfoundations. If 'modern macro' is indeed ideology, it is also a *dangerous* ideology. I am writing this final chapter in January 2012, with the European debt crisis (or cris*es*) still unresolved and the paradox of thrift being demonstrated on a daily basis in Greece, Ireland, Italy, Portugal, Spain and elsewhere as attempts to increase government saving simply intensify the decline in output, income and tax receipts and so become self-defeating. As one Austrian Keynesian notes, the problem has been made much worse by 'the neoliberal smog in the heads of the elites' (Schulmeister 2011, p. 31). The microfoundations dogma has been an important source of this ideological smog, which is bad for the long-term health of the system, impairs vision in the short term and may yet prove extremely damaging to the prospects of global capitalism.

Thus neither of Solow's two explanations is entirely satisfactory, and I cannot claim to have a better alternative. Possibly Solow dismisses the third possibility just a shade too easily, when he writes of the mainstream's 'relaxed approach to empirical validity'. This is true as far as it goes, but it is not the whole story. As we saw in Chapter 10, mid-twentieth century writers on economic methodology often pointed to Keynesian macroeconomics and related econometric modelling as providing one (indeed, perhaps the only) important example of successful empirical work in economics. Thus the apparent empirical and policy failures of Keynesianism in the years of stagflation (roughly, from 1973 to 1992) must have served to discredit macroeconomics in any form, including the monetarist and New Classical challengers to Keynes, whose predictive record proved to be little better than the Keynesian orthodoxy that they sought to replace. The apparent collapse of *all* pre-Real Business Cycle macroeconomic models in the 1970s must also have had some influence in giving 'macro' a bad name, which 'micro' did not have.

Only the fourth possible explanation for the triumph of the microfoundations dogma can be completely dismissed: a well-argued and well-documented case based on methodological considerations, justifying micro-reduction as an authoritative position in the philosophy of science. As we have seen, this has never been seriously attempted by the defenders of the microfoundations dogma.

11.3 THE AUTONOMY OF THE 'SPECIAL SCIENCES'

The failure of the microfoundations project implies the continued existence of a relatively autonomous discipline – a 'special science' – of macroeconomics. Philosophers of science have paid a considerable amount of attention to Fodor's question: why *is* there anything except physics? Why *are* the special sciences autonomous?

Note first that 'autonomy' is a slippery word. Both of my dictionaries give three meanings. For the one-volume *Concise Oxford Dictionary*, autonomy is defined as 'right of self-government; personal freedom; freedom of the will'. In the very much larger, two-volume *Shorter Oxford Dictionary*, it means, first, 'the right or condition of self-government (frequently only in specified matters) of a State, community, institution, etc.'; second, 'freedom of the will'; and, third, 'independence, freedom from external control or influence, personal liberty'. In the present context, 'freedom of the will' is irrelevant, and 'independence' is clearly too strong; 'self-government' comes closest to the meaning of autonomy for the special sciences.

Fodor himself treats 'autonomous' as being synonymous in this context with 'irreducible' (Fodor 1997, p. 162 n5): 'I will say that a law or theory that figures in bona fide empirical explanations, but is not reducible to a law or theory of physics, is ipso facto *autonomous*' (ibid., p. 149; original stress). He offers as examples the scientific study of mental states (ibid., p. 150; here Jaegwon Kim is his target) and the laws of biology (ibid., p. 162 n7). 'The very *existence* of the special sciences', Fodor argues,

> testifies to reliable macrolevel regularities that are realized by mechanisms whose physical substance is quite typically heterogeneous. Does anybody really doubt that mountains are made of all sorts of stuff? Does anybody really think that, since they are, generalizations about mountains-as-such won't continue to serve geology in good stead? Damn near everything we know about the world suggests that unimaginably complicated to-ings and fro-ings of bits and pieces at the extreme *micro*level manage somehow to converge on stable *macrolevel* properties. (Ibid., p. 160; original stress)

For Fodor this is an empirical question: 'I am suggesting, roughly, that there are special sciences not because of the nature of our epistemic relation to the world, but because of the way the world is put together' (Fodor 1991, p. 439).

Similarly, J.D. Trout suggests that, if reduction had succeeded, the special sciences would have disappeared, whereas in fact they have proliferated (Trout 1991, p. 390). And this is a matter of fact, not of principle; the opponent of reductionism claims simply that 'causal features of the world determine which explanatory practices are appropriate' (ibid., p. 391). But it does have clear implications for scientific method, as Steven Horst emphasizes:

> In philosophy of science the aprioristic normative agenda of the Positivists has been abandoned in favor of approaches that study the various methods and models of individual sciences, and the prevailing view is that the special sciences are autonomous and not in need of vindication by proving their reducibility to physics. (Horst 2007, p. 47)

Thus Horst defends 'the *methodological autonomy* of the special sciences' (his stress), as urged by those advocating a 'historicist turn' in the philosophy of science (here he cites Larry Laudan, Dudley Shapere and Stephen Toulmin).

'Two features of this historicist turn seem particularly important for our purposes', Horst continues:

> the domain-specificity of scientific methodology and the central importance of progress *within* a scientific domain in the maturation of that science. Indeed, the historicist turn forces us away from a global notion of 'Science' and toward a more pluralistic notion of scienc*es*, each of which may have features that are significantly different from those of other sciences, and is largely justified by its own internal successes. (Ibid., p. 57; original stress)

And 'there can be a variety of separate good-making qualities or explanatory virtues, each of which contributes to the epistemic quality of scientific understanding' (ibid., p. 58), and also a variety of interdomain relations, since:

> The rejection of the paradigm of intertheoretic reduction and the acknowledgement of the justificatory and methodological autonomy of individual scientific domains ought not to lead to the conclusion that the various sciences are each free-spinning wheels, unconnected to one another. Rather, it opens the door to investigation of what kinds of relations are actually to be found through a historically faithful examination of cross-disciplinary work. (Ibid., p. 58)

This is not a question of unacceptable post-modernist laxity or in any way 'anti-science', he continues, despite E.O. Wilson's allegations to the contrary (ibid., p. 60). Here Horst cites Ian Hacking (1996), who contrasts 'unity as singleness' with 'unity as harmonious integration', and Nancy Cartwright (1999), 'who characterizes the relations between the sciences as a patchwork, portraying a "dappled world"' (ibid., p. 61; no page references are given to either source). Horst's own 'cognitive pluralism' is pragmatist as well as pluralist: 'Indeed, if a worldview is anything like an all-encompassing axiomatic system, we do not have anything as global as a worldview at all. Instead, we triangulate the world by deploying various models, each of which is good enough for particular things' (ibid., p. 128).

What does this imply for economics? Daniel Hausman notes, without comment, that '[e]conomics resembles individual theories such as Newtonian dynamics or Mendelian population genetics more closely than it resembles disciplines such as physics or biology. For an orthodox theorist, *it is in effect a one-theory science*' (Hausman 1992, p. 95; stress added). The role of methodological individualism is critical in this regard (ibid., pp. 97–8). It is a relatively short step from this to the position that macroeconomics is a mere branch or application of the 'one-theory science' of RARE microeconomics, as David Colander and Daniel Hamermesh have claimed (see above, p. 2). To cite Hamermesh again, 'the creation of a microfoundation for macro means that it is now an applied field, no longer central'. Hence it should be removed from the core of postgraduate training in economics: 'the atavistic inclusion of macro in the core may be based less in intellectual rigor and more in the job-security concerns of macroeconomists and their Ph.D. students' (Hamermesh 2008, p. 409). Indeed, one interpretation of the early literature on microfoundations that was discussed in Chapter 5 is that Hicks and some others were seeking, as early as the 1930s, to *prevent* macroeconomics from becoming a separate science. This is perhaps what Joan Robinson had in mind when she accused the inventors of the (original) neoclassical synthesis of 'putting Keynes to sleep' (Robinson 1972, p. 4).

11.4 THE FUTURE OF MACROECONOMICS

Mainstream economists, too, would do well to reconsider the potential dangers of the microfoundations dogma, since it might well prove to have unpleasant unintended consequences. Even if the principle of hierarchical (downward) reduction is accepted, there is no obvious reason why it should stop at the individual. Howard and King (1989) made precisely this point almost twenty years ago in a critical appraisal of Rational Choice Marxism. Why not go down even further, to the gene (Dawkins 1976) or the subatomic particle (Wilson 1998)? If this seems fanciful, consider the implications of the burgeoning science of neuroeconomics, which seeks to explain individual behaviour through studying small areas of the individual's brain and seems to have discovered that there are distinct neurological grounds for doubting the relevance of 'rational economic man' (Camerer, Loewenstein and Pelec 2005; Marchionni and Vromen 2010).

The alternative, as advocated by Keynesian theorists like Robert Skidelsky (2009) and John Smithin (2009), is the retention of macroeconomics as a relatively autonomous discipline, a 'special science', in its own right. There are some significant implications. Skidelsky has proposed two specific reforms. First, undergraduate economics teaching should be 'broadly based'; that is to say, it should be multi-disciplinary, with more history than there is at present and less maths (Skidelsky 2009, p. 99). His second proposal is more controversial:

> My second reform would be to separate the postgraduate study of microeconomics from macroeconomics. Taught postgraduate courses in microeconomics should concern themselves, as at present, with the building and testing of models based on a narrow set of assumptions. Such courses could probably best be taught in business schools, where they could be combined with wider business studies. By contrast, masters degrees in macroeconomics should be joint degrees, with an equally weighted non-economic component. It could be history, philosophy, sociology, politics, international relations, biology, or anthropology. There is something to be said for locating such degrees in the departments of the non-economic disciplines which contribute to them. It would be splendid if teachers and students of economics could be forced to talk to teachers and students of philosophy or history; better still if they were partly knowledgeable in matters outside their specialist disciplines. Both sides would benefit. A broadly based postgraduate course in macroeconomics would study not just the implications of particular policies for economic stability, growth and development, but also their social and moral implications.
>
> *The obvious aim of such a reconstruction is to protect macroeconomics from the encroachment of the methods and habits of thought of microeconomics.* (Ibid., pp. 99–100; stress added)

This, I think, is a sensible short-term suggestion, while the damage done to macroeconomics by the microfoundations dogma is repaired. To revert to an earlier metaphor (above, p. 26), unrestricted movement between the micro and the macro buildings is not possible right now, and the bridges between them need to be patrolled. Once the relative autonomy of macroeconomics and the self-confidence of its practitioners have been restored, freedom of movement will soon follow.

11.5 A FINAL WORD

Finally, here are some reflections on the lessons that a younger generation of economists might learn from the mistakes of their predecessors. I have put them in the second person, for dramatic effect, but they apply also to me.

First, mind your language. Metaphors are not mere rhetorical adornments. They can have substantive consequences, not always for the good. Be especially careful with constructional analogies, which have proved to be misleading and a source of serious confusion. Do not be tempted to replace ‘microfoundations’ with ‘macrofoundations’, which is not much better. Use horizontal rather than vertical metaphors: 'bridges' or 'links', rather than 'underpinnings' or 'cornerstones'.

Second, be a good neighbour. Do not treat your colleagues in the other social sciences as colonial subjects, or feudal vassals, or disobedient children. Economics imperialism was always a bad idea. It was never going to succeed, and it should be abandoned now. Your neighbours in anthropology, political science, social psychology and sociology have a lot to teach you, and probably also much to learn. Cooperation will be beneficial to all concerned, but conquest is an idle dream. Remember Edgar Kiser's metaphor, and be prepared to take part in *two-way* trade with the other social sciences.

Third, be kind to methodologists and philosophers of science. They do not bite, unless severely provoked, and they have a lot to teach you. They are for the most part modest folk, who are also prepared to learn from you. Perhaps in the future, when the dust has settled on the ruins of the microfoundations project, they will write it up as a salutary lesson: a case study in how *not* to do social science.

Fourth, and most important, be happy. The end of the microfoundations dogma is good news. Read up on the recent history of the other social sciences, where intellectual pluralism is alive and well, as confirmed by several contributors to the recent volume edited by Roger Backhouse and Philippe Fontaine (2010). Send your DSGE texts to be re-filed on the science fiction or science fantasy shelves of your library, and get ready to read up on some real macroeconomics. Treat yourself to a copy of *Maynard's Revenge* (Taylor 2010), *Post Keynesian Macroeconomic Theory* (Davidson 2011) and *A Modern Guide to Keynesian Macroeconomics and Economic Policies* (Hein and Stockhammer 2011), and see how it might be done.

References

Acemoglu, D. (2009), *Introduction to Modern Economic Growth*, Princeton, NJ: Princeton University Press.

Achen, C.H. (2002), 'Toward a new political methodology: microfoundations and ART', *Annual Review of Political Science*, **5**, 423–50.

Ackley, G. (1961), *Macroeconomic Theory*, New York: Macmillan, 1966.

Addis, L. (1966), 'The individual and the Marxist philosophy of history', *Philosophy of Science*, **33** (1/2), 101–17, cited from M. Brodbeck (ed.) (1968), *Readings in the Philosophy of the Social Sciences*, New York: Macmillan, pp. 317–35.

Agassi, J. (1960), 'Methodological individualism', *British Journal of Sociology*, **11** (3), 244–70.

Agassi, J. (1975), 'Institutional individualism', *British Journal of Sociology*, **26** (2), 144–55.

Akerlof, G.A. and R.J. Shiller (2009), *Animal Spirits: How Human Psychology Drives the Economy, and why it Matters for Global Capitalism*, Princeton, NJ: Princeton University Press.

Alexander, J.C., B. Giesen, R. Münch and N.J. Smelser (eds) (1987), *The Micro–Macro Link*, Berkeley, CA: University of California Press.

Amadae, S.M. and B. Bueno de Mesquita (1997), 'The Rochester School: the origins of positive political theory', *Annual Review of Political Science*, **2**, 269–95.

Amin, A. (ed.) (1997), *Post-Fordism: A Reader*, Oxford: Blackwell.

Anderson, P.W. (1972), 'More is different: broken symmetry and the nature of the hierarchical structure of science', *Science*, **177**, 393–6; reprinted in M.A. Bedau and P. Humphreys (eds), *Emergence: Contemporary Readings in Philosophy and Science*, Cambridge, MA: MIT Press, 2008, pp. 221–9.

Arestis, P. (1992), *The Post-Keynesian Approach to Economics: An Alternative Analysis of Economic Theory and Policy*, Aldershot, UK and Brookfield, VT, USA: Edward Elgar.

Arestis, P. and M. Sawyer (eds) (2006), *A Handbook of Alternative Monetary Economics*, Cheltenham, UK and Northampton, MA, USA: Edward Elgar.

Arrow, K.J. (1950), Review of Duesenberry (1949), *American Economic* Review, **40** (5), 906–11.

Arrow, K.J. (1951a), 'Mathematical models in the social sciences', in D. Lerner and A.D. Laswell (eds), *The Policy Sciences*, Stanford, CA: Stanford University Press, pp. 129–54, reprinted in M. Brodbeck (ed.), *Readings in the Philosophy of the Social Sciences*, New York: Macmillan, 1968, pp. 635–67.

Arrow, K.J. (1951b), *Social Choice and Individual Values*, New Haven, CT: Yale University Press.

Arrow, K.J. (1967), 'Samuelson collected', *Journal of Political Economy*, **75** (5), 730–37.

Arrow, K.J. (1968), 'Economic equilibrium', in D.L. Sills (ed.), *International Encyclopaedia of the Social Sciences, Volume 3*, London: Collier-Macmillan, pp. 378–9.

Arrow, K.J. (1986), 'Rationality of self and others in an economic system', *Journal of Business*, **59** (4:2), S385–S399.

Arrow, K.J. (1994), 'Methodological individualism and social knowledge', *American Economic Review*, **84** (2), 1–9.

Arrow, K.J. and F.H. Hahn (1971), *General Competitive Analysis*, San Francisco: Holden-Day.

Asimakopulos, A. (1975), 'A Kaleckian theory of income distribution', *Canadian Journal of Economics*, **8** (3), 313–33.

Backhouse, R.E. (1998), *Explorations in Economic Methodology: From Lakatos to Empirical Philosophy of Science*, London: Routledge.

Backhouse, R.E. (2000), Review of Kincaid (1997), *Economic Journal*, **110** (461), F193–F195.

Backhouse, R.E. (2010), *The Puzzle of Modern Economics: Science or Ideology?*, Cambridge: Cambridge University Press.

Backhouse, R.E. and P. Fontaine (eds) (2010), *The History of the Social Sciences since 1945*, Cambridge: Cambridge University Press.

Bailey, R.W. (2002), Review of Hoover (2001b), *Economic Journal*, **112** (423), F584–F586.

Baranzini, M. (ed.) (1982), *Advances in Economic Theory*, Oxford: Basil Blackwell.

Barba, A. and M. Pivetti (2009), 'Rising household debt: its causes and macroeconomic implications – a long-period analysis', *Cambridge Journal of Economics*, **33** (1), 113–37.

Baron, J.N. and M.T. Hannan (1994), 'The impact of economics on contemporary sociology', *Journal of Economic Literature*, **32** (3), 1111–46.

Baumol, W.J. (2009), 'Endogenous growth: valuable advance, substantive misnomer', in M. Boianovsky and K.D. Hoover (eds), *Robert Solow and the Development of Growth Economics*, Durham, NC: Duke University Press, pp. 304–14.

Bechtel, W. and R.C. Richardson (1992), 'Emergent phenomena and complex systems', in A. Beckerman, H. Flohr and J. Kim (eds), *Emergence or Reduction? Essays on the Prospects of Non-reductive Physicalism*, Berlin: De Gruyter, 1992, pp. 257–88.

Becker, H.S. (1998), *Tricks of the Trade: How to Think About Your Research While You're Doing It*, Chicago: Chicago University Press.

Beckerman, A., H. Flohr and J. Kim (eds) (1992), *Emergence or Reduction? Essays on the Prospects of Non-reductive Physicalism*, Berlin: De Gruyter.

Bedau, M.A. (2003), 'Downward causation and autonomy in weak emergence', in M.A. Bedau and P. Humphreys (eds), *Emergence: Contemporary Readings in Philosophy and Science*, Cambridge, MA: MIT Press, 2008, pp. 155–88.

Bedau, M.A. and P. Humphreys (2008), 'Introduction to philosophical perspectives on emergence', in M. Bedau and P. Humphreys (eds), *Emergence: Contemporary Readings in Philosophy and Science*, Cambridge, MA: MIT Press, pp. 9–18.

Beinhocker, E.D. (2006), *The Origin of Wealth: Evolution, Complexity, and the Radical Remaking of Economics*, Boston, MA: Harvard Business School Press.

Belongia, M.T. and M.R. Garfinkel (eds) (1992), *The Business Cycle: Theories and Evidence*, Boston: Kluwer.

Bhargava, R. (1992), *Individualism in Social Science: Forms and Limits of a Methodology*, Oxford: Clarendon Press.

Bhaskar, R. (1998), *The Possibility of Naturalism: A Philosophical Critique of the Contemporary Human Sciences*, London: Routledge, third edition.

Bicchieri, C. (1988), 'Should a scientist abstain from metaphor?', in A. Klamer, D.N. McCloskey and R.M. Solow (eds), *The Consequences of Economic Rhetoric*, Cambridge: Cambridge University Press, pp. 100–114.

Black, F. (1987), *Business Cycles and Equilibrium*, Oxford: Basil Blackwell.

Blanchard, O.J. (1992), 'For a return to pragmatism', in M.T. Belongia and M.R. Garfinkel (eds), *The Business Cycle: Theories and Evidence*, Boston, MA: Kluwer, pp. 121–32.

Blanchard, O.J. (1997), 'Is there a core of usable macroeconomics?', *American Economic Review*, **87** (2), 244–6.

Blanchard, O.J. (2000), 'What do we know about macroeconomics that Fisher and Wicksell did not?', *Quarterly Journal of Economics*, **115** (4), 1375–1409.

Blanchard, O.J. (2008), 'The state of macro', New York: National Bureau of Economic Research, Working Paper 14259, August.

Blanchard, O.J., G. Dell'Arica and P. Mauro (2010), 'Rethinking Macroeconomic Policy', Washington, DC: IMF Staff Position Note, SPN/10/03, February 12.

Blanchard, O.J. and S. Fischer (1989), *Lectures on Macroeconomics*, Cambridge, MA: MIT Press.

Blaug, M. (1962), *Economic Theory in Retrospect*, London: Heinemann.

Blaug, M. (1968), *Economic Theory in Retrospect*, London: Heinemann, second edition.

Blaug, M. (1980), *The Methodology of Economics*, Cambridge: Cambridge University Press.

Blaug, M. (1985), *Economic Theory in Retrospect*, Cambridge: Cambridge University Press, fourth edition.

Blaug, M. (1992), *The Methodology of Economics*, Cambridge: Cambridge University Press, second edition.

Blaug, M. (1996), *Economic Theory in Retrospect*, Cambridge: Cambridge University Press, fifth edition.

Blaug, M. (1997), Review of Boland (1996), *Economic Journal*, **197** (445), 1945.

Blaug, M. (1999), Review of Kincaid (1997), *Manchester School*, **67** (2), 249–50.

Blecker, R.A. (2002), 'Distribution, demand and growth in neo-Kaleckian macro-models', in M. Setterfield (ed.), *The Economics of Demand-Led Growth*, Cheltenham, UK and Northampton, MA, USA: Edward Elgar, pp. 129–52.

Blinder, A.S. (1982), 'Inventories and sticky prices: more on the microfoundations of macroeconomics', *American Economic Review*, **72** (3), 334–48.

Blinder, A.S. (1986), 'Keynes after Lucas', *Eastern Economic Journal*, **12** (3), 209–16.

Blinder, A.S. (1987), 'Keynes, Lucas, and scientific progress', *American Economic Review*, **77** (2), 130–36.

Blinder, A.S. (1997), 'Is there a core of practical macroeconomics that we should all believe?', *American Economic Review*, **87** (2), 240–43.

Boettke, P.J. and P.T. Leeson (2003), 'The Austrian school of economics: 1950–2000', in W.J. Samuels, J.E. Biddle and J.B. Davis (eds), *A Companion to the History of Economic Thought*, Oxford: Blackwell, pp. 445–53.

Böhm-Bawerk, E. von (1891), 'The historical versus the deductive method in political economy', *Annals of the American Academy of Political and Social Science*, **1**, http://socserv2.mcmaster.ca/~econ/ugcm/3113/bawerk/bohm001.html (consulted 21 August 2003).

Boland, L.A. (1982), *The Foundations of Economic Method*, London: Allen & Unwin.

Boland, L.A. (1996), *Critical Economic Methodology: A Personal Odyssey*, London: Routledge.
Boland, L.A. (2003), *The Foundations of Economic Method*, London: Routledge, second edition.
Booth, W.J. (1993), 'Marx's two logics of capitalism', in W.J. Booth, P. James and H. Meadwell (eds), *Politics and Rationality*, Cambridge: Cambridge University Press, 1993, pp. 61–85.
Booth, W.J., P. James and H. Meadwell (eds) (1993a), *Politics and Rationality*, Cambridge: Cambridge University Press.
Booth, W.J., P. James and H. Meadwell (1993b), 'Introduction', in W.J. Booth, P. James and H. Meadwell (eds), *Politics and Rationality*, Cambridge: Cambridge University Press, pp. 61–85.
Borger, R. and F. Cioffi (eds) (1970), *Explanation in the Behavioural Sciences*, Cambridge: Cambridge University Press.
Boudon, R. (1979), *Effets Pervers et Ordre Sociale*, Paris: Presses Universitaires de France, second edition.
Boulding, K.E. (1939), Review of Hicks (1939), *Canadian Journal of Economics and Political Science*, **5** (4), 521–8.
Boumans, M. and Davis, J.B. (2010), *Economic Methodology: Understanding Economics as a Science*, Basingstoke: Palgrave Macmillan.
Boyd, R. (1983), 'On the current state of the issue of scientific realism', *Erkenntnis*, **19** (1/3), 45–90, reprinted in R. Boyd, P. Gasper and J.D. Trout (eds), *The Philosophy of Science*, Cambridge, MA: MIT Press, 1991, pp. 195–222.
Boyd, R., P. Gasper and J.D. Trout (eds) (1991), *The Philosophy of Science*, Cambridge, MA: MIT Press.
Bradie, M. (2000), Review of Kincaid (1997), *Economics and Philosophy*, **16** (1), 147–59.
Brodbeck, M. (1954), 'On the philosophy of the social sciences', *Philosophy of Science*, **21** (2), 140–56.
Brodbeck, M. (1958), 'Methodological individualisms: definition and reduction', *Philosophy of Science*, **25** (1), 1–22.
Brodbeck, M. (1968), 'Introduction', to section 3 of M. Brodbeck (ed.), *Readings in the Philosophy of the Social Sciences*, New York: Macmillan, pp. 139–43.
Bronfenbrenner, M. (1981), Review of Negishi (1979), *Journal of Economic Literature*, **19** (2), 573–4.
Bronk, R. (2009), *The Romantic Economist: Imagination in Economics*, Cambridge: Cambridge University Press.
Brown, A. (2012), 'Critical realism', in J.E. King (ed.), *The Elgar Companion to Post Keynesian Economics*, Cheltenham, UK and Northampton, MA, USA: Edward Elgar, second edition, pp. 121–6.

Brown, R. (1970), 'Comment' [on J.O. Wisdom], in R. Borger and F. Cioffi (eds), *Explanation in the Behavioural Sciences*, Cambridge: Cambridge University Press, pp. 297–305.

Brown, R.D. (2003), 'Microhistory and the post-modern challenge', *Journal of the Early Republic*, **23** (1), 1–20.

Browning, M., L.P. Hansen and J.J. Heckman (2000), 'Micro data and general equilibrium models', in J. Taylor and M. Woodford (eds), *Handbook of Macroeconomics*, Volume 1C, Amsterdam: North-Holland, pp. 543–625.

Brunner, K. (1971), '"Yale" and money', *Journal of Finance*, **26** (1), 165–74.

Bryan, W.R. and W.T. Carleton (1967), 'Short-run adjustments of an individual bank', *Econometrica*, **35** (2), 321–47.

Bryant, J. (1985), Review of Laidler (1982), *Journal of Economic Literature*, **23** (1), 122–4.

Bueno de Mesquita, B. (1981), *The War Trap*, New Haven, CT: Yale University Press.

Bunge, M. (1996), *Finding Philosophy in Social Science*, New Haven, CT: Yale University Press.

Bunge, M. (1998), *Social Science under Debate: A Philosophical Perspective*, Toronto: Toronto University Press.

Bunge, M. (2000), 'Systemism: the alternative to individualism and holism', *Journal of Socio-Economics*, **29** (2), 147–57.

Bürger, H. and K.W. Rothschild. (2009), *Wie Wirtschaft die Welt bewegt: die grossen ökonomischen Modelle auf dem Prüfstand* (*How Economics Makes the World Go Round: The Great Economic Models Put to the Test*), Vienna: Lesethek.

Caballero, R.J. (1992), 'A fallacy of composition', *American Economic Review*, **82** (5), 1279–92.

Cagan, P. (1987), 'Monetarism', in J. Eatwell, M. Milgate and P. Newman (eds), *The New Palgrave: A Dictionary of Economics*, Volume 3, London: Macmillan, pp. 492–7.

Camerer, C., G. Loewenstein and D. Prelec (2005), 'Neuroeconomics: how neuroscience can inform economics', *Journal of Economic Literature*, **43** (1), 9–64.

Carabelli, A. (1994), 'The methodology of the critique of classical theory: Keynes on organic interdependence', in A. Marzola and F. Silva (eds), *John Maynard Keynes: Language and Method*, Aldershot, UK and Brookfield, VT, USA: Edward Elgar, 1994, pp. 128–54.

Cartwright, N. (1999), *The Dappled World: A Study of the Boundaries of Science*, Cambridge: Cambridge University Press.

Cartwright, N., J. Cat, L. Fleck and T.E. Webel (1996), *Otto Neurath: Philosophy Between Science and Politics*, Cambridge: Cambridge University Press.

Cass, D. (1965), 'Optimal growth in an aggregate model of capital accumulation', *Review of Economic Studies*, **32** (3), 233–40.

Cass, D. and M.E. Yaari (1966), 'A re-examination of the pure consumption loans model', *Journal of Political Economy*, **74** (4), 353–67.

Causey, R.L. (1972), 'Attribute-identities in microreductions', *Journal of Philosophy*, **69** (14), 407–22.

Chandra, R. and R.J. Sandilands (2010), 'Reply to Roy H. Grieve on increasing returns', *Review of Political Economy*, **22** (1), 141–50.

Chick, V. (1983), *Macroeconomics after Keynes: A Reconsideration of the General Theory*, Cambridge, MA: MIT Press.

Chick, V. (2002), 'Keynes's theory of investment and necessary compromise', in S.C. Dow and J.V. Hillard (eds), *Keynes, Uncertainty and the Global Economy: Beyond Keynes, Volume Two*, Cheltenham, UK and Northampton, MA, USA: Edward Elgar, pp. 55–67.

Chilosi, A. (1989), 'Kalecki's quest for the microeconomic foundations of his macroeconomic theory', in M. Sebastiani (ed.), *Kalecki's Relevance Today*, London: Macmillan, pp. 101–20.

Clower, R.W. (1965), 'The Keynesian counter-revolution: a theoretical appraisal', cited from D.A. Walker (ed.), *Money and Markets: Essays by Robert W. Clower*, Cambridge: Cambridge University Press, 1984, pp. 34–58.

Clower, R.W. (1967), 'A reconsideration of the microfoundations of monetary theory', *Western Economic Journal*, **6** (1), 1–8.

Coates, J. (1996), *The Claims of Common Sense*, Cambridge: Cambridge University Press.

Cohn, S. (1985), Review of Hechter (1983), *Social Forces*, **64** (1), 221–3.

Colander, D. (1994), 'Foreword', in J. Cornwall, *Economic Breakdown and Recovery: Theory and Policy*, Armonk, NY: M.E. Sharpe, pp. xiii–xviii.

Colander, D. (1996), 'The macro foundations of micro', in D. Colander (ed.), *Beyond Microfoundations: Post Walrasian Economics*, Cambridge: Cambridge University Press, pp. 57–68.

Colander, D. (1998), Review of Hartley (1997), *Journal of Economic Literature*, **36** (4), 2172–3.

Colander, D. (1999), 'Conversations with James Tobin and Robert Shiller on the "Yale tradition" in macroeconomics', *Macroeconomic Dynamics*, **3** (1), 116–43.

Colander, D. (ed.) (2006), *Post Walrasian Macroeconomics: Beyond the Dynamic Stochastic General Equilibrium Model*, Cambridge: Cambridge University Press.

Colander, D. (2007), *The Making of an Economist: Redux*, Princeton, NJ: Princeton University Press.
Colander, D. (2009), 'How did macro theory get so far off track, and what can heterodox macroeconomists do to get it back on track?', in E. Hein, T. Niechoj and E. Stockhammer (eds), *Macroeconomic Policies on Shaky Foundations: Whither Mainstream Economics?*, Marburg: Metropolis, pp. 55–73.
Colander, D., P. Howitt, A. Kirman, A. Leijonhufvud and P. Mehrling (2008), 'Beyond DSGE models: toward an empirically based macroeconomics', *American Economic Review*, **98** (2), 26–40.
Colander, D. and H. Landreth (1996), *The Coming of Keynesianism to America: Conversations with the Founders of Keynesian Economics*, Cheltenham, UK and Brookfield, VT: Edward Elgar.
Colander, D. and C. Rothschild (2009), 'Complexity and macro pedagogy: the complexity vision as a bridge between graduate and undergraduate macro', in G. Fontana and M. Setterfield (eds), *Macroeconomic Theory and Macroeconomic Pedagogy*, Basingstoke: Palgrave Macmillan, pp. 118–28.
Colander, D., H. Föllmer, A. Haas, M. Goldberg, K. Juselius, A. Kirman, T. Lux and B. Sloth (2009), 'The financial crisis and the systemic failure of academic economics', University of Kiel, mimeo.
Coleman, J.S. (1986), 'Psychological structure and social structure in economic models', *Journal of Business*, **59** (4, part 2), S365–S369.
Coleman, J.S. (1987), 'Microfoundations and macrosocial behavior', in J.C. Alexander, B. Giesen, R. Münch and N.J. Smelser (eds), *The Micro–Macro Link*, Berkeley, CA: University of California Press, pp. 153–73.
Coleman, J.S. (1990), *Foundations of Social Theory*, Cambridge, MA: Harvard University Press.
Collins, R. (1981), 'On the microfoundations of macrosociology', *American Journal of Sociology*, **86** (5), 984–1014.
Collins, R. (1985), Review of Hechter (1983), *Contemporary Sociology*, **14** (1), 132–3.
Collins, R. (1987), 'Interaction ritual chains, power and property: the micro–macro connection as an empirically based theoretical problem', in J.C. Alexander, B. Giesen, R. Münch and N.J. Smelser (eds), *The Micro–Macro Link*, Berkeley, CA: University of California Press, pp. 193–206.
Cook, K.S. (2000), 'Advances in the microfoundations of sociology: recent developments and new challenges for social psychology', *Contemporary Sociology*, **29** (5), 685–92.
Cornwall, J. (1977), *Modern Capitalism: Its Growth and Transformation*, New York: St. Martin's Press.

Cornwall, J. and W. Cornwall (2001), *Capitalist Development in the Twentieth Century: An Evolutionary Keynesian Analysis*, Cambridge: Cambridge University Press.
Crace, J. (2009), 'At the heart of physiology', *Guardian Weekly*, 9 January, 30–31.
Crotty, J.R. (1980), 'Post Keynesian economic theory: an overview and evaluation', *American Economic* Review, **70** (2), 20–25.
Crotty, J.R. (1994), 'Are Keynesian uncertainty and macrotheory incompatible? Conventional decision making, institutional structures and conditional stability in Keynesian macromodels', in G. Dymski and R. Pollin (eds), *New Perspectives in Monetary Macroeconomics: Explorations in the Tradition of Hyman Minsky*, Ann Arbor: University of Michigan Press, pp. 105–42.
Crotty, J.R. (1996), 'Is New Keynesian investment theory really "Keynesian"? Reflections on Fazzari and Variato', *Journal of Post Keynesian Economics*, **18** (3), 333–57.
Courvisanos, J. (1996), *Investment Cycles in Capitalist Economies: A Kaleckian Behavioural Contribution*, Cheltenham, UK and Northampton, MA, USA: Edward Elgar.
Cunningham, B. (2001), 'The reemergence of "emergence"', *Philosophy of Science*, **68** (3), Supplement: Part I, S62–S75.
Currie, G. (1984), 'Individualism and global supervenience', *British Journal for the Philosophy of Science*, **35** (4), 345–58.
Dasgupta, P. (2002), 'Modern economics and its critics', in U. Mäki (ed.), *Fact and Fiction in Economics: Models, Realism, and Social Construction*, Cambridge: Cambridge University Press, pp. 57–89.
Davidson, P. (1977), 'Money and general equilibrium', *Économie Appliquée*, **30** (4), 541–63, reprinted in P. Davidson, *Money and Employment: The Collected Writings of Paul Davidson, Volume 1*, London: Macmillan, 1991, pp. 196–217.
Davidson, P. (1978), *Money and the Real World*, London: Macmillan, second edition.
Davidson, P. (1980), '*Causality in Economics*: a review', *Journal of Post Keynesian Economics*, **2** (4), 576–84.
Davidson, P. (2011), *Post Keynesian Macroeconomic Theory, Second Edition: A Foundation for Successful Economic Policies for the Twenty-First Century*, Cheltenham, UK and Northampton, MA, USA: Edward Elgar.
Davis, J.B. (2003), *The Theory of the Individual in Economics: Identity and Value*, London: Routledge.
Dawkins, R. (1976), *The Selfish Gene*, Oxford: Oxford University Press.
Dawkins, R. (1996), *The Blind Watchmaker*, Harmondsworth: Penguin.
Denis, A. (2009), 'A century of methodological individualism. Part 1: Schumpeter and Menger', London: City University, June, mimeo.

Denis, A. (2010), 'A century of methodological individualism. Part 2: Mises and Hayek', London: City University, January, mimeo.

Dennett, D.C. (1996), *Darwin's Dangerous Idea: Evolution and the Meanings of Life*, London: Penguin.

De Wolff, P. (1941), 'Income elasticity of demand, a micro-economic and a macro-economic interpretation', *Economic Journal*, **51** (201), 140–45.

Dex, S. (1985), Review of Hechter (1983), *British Journal of Sociology*, **36** (2), 301.

Diamond, P. (1984), *An Equilibrium Approach to the Micro Foundations of Macroeconomics: The Wicksell Lectures, 1982*, Cambridge, MA: MIT Press.

Dixon, H. (1994), Review of Janssen (1993), *Economic Journal*, **104** (425), 946–8.

Dobb, M.H. (1973), *Theories of Value and Distribution Since Adam Smith: Ideology and Economic Theory*, Cambridge: Cambridge University Press.

Dolan, E.G. (1976), 'Austrian economics as extraordinary science', in E.G. Dolan (ed.), *The Foundations of Modern Austrian Economics*, Kansas City, MO: Sheen & Ward, pp. 3–15.

Dopfer, K. and J. Potts (2008), *The General Theory of Economic Evolution*, London and New York: Routledge.

Dore, M.H.I. (1993), *The Macrodynamics of Business Cycles: A Comparative Evaluation*, Oxford: Blackwell.

Dore, M.H.I. (2002), 'Representative agent model', in B. Snowdon and H.R. Vane, *Encyclopedia of Macroeconomics*, Cheltenham, UK and Northampton, MA, USA: Edward Elgar, pp. 623–8.

Dotsey, M. and R.G. King (1987), 'Business cycles', in J. Eatwell, M. Milgate and P. Newman (eds), *The New Palgrave: A Dictionary of Economics*, Volume 1, London: Macmillan, pp. 302–10.

Dow, S.C. (1981), 'Weintraub and Wiles: the methodological basis of conflict', *Journal of Post Keynesian Economics*, **3** (1), 325–39.

Dow, S.C. (1982–3), 'Substantive mountains and methodological molehills: a rejoinder' [to E.R. Weintraub], *Journal of Post Keynesian Economics*, **5** (2), 304–8.

Dow, S.C. (1985a), 'Microfoundations: a diversity of treatments', *Eastern Economic Journal*, **11** (4), 342–60.

Dow, S.C. (1985b), *Macroeconomic Thought: A Methodological Approach*, Oxford: Blackwell.

Dow, S.C. (1996), *The Methodology of Macroeconomic Thought*, Cheltenham, UK and Northampton, MA, USA: Edward Elgar.

Dow, S.C. (2002), *Economic Methodology: An Inquiry*, Oxford: Oxford University Press.

Dow, S.C. (2010), 'Keynes on knowledge, expectations and rationality', University of Stirling, mimeo.
Dow, S.C. and P.E. Earl (1982), *Money Matters: A Keynesian Approach to Monetary Economics*, Oxford: Martin Robertson.
Downing, B.M. (1990), Review of Taylor (1988), *Ethics*, **100** (3), 679–81.
Downs, A. (1957), *An Economic Theory of Democracy*, New York: Harper & Row.
Duarte, P.G. (2010), 'Not going away? Microfoundations in the making of a new consensus in macroeconomics', University of São Paulo, mimeo.
Duesenberry, J.S. (1949), *Income, Saving and the Theory of Consumer Behavior*, Cambridge, MA: Harvard University Press, 1962.
Dullien, S. (2011), 'The New Consensus from a traditional Keynesian and Post-Keynesian perspective: a worthwhile foundation for research or just a waste of time?', *Économie Appliquée*, **44** (1), 173–200.
Durkheim, E. (1898), *Sociology and Philosophy*, New York: Free Press, 1974.
Dutt, A.K. (2006), 'Is there a place for microfoundations for heterodox macroeconomics?', University of Notre Dame, mimeo.
Eichner, A.S. (1976), *The Megacorp and Oligopoly: Micro Foundations of Macro Dynamics*, Cambridge: Cambridge University Press.
Eichner, A.S. (1983), 'Why economics is not yet a science', in A.S. Eichner (ed.), *Why Economics is not Yet a Science*, London: Macmillan, pp. 205–41.
Eichner, A.S. (1985), *Toward a New Economics: Essays in Post-Keynesian and Institutionalist Theory*, Armonk, NY: M.E. Sharpe.
Eldredge, N. (1995), *Reinventing Darwin: The Great Evolutionary Debate*, London: Weidenfeld & Nicolson.
Elster, J. (1978), *Logic and Society: Contradictions and Possible Worlds*, Chichester: Wiley.
Elster, J. (1985), *Making Sense of Marx*, Cambridge: Cambridge University Press.
Emmeche, C., S. Køppe and F. Stjernfelt (2000), 'Levels, emergence, and three versions of downward causation', in P.B. Andersen, C. Emmeche, N.O. Finneman and P.V. Christiansen (eds), *Downward Causation: Mind, Bodies and Matter*, Aarhus: Aarhus University Press, pp. 13–34.
Endres, A.M. and Harper, D.A. (2011), 'Carl Menger and his followers in the Austrian tradition on the nature of capital and its structure', *Journal of the History of Economic Thought*, **33** (3), 357–84.
Epstein, J.M. and Axtell, R. (1996), *Growing Artificial Societies: Social Science from the Bottom Up*, Washington, DC: Brookings Institution Press and Cambridge, MA: MIT Press.

Evans, R. (1997), 'Soothsaying or science? Falsification, uncertainty and social change in macroeconomic modelling', *Social Studies of Science*, **27** (3), 395–438.

Fan, L.-S. (1966), 'A study in the maturity structure of interest rates', *Journal of Finance*, **21** (1), 131.

Farmer, R.A.E. (ed.) (2008), *Macroeconomics in the Small and the Large: Essays on Microfoundations, Macroeconomic Applications and Economic History in Honour of Axel Leijonhufvud*, Cheltenham, UK and Northampton, MA, USA: Edward Elgar.

Feiwel, G.R. (1975), *The Intellectual Capital of Michał Kalecki: A Study in Economic Theory and Policy*, Knoxville, TE: University of Tennessee Press.

Feiwel, G.R. (1989), 'The legacies of Kalecki and Keynes', in M. Sebastiani (ed.), *Kalecki's Relevance Today*, London: Macmillan, pp. 45–80.

Fernández-Huerga, E. (2008), 'The economic behavior of human beings: the institutional/Post-Keynesian model', *Journal of Economic Issues*, **42** (3), 709–26.

Fine, G.A. (1991), 'On the macrofoundations of microsociology: constraint and the exterior reality of structure', *Sociological Quarterly*, **33** (2), 161–72.

Fine, G.A. and B. Harrington (2004), 'Tiny publics: small groups and civil society', *Sociological Theory*, **22** (3), 341–56.

Fine, B. and D. Milonakis (2009), *From Economics Imperialism to Freakonomics: The Shifting Boundaries between Economics and other Social Sciences*, London: Routledge.

Fischer, S. (1977), 'Long-term contracts, rational expectations, and the optimal money supply rule', *Journal of Political Economy*, **85** (1), 191–205.

Fisk, M. (1991), 'Elster, Marx and method', *Noûs*, **25** (2), 215–20.

Fleming, J.M. (1938), 'The determination of the rate of interest', *Economica*, n.s., **5** (18), 333–41.

Fodor, J. (1991), 'Special sciences (or: the disunity of science as a working hypothesis', in R. Boyd, P. Gasper and J.D. Trout (eds), *The Philosophy of Science*, Cambridge, MA: MIT Press, pp. 429–41.

Fodor, J. (1997), 'Special sciences: still autonomous after all these years', *Noûs*, **31**, Supplement: 'Philosophical Perspectives, 11: Mind, Causation, and Worlds, 1997', 149–63.

Foley, D.K. and M. Sidrauski (1971), *Monetary and Fiscal Policy in a Growing Economy*, London: Collier-Macmillan.

Fontana, G. (2009), *Money, Uncertainty and Time*, London: Routledge.

Forni, M. and M. Lippi (1997), *Aggregation and the Microfoundations of Dynamic Macroeconomics*, Oxford: Clarendon Press.

Foster, J. (1984), Review of Chick (1983), *Economica*, **51** (203), 360–61.

Frank, R.H. (1992), 'Melding sociology and economics: James Coleman's *Foundations of Social Theory*', *Journal of Economic Literature*, **30** (1), 147–70.

Friedman, M. (1940), Review of Tinbergen (1939), *American Economic Review*, **30** (3), 657–60.

Friedman, M. (1946), 'Lange on price flexibility and employment: methodological criticisms', *American Economic Review*, **36** (4), 613–31.

Friedman, M. (1953), 'The methodology of positive economics', in M. Friedman, *Essays in Positive Economics*, Chicago, IL: Chicago University Press, pp. 3–43.

Friedman, M. (1956), 'The quantity theory of money: a restatement', in M. Friedman, *The Optimum Quantity of Money and Other Essays*, Chicago: Aldine, 1969, pp. 51–68.

Friedman, M. (1957), *A Theory of the Consumption Function*, Princeton, NJ: Princeton University Press.

Friedman, M. (1970), 'The counter-revolution in monetary theory', in M. Friedman, *Monetarist Economics*, Oxford: Blackwell, 1990, pp. 1–20.

Friedman, M. (1976), 'Comment' [on Tobin and Buiter], in J.L. Stein (ed.), *Monetarism*, Amsterdam: North-Holland, pp. 310–17.

Friedman, M. and G.S. Becker (1957), 'A statistical illusion in judging Keynesian models', *Journal of Political Economy*, **65** (1), 64–75.

Friedman, M. and A. Schwartz (1963), *A Monetary History of the United States 1867–1960*, Princeton, NJ: Princeton University Press, 1993.

Frisch, R. (1933), 'Propagation problems and impulse problems in dynamic economics', in *Economic Essays in Honour of Gustav Cassel, October 20th, 1933*, London: George Allen & Unwin, pp. 171–205.

Fullbrook, E. (2003), *The Crisis in Economics: The Post-autistic Economics Movement: The First 600 Days*, London: Routledge.

Garfinkel, A. (1981), 'Reductionism', Chapter 2 of A. Garfinkel, *Forms of Explanation*, New Haven, CT: Yale University Press, 1981, pp. 49–74, reprinted in R. Boyd, P. Gasper and J.D. Trout (eds), *The Philosophy of Science*, Cambridge, MA: MIT Press, 1991, pp. 443–59.

Garretsen, H. (1992), *Keynes, Coordination and Beyond: The Development of Macroeconomic and Monetary Theory since 1945*, Aldershot, UK and Brookfield, VT, USA: Edward Elgar.

Garrison, R.W. (1978), 'Austrian macroeconomics: a diagrammatical exposition', in L.M. Spadaro (ed.), *New Directions in Austrian Economics*, Kansas City, MO: Sheed Andrews and McMeel, pp. 167–204.

Garrison, R.W. (2001), *Time and Money: The Macroeconomics of Capital Structure*, London: Routledge.

Gellner, E.A. (1956), 'Symposium: explanation in history', *Proceedings of the Aristotelian Society, Supplementary Volumes*, **30**, 157–76.

Gerstein, D. (1987), 'To unpack micro and macro: link small with large and part with whole', in J.C. Alexander, B. Giesen, R. Münch and N.J. Smelser (eds), *The Micro–Macro Link*, Berkeley, CA: University of California Press, pp. 86–111.

Gibbs, R.W. Jr (ed.) (2008), *The Cambridge Handbook of Metaphor and Thought*, Cambridge: Cambridge University Press.

Gibson, B. (2009), 'The current crisis in macroeconomic theory', in J.P. Goldstein and M.G. Hillard (eds), *Heterodox Macroeconomics: Keynes, Marx and Globalization*, Abingdon and New York: Routledge, pp. 85–98.

Ginzburg, C. (1993), 'Microhistory: two or three things that I know about it', *Critical Inquiry*, **20** (1), 10–35.

Goldstein, J.P. (2009), 'An introduction to a unified heterodox macroeconomic theory', in J.P. Goldstein and M.G. Hillard (eds), *Heterodox Macroeconomics: Keynes, Marx and Globalization*, Abingdon and New York: Routledge, pp. 36–53.

Goldstein, L.J. (1956), 'The inadequacy of the principle of methodological individualism', *Journal of Philosophy*, **53** (25), 801–13.

Goldstein, L.J. (1958), 'The two theses of methodological individualism', *British Journal for the Philosophy of Science*, **9** (33), 1–11.

Goldstein, L.J. (1959), 'Mr. Watkins on the two theses', *British Journal for the Philosophy of Science*, **10** (39), 240–41.

Goodfriend, M. and R.G. King (1997), 'The new neoclassical synthesis and the role of monetary policy', *NBER Macroeconomics Annual*, **12**, 231–83.

Gordon, R.J. (1990), 'What is New-Keynesian economics?', *Journal of Economic Literature*, **28** (3), 1115–71.

Gordon, S. (1991), *The History and Philosophy of Science*, London: Routledge.

Gould, S.J. (2007), *The Richness of Life: The Essential Stephen Jay Gould*, ed. P. McGarr and S. Rose, New York: Norton.

Grafen, A. and M. Ridley (eds) (2006), *Richard Dawkins: How a Scientist Changed the Way We Think*, Oxford: Oxford University Press.

Green, D.P. and I. Shapiro (1994), *Pathologies of Rational Choice Theory: A Critique of Applications in Political Science*, New Haven, CT: Yale University Press.

Green, E.J. (1981), Review of Katouzian (1980), *Journal of Economic Literature*, **19** (4), 1582–4.

Green, H.A.J. (1964), *Aggregation in Economic Analysis: An Introductory Survey*, Princeton, NJ: Princeton University Press.

Greenwald, B. and J. Stiglitz (1987), 'Keynesian, New Keynesian and New Classical economics', *Oxford Economic Papers*, **39** (1), 119–32.

Greenwald, B. and J. Stiglitz (1993), 'New and old Keynesians', *Journal of Economic Perspectives*, **7** (1), 23–44.

Haberler, G. (1937), *Prosperity and Depression*, Geneva: League of Nations.

Hacking, I. (1996), 'The disunities of the sciences', in P. Gallison and D. Stump (eds), *The Disunity of Science: Boundaries, Contexts, and Power*, Stanford, CA: Stanford University Press, 1996.

Hahn, F.H. (1974), 'On the notion of equilibrium in economics', in F.H. Hahn, *Equilibrium and Macroeconomics*, Oxford: Blackwell, 1984, pp. 43–71.

Hahn, F.H. (1977), 'Keynesian economics and general equilibrium theory: reflections on some current debates', in G.C. Harcourt (ed.) (1977), *The Microeconomic Foundations of Macroeconomics:Proceedings of a Conference, Held by the International Economic Association at S'Agaro, Spain*, London: Macmillan, pp. 25–40, reprinted in F.H. Hahn, *Equilibrium and Macroeconomics*, Oxford: Blackwell, 1984, pp. 175–94.

Hahn, F.H. (1980), Review of Weintraub (1980), *Economic Journal*, **90** (357), 187–8.

Hahn, F.H. (1982), 'Why I am not a monetarist', in F.H. Hahn, *Equilibrium and Macroeconomics*, Oxford: Blackwell, 1984, pp. 307–26.

Hahn, F.H. (1983), 'Comment' [on Leijonhufvud], in R. Frydman and E.S. Phelps (eds), *Individual Forecasting and Aggregate Outcomes: 'Rational Expectations' Examined*, Cambridge: Cambridge University Press, pp. 223–30.

Hahn, F.H. (1984), *Equilibrium and Macroeconomics*, Oxford: Blackwell.

Hahn, F.H. (1988), Review of Lucas (1987), *Economica*, **55** (218), 283–4.

Haley, B.F. (1939), Review of Hicks (1939), *American Economic Review*, **29** (3), 557–60.

Hall, R.E. (1971), 'The dynamic effects of fiscal policy in an economy with foresight', *Review of Economic Studies*, **38** (2), 229–44.

Halliday, F. (1992), 'Bringing the "economic" back in: the case of nationalism', *Economy and Society*, **21** (4), 483–90.

Hamermesh, D.S. (2008), 'A Review of David Colander's *The Making of an Economist: Redux*', *Journal of Economic Literature*, **46** (2), 407–11.

Hands, D.W. (1993), *Testing, Rationality, and Progress: Essays on the Popperian Tradition in Economic Methodology*, Lanham, MD: Rowman & Littlefield.

Hands, D.W. (2001), *Reflection without Rules: Economic Methodology and Contemporary Science Theory*, Cambridge: Cambridge University Press.

Hands, D.W. (2008), 'Introspection, revealed preference, and neoclassical economics: a critical response to Don Ross on the Robbins–Samuelson argument pattern', *Journal of the History of Economic Thought*, **30** (4), 453–78.

Harcourt, G.C. (ed.) (1977), *The Microeconomic Foundations of Macroeconomics: Proceedings of a Conference, Held by the International Economic Association at S'Agaro, Spain*, London: Macmillan.

Harcourt, G.C. (1980), 'Discussion' [of Crotty], *American Economic Review*, **70** (2), 27–8.

Harcourt, G.C. (2006), *The Structure of Post-Keynesian Economics*, Cambridge: Cambridge University Press.

Harcourt, G.C. (2010), 'The crisis in mainstream economics', *Real-World Economics Review*, 53, 26 June, pp. 47–51, http://www.paecon.net/PAEReview/Issue53/Harcourt53.pdf (consulted 6 September 2010).

Harcourt, G.C. and P. Kenyon (1976), 'Pricing and the investment decision', *Kyklos*, **29** (3), 449–77.

Harper, D.A. and A.M. Endres (2011), 'The anatomy of emergence, with a focus upon capital formation', *Journal of Economic Behavior and Organization* (2011), doi: 10.1016/j.jebo.2011.03.103, pp. 1–16 (consulted 13 January 2012).

Harrod, R.F. (1939), Review of Hicks (1939), *Economic Journal*, **49** (194), 294–300.

Hartley, J.E. (1997), *The Representative Agent in Macroeconomics*, London: Routledge.

Hartley, J.E. (1999), Review of Forni and Lippi (1997), *Economic Journal*, **109** (453), F224–F226.

Hartley, J.E., K.D. Hoover and K.D. Salyer (eds) (1998), *Real Business Cycles: A Reader*, London: Routledge.

Hausman, D.M. (1992), *The Inexact and Separate Science of Economics*, Cambridge: Cambridge University Press.

Hausman, D.M. (ed.) (2008), *The Philosophy of Economics: An Anthology*, Cambridge: Cambridge University Press, third edition.

Hayek, F.A. (1955), *The Counter Revolution of Science: Studies on the Abuse of Reason*, London: Free Press and Collier-Macmillan.

Hayek, F.A. (1963), 'The economics of the 1930s as seen from London', cited from B. Caldwell (ed.), *The Collected Works of F.A. Hayek. Volume IX: Contra Keynes and Cambridge. Essays, Correspondence*, London: Routledge, 1995, pp. 49–73.

Hayek, F.A. (1966), 'Personal recollections of Keynes and the "Keynesian revolution"', *The Oriental Economist*, **34** (663), 78–80, cited from B. Caldwell (ed.), *The Collected Works of F.A. Hayek. Volume IX: Contra Keynes and Cambridge. Essays, Correspondence*, London: Routledge, 1995, pp. 240–46.

Hayek, F.A. (1972), *A Tiger By The Tail: A 40-years' Running Commentary on Keynesianism by Hayek*, London: Institute of Economic Affairs.

Heath, J. (2009), 'Methodological individualism', *Stanford Encyclopedia of Philosophy*, online edition, 12 March, http://plato.stanford.edu/entries/ methodological individualism/ (consulted 2 February 2010).

Hechter, M. (ed.) (1983), *The Microfoundations of Macrosociology*, Philadelphia, PA: Temple University Press.

Hechter, M. and S. Kanazawa (1997), 'Sociological rational choice theory', *Annual Review of Sociology*, **23**, 191–214.

Heilbroner, R. (1988), *Behind the Veil of Economics: Essays in the Worldly Philosophy*, New York: Norton.

Heilbroner, R. and W. Milgate (1995), *The Crisis of Vision in Modern Economic Thought*, Cambridge: Cambridge University Press.

Hein, E. and T. van Treeck (2010), 'Financialisation and rising shareholder power in Kaleckian/Post-Kaleckian models of distribution and growth', *Review of Political Economy*, **22** (2), 205–33.

Hein, E. and E. Stockhammer (eds) (2011), *A Modern Guide to Keynesian Macroeconomics and Economic Policies*, Cheltenham, UK and Northampton, MA, USA: Edward Elgar.

Hempel, C. and P. Oppenheim (1965), 'On the idea of emergence', in C. Hempel, *Aspects of Scientific Explanation and Other Essays in the Philosophy of Science*. Glencoe, IL: Free Press, 1965, pp. 258–64, reprinted in M.A. Bedau and P. Humphreys (eds), *Emergence: Contemporary Readings in Philosophy and Science*, Cambridge, MA: MIT Press, 2008, pp. 61–7.

Henderson, W. (1986), 'Metaphors in economics', in M. Coulthard (ed.), *Talking about Text: Studies Presented to David Brazil on his Retirement*, Birmingham: English Language Research, University of Birmingham, pp. 109–27.

Henderson, W. (1993), 'The problem of Edgeworth's style', in W. Henderson (ed.), *Economics and Language*, London: Routledge, pp. 200–222.

Henderson, W. (1995), *Economics as Literature*, London: Routledge.

Hendry, D.F. (2003), Review of Hoover (2001b), *Economica*, **70** (278), 375–7.

Hesse, M. (1966), *Models and Analogies in Science*, Notre Dame, IN: University of Notre Dame Press.

Hester, D.D. (1972), Review of Foley and Sidrauski (1971), *Journal of Finance*, **27** (5), 1186–8.

Hewitson, G. (2012), 'Banking', in J.E. King (ed.), *The Elgar Companion to Post Keynesian Economics*, Cheltenham, UK and Northampton, MA, USA: Edward Elgar, second edition, pp. 24–9.

Hicks, J.R. (1935), 'A suggestion for simplifying the theory of money', *Economica*, n.s., **2** (5), 1–19.

Hicks, J.R. (1939), *Value and Capital: An Inquiry into Some Fundamental Principles of Economic Theory*, Oxford: Clarendon Press.

Hicks, J. (1965), *Capital and Growth*, Oxford: Oxford University Press.
Hicks, J. (1974), *The Crisis in Keynesian Economics*, Oxford: Blackwell.
Hicks, J. (1979), Review of Weintraub (1979), *Journal of Economic Literature*, **17** (4), 1451–4.
Hicks, J. (1980–81), 'IS-LM: an explanation', *Journal of Post Keynesian Economics*, **3** (2), 139–54.
Hodgson, G.M. (1986), 'Behind methodological individualism', *Cambridge Journal of Economics*, **10** (3), 211–24.
Hodgson, G.M. (2000), 'From micro to macro: the concept of emergence and the role of institutions', in L. Burlamaqui, A.C. Castro and H.-J. Chang (eds), *Institutions and the Role of the State*, Cheltenham, UK and Northampton, MA, USA, pp. 103–26.
Hodgson, G.M. (2001), *How Economics Forgot History: The Problem of Historical Specificity in Social Science*, London: Routledge.
Hodgson, G.M. (2002), 'Reconstitutive downward causation: social structure and the development of individual agency', in E. Fullbrook (ed.), *Intersubjectivity in Economics: Agents and Structures*, London: Routledge, pp. 159–80.
Hodgson, G.M. (2007), 'Meanings of methodological individualism', *Journal of Economic Methodology*, **14** (2), 57–68.
Hollis, M. and E.J. Nell (1975), *Rational Economic Man: A Philosophical Critique of Neo-Classical Economics*, Cambridge: Cambridge University Press.
Holmes, J. (2003), Review of Hoover (2001b), *Journal of Economic Literature*, **41** (2), 592–3.
Homans, G.C. (1984), Review of Hechter (1983), *Theory and Society*, **13** (6), 877–80.
Hoover, K.D. (1988), *The New Classical Macroeconomics: A Sceptical Inquiry*, Oxford: Blackwell.
Hoover, K.D. (1995a), 'Why does methodology matter for economics?', *Economic Journal*, **105** (430), 715–34.
Hoover, K.D. (1995b), 'The problem of macroeconometrics', in K.D. Hoover (ed.), *Macroeconometrics: Developments, Tensions, and Prospects*, Boston, MA: Kluwer, pp. 1–12.
Hoover, K.D. (1995c), 'Is macroeconomics for real?', *The Monist*, **78** (3), 235–57, reprinted in U. Mäki (ed.), *The Economic World View: Studies in the Ontology of Economics*, Cambridge: Cambridge University Press, 2001, pp. 225–45.
Hoover, K.D. (2001a), *The Methodology of Empirical Macroeconomics*, Cambridge: Cambridge University Press, part reprinted in D.M. Hausman (ed.), *The Philosophy of Economics: An Anthology*, Cambridge: Cambridge University Press, third edition, 2008, pp. 315–33.

Hoover, K.D. (2001b), *Causality in Macroeconomics*, Cambridge: Cambridge University Press.

Hoover, K.D. (2003), 'A history of postwar monetary economics and macroeconomics', in W.J. Samuels, J.E. Biddle and J.B. Davis (eds), *A Companion to the History of Economic Thought*, Oxford: Blackwell, pp. 411–27.

Hoover, K.D. (2006), 'The past as the future: the Marshallian approach to Post Walrasian economics', in D. Colander (ed.), *Post Walrasian Macroeconomics: Beyond the Dynamic Stochastic General Equilibrium Model*, Cambridge: Cambridge University Press, pp. 239–57.

Hoover, K.D. (2009), 'Microfoundations and the ontology of macroeconomics', in H. Kincaid and D. Ross (eds), *The Oxford Handbook of Philosophy of Economics*, Oxford: Oxford University Press, pp. 386–409.

Hoover, K.D. (2010a), 'Idealizing reduction: the microfoundations of macroeconomics', *Erkenntnis*, **73** (3), 329–47.

Hoover, K.D. (2010b), 'Microfoundational programs', Duke University, 14 January, mimeo.

Horn, K.I. (2009), *Roads to Wisdom: Conversations with Ten Nobel Laureates in Economics*, Cheltenham, UK and Northampton, MA, USA: Edward Elgar.

Horst, S. (2007), *Beyond Reduction: Philosophy of Mind and Post-reductionist Philosophy of Science*, Oxford: Oxford University Press.

Horwitz, S. (2000), *Microfoundations and Macroeconomics: An Austrian Perspective*, London: Routledge.

Horwitz, S. (2010), 'The microeconomic foundations of macroeconomic disorder: an Austrian perspective on the Great Recession of 2008', in S. Kates (ed.), *Macroeconomic Theory and its Failings: Alternative Perspectives on the Global Financial Crisis*, Cheltenham, UK and Northampton, MA, USA: Edward Elgar, pp. 112–26.

Howard, M.C. and J.E. King (1989), 'The rational choice Marxism of John Roemer: a critique', *Review of Social Economy*, **47** (4), 392–414.

Howard, M.C. and J.E. King (1992), *A History of Marxian Economics: Volume II, 1929–1990*, Basingstoke: Macmillan and Princeton, NJ: Princeton University Press.

Howitt, P. (1986), 'The Keynesian recovery', *Canadian Journal of Economics*, **19** (4), 626–41.

Howitt, P. (1987), 'Macroeconomics: relations with microeconomics', in J. Eatwell, M. Milgate and P. Newman (eds), *The New Palgrave: A Dictionary of Economics*, Volume 3, London: Macmillan, pp. 273–6.

Howitt, P. (2006), 'The microfoundations of the Keynesian multiplier process', *Journal of Economic Interaction and Coordination*, **1** (1), 33–44.

Howitt, P. (2008), 'Macroeconomics with intelligent autonomous agents', in R.A.E. Farmer (ed.), *Macroeconomics in the Small and the Large: Essays on Microfoundations, Macroeconomic Applications and Economic History in Honour of Axel Leijonhufvud*, Cheltenham, UK and Northampton, MA, USA: Edward Elgar, pp. 157–77.

Huber, J. (1990), 'Macro–micro links in gender stratification', *American Sociological Review*, **55** (1), 1–10.

Hudík, M. (2011), 'Why economics is not a science of behaviour', *Journal of Economic Methodology*, **18** (2), 147–62.

Hutchison, T.W. (1938), *The Significance and Basic Postulates of Economic Theory*, New York: Kelley, 1960.

Hutchison, T.W. (1981), *The Politics and Philosophy of Economics: Marxians, Keynesians, and Austrians*, New York: New York University Press.

Hutchison, T.W. (1994), *The Uses and Abuses of Economics: Contentious Essays on History and Method*, London: Routledge.

Hutchison, T.W. (2000), *On the Methodology of Economics and the Formalist Revolution*, Cheltenham, UK and Northampton, MA, USA: Edward Elgar.

Hynes, J.A. (1998), 'The emergence of the neoclassical consumption function: the formative years, 1940–1952', *Journal of the History of Economic Thought*, **20** (1), 25–51.

Ibáñez, C.U. (1999), *The Current State of Macroeconomics: Leading Thinkers in Conversation*, Basingstoke: Palgrave.

Ingham, G. (1996), 'Some recent changes in the relationship between economics and sociology', *Cambridge Journal of Economics*, **20** (2), 243–75.

James, S. (1984), *The Content of Social Explanation*, Cambridge: Cambridge University Press.

Janssen, M.C.W. (1993), *Microfoundations: A Critical Inquiry*, London: Routledge.

Jarvie, I.C. (1972), *Concepts and Society*, London: Routledge & Kegan Paul.

Jespersen, J. (2009), *Macroeconomic Methodology: A Post-Keynesian Perspective*, Cheltenham, UK and Northampton, MA, USA: Edward Elgar.

Jo, T.-H. (2011), 'Social provisioning process and socio-economic modeling', *American Journal of Economics and Sociology*, **70** (5), 1094–1116.

Jo, T.-H. (2012), 'Welfare economics', in J.E. King (ed.), *The Elgar Companion to Post Keynesian Economics*, Cheltenham, UK and Northampton, MA, USA: Edward Elgar, second edition, pp. 593–8.

Jorgenson, D.W. (1963), 'Capital theory and investment behavior', *American Economic Review*, **53** (2), 247–59.

Kaldor, N. (1956), 'Alternative theories of distribution', *Review of Economic Studies*, **23** (2), 83–100.

Kaldor, N. (1966), *Causes of the Slow Rate of Economic Growth in the United Kingdom: An Inaugural Lecture*, Cambridge: Cambridge University Press.

Kaldor, N. (1978), 'Introduction' to N. Kaldor, *Further Essays on Economic Theory, Volume I*, London: Duckworth, pp. vii– xxix.

Kaldor, N. (1983), 'Keynesian economics after fifty years', in D. Worswick and J. Trevithick (eds), *Keynes and the Modern World*, Cambridge: Cambridge University Press, pp. 1–28.

Kalecki, M. (1935), 'A macrodynamic theory of business cycles', *Econometrica*, **3** (3), 327–44.

Kalecki, M. (1942), 'A theory of profits', *Economic Journal*, **52** (206–7), 258–67.

Kalecki, M. (1943), 'Political aspects of full employment', *Political Quarterly*, **14** (4), 322–31.

Katouzian, H. (1980), *Ideology and Method in Economics*, London: Macmillan.

Kaufman, B.E. (2007), 'The impossibility of a perfectly competitive labour market', *Cambridge Journal of Economics*, **31** (5), 775–87.

Kemeny, J. (1976), 'Perspectives on the micro–macro distinction', *Sociological Review*, **24** (4), 731–52.

Kemeny, J.G. and P. Oppenheim (1956), 'On reduction', *Philosophical Studies*, **7** (1/2), 6–19.

Keynes, J.M. (1926), 'Francis Ysidro Edgeworth, 1845–1926', *Economic Journal*, **36** (141), 140–53.

Keynes, J.M. (1936), *The General Theory of Employment, Interest and Money*, London: Macmillan.

Keynes, J.M. (1937), 'The general theory of employment', *Quarterly Journal of Economics*, **51** (2), 209–23.

Keynes, J.M. (1939), 'Preface to the French edition', in *The Collected Works of John Maynard Keynes. Volume VII: The General Theory of Employment, Interest and Money*, London: Macmillan for the Royal Economic Society, 1973, pp. xxxi–xxxv.

Keynes, J.M. (1972), *The Collected Writings of John Maynard Keynes, Volume X: Essays in Biography*, London: Macmillan for the Royal Economic Society.

Keynes, J.N. (1890), *The Scope and Method of Political Economy*, London: Macmillan.

Kim, J. (1999), 'Making sense of emergence', *Philosophical Studies*, **95** (1/2), 3–36, reprinted in M.A. Bedau and P. Humphreys (eds), *Emergence: Contemporary Readings in Philosophy and Science*, Cambridge, MA: MIT Press, 2008, pp. 127–54.

Kim, J. (2005), *Physicalism, or Something Near Enough*, Princeton, NJ: Princeton University Press.
Kincaid, H. (1997), *Individualism and the Unity of Science: Essays on Reduction, Explanation, and the Special Sciences*, Lanham, MD: Rowman & Littlefield.
Kincaid, H. (1998), 'Methodological individualism/atomism', in J.B. Davis, D.W Hands and U. Mäki (eds), *The Handbook of Economic Methodology*, Cheltenham, UK and Northampton, MA, USA: Edward Elgar, pp. 294–300.
King, J.E. (1995), *Conversations with Post Keynesians*, Basingstoke: Macmillan.
King, J.E. (1998), 'From Giblin to Kalecki: the export multiplier and the balance of payments constraint on economic growth, 1930–1933', *History of Economics Review*, **28**, 62–71.
King, J.E. (2002), *A History of Post Keynesian Economics since 1936*, Cheltenham, UK and Northampton, MA, USA: Edward Elgar.
King, J.E. (2009), 'Microfoundations?', in E. Hein, T. Niechoj and E. Stockhammer (eds), *Macroeconomic Policies on Shaky Foundations: Whither Mainstream Economics?*, Marburg: Metropolis, pp. 33–53.
King, R.G. and C.I. Plosser (1984), 'Money, credit, and prices in a real business cycle', *American Economic Review*, **74** (3), 363–80.
King, R.G., C.I. Plosser and S.T. Rebelo (1988), 'Production, growth and business cycles', *Journal of Monetary Economics*, **21** (2–3), 195–232.
Kirman, A. (1989), 'The intrinsic limits of modern economic theory: the emperor has no clothes', *Economic Journal*, **99** (395), Supplement, 126–39.
Kirman, A. (1992), 'Whom or what does the representative individual represent?', *Journal of Economic Perspectives*, **6** (2), 117–36.
Kirman, A. (1999a), 'Introduction', in M. Gallegati and A. Kirman (eds), *Beyond the Representative Agent*, Cheltenham, UK and Northampton, MA, USA: Edward Elgar, pp. ix–xvi.
Kirman, A. (1999b), 'Interaction and markets', in M. Gallegati and A. Kirman (eds), *Beyond the Representative Agent*, Cheltenham, UK and Northampton, MA, USA: Edward Elgar, pp. 1–39.
Kirman, A. (2011a), *Complex Economics: Individual and Collective Rationality*, London: Routledge.
Kirman, A. (2011b), 'The economic entomologist: an interview with Alan Kirman', *Erasmus Journal for Philosophy and Economics*, **4** (2), 42–66, http://ejpe.org/pdf/4–2–int.pdf (consulted 6 December 2011).
Kiser, E. (1999), 'Comparing varieties of agency theory in economics, political science and sociology: an illustration from state policy implementation', *Sociological Theory*, **17** (2), 146–70.

Klamer, A. and D. Colander (1989), *The Making of an Economist*, Boulder, CO: Westview Press.
Klamer, A. and T.C. Leonard (1994), 'So what's an economic metaphor?', in P. Mirowski (ed.), *Natural Images in Economic Thought: Markets Read in Tooth and Claw*, Cambridge: Cambridge University Press, pp. 20–51.
Klein, L.R. (1946), 'Macroeconomics and the theory of rational behavior', *Econometrica*, **14** (2), 93–108.
Klein, L.R. (1947), *The Keynesian Revolution*, New York: Macmillan.
Klein, L.R. (1993), 'What is macroeconomics?', in H. Barkai, S. Fischer and N. Liviatan (eds), *Monetary Theory and Thought: Essays in Honour of Don Patinkin*, Basingstoke: Macmillan, pp. 35–54.
Klein, L.R. (2006), 'Paul Samuelson as a "Keynesian" economist', in M. Szenberg, L. Ramrattan and A.A. Gottesman (eds), *Samuelsonian Economics and the Twenty-First Century*, Oxford: Oxford University Press, pp. 165–77.
Knapp, P. (1990), 'The revival of macrosociology: methodological issues of discontinuity in comparative historical theory', *Sociological Forum*, **5** (4), 545–67.
Koopmans, T.C. (1947), 'Measurement without theory', *Review of Economics and Statistics*, **29** (3), 161–72.
Koopmans, T.C. (1949), 'A reply' [to R. Vining], *Review of Economics and Statistics*, **31** (2), 86–91.
Kregel, J.A. (1985), 'Sidney Weintraub's macrofoundations of microeconomics and the theory of distribution', *Journal of Post Keynesian Economics*, **7** (4), 540–58.
Kregel, J.A. (1987), 'Rational spirits and the Post Keynesian macrotheory of microeconomics', *De Economist*, **135** (4), 520–32.
Kriesler, P. (1989), 'Methodological implications of Kalecki's microfoundations', in M. Sebastiani (ed.), *Kalecki's Relevance Today*, Basingstoke: Macmillan, pp. 121–41.
Kriesler, P. (1996), 'Microfoundations: a Kaleckian perspective', in J.E. King (ed.), *An Alternative Macroeconomic Theory: The Kaleckian Model and Post-Keynesian Economics*, Boston, MA: Kluwer, pp. 55–72.
Kropotkin, P. (1902), *Mutual Aid*, Harmondsworth: Penguin, 1939.
Krugman, P. (2009), 'How did economists get it so wrong?', *New York Times*, 6 September.
Kuipers, T.A.F. (2001), *Structures in Science: Heuristic Patterns Based on Cognitive Structures*, Dordrecht: Kluwer.
Küppers, B.-O. (1992), 'Understanding complexity', in A. Beckerman, H. Flohr and J. Kim (eds), *Emergence or Reduction? Essays on the Prospects of Non-reductive Physicalism*, Berlin: De Gruyter, pp. 241–56.

Kurz, H.D. (2008), 'Sraffa, Piero 1898–1983', in W.A. Darity Jr (ed.), *International Encyclopedia of the Social Sciences, 2nd Edition*, Detroit: Macmillan Reference, volume 7, pp. 70–72.

Kydland, F.E. and E.C. Prescott (1982), 'Time to build and aggregate fluctuations', *Econometrica*, **50** (2), 1345–70.

Lachmann, L.M. (1969), 'Methodological individualism and the market economy', in L.M. Lachmann (ed.), *Roads to Freedom: Essays in Honour of Friedrich A. von Hayek*, London: Routledge & Kegan Paul, pp. 89–105.

Lachmann, L.M. (1973), *Macro-economic Thinking and the Market Economy: An Essay on the Neglect of the Micro-foundations and its Consequences*, London: Institute of Economic Affairs.

Lachmann, L.M. (1976a), 'On Austrian capital theory', in E.G. Dolan (ed.), *The Foundations of Modern Austrian Economics*, Kansas City, MO: Sheen & Ward, pp. 145–51.

Lachmann, L.M. (1976b), 'Towards a critique of macroeconomics', in E.G. Dolan (ed.), *The Foundations of Modern Austrian Economics*, Kansas City, MO: Sheen & Ward, pp. 152–9.

Lachmann, L.M. (1978), 'An Austrian stocktaking: unsettled questions and tentative answers', in L.M. Spadaro (ed.), *New Directions in Austrian Economics*, Kansas City: Sheed Andrews & McMeel, pp. 1–18.

Lagueux, M. (1999), 'Do metaphors affect economic theory?', *Economics and Philosophy*, **15** (1), 1–22.

Laidler, D. (1982), *Monetarist Perspectives*, Oxford: Philip Allan.

Laidler, D. (1986), Review of Walker (1984), *Economic Journal*, **96** (382), 547–9.

Laidler, D. (1990), *Taking Money Seriously and Other Essays*, Oxford: Philip Allan.

Laidler, D. (1992), 'The cycle before New Classical economics', in M.T. Belongia and M.R. Garfinkel (eds), *The Business Cycle: Theories and Evidence*, Boston, MA: Kluwer, pp. 85–112.

Laidler, D. (1997), 'Notes on the microfoundations of monetary economics', *Economic Journal*, **107** (443), 1213–23.

Laidler, D. (1999), *Fabricating the Keynesian Revolution: Studies of the Inter-war Literature on Money, the Cycle and Unemployment*, Cambridge: Cambridge University Press.

Laidler, D. (2008), 'Axel Leijonhufvud and the quest for microfoundations', in R.E.A. Farmer (ed.), *Macroeconomics in the Small and the Large: Essays on Microfoundations, Macroeconomic Applications and Economic History in Honour of Axel Leijonhufvud*, Cheltenham, UK and Northampton, MA, USA: Edward Elgar, pp. 1–23.

Laidler, D. (2010), 'Chicago monetary traditions', in R. Emmett (ed.), *The Elgar Companion to the Chicago School of Economics*, Cheltenham, UK and Northampton, MA, USA: Edward Elgar, pp. 70–80.
Lakoff, G. and M. Johnson (1980), *Metaphors We Live By*, Chicago, IL: University of Chicago Press.
Lamoreaux, N.R. (2006), 'Rethinking microhistory: a comment', *Journal of the Early Republic*, **26** (4), 555–61.
Lange, O. (1945), *Price Flexibility and Employment*, San Antonio, TX: Principia Press of Trinity University.
Lange, P. and G. Tsebelis (1993), 'Wages, strikes, and power: an equilibrium analysis' in W.J. Booth, P. James and H. Meadwell (eds), *Politics and Rationality*, Cambridge: Cambridge University Press, pp. 132–64.
Latham, J. (2011), 'Genome doesn't have the answers', *Guardian Weekly*, 28 April, 20–21.
Lavoie, M. (1996), 'Horizontalism, structuralism, liquidity preference and the principle of increasing risk', *Scottish Journal of Political Economy*, **43** (3), 275–300.
Lavoie, M. and M. Seccareccia (2001), 'Minsky's financial fragility hypothesis: a missing macroeconomic link?', in R. Bellofiore and P. Ferri (eds), *Financial Fragility and Investment in the Capitalist Economy: The Economic Legacy of Hyman Minsky, Volume II*, Cheltenham, UK and Northampton, MA, USA: Edward Elgar, pp. 76–96.
Lawson, T. (1997), *Economics and Reality*, London: Routledge.
Lawson, T. (2003), *Reorienting Economics*, London: Routledge.
Lazear, E.P. (2000), 'Economic imperialism', *Quarterly Journal of Economics*, **115** (1), 99–146.
Lee, F. (2011), 'Heterodox microeconomics and the foundation of heterodox macroeconomics', http://mpra.ub.uni-muenchen.de/30491/ (consulted 22 June 2011).
Lerner, A.P. (1940), 'Professor Hicks's dynamics', *Quarterly Journal of Economics*, **54** (2), 298–306.
Lerner, A.P. (1943), 'Functional finance and the federal debt', *Social Research*, **10** (1), 38–51.
Lerner, A.P. (1962), 'Microeconomics and macroeconomics', in E. Nagel, P. Suppes and A. Tarski (eds), *Logic, Methodology and Philosophy of Science: Proceedings of the 1960 International Congress*, Stanford, CA: Stanford University Press, pp. 474–83.
Levy, D.M. (1985), 'The impossibility of a complete methodological individualist: reduction when knowledge is imperfect', *Economics and Philosophy*, **1** (1), 101–8.
Lewontin, R.C. (1993), *Biology as Ideology*, Harmondsworth: Penguin.
Lewontin, R.C., S. Rose and L.J. Kamin (1984), *Not in Our Genes: Biology, Ideology, and Human Nature*, Harmondsworth: Penguin.

Lipsey, R.G. (1962), *An Introduction to Positive Economics*, London: Weidenfeld and Nicolson.
Liska, A.E. (1990), 'The significance of aggregate dependent variables and contextual independent variables for linking macro and micro theories', *Social Psychological Quarterly*, **53** (4), 292–301.
Little, D. (1998), *On the Philosophy of the Social Sciences: Microfoundations, Method, and Causation*, New Brunswick, NJ: Transaction Publishers.
Little, D. (2009), 'The heterogeneous social: new thinking about the foundations of the social sciences', in C. Mantzavinos (ed.), *Philosophy of the Social Sciences: Philosophical Theory and Scientific Practice*, Cambridge: Cambridge University Press, pp. 154–78.
Ljungkvist, L. and Sargent, T.J. (2004), *Recursive Macroeconomic Theory*, Cambridge, MA: MIT Press, second edition.
Long, J.B. Jr and C.I. Plosser (1983), 'Real business cycles', *Journal of Political Economy*, **91** (1), 39–69.
Lucas, R.E. Jr (1973), 'Some international evidence on output–inflation tradeoffs', *American Economic Review*, **63** (3), 326–34.
Lucas, R.E. Jr (1975), 'An equilibrium model of the business cycle', *Journal of Political Economy*, **83** (6), 1113–44.
Lucas, R.E. Jr (1977), 'Understanding business cycles', in K. Brunner and A.H. Meltzer (eds), *Stabilization of the Domestic and International Economy*, New York: North-Holland, 1977, pp. 7–29, reprinted in R.E. Lucas Jr, *Studies in Business-Cycle Theory*, Cambridge, MA: MIT Press, 1987, pp. 215–39.
Lucas, R.E. Jr (1981), *Studies in Business-Cycle Theory*, Cambridge, MA: MIT Press, 1987.
Lucas, R.E. Jr (1987), *Models of Business Cycles: Yrjö Jahnsson Lectures 1985*, Oxford: Blackwell.
Lukes, S. (1968), 'Methodological individualism reconsidered', *British Journal of Sociology*, **19** (2), 119–29.
Machlup, F. (1940), 'Professor Hicks's statics', *Quarterly Journal of Economics*, **54** (2), 277–97.
Machlup, F. (1963), *Essays on Economic Semantics*, cited from the second edition, with the title *Economic Semantics*, New Brunswick, NJ: Transaction Publishers, 1991.
Magnússon, S.G. (2003), 'The singularization of history: social history and microhistory within the postmodern state of knowledge', *Journal of Social History*, **36** (3), 710–35.
Mäki, U. (2011), 'Scientific realism as a challenge to economics (and vice versa)', *Journal of Economic Methodology*, **18** (1), 1–12.
Malinvaud, E. (1977), *The Theory of Unemployment Reconsidered*, Oxford: Blackwell.

Mandelbaum, M. (1955), 'Societal facts', *British Journal of Sociology*, **6** (4), 305–17.
Mandelbaum, M. (1957), 'Societal laws', *British Journal for the Philosophy of Science*, **8** (31), 211–24.
Manning, A. (2003), *Monopsony in Motion*, Princeton, NJ: Princeton University Press.
Manolio, T.A. and 26 co-authors (2009), 'Finding the missing heritability of complex diseases', *Nature*, **461**, 747–53.
Marchionni, C. and J. Vromen (2010), 'Introduction: "Neuroeconomics: hype or hope?"', *Journal of Economic Methodology*, **17** (2), 103–6.
Marschak, J. (1934), 'The meetings of the Econometric Society in Leyden, September–October 1933', *Econometrica*, **2** (2), 187–203.
Marx, K. (1852), 'The eighteenth Brumaire of Louis Bonaparte', in K. Marx and F. Engels, *Selected Works, Volume 1*, Moscow: Foreign Languages Publishing House, 1962, pp. 247–344.
Mata, T. (2011), 'Godley works in mysterious ways: the craft of economic judgment in postwar Britain', Durham, NC: Duke University, Center for the History of Political Economy, mimeo.
Mayer, T. (1994), *Analytical Marxism*, Thousand Oaks, CA: Sage.
McCandless, G.T. Jr and N. Wallace (1991), *Introduction to Dynamic Macroeconomic Theory: An Overlapping Generations Approach*, Cambridge, MA: Harvard University Press.
McCloskey, D. (1985), *The Rhetoric of Economics*, Madison: University of Wisconsin Press.
McDonald, I.M. (2008), 'Behavioural macroeconomics and wage and price setting: developing some early insights of John Maynard Keynes and Joan Robinson (with appendix)', University of Melbourne, mimeo.
McDonald, I.M. (2010), 'Beyond Krugman to behavioural Keynes', *Agenda*, **17** (1), 89–118.
McKenna, E.J. and Zannoni, D.C. (2012), 'Agency', in J.E. King (ed.), *The Elgar Companion to Post Keynesian Economics*, Cheltenham, UK and Northampton, MA, USA: Edward Elgar, second edition, pp. 1–5.
McLaughlin, B.P. (1992), 'The rise and fall of British emergentism', in A. Beckerman, H. Flohr and J. Kim (eds), *Emergence or Reduction? Essays on the Prospects of Non-reductive Physicalism*, Berlin: De Gruyter, pp. 49–93.
Meade, J.E. (1936), *An Introduction to Economic Analysis and Policy*, Oxford: Oxford University Press.
Meade, J.E. (1975), 'The Keynesian revolution', in M. Keynes (ed.), *Essays on John Maynard Keynes*, Cambridge: Cambridge University Press, pp. 82–8.
Means, G.C. (1947), *A Monetary Theory of Employment*, Armonk, NY: M.E. Sharpe, 1994.

Mearman, A. (2009), 'Why have Post-Keynesians (perhaps) inadequately dealt with issues related to the environment?', in P. Lawn (ed.), *Environment and Employment: A Reconciliation*, Abingdon and New York: Routledge, pp. 97–125.

Mehrling, P. (2005), *Fischer Black and the Revolutionary Idea of Finance*, New York: Wiley.

Mellor, D.H. (1982), 'The reduction of society', *Philosophy*, **57** (219), 51–75.

Merton, R.K. (1957), *Social Theory and Social Structure*, Glencoe, IL: Free Press.

Messori, M. (ed.) (1999), *Financial Constraints and Market Failures: The Microfoundations of the New Keynesian Macroeconomics*, Cheltenham, UK and Northampton, MA, USA: Edward Elgar.

Midgley, M. (2010), *The Solitary Self: Darwin and the Selfish Gene*, Durham, UK: Acumen Press.

Mill, J.S. (1974), *A System of Logic*, volume 8 of J.M. Robson (ed.), *The Collected Works of John Stuart Mill*, Toronto: University of Toronto Press.

Miller, M.H. and C.W. Upton (1974), *Macroeconomics: A Neoclassical Introduction*. Homewood, IL: Irwin.

Miller, R.W. (1978), 'Methodological individualism and social explanation', *Philosophy of Science*, **45** (3), 387–414.

Minsky, H.P. (1954 [2004]), *Induced Investment and Business Cycles*, edited and with an introduction by D.B. Papadimitriou, Cheltenham, UK and Northampton, MA, USA: Edward Elgar.

Mirowski, P. (1989a), *More Heat Than Light: Economics as Social Physics, Physics as Nature's Economics*, Cambridge: Cambridge University Press.

Mirowski, P. (1989b), 'The measurement without theory controversy: defeating rival research programs by accusing them of naïve empiricism', *Économies et Sociétés*, **11** (1), 65–87.

Mirowski, P. (2010), 'Inherent vice: Minsky, markomata and the tendency of markets to undermine themselves', *Journal of Institutional Economics*, **6** (4), 415–43.

Mises, L. von (1949), *Human Action: A Treatise on Economics*, Irvington-on-Hudson, NY: Foundation for Economic Education, fourth edition, 1996.

Mitchell, W.C. (1913), *Business Cycles*, Berkeley, CA: University of California Press.

Modigliani, F. (1954), 'Utility analysis and the consumption function: an interpretation of cross-section data', in K.K. Kurihara (ed.), *Post-Keynesian Economics*, New Brunswick, NJ: Rutgers University Press, pp. 388–436.

Modigliani, F. (2001), *Adventures of an Economist*, New York: Textere.

Morgan, G. (1997), *Images of Organization*, Thousand Oaks, CA: Sage, second edition.

Morgan, M.S. (1990), *The History of Econometric Ideas*, Cambridge: Cambridge University Press.

Morgenstern, O.M. (1941), 'Professor Hicks on value and capital', *Journal of Political Economy*, **49** (3), 361–93.

Morgenstern, O.M. (1972), 'Thirteen critical points in contemporary economic theory: an interpretation', *Journal of Economic Literature*, **10** (4), 1163–89.

Morrow, J.D. (1988), 'Social choice and system structure in world politics', *World Politics*, **41** (1), 75–97.

Mouzelis, N. (1995), *Sociological Theory: What Went Wrong?*, London: Routledge.

Münch, R. (1987), 'The interpenetration of microinteraction and macrostructures in a complex and contingent institutional order', in J.C. Alexander, B. Giesen, R. Münch and N.J. Smelser (eds), *The Micro–Macro Link*, Berkeley, CA: University of California Press, pp. 319–36.

Münch, R. and N.J. Smelser (1987), 'Relating the micro and macro', in J.C. Alexander, B. Giesen, R. Münch and N.J. Smelser (eds), *The Micro–Macro Link*, Berkeley, CA: University of California Press, pp. 356–85.

Murphy, J.B. (1994), 'The kinds of order in society', in P. Mirowski (ed.), *Natural Images in Economic Thought: Markets Read in Tooth and Claw*, Cambridge: Cambridge University Press, pp. 536–82.

Nader, R. (1965), *Unsafe at any Speed: The Designed-in Dangers of the American Automobile*, New York: Pocket Books.

Nagel, E. (1961), *The Structure of Science: Problems in the Logic of Scientific Explanation*, London: Routledge & Kegan Paul.

Negishi, T. (1979), *Microeconomic Foundations of Keynesian Macroeconomics*, Amsterdam: North-Holland.

Neher, P.A. (1966), 'An implication of the labor-surplus assumption', *American Economic Review*, **56** (4), 855–7.

Nelson, A. (1984), 'Some issues surrounding the reduction of macroeconomics to microeconomics', *Philosophy of Science*, **51** (4), 573–94.

Nelson, R.R. and S.G. Winter (1974), 'Neoclassical vs. evolutionary theories of economic growth: critique and prospectus', *Economic Journal*, **84** (336), 886–905.

Nelson, R.R. and S.G. Winter (1982), *An Evolutionary Theory of Economic Change*, Cambridge, MA: Belknap Press of Harvard University Press.

Neurath, O. (1944), *Foundations of the Social Sciences*, Chicago, IL: Chicago University Press.

Nickles, T. (1973), 'Two concepts of intertheoretic reduction', *Journal of Philosophy*, **70** (7), 181–201.

Norkus, Z. (2005), 'Mechanisms as miracle makers? The rise and inconsistencies of the "mechanistic approach" in social science and history', *History and Theory*, **44** (3), 348–72.

O'Donnell, R.M. (1989), *Keynes: Philosophy, Economics and Politics*, Basingstoke: Macmillan.

O'Driscoll, G.P. and S.R. Shenoy (1976), 'Inflation, recession, and stagflation', in E.G. Dolan (ed.), *The Foundations of Modern Austrian Economics*, Kansas City, MO: Sheen & Ward, pp. 185–212.

Okun, A.M. (1981), *Prices and Quantities: A Macroeconomic Analysis*, Washington, DC: Brookings Institution.

Olson, M. (1965), *The Logic of Collective Action*, Cambridge, MA: Harvard University Press.

O'Neill, J. (ed.) (1973), *Modes of Individualism and Collectivism*, London: Heinemann.

O'Neill, J. (2004), 'Ecological economics and the politics of knowledge: the debate between Hayek and Neurath', *Cambridge Journal of Economics*, **24** (3), 431–47.

Opp, K.-D. (1985), Review of Hechter (1983), *Ethics*, **95** (2), 360–62.

Oppenheim, P. and H. Putnam (1958), 'Unity of science as a working hypothesis', in H. Feigl, M. Scriven and G. Maxwell (eds), *Minnesota Studies in the Philosophy of Science*, Minneapolis: University of Minnesota Press, volume 2, pp. 3–36.

Ormerod, P. (2009), 'The current crisis and the culpability of macroeconomic theory', London: Volterra Consulting, mimeo.

Packard, V. (1957), *The Hidden Persuaders*, New York: McKay.

Papineau, D. (2009), 'Physicalism and the human sciences', in C. Mantzavinos (ed.), *Philosophy of the Social Sciences: Philosophical Theory and Scientific Practice*, Cambridge: Cambridge University Press, pp. 103–23.

Parkin, M. and R. Bade (1982), *Modern Macroeconomics*, Deddington: Philip Allan.

Parsons, T. (1937), *The Structure of Social Action: A Study in Social Theory with Special Reference to a Group of Recent European Writers*, New York: The Free Press, second edition, 1949.

Pasinetti, L.L. (1962), 'Rate of profit and income distribution in relation to the rate of economic growth', *Review of Economic Studies*, **29** (4), 267–79.

Pasinetti, L.L. (2005), 'The Cambridge school of Keynesian economics', *Cambridge Journal of Economics*, **29** (6), 837–48.

Pasinetti, L.L. (2007), *Keynes and the Cambridge Keynesians: A "Revolution in Economics" to be Accomplished*, Cambridge: Cambridge University Press.

Patinkin, D. (1956), *Money, Interest, and Prices: An Integration of Monetary and Value Theory*, New York: Harper & Row, 1965.
Peltonen, M. (2001), 'Clues, margins, and monads: the micro–macro link in historical research', *History and Theory*, **40** (3), 347–59.
Penn, M. and S. Gudeman (1999), Review of Kincaid (1999), *American Anthropologist*, **101** (4), 902–3.
Peston, M.H. (1959), 'A view of the aggregation problem', *Review of Economic Studies*, **27** (1), 58–64.
Pheby, J. (1987), *The Methodology of Economics: A Critical Introduction*, Basingstoke: Macmillan.
Phelps, E.S. (1965), *Golden Rules of Economic Growth: Studies of Efficient and Optimal Investment*, Amsterdam: North-Holland.
Phelps, E.S. (1969), 'The new microeconomics in inflation and employment theory', *American Economic Review*, **59** (2), 147–60.
Phelps, E.S. (1987), 'Equilibrium: an expectational concept', in J. Eatwell, M. Milgate and P. Newman (eds), *The New Palgrave: A Dictionary of Economics*, Volume 1, London: Macmillan, pp. 177–8.
Phelps, E.S. (1990), *Seven Schools of Macroeconomic Thought: The Arne Ryde Memorial Lectures at Lund 1988*, Oxford: Clarendon Press.
Phelps, E.S. and J.B. Taylor (1977), 'Stabilizing powers of monetary policy under rational expectations', *Journal of Political Economy*, **85** (1), 163–90.
Phelps, E.S. and others (1970), *Microeconomic Foundations of Employment and Inflation Theory*, New York: Norton.
Philp, B. and D. Young (2002), 'Preferences, reductionism and the microfoundations of Analytical Marxism', *Cambridge Journal of Economics*, **26** (3), 313–29.
Pinker, S. (2005), *The Blank Slate: The Modern Denial of Human Nature*, Harmondsworth: Penguin.
Plosser, C.I. (1989), 'Understanding real business cycles', *Journal of Economic Perspectives*, **3** (3), 51–77.
Polanyi, M. (1958), *Personal Knowledge: Towards a Post-Critical Philosophy*, Chicago, IL: University of Chicago Press.
Pomata, G. (2000), 'Telling the truth about micro-history: a memoir (and a few reflections)', Copenhagen: Netvaerk for Historieteori, Working Paper No. 3.
Popper, K.R. (1957), *The Poverty of Historicism*, London: Routledge & Kegan Paul.
Popper, K.R. (1979), *Objective Knowledge: An Evolutionary Approach*, Oxford: Clarendon Press, second edition.
Qin, D. (1993), *The Formation of Econometrics: A Historical Perspective*, Oxford: Clarendon Press.

Quiggin, J. (2010a), 'Beauty – truth? Thoughts on Krugman's "How did economists get it so wrong?"', *Agenda*, **17** (1), 113–18.
Quiggin, J. (2010b), *Zombie Economics: How Dead Ideas Still Walk Among Us*, Princeton, NJ: Princeton University Press.
Ramsey, F.P. (1928), 'A mathematical theory of saving', *Economic Journal*, **38** (152), 543–59.
Rapping, L.A. (1990), Review of Hoover (1988), *Journal of Economic Literature*, **28** (1), 71–3.
Redman, D.A. (1991), *Economics and the Philosophy of Science*, Oxford: Oxford University Press.
Reiss, J. (2004), Review of Hoover (2001a), *Economics and Philosophy*, **20** (1), 226–33.
Richardson, G.B. (1959), 'Equilibrium, expectations and information', *Economic Journal*, **69** (274), 223–37.
Riker, W.H. and P.C. Ordeshook (1973), *An Introduction to Positive Political Theory*, Englewood Cliffs, NJ: Prentice-Hall.
Rizvi, S.A.T. (1994), 'The microfoundations project in general equilibrium theory', *Cambridge Journal of Economics*, **18** (4), 357–77.
Robbins, L. (1934), *The Nature and Significance of Economic Science*, London: Macmillan.
Roberts, M. (1996), *Analytical Marxism: A Critique*, London: Verso.
Robinson, J. (1956), *The Accumulation of Capital*, London: Macmillan.
Robinson, J. (1972), 'The second crisis of economic theory', *American Economic Review*, **62** (2), Papers and Proceedings, 1–10.
Robinson, J. (1977), 'What are the questions?', *Journal of Economic Literature*, **15** (4), 1318–39.
Roemer, J.E. (1979), 'Divide and conquer: microfoundations of the Marxian theory of wage discrimination', *Bell Journal of Economics*, **10** (2), 695–705.
Roemer, J.E. (1981), *Analytical Foundations of Marxian Economic Theory*, Cambridge: Cambridge University Press.
Roemer, J.E. (1982), 'Methodological individualism and deductive Marxism', *Theory and Society*, **11** (4), 513–20.
Rogowski, R. (1978), 'Rationalist theories of politics', *World Politics*, **30** (2), 296–323.
Romer, D. (1993), 'The New Keynesian synthesis', *Journal of Economic Perspectives*, **7** (1), 5–22.
Roncaglia, A. (1978), *Sraffa and the Theory of Prices*, Chichester: Wiley.
Rose, S. (2005), *Lifelines: Life beyond the Gene*, London: Vintage, second edition.
Rosenberg, A. (1992), *Economics: Mathematical Politics or Science of Diminishing Returns?*, Chicago, IL: University of Chicago Press.

Rosenberg, A. (1994), 'Does evolutionary theory give inspiration to economics?, in P. Mirowski (ed.), *Natural Images in Economic Thought: Markets Read in Tooth and Claw*, Cambridge: Cambridge University Press, pp. 384–407.

Rosenof, T. (1997), *Economics in the Long Run: New Deal Economists and Their Legacies, 1933–1993*, Chapel Hill, NC: University of North Carolina Press.

Ross, D. (2009), Review of Hausman (2008), *Journal of Economic Literature*, **47** (1), 174–7.

Rossi, S. (2010), 'Financial stability requires macroeconomic foundations of macroeconomics', *Journal of Philosophical Economics*, **III** (2), 58–73.

Rotheim, R. (2006), 'Credit rationing', in P. Arestis and M. Sawyer (eds), *A Handbook of Alternative Monetary Economics*, Cheltenham, UK and Northampton, MA, USA, Edward Elgar, pp. 307–27.

Rothschild, K.W. (1947), 'Price theory and oligopoly', *Economic Journal*, **57** (227), 299–320.

Rothschild, K.W. (1988), 'Microfoundations, ad hocery, and Keynesian theory', *Atlantic Economic Journal*, **16** (2), 12–21.

Russell, B. (1956), *Portraits from Memory, and Other Essays*, London: Allen & Unwin.

Ryan, M. (2005), 'Micro-macro integration', in G. Ritzer (ed.), *Encyclopedia of Social Theory. Volume I*, Thousand Oaks, CA: Sage, pp. 501–3.

Samuelson, P.A. (1947), *Foundations of Economic Analysis*, Harvard, MA: Harvard University Press.

Samuelson, P.A. (1948), *Economics: An Introductory Analysis*, New York: McGraw-Hill.

Samuelson, P.A. (1963), 'Problems of methodology: discussion', *American Economic Review*, **53** (2), 231–6.

Samuelson, P.A. (1996), 'Paul Anthony Samuelson (b. 1915)', in D.C. Colander and H. Landreth (eds), *The Coming of Keynesianism to America: Conversations with the Founders of Keynesian Economics*, Cheltenham, UK and Northampton, MA, USA: Edward Elgar, pp. 145–78.

Samuelson, P.A. (1998), 'How foundations came to be', *Journal of Economic Literature*, **36** (3), 1375–86.

Samuelson, P.A. and F. Modigliani (1966), 'The Pasinetti paradox in neoclassical and more general models', *Review of Economic Studies*, **33** (96), 269–301.

Samuelson, P.A. and R.M. Solow (1956), 'A complete capital model involving heterogeneous capital goods', *Quarterly Journal of Economics*, **70** (4), 537–62.

Sandilands, R.J. (2009), 'Solovian and new growth theory from the perspective of Allyn Young on macroeconomic increasing returns', in M. Boianovsky and K.D. Hoover (eds), *Robert Solow and the Development of Growth Economics*, Durham, NC: Duke University Press, pp. 285–303.

Sardoni, C. (2002), 'On the microeconomic foundations of macroeconomics: a Keynesian perspective', in P. Arestis, M. Desai and S. Dow (eds), *Essays in Honour of Victoria Chick*, London: Routledge, pp. 4–14.

Sawyer, M.C. (2010), 'Crises and paradigms in macroeconomics', *Intervention. European Journal of Economics and Economic Policies*, **7** (2), 283–302.

Schabas, M. (2009), 'Constructing "the economy"', *Philosophy of the Social Sciences*, **39** (1), 3–19.

Schaffner, K.F. (1967), 'Approaches to reduction', *Philosophy of Science*, **34** (2), 137–47.

Schlicht, E. (1985), *Isolation and Aggregation in Economics*, Berlin: Springer-Verlag.

Schneider, M.P. (2010), 'Keynesian income determination diagrams', in M. Blaug and P.J. Lloyd (eds), *Famous Figures and Diagrams in Economics*, Cheltenham, UK and Northampton, MA, USA: Edward Elgar, pp. 337–47.

Schohl, F. (1998), Review of Hartley (1997), *Journal of Evolutionary Economics*, **8** (3), 7–20.

Schohl, F. (1999), 'The paradoxical fate of the representative firm', *Journal of the History of Economic Thought*, **21** (1), 65–80.

Schulmeister, S. (2011), 'Hellas-Referendum als Chance für eine Systemtherapie' ('Greek referendum as a chance for system therapy'), *Der Standard*, 3 November, p. 31.

Schultze, C.L. (1981), 'Some macro foundations for micro theory', *Brookings Papers on Economic Activity*, **2**, 521–92.

Schumpeter, J.A. (1954), *History of Economic Analysis*, London: Allen & Unwin.

Scitovsky, T. (1952), *Welfare and Competition: The Economics of a Fully Employed Economy*, London: Unwin University Books, 1968.

Scott, K.J. (1961), 'Methodological and epistemological individualism', *British Journal for the Philosophy of Science*, **11** (44), 331–6.

Scull, A. (2007), 'Mind, brain, law and culture', *Brain*, **130** (2), 585–91.

Searle, J.R. (1995), *The Construction of Social Reality*, Harmondsworth: Penguin.

Sebastiani, M. (ed.) (1989), *Kalecki's Relevance Today*, London: Macmillan.

Setterfield, M. and A.P. Thirlwall (2010), 'Macrodynamics for a better society: the economics of John Cornwall', *Review of Political Economy*, **22** (4), 481–98.
Shackle, G.L.S. (1954), 'The complex nature of time as a concept in economics', *Economia Internazionale*, **7**, 743–53.
Shubik, M. (1975), 'The general equilibrium model is incomplete and not adequate for the reconciliation of micro and macroeconomic theory', *Kyklos*, **28** (3), 545–73.
Sidrauski, M. (1967), 'Rational choice and patterns of growth in a monetary economy', *American Economic Review*, **57** (2), 534–44.
Simon, H.A. (1962), 'The architecture of complexity', *Proceedings of the American Philosophical Society*, **106** (6), 467–82.
Simon, H.A. (1996), 'Alternative views of complexity', in H.A. Simon, *The Sciences of the Artificial*, third edition, Cambridge, MA: MIT Press, reprinted in M.A. Bedau and P. Humphreys (eds), *Emergence: Contemporary Readings in Philosophy and Science*, Cambridge, MA: MIT Press, 2008, pp. 249–58.
Skidelsky, R. (2009), *Keynes: The Return of the Master*, London: Allen Lane.
Sklar, L. (1967), 'Types of inter-theoretic reduction', *British Journal for the Philosophy of Science*, **18** (2), 109–24.
Smelser, N. (1990), 'Can individualism yield a sociology?', *Contemporary Sociology*, **19** (6), 778–83.
Smithin, J. (2004), 'Macroeconomic theory, (critical) realism and capitalism', in P. Lewis (ed.), *Transforming Economics: Perspectives on the Critical Realist Project*, London and New York: Routledge, pp. 55–75.
Smithin, J. (2009), *Money, Enterprise and Income Distribution: Towards a Macroeconomic Theory of Capitalism*, London: Routledge.
Snowdon, B. (1993), Review of Belongia and Garfinkel (1992), *Economic Journal*, **103** (421), 1565–7.
Snowdon, B. and H.R. Vane (eds) (1999), *Conversations with Leading Economists: Interpreting Modern Macroeconomics*, Cheltenham, UK and Northampton, MA, USA: Edward Elgar.
Snowdon, B. and H.R. Vane (eds) (2002), 'Business cycles: new classical approach', in B. Snowdon and H.R. Vane, *Encyclopedia of Macroeconomics*, Cheltenham, UK and Northampton, MA, USA: Edward Elgar, pp. 83–9.
Snowdon, B., H. Vane and P. Wynarczyk (1994), *A Modern Guide to Macroeconomics: An Introduction to Competing Schools of Thought*, Cheltenham, UK and Northampton, MA, USA: Edward Elgar.
Sober, E. (1984), *The Nature of Selection: Evolutionary Theory in Philosophical Focus*, Cambridge, MA: MIT Press.

Sober, E. (1999), 'The multiple realizability argument against reductionism', *Philosophy of Science*, **66** (4), 542–64, reprinted in E. Sober (ed.), *Conceptual Issues in Evolutionary Biology*, Cambridge, MA: MIT Press, 2006, pp. 301–22.

Sober, E. (ed.) (2006), *Conceptual Issues in Evolutionary Biology*, Cambridge, MA: MIT Press.

Solow, R.M. (1979), 'Alternative approaches to macroeconomic theory: a partial view', *Canadian Journal of Economics*, **12** (3), 339–54.

Solow, R.M. (1986), 'What is a nice girl like you doing in a place like this? Macroeconomics after fifty years', *Eastern Economic Journal*, **12** (3), 191–8.

Solow, R.M. (1997), 'Is there a core of usable macroeconomics we should all believe in?', *American Economic Review*, **87** (2), 230–32.

Solow, R.M. (1998), *Monopolistic Competition and Macroeconomic Theory*, Cambridge: Cambridge University Press.

Solow, R.M. (1999), 'Neoclassical growth theory', in J.B. Taylor and M. Woodford (eds), *Handbook of Macroeconomics. Volume 1A*, Amsterdam: Elsevier, pp. 637–67.

Solow, R.M. (2007), 'Reflections on the survey', in D. Colander (ed.), *The Making of an Economist: Redux*, Princeton, NJ: Princeton University Press, pp. 234–8.

Solow, R.M. (2008), 'The state of macroeconomics', *Journal of Economic Perspectives*, **22** (1), 243–6.

Sørensen, A.B. (1999), Review of Little (1998), *Contemporary Sociology*, **28** (4), 482–3.

Spadaro, L.M. (1978), 'Towards a program of research and development for Austrian economics', in L.M. Spadaro (ed.), *New Directions in Austrian Economics*, Kansas City, MO: Sheed Andrews & McMeel, pp. 205–27.

Steele, G.R. (2007), 'Are macroeconomic theorists rational?', *Quarterly Journal of Austrian Economics*, **10** (2), 3–13.

Steindl, J. (1976), *Maturity and Stagnation in American Capitalism*, New York: Monthly Review Press, second edition.

Stiglitz, J.E. (1991), 'Alternative approaches to macroeconomics: methodological issues and the New Keynesian economics', Cambridge, MA: National Bureau of Economic Research Working Paper No. 3586, January.

Stiglitz, J.E. (1992), 'Methodological issues and New Keynesian economics', in A. Vercelli and N. Dimitri (eds), *Macroeconomics: A Survey of Research Strategies*, Oxford: Oxford University Press, pp. 38–86.

Stiglitz, J.E., J.A. Ocampo, S. Spiegel, R. Ffrench-Davis and D. Nayyar (2006), *Stability with Growth: Macroeconomics, Liberalization, and Development*, Oxford: Oxford University Press.

Stone, R. (1962), 'Three models of economic growth', in E. Nagel, P. Suppes and A. Tarski (eds), *Logic, Methodology and Philosophy of Science: Proceedings of the 1960 International Congress*, Stanford, CA: Stanford University Press, pp. 494–506.

Tamborini, R. (1999), Review of Rotheim (1998), *Economic Journal*, **109** (459), F791–F792.

Tarshis, L. (1980), 'Post Keynesian economics: a promise that bounced?', *American Economic Review*, **70** (2), 10–14.

Tawney, R.H. (1926), *Religion and the Rise of Capitalism: A Historical Study*, London: J. Murray.

Taylor, J.B. (1997), 'A core of practical macroeconomics', *American Economic Review*, **87** (2), 233–5.

Taylor, L. (2004), *Reconstructing Macroeconomics: Structuralist Proposals and Critiques of the Mainstream*, Cambridge, MA: Harvard University Press.

Taylor, L. (2010), *Maynard's Revenge: The Collapse of Free Market Macroeconomics*, Cambridge, MA: Harvard University Press.

Taylor, M. (1993), 'Structure, culture, and action in the explanation of social change', in W.J. Booth, P. James and H. Meadwell (eds), *Politics and Rationality*, Cambridge: Cambridge University Press, pp. 89–131.

Taylor, M. (ed.) (1988), *Rationality and Revolution*, Cambridge: Cambridge University Press.

Tilly, C. (1985), Review of Hechter (1983), *American Journal of Sociology*, **90** (5), 1094–6.

Tinbergen, J. (1939), *Business Cycles in the United States of America, 1919–1932*, Geneva: League of Nations.

Tobin, J. (1958), 'Liquidity preference as behaviour towards risk', *Review of Economic Studies*, **25** (2), 65–86.

Tobin, J. (1970), 'Macroeconomics', in N. Ruggles (ed.), *Economics*, Englewood Cliffs, NJ: Prentice-Hall, pp. 44–54.

Tobin, J. (1993), 'Price flexibility and output stability: an Old Keynesian view', *Journal of Economic Perspectives*, **7** (1), 45–65.

Togati, T.D. (1998), *Keynes and the Neoclassical Synthesis: Einsteinian versus Newtonian Macroeconomics*, London: Routledge.

Toporowski, J. (2008), 'Minsky's "induced investment and business cycles"', *Cambridge Journal of Economics*, **32** (5), 725–37.

Trout, J.D. (1991), 'Section III: reductionism and the unity of science', in R. Boyd, P. Gasper and J.D. Trout (eds), *The Philosophy of Science*, Cambridge, MA: MIT Press, pp. 387–92.

Tsou, T. (2000), 'Interpreting the revolution in China: macrohistory and micromechanisms', *Modern China*, **26** (2), 205–38.

Udehn, L. (2001), *Methodological Individualism: Background, History and Meaning*, London: Routledge.

Udehn, L. (2002), 'The changing face of methodological individualism', *Annual Review of Sociology*, **28**, 479–508.
Van den Bergh, J.C.J.M. and J.M. Gowdy (2003), 'The microfoundations of macroeconomics: an evolutionary perspective', *Cambridge Journal of Economics*, **27** (1), 65–84.
Van den Berghe, P.L. (1998), Review of Kincaid (1997), *Contemporary Sociology*, **27** (6), 655–7.
Varian, H.R. (1987), 'Microeconomics', in J. Eatwell, M. Milgate and P. Newman (eds), *The New Palgrave: A Dictionary of Economics*, Basingstoke: Macmillan, Volume 3, pp. 461–3.
Varoufakis, Y., J. Halevi and T. Theocarakis (2011), *Modern Political Economics: Making Sense of the Post-2008 World*, London: Routledge.
Veneziani, R. (2012), 'Analytical Marxism', *Journal of Economic Surveys*, forthcoming.
Vercelli, A. (2008), *Methodological Foundations of Macroeconomics: Keynes and Lucas*, Cambridge: Cambridge University Press, first published in 1991.
Vines, D. (2010), 'What Keynes missed and Krugman is missing: the short/long choice', *Agenda*, **17** (1), 101–111.
Vining, R. (1949a), 'Koopmans on the choice of variables to be studied and of methods of measurement', *Review of Economics and Statistics*, **31** (2), 77–86.
Vining, R. (1949b), 'A rejoinder' [to Koopmans], *Review of Economics and Statistics*, **31** (2), 91–4.
Walker, D.A. (ed.) (1984), *Money and Markets: Essays by Robert W. Clower*, Cambridge: Cambridge University Press.
Walther, H. (2011), 'Kurt Rothschild und der Theorie der Arbeitslosigkeit' ('Kurt Rothschild and the theory of unemployment'), *Kurswechsel*, 2/2011, 27–40.
Waters, C.K. (1990), 'Why the antireductionist consensus won't survive the case of classical Mendelian genetics', in E. Sober (ed.), *Conceptual Issues in Evolutionary Biology*, Cambridge, MA: MIT Press, 2006, pp. 283–300.
Watkins, J.W.N. (1952a), 'Ideal types and historical explanation', *British Journal for the Philosophy of Science*, **3** (9), 22–43, reprinted in J. O'Neill (ed.), *Modes of Individualism and Collectivism*, London: Heinemann, 1973, pp. 143–65.
Watkins, J.W.N. (1952b), 'The principle of methodological individualism', *British Journal for the Philosophy of Science*, **3** (10), 186–9.
Watkins, J.W.N. (1955), 'Methodological individualism: a reply' [to M. Brodbeck], *Philosophy of Science*, **22** (1), 58–62, reprinted in J. O'Neill (ed.), *Modes of Individualism and Collectivism*, London: Heinemann, 1973, pp. 179–84.

Watkins, J.W.N. (1957), 'Historical explanation in the social sciences', *British Journal for the Philosophy of Science*, **8** (30), 104–17, reprinted in J. O'Neill (ed.), *Modes of Individualism and Collectivism*, London: Heinemann, 1973, pp. 166–78.

Watkins, J.W.N. (1958), 'The alleged inadequacy of methodological individualism', *Journal of Philosophy*, **55** (9), 390–95.

Watkins, J.W.N. (1959a), 'The two theses of methodological individualism', *British Journal for the Philosophy of Science*, **9** (36), 319–20.

Watkins, J.W.N. (1959b), 'Third reply to Mr. Goldstein', *British Journal for the Philosophy of Science*, **10** (39), 242–4.

Weber, M. (1930), *The Protestant Ethic and the Spirit of Capitalism*, London: Allen & Unwin.

Weintraub, E.R. (1977), 'The microfoundations of macroeconomics: a critical survey', *Journal of Economic Literature*, **15** (1), 1–23.

Weintraub, E.R. (1979), *Microfoundations: The Compatibility of Microeconomics and Macroeconomics*, Cambridge: Cambridge University Press.

Weintraub, E.R. (1982–3), 'Substantive mountains and methodological molehills', *Journal of Post Keynesian Economics*, **5** (2), 295–303.

Weintraub, E.R. (2002), *How Economics Became a Mathematical Science*, Durham, NC: Duke University Press.

Weintraub, S. (1956), 'A macroeconomic approach to the theory of wages', *American Economic Review*, **46** (5), December, 835–56.

Weintraub, S. (1957), 'The micro-foundations of aggregate demand and supply', *Economic Journal*, **67** (267), 455–70.

Weitzman, M.L. (1982), 'Increasing returns and the foundations of unemployment theory', *Economic Journal*, **92** (368), 781–809.

Weldes, J. (1989), 'Marxism and methodological individualism: a critique', *Theory and Society*, **18** (3), 353–86.

Wickens, M. (2008), *Macroeconomic Theory: A Dynamic General Equilibrium Approach*, Princeton, NJ: Princeton University Press.

Wilson, E.O. (1998), *Consilience: The Unity of Knowledge*, New York: Knopf.

Wimsatt, W.C. (1979), 'Reduction and reductionism', in P.D. Asquith and H.E. Kyburg Jr (eds), *Current Research in Philosophy of Science*, East Lansing, MI: Philosophy of Science Association, pp. 352–77.

Wimsatt, W.C. (1997), 'Aggregativity: reductive heuristics for finding emergence', *Philosophy of Science*, **64** (4), Supplement 2, S372–S384, reprinted in M.A. Bedau and P. Humphreys (eds), *Emergence: Contemporary Readings in Philosophy and Science*, Cambridge, MA: MIT Press, 2008, pp. 99–110.

Wisdom, J.O. (1970a), 'Situational individualism and the emergent group properties', in R. Borger and F. Cioffi (eds), *Explanation in the Behavioural Sciences*, Cambridge: Cambridge University Press, pp. 271–96.

Wisdom, J.O. (1970b), 'Reply' [to R. Brown], in R. Borger and F. Cioffi (eds), *Explanation in the Behavioural Sciences*, Cambridge: Cambridge University Press, pp. 306–11.

Wood, A. (1975), *A Theory of Profits*, Cambridge: Cambridge University Press.

Woodford, M. (1999), 'Revolution and evolution in twentieth-century macroeconomics', Columbia University, mimeo, http://www.columbia.edu/~mw2230/ (consulted 30 March 2010).

Woodford, M. (2003), *Interest and Prices: Foundations of a Theory of Monetary Policy*, Princeton, NJ: Princeton University Press.

Wren-Lewis, S. (2007), 'Are there dangers in the microfoundations consensus?', in P. Arestis (ed.), *Is There a New Consensus in Macroeconomics?*, Basingstoke: Palgrave Macmillan, pp. 43–60.

Wren-Lewis, S. (2011), 'Internal consistency, price rigidity and the microfoundations of macro-economics', *Journal of Economic Methodology*, **18** (2), 129–46.

Wright, E.O., A. Levine and E. Sober (1992), *Reconstructing Marxism: Essays on Explanation and the Theory of History*, London: Verso.

Name index

Subject index